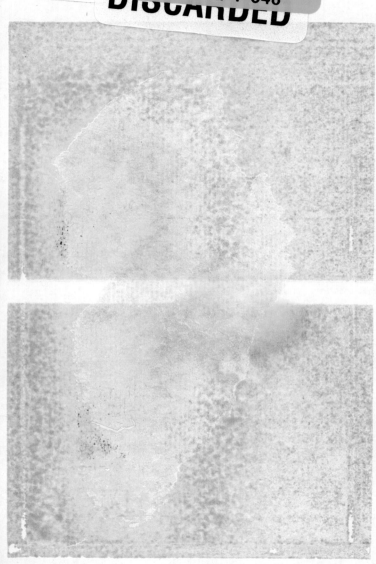

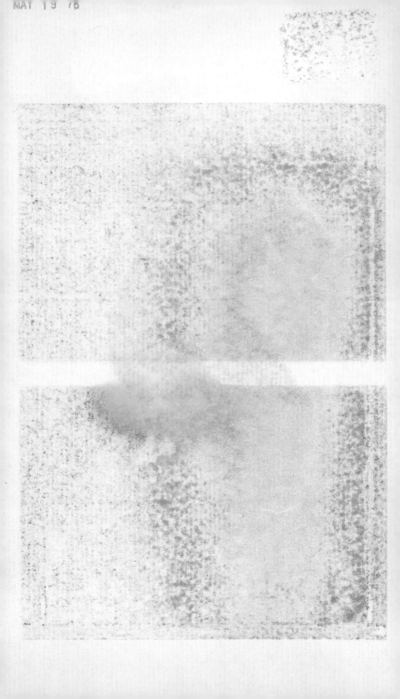

ENGLISH RECUSANT LITERATURE
1558–1640

Selected and Edited by
D. M. ROGERS

Volume 295

LUIS DE LA PUENTE
Meditations upon the Mysteries
of our Faith . . . Abbridged
1624

LUIS DE LA PUENTE

Meditations upon the Mysteries
of our Faith . . . Abbridged
1624

The Scolar Press
1976

ISBN 0 85967 296 4

*Published and printed in Great Britain by
The Scolar Press Limited, 59-61 East Parade,
Ilkley, Yorkshire and
39 Great Russell Street,
London WC1*

1900749

NOTE

Reproduced (original size) from a copy in the library of Stonyhurst College, by permission of the Rector.

References : Allison and Rogers 699; STC 20487.

MEDITATIONS
VPON THE
MYSTERIES
OF OVR FAITH.

Corresponding to the three
Wayes, *Purgatiue*, *Illumi-*
natiue, and *Vnitiue*.

Composed in Spanish by the Reuerend Father,
L V Y S   D E   L A   P V E N T E,
of the Society of I E S V S.

Abbridged, and translated into English by
a Father of the same S O C I E T Y.

Permissu Superiorum. M. DC. XXIIII.

TO

THE RIGHT

HONORABLE

THE LADY

ELIZABETH

VISCOVNTESSE

VVALLINGFORD,

WIFE TO THE

RIGHT HONORABLE

VVILLIAM LORD

KNOLLYS

BARON OF GRAYES,

VISCOVNT

VVALLINGFORD,

KNIGHT OF THE

NOBLE ORDER

OF GARTER

AND ONE OF HIS

MAIESTIES

MOST HONORABLE

PRIVY

COVNSELL.

IGHT HO-
NORABLE,

T H E great
Affection & De-
uotion, which you are knowne
to haue vnto Mentall Prayer,
and Contemplation of heauenly Thinges, hath (amongſt o-
ther no leſſe forcible Motiues)
moued me to dedicate this A-
BRIDGEMENT of moſt Ex-
cellent & Diuine Meditations
vnto your H O N O V R; not
doubting,

doubting, but that you will patronize the same, as it deserueth.

The Author is well known, and renowned throughout the Christian World, for his Learning, Piety, Humility, & other eminent Parts; as hauing byn trayned vp, from his youth, in the Schoole of Vertue, vnder the best, & most expert Maisters of Spirit, that are this day in the world.

The Translation it selfe is purposely clad in a playne & hūble Style, as best suting with so high and heauenly a subiect as Contemplation is; wherein ouer-fine & eloquent Speach, is not so much to be regarded,

as

as the Doctrine it selfe, vttered in a more humble Language.

The Variety of matter, togeather with pious Documents for the direction, and spirituall profit of the soule, & the plaine and easy methode of treating the same, will breed dayly new delightes, without tediousnes. For heerein the Deuout Contemplant shall behould as in a Christall Glasse, the vvhole Tract, and Processe of the life of our Lord and Sauiour Iesus Christ, liuely represented vnto him; togeather with the B. Virgins admirable Vertues, & rare examples of Humility, for imitation.

Heere are to be found Prin-

* 4   ciples

ciples and Precepts of Good Life, the vſe and practiſe of Prayer, Faſting, Almeſdeeds, and all other, as well ſpirituall as corporall Exerciſes of Vertue. Heere alſo are deliuered ſundry Aduertiſments for the profitably receauing of the Sacraments, the benefits thereof, & the manner of worthy preparation thereunto. Heere are ſet downe Remedyes agaynſt Tentation, Comfortes in Affliction, Inſtructions for Security, Forewarnings againſt danger; and in a word, what to feare, what to follow, what to fly.

So as this Booke, to ſuch as will make vſe thereof (as
all

all, who will take but a little paines, may) and frame their liues according to the prescript therein set downe, may well be termed a Rich Iewell, or rather a Cabbinet full of Heauenly Treasure; & wherof may truly be said, that which Salomon pronounced, *Procul & de vltimis finibus pretium eius*.

I will not ouerweary your HONOVR vvith a longer Epistle, since your Bountifulnes & Piety assure me of the gratefull Acceptance of this meane Oblation, which your knowne Vertues & Deserts, haue, as it were, inforced me, through want of a more worthy Preset, to offer into the Treasury of

your

THE EPISTLE

your Spirituall Iewells;and my
selfe to your Gratious. Fauour
and Protection, resting euer,

*Your Honours deuoted ser-
uant in Christ Iesus.*

I. W.

THE PREFACE,

Or Aduertisment of the Abridger, to the Reader.

§. I.

READING of late with attention the meditations of Fa. *Luys dela Puente* of our Society, which I found full of excellent doctrine and instructions conuenient for them, who desire to profit in spirit, to purge & cleanse their soules from al vice, to mortify their disordered, & vnbridled passions, to get the vse & habit of vertue, and finally to vnite themselues with God (for there is to be found in this Treatise much matter both of learning & piety for all these points, drawne from the Authours owne continuall reading, meditation, and mortification) and considering the misery of the corrupted tymes, in which we now liue, and also the fraylty of our peruerted Nature, that liketh not to read long discourses, be they neuer so profitable, but contenting our selues rather with breuity, though the sayings & sentences

tences for variety be neuer so solid, good, & holy; it seemed to me, that it would be a thing, much pleasing vnto God, and profitable for the aduancement of deuout soules, and also for religious persons, to contract into short points all that doctrine, dispersed in the sayd Fathers larger works, to the end that by the abbreuiating of so many good & profitable documents and instructions, and reducing the same into order, euery one might make his aduantage and profit thereof with more facility; and all excuse might be taken away from the negligent, who might giue matter to their doubtfull lukewarmenes, that vnder pretence of the length of the worke, would exempt themselues from the practise thereof. In the meane time nothing shall in this briefe Collection be omitted, that may be of importance, to the end the Memory (which is a Faculty of the Soule, that hath the first place in the exercise of Prayer) may not be ouercharged, but rather with facility cary away the matter of the meditation; & that for want therof, the spirit take not occasion to conuert it selfe to superfluous, & distractiue thoughts, with the losse of the fruite of prayer, so profitable, and necessary to the Soule.

I haue been further moued to vndertake this worke for another reason, with our Holy Father S. Ignatius toucheth in the second Annotation of the twenty, which he hath in the beginning of his Spirituall Exercises, where speaking of the manner which the Directour should vse & obserue, he insinuateth, that he must propose

the

the matter of meditation in few wordes , together with some short explication thereof. And
to the end euery one may beare & vnderstand
our sayd B. Fathers owne wordes, he being one
of the most excellent Maysters of deuotion, that
Gods Church euer had , as is to be seene by the
golden booke of his Exercises, it will be good to
set them downe as they lye thus : He (the Dire-
&our) must briefly and faythfully (sayth he)
propose the matter of meditation to him, that is
to take it, that hauing cleerly & well conceyued
the subiect of the history, he may himselfe afterwardes discourse thereon. Whereof this will
follow , that hauing found out some thing, that
giueth him a better knowledge , & vnderstanding of that , which he meditateth , whether ,
through his owne vnderstanding , holpen by
Gods grace, or by some particular illustration
from heauen , he will reape more profit, & contentment , then he should doe if another should
explicate vnto him at large the whole subiect of
the Meditation, by laying that open vnto him ,
which himselfe might haue found out . For the
knowledge of many things is not that, which sa-
tisfyeth & contenteth the deuout soule, but the
experimentall vnderstanding thereof, & the inward pleasure, that he draweth thereout &c.

It is not heere forbidden to explicate the
matter , more or lesse , according to the capacity
of him, to whome it is giuen, or according to the
disposition he shall see in him ; for it is for this
reaso, that the same Father putteth down his meditations at length, that euery one may take that

* *
which

which shall be for him most conuenient & proper: but because all cannot haue them commodiously, & though they had them, all could not haue tyme to read them, nor, as I sayd before, all take pleasure in reading long discourses, be they neuer so good & profitable, I haue thought good to make a briefe Collection & Abbridgement, in forme of a Manuall, that as well those who remayne quiet at home, as those whose affayres call forth abroad, those also who haue imployments, & those agayne that haue none, yea the beginners themselues in this holy exercise, & they who haue been practised therein, may make profitable vse thereof: & in particular that the brethren of our Society for whose sake I haue chiefly vndertaken this labour, as well Students, as Coadiutors & Neuices, may with the more facility make particular vse thereof in their dayly exercise of prayer. And if any desire to haue fuller or more ample vnderstanding of the mystery that is proposed vnto him for his meditation, he may recurre to the same in the Fathers larger volumes, if he please.

§. 2.

Though I haue in this Abridgement, endeauoured to follow the foresayd meditations, as neere as I could, yet haue I added some things heere and there, and in some places I haue altogeather chaunged the order of them, endeauouring to accommodate the meditations to the foure Weekes of our B. Father S. Ignatius, set downe in his booke of spirituall Exercises, of which we ought to make as great esteeme, as it

meriteth,

meriteth : for as it was left vs by him who , as
we may perſwade our ſelues, receyued it from
God, ſo his pleaſure no doubt is that the childrē
recevuing from their Father the gift of prayer ,
ſhould be wholy deuoted to the exerciſe therof.
And therefore, becauſe this little worke is principally directed to the religious of our Society ,
I haue thought it good , as occaſion often offereth it ſelfe , to remit them to the ſayd booke of
Exerciſe , in many things, that I might haue ſet
downe at length , that ſo the reading of this diuine Booke , approued by the holy Sea Apo-
ſtolike, to the great good of the Church , might
be more frequēt with vs, perſwading our ſelues,
that whatſoeuer may be ſayd touching piety &
deuotion, is aptly treated in it , with admirable
propriety of wordes, & fit order .

It is to be noted alſo , that though all the
meditations be diſtributed into foure Weekes ,
it is not to be vnderſtood, that we haue comprehended in euery one of them all , that might
haue been ſayd thereof in that kinde; but that
they haue been ſo deuided , to diſtinguiſh their
kindes and differences, which muſt ſo long time
be exerciſed as ſhall be neceſſary to meditate thē
ouer at leaſure , vnleſſe (as we ſhall ſay afterwards) one ſhould be forced by neceſſity to in-
terrupt them , or by counſayle of his ſpirituall
Father to leaue them off .

§. 3.

Beſides this we haue made a collection of
fiue other Treatiſes of diuers meditations; One
of the B. Sacrament of the Altar,& of Confeſſi-

on;

⁂ 2

on, & two other of our B Lady, the former of her life and vpon her festiuities, the latter touching her vertues. And this I was iuduced to do, for that many affected to the honor of that glorious Queene of heauen, take singular delight & pleasure in meditating of her life and vertues: & therefore would happily be glad to find all these matters comprised in some short forme. The fourth is of diuers perfections & benefits which we receyue, as well naturall as supernaturall, & which may be accommodated to the fourth Weeke, that apperteyneth to the vnitiue life, in which our Blessed Father hath put the Exercise of the *Loue of God*. The last contayneth certayne particular meditations, chiefly vpon the lyues of Saints, to the end that out of them we may draw a modell, and forme to meditate of others, as often as our deuotion would please to walke & recreate it selfe in the garden of the diuine flowers of holy Church, since euery Saint is a most fayre and odoriferous flower, the beauty and fragrancy wherof recreateth the soule of a deuout person, that meditateth vpon their lyues, & vertues.

Moreouer in the first Weeke be proposed and taught three manners of Prayer, which also our B. Father S. Ignatius putteth down in his Booke of Exercise: & hath further deliuered in forme of meditation, how one should make his prayer for the ouercomming of some vice, or for the purchasing of some vertue. In the beginning are put downe two dayly and ordinarily Examens, to wit, a generall, and a particular, as also a
third

third more ample then the other, wherein all the actions, and houres of the day, are examined conformably to euery ones state and condition of life : and all are deuided by paragraphes and points, that he who desireth his souls good, may easily see wherein he fayleth of his duty, & vnderstand whether he profiteth in spirit, or no . And this he may easily doe once a weeke , or as often as his other imployments will giue him leaue .

§. 4.

The tymes into which one may distribute the meditations of the foure Weekes , and the rest, speaking in generall, if particular necessity, or our deuotion require not otherwise, be these, to wit : The Exercises of the first Weeke, which appertaine to the Purgatiue Way, may be made after the feast of the Octaue of *Corpus Christi* , in the moneths of Iune , & Iuly . Those of the second Weeke , which appertayne to the Illuminatiue Way, may begin with the moneth of August, and be continued vntill Aduent beginning with the meditation of the *Baptisme of our Sauiour,* & continuing the meditations of his whole life. The first Sunday of Aduent , and the dayes following meditate vpon the last iudgement, conformably to the office of holy Church . Then begin to meditate of the Incarnation, & Infancy of our Sauior, continuing vntill the octaue of the Epiphany, according to the misteries represented by the Church. After the octaue, vou may return to the rest of our Sauiours life, & meditate theron. Frō the beginning of Lent you may meditate

* 3   vpon

vpon the third Weeke, which appertayneth also to the Illuminatiue Way. From Easter day vntill Whit-Sunday he may take those meditations of the fourth Weeke, of the Resurrection, Ascension, & Glory of our Sauiour, with the cōming of the holy Ghost : & this Weeke is referred to the Vnitiue way.

Vpon the feast of the B. Sacrament the meditations of the same mystery must be vsed , & of them also one may make his prayer all the dayes of Communion , as is insisuated in the Tract of that mystery .

One may also meditate vpon the life of our B. Lady , & make his prayers theron vpon all the Sondayes, in honour of her : & if his deuotion serue him , he may continue all the Saturdayes in the meditation of her vertues, as is mētioned in the second Tract of the glorious Virgin, & is the third in order .

Vpon the principall feasts of Saints he may make his meditation of their priuiledges, & vertues , as is declared in the beginning of the last Tract .

§. 5. *The Dayly Examen of our Conscience, especially at Night .*

To giue God thanks for all benefits formerly receaued, & especially of that present day .

2. To demaund grace & true light, to know & hate our sinnes.

2 . To call our soules to accompt, wherin we may haue that day offended God: hauing speciall cōsideration of such defects wherunto we are most inclined .

4. To

4. To craue pardon hûbly of God for all fins & defects wherof we find our felues guilty.

5. To make a firme purpose, through Gods grace to auoid finne heerafter, with intention to côfeſſe thoſe wherin we haue tranſgreſſed. Laſtly, ſay *Pater noſter* . *Aue-Maria*. *Credo* .

§. 6. *The Particular Examen to be made at three tymes, very neceſſary for the better diſpoſing, & ſearching into our felues.*

THE 1. is in the morning, when aſſoone as we awake, we muſt purpoſe to keep a diligent watch that day ouer our felues, for the auoyding of ſome finne or imperfection which we are deſirous to amend .

The 2. is at Noone, when we muſt demaund Gods geace, that we may remember how often we haue fallen into that particuler fin or defect, & be more heedfull heerafter. Then let vs make our firſt Examen, calling our foule to accôpt, & rûning ouer euery houre of the day to that preſent, how often we haue fallen therinto : & let vs make ſo many markes in the former lyne of the enſuing table . This done let vs purpoſe to keep our felues more warily the reſt of the day.

The 3. Time, ſhalbe at Night after ſupper, when we muſt make the ſecond Examen, running ouer euery houre from the former examination vntill that, calling to mind, & nûbring the times wherein we haue offended, making ſo many markes in the ſecond line of the table mêtioned before .

§. 7. *Foure additions very profitable for the more easy & ſpeedy rooting out of any vice, or ſinne.*

THE 1. is, that as often we commit that particuler ſinne, we be ſory for it frō our hart, in witnes wherof let vs lay our hand vpon our breſt: which may be done at all tymes, without being perceaued by others.

The 2. is, that at Night we number & compare the markes of both lines togeather, the former line being appointed for the firſt examen, & the later for the ſecond: & let vs ſee, if from the former hath followed any amendment.

The 3. is, that we compare the examinations of the firſt & ſecond day togeather, & marke whether any amendment hath byn made.

The 4. is, that by comparing two weeks togeather, it may appeare what amendment hath byn made, or omitted.

It is alſo to be noted, that the firſt of the lines following, which is longer then the reſt, is appointed for the firſt day, the ſecond ſomewhat ſhorter for the ſecond day, & ſo likewiſe for euery day, ſhorter & ſhorter. It being meet that the number of our faults be dayly diminiſhed.

Sunday ———————————————
Mundy ————————————————
Tweſday ———————————————
Wedneſday—————————————
Thurſday ——————————
Friday ————————
Saturday ————

Certayne

§. 8. Certayne Aduertisments necessary for the better making of our Prayer.

BEfore prayer the Soule must exercise it selfe in some acts of humility, by considering its own basenes, & the greatnes of God, with whō it is to treate, & falling downe vpon our knees we must begin with the signe of the Crosse, in blessing our selues, & crauing of the diuine maiesty grace to spend that short tyme well, which we are to imploy in that holy exercise, so as all our thoughts, words, & works may be sincerely address'd to the greater glory of God. Morouer we must imagine a certaine Cōposition of place; & therin accōmodate our selues in such manner as is insinuated in the first Exercise of the first Weeke following. Finally we must perswade our selues, that we stand in the presence of God, who is both within vs, & round about vs, to the end that the imagination therof may incite vs to greater attention, confidence, & reuerence. Next we must aske of the diuine goodnes that, which we desire, answerable to the matter wherof the meditation is to be made. For example, if I meditate of sin, I will craue pardō for my own &c.

We must also make one, or more Colloquies at the end, according to the motions, & affection which the soule shall feele in it selfe, in speaking sometymes to the B. Trinity, sometimes to euery one of the three Diuine Persons, or to the B. Virgin, or the Saints, giuing thanks otherwhiles for benefitts receiued, other whils crauing Gods help, for getting of some one vertue in particular.   The

The repetitions, that our B. Father teacheth in the firſt Week of his ſpirituall Exerciſes muſt be made after two, or, three meditations, in ſuch manner, as is ſpecifyed in the ſame place, making three Colloquies, to the Father, to the Son, & to the B. Virgin.

§. 9. *Other Additions concerning Prayer.*

AT night before I compoſe my ſelfe to ſleepe I will bethinke me for the ſpace of one Aue Maria, at what houre I am to riſe in the morning, & what Exerciſe I am to make.

As ſoone as I am riſen, before any other thought enter into my minde, I will thinke on the matter I am to meditate: & for the more Confuſion of my ſelfe, I will vſe this example, or the like: With what a confuſion of countenance would a Gentleman appeare before his Prince & Soueraygne Lord, if after hauing receyued many exceeding great benefits of him, he ſhould ſee himſelfe conuicted of ſome enormous crime agaynſt his maieſty. Then turning to my ſelfe, who am ſo vile a ſinner, I will imagine myſelfe to be bound in chaines & loaden with bolts & irons, & in that manner brought before the throne of my ſupreme Iudge, as they vſe to do a cryminall perſő & culpable of death, before a temporall Iudge. This, or the like example will I propoſe to my ſelfe, conformably to the matter I am to meditate.

Thus ſtanding a pace or two from the place, where I am to make my praier, I will lift vp my mind to God, for the time of one *Pater noſter*, & I will conſider my Lord Ieſus preſent, & looking

king vpon me, & beholding what I am to do, to whome I will make reuerence with all humble gesture.

Then I will begin my prayer in that composition of body, that I shall thinke best, for the more easy obtaining of what I desire, whether lying prostrate on the groud, kneeling, standing or sitting, or in what other manner soeuer. And heere I am to obserue two things. The one, if either by kneeling, or by any other cōposition of body, i find what I seeke for or desire, that thē I make no other chaunge. The other is, that if in meditating of one point, I find the deuotion I seeke for, I ought to continue therein, without care to passe further to any other point, vntill I shall haue fully satisfyed my selfe therein.

My prayer ended, eyther sitting, or walking, I will for a quarter of an houre bethinke me, what successe my meditation hath had. If bad, I will with sorrow search out the causes, & purpose amendment : if good, I will thanke God for it, with intention to do the like, or better, if I can, for the tyme to come.

As long as the Exercises of the first Weeke last, I must shunne all cogitations that cause ioy, as those of the glorious Resurrection &c. because euery such thought hindreth teares & sorrow for my sinnes, which is euer to be sought during this tyme: & for this cause I may depriue my selfe of light, by shutting of the dores and windowes, except whē I am to read, or take my refection.

I must forbeare all occasions of laughter, or
mirth

mirth; neither muſt I caſt myne eyes vpon any, vnles neceſſary occaſion require the ſame. And alſo during thoſe dayes, I may add ſome pennance or ſatisfaction, which is both inward, & outward. The inward is ſorrow for ſinns committed, with a full & firme purpoſe to beware both of them, & all other, for the time to come. The outward is the fruit of the inward, & that is ſome chaſtiſement, or puniſhing of the body voluntarily done, for my committed ſinnes: and this conſiſteth in three manners ſpecially. The firſt in our dyet, by withdrawing from it ſome things, not only ſuperfluous (which is an act of Temperance) but alſo conuenient, & neceſſary for our nutriment. And the more we ſhall take from our ſelues, the better it is, ſo long as we neyther preiudice nature, nor bring our bodyes into any great weaknes, or infirmity thereby. The ſecond conſiſteth in our ſleep, & manner of lodging, by depriuing our ſelues, not only of what is ſoft & delicate, but alſo of ſom what that is conuenient and needfull; yet all muſt be done without endomaging our health. And therfore we muſt not depriue our ſelues of neceſſary ſleep, further then tor a time, for the moderating of a cuſtome of ouermuch ſleeping. The third manner is by inflicting ſome payne vpon our Body it ſelfe, as in wearing of hairecloath, cords, braceletts of iron, diſciplining our ſelues, or in practice of ſome other auſterity of that kinde: but ſo, as without the detriment of our health.

MEDI-

MEDITATIONS
OF THE FIRST
WEEKE.

I. MEDITATION.

Of the End for which Man was created.

ONSIDER, that man was created in the beginning to prayse,
honour and serue God, and therby to obtaine beatitude. Hereupon I must meditate first, how
God created me of nothing, making me the
perfectest creature on earth, giuing me a body
so perfect, togearher with fiue senses, for euery one whereof he created a great multitude of
different obiects: he gaue me further a reasonable, spirituall, and mortall soule, beautified with so noble powers, such as be the Memory, the Vnderstanding, and the Will. And
all these he gaue me out of his only goodnesse
without any merit of myne, to the end, that
seruing

A

seruing him I may arriue to my last end. Vpō
this I will consider, how much I am bound to
vse well all the foresayd perfections, and how
much I haue offended in vsing them yll. I will
apprehend the domage and hurt that will befall me, if I fayle to come to this my end. I will
consider, that I was not created, to follow mine
owne appetite, to liue voluptuously, nor to
seeke after honours, & riches of the world I
will meditate, that God hath giuen me a soule
to his owne Image and likenes, for two
reasons. The one, that I should carry a continuall remembrance of his diuine maiesty, sith
I carry the resemblance of him in my selfe: the
other, to the end I should haue a care of the
preseruing of my soule, because it is the Image
of God, sith the contempt causeth the affront,
and the affront offered to the Image of the
King, redoundeth to his person: and to the
end I may set it forth and beautify it with the
ornaments of all vertues.

    2. I wil call to remembrance, that
my soule hath a certaine alliance and affinity
with the Holy Angells, and thereof I will take
an occasion to vse it well. I will consider, how
great a fauour it pleased the diuine Goodnes to
shew me, in creating me to so honorable an office, as to serue the same Goodnes, and how
carefull I ought to be to discharge my selfe of
this duty. Finally I will thinke, that God hath
giuen me the same office heere on earth, that
the Angells exercise in heauen, which is to
serue, and prayse him, and to enioy him after

                         for

for all eternity.

3.   I will confider, how God hath created, and made all the reft of the creaturs of the earth for the help of Man to the attayning of his end. Where I will firft confider Gods great liberality in building an houfe, fo abundantly furnifhed of all thinges for mans vfe, euen before his creation, making him fo many obiects for his recreation. And this will excite me, and giue me a more earneft defire to ferue him. I will alfo ponder, by difcourfing ouer all creatures, how directly they tend, and labour to the end, for which God hath made them, in doing their reftles feruice ro man: how I haue abufed them, in taking occafion to offend my God by that, whereby I fhould draw an argument of feruing him, ingulfing myne affection and loue in their inftability, & placing mine end in them, with the exceeding contempt of his diuine Maiefty. I will confider, that the creatures are but the meanes only for the attaining of my laft end, & as ladders to get vp to the knowledge of God, both the one and the other beeing as fingars, that point out the perfections of God, teaching me that all that, which is found good and perfect in them, is much more excellent, and more perfect in their Creatour.

4.   Of what is heere aboue fayd, I will gather, that I am to vfe Gods creatures with fobriety, and with an indifferency, nor any more of them, then what fhall be precifely profitable, and neceffary for the compaffing

of my laſt end, deſiring neither riches, nor pouerty; neither honour nor contempt : neither health nor ſicknes &c, euen as we take not a medicine but, with moderation and meaſure, leaſt that thing whereof we make vſe for our profit, turne to our domage and hurt : and as a trauailler, who goeth a iourney in haſt, taketh no more for his refection, then what he needeth for the making of his iourney, for feare leaſt if he ſhould take ouermuch, he ſhould find himſelfe hindred in the way. Heere I will endeauour alſo to reſolue my ſelfe to vſe a great indifferency in all that which God wold pleaſe to do with me, either for his ſeruice, or for my Superiors ; I will further endeauour to haue as little to doe with the creatures, as I may, baniſhing all fooliſh and prepoſterous affection out of my hart : and I will conceiue an irreconciliable deteſtation againſt mortall ſin, which alone, and nothing els, is able to withhold me from the attayning of my laſt end.

Meditation II. *Of the grieuouſnes of Sinne.*

TO know, how accurſed ſinne is, & how worthily to be deteſted, I will conſider, how much God hateth it, as neere as I may gheſſe by the ſeuere puniſhments of ſome ſinnes. And firſt the puniſhment of the bad Angells, who after they were created in heauen, were for their pride precipitated into hell, and chaunged into vgly Diuells. Hoere I will ponder firſt, how liberall God ſhewed himſelfe
towards

towards his Angells, in creating them to his I-
mage and likenes, and imparting vnto them
rare and singular gifts both of nature & grace,
for which they were on their part bound to a
certaine soueraigne acknowledgement for the
same. Secondly, I will consider, how ingrate
they shewed themselues, by rebelling against
God, & offending him in the very same, wherin they ought to haue serued him. Thirdly, I
will consider, how abhominable sinne is, sith
the same was inough to change so noble creatures, & to make them, who were so beautifull, the most foule, & vgly, that possibly could
be. Fourthly, I wil consider, how God detesteth sinne, seeing that for one sinne alone,
which they committed, he threw them downe
from heauen into the euerlastng flames of hell,
spoyling them of the grace, which he had bestowed vpon them, without regard of their
beautifull nature, or of the greatnes and dignity of their estate &c. Finally, I will thinke,
how foule and heauy a burden mortall sinne
is, which did so sodainly cast downe the Angells into hell: where I will represent to my
selfe also, how foule, and stincking, & hideous my soule is, by the infection of so many
sinnes I haue committed, when for one alone
the Angells were conuerted into diuells.

2. I will consider the punishment,
that God exercised vpon our first Parents A-
dam and Eue for their disobedience in eating
of the forbidden fruit. Where I will ponder
first, how liberall God shewed himselfe in their

behalfe, in creating them out of his own goodnes alone, to his owne Image and likenes, placing them in the terestriall Paradise, a place of pleasure and contentment, giuing them his grace, honouring them with originall iustice, & graunting them an happy, & quiet life both for themselues, & their posterity &c. Secondly, how ingrate they became to their benefa-ctour, by contemning his commaundements, & obeying the Diuell, who beguiled them by false promises, and caused Eue to eate the fruit first, and after Adam, who to please his wife made no difficulty to displease God. Thirdly, how terrible and dreadfull God shewed himselfe, though iustly, in punishing them, in banishing them out of paradise for euer, depriuing them of grace & originall iustice, condemning them to death, not only to temporall of the body, but also to eternall of the soule, both themselues, & all their posterity, & for this cause we al, as children of wrath, come into the world. Fourthly, I will consider, how all the euills, and myseries, that euer haue been, or shall be in the world, receiue their roote and beginning from sinne: whence I will conceiue the quality of the tree, by consideration of the fruit, that beareth so many & so great euills, & spoileth vs of so many and so great goods. Finally I will weigh the long pennance, that our first parents did, how deerly they bought this deadly morsell, that wrought so much bitternes vnto them. For Adam spent his whole life, which contayned aboue nine hundred yeares

yeares , in continuall labour, teares , sighes , and groanes .

3. I will meditate , that for one only mortall sinne , vvbat an infinite number be damned for all eternity to hell , where they are and shall be tormented for euer. And heerupon I will wonder at the grieuousnes of mortall sin, sith he, who is an vpright Iudge , punisheth it grieuously . I will consider also , how iustly God might haue condemned me long since to the like pains, not for one, but for many heinous sins, without expecting me to penance: & I will represent to my selfe that, which is true, that I am no lesse obliged vnto him , that he hath not throwne me headlong into hell, when I first deserued the same by sinne , then if he had drawne me out thence , if I had beene there .

4. I will consider , that the grieuousnes of sinne appeared much more in that most rigorous punishment, which the Eternall Father exercised vpon his most Blessed & most innocent Son for the offences of men, then in all other the punishments , that he euer exercised , how strange & seuere soeuer they were . I will represent to my selfe my Sauiour Iesus Christ, hanging vpon the Crosse, & I wil consider him wounded all his body ouer from head to foot, & I will meditate with a thousand sighes , that which sorrow and feare shall wrest from me . *Yf such punishment was exercised in greene wood , what shall be done vpon the dry?* such as I am , whome the drynesse of an infinite number of

A 4 grieuous

grieuous finns hath difpofed to fire euerlafting.

Meditation III. *Of the grieuoufnes of finnes, as they are many in number, and committed against Reafon.*

I Will thinke vpon the finnes I haue committed, reflecting vpon the tymes, the places, the offices, & exercifes I haue been imployed, & liued in. And this I will doe with fhame, confufion, and forrow, for hauing offended my God, crauing humbly pardon of his diuine maiefty as well for thofe, which I fhall remember, as for thofe, that I cannot call to minde, faying with the Prophet Dauid : *Pardon me my fecret finnes, O God*. And therefore I will wonder at the patience of my Lord God, who hath tolerated fuch a finner as I am, engulfed in the bottomles pit of fo many offeces & fo often reiterated.

2. I will further confider, who I am, & what fruits I haue brought forth, which be my finnes, & which I will behold as fo many vgly, & abhominable figures, that I haue drawne vpon the table of my life. Againe I will reprefent to my felfe finne, like vnto an huge heauy milftone, tyed to the finners neck, which of it owne weight is carryed downe into hell : or as a chaine compofed of an infinite number of lincks, at the one end whereof the infernall fpirits are pulling : or as a Great Gable-rope tyed to a thoufand leffer ropes : or as an army of enraged & mad dogges, or
                                    furious

furious bulls, of roaring Lions, of venemous serpents, & of other fierce & cruell beasts, that rent the sinnefull soule ; and thereby I will stir vp in my selfe feare and confusion.

3.   I will consider the obscenity and foulnes of sinne, committed against naturall Reason, for that it is hatefull, though there were no hell to punish it. First, because man doth sinne against Reason, according wherevnto he ought to order all his actions, & therfore all mortall sinne may be said to be against nature. For by it the sinner chaungeth himselfe into a beast, liueth a beast-like life, & maketh himselfe a slaue to sinne, & to the Diuell. Secondly, for the ignominy, and confusion, that sinne draweth with it, as is to be daily seene in such as commit it, who seeke darknes, & shunne the light, & search out secret places for auoiding of the shame, which might come vnto them by the foulenes thereof. Thirdly, in regard of the bitternes, it leaueth behind in the sinners hart, arising of the gnawing worme of conscience.

4.   I will consider, what man is, who is so hardy as to offéd the diuine maiesty, his Creatour, and I shall see, that as touching his body he is nothing but a peece of clay, and composed of ashes, subiect to infinite miseries, maladies, & trauailes, a sacke of worms, and a fountaine of putrifaction. Touching the soule, that it was created of nothing, & that consequently it cannot doe any thing of it owne being, being clad with ignorance, errour,

&

& darkenes, enuironed with tentatiõs not to be numbred, without & within, infested & assayled with enemies both visible & inuisible, inconstant & fraile, & to say in one word, inclined & propense to all kind of vices & sinnes. I will consider, my selfe to resemble a dogge dead, putrified, stincking, & abhominable, & I will meruaile with my selfe, that a thing, so vile, hath had the hardines to oppugne the infinite maiesty of God. I will conioine my littlenes with his incomparable greatnes: my ignorãce with the infinity of his wisdom: my weaknes with his illimited and endles power: mine excessiue naughtines with his immeasurable goodnes, meruailing that such vility, such frailty & basenes, hath had the boldnes to oppose against the incomprehensible excellécy, greatnes, & maiesty of God, considering a crime is so much the greater, & more exhorbitant, by how much more vile the person is that cõmitteth it, and the person more noble who is offended. I will meruaile yet much more, wherefore the Angells who are the ministers of Gods iustice, & who togeather therewith are so zealous of his honour, haue not rent & dismembred me into a thousand peeces. You may in this meditation, & the two following, see the Exercise of the first Weeke vpon the sinnes.

                              Medita-

Meditation IIII. *Of the grieuousnes of sinne, in regard of the Maiesty & infinite goodnes of God, who is thereby offended.*

IF the penitēt soule desire to stir vp in it selfe a greatest sorrow for his owne sinnes, to confound himselfe the more, & to procure a more cleare knowledge & vnderstanding of himselfe, it will be good to consider some one or other of the infinite perfections of God, especially those against which sinns are cōmitted. The first is his infinite Goodnesse, which maketh him in the highest degree amiable. The secōd is his Immēsity, by which he is present euery where: his incomprehensible Wisdome, by which he knoweth and seeth all thinges: his Omnipotency, which giueth being, & conserueth all things, yea the very sinner himselfe when he committeth the sinne. And hereby I come to vnderstand, that if there be not a man so desperate vpon earth, which is so hardy, as to commit a sinne before him who hath power to punish him for it; how much more ought we to stand in feare of the sight of this great King, who seeth and penetrateth all things, be the same neuer so hidden, and secret?

2. Wherefore I will in the second place consider the fauours & graces, I haue receiued from the liberall hand of such a benefactour, as God is; & I will ponder the beneefits of my Creation, Conseruation, & other

with

without number, that concerne my being, of
Nature, both of body and soule, and vpon this
I will gather that if the offence which the Son
committeth agaynst the Father be very grieuous, what may worthily be said of the creature, that hath offended the Creatour by those
very giftes which he hath receyued to honour
and serue him? Secondly, I will thinke vpon
the good of our Redemption, beginning from
our Sauiours Incarnation vntill his Ascension:
& vpon those of our Sanctification, such as be
the holy Sacraments, and other most singular
gifts and graces besides. I will wonder at my
selfe, that I haue so ill answered to so many o-
bligations by so many my sinnes, and the com-
pact which seemeth to haue been betweene his
diuine Maiesty, (who hath neuer ceased to do
me good, and to heape benefits vpon me) &
my selfe, who haue alwayes been obstinate in
rending him euill for good.

3.   I wil thinke vpon the Motiues,
that haue giuen me occasion of offending God,
and I shall find, that the same were thinges
most vile, that passe as doth the smoke, for the
loue whereof I haue contemned my louing
Lord God, committing Idolatry with them,
and preferring Barabbas before my Sauiour
Iesus, a folly or madnes not to be expressed by
wordes. I will thinke, what a blindnes it is to
belieue what fayth teacheth me, & yet to liue
as I doe; and to perswade my selfe, that sinne
is a thing so detestable, and yet to commit the
same without scruple; to hold for certaine, that
God

God foueraigne is my good, & withall iuſt, & yet to make no difficulty to offēd him. Wher-upon I wil breake into admiratiō with my ſelf, how all creatures haue not conſpired, & riſen againſt me: that the earth hath not opened to ſwallow me vp; that fire from heauen hath not burnt me to aſhes, as it did *Sodome,* & *Gomorrha,* that the beaſtes, plants, and all liuing thinges &c. haue not refuſed to do me ſeruice.

Meditat. V. Of the grieuouſnes of ſynne, by a compariſon of the paynes temporall and eternall, wherewith it is punished.

TO conſider, how ſinne is the cauſe of the ruyne and loſſe of all good, God ſpoiling ſinners thereof: Of honour as *Hely,* and his Sonnes: Of Royalties and Kingdomes, as *Saul,* & *Nabuchodonoſor* : Of Health of body, contentment & repoſe of ſpirit, ioy, and the life of body, in place whereof he ſendeth incurable diſeaſes, deadly ſorrow, ſodaine and ſhamefull deathes, famine, warre, peſtilence, and other euills that conſume the world.

2. To conſider, that beſides theſe afflictions cauſed by ſinne, it depriueth the ſinner further of the infinite and ſoueraigne good of all, which is God, the fountaine of all goodnes, the looſing of whome bringeth with it the greateſt euil of al, & ſo ſinne may be called the very ſame euill, & diſaſtre, and the very quinteſſence of all, that may be imagined pernicious, and domageable, becauſe it is an euill of

B   fault,

fault, that exceeds the euill of paine by infinit
degrees, and by this I wil conceiue an extreme
hatred and horrour of sinne. I will consider
also, how the infinite wisdome and prouidence
of God disposeth and ordaineth the euills of
payne to cure, as a medicine, those euills of
fault, whereby I will conceyue how straunge
this malady must needes be, for cure whereof
the vse of so bitter remedies is required, & necessary.

3.   I will consider, that this is not all, for
as much as sinne draweth yet other miseries after it, as those euen of hel that depriue the soule
of the infinite good, and of the vision of God
for all eternity: a paine and euill, that goeth
beyond al imagination. Moreouer I will consider, that sinne of it selfe is an euill greater then
be all those of this present life, yea and of hell
it selfe put togeather, in so much as if a man
hauing but one mortall sinne, should not suffer any paine, & that another free from sinne,
suffer himselfe alone all the torments of this
world and of hell, that other should be more
vnhappy, and more miserable, then this man.
Wherefore if it should be put in election to
commit a mortall sinne, or to suffer whatsoeuer
punishment, it were better to dye therby then
to sinne. I must ponder all this, to the end I
may the better apprehend the foulnes of sinne,
haue an horrour thereof, and be in a most high
degree sory for hauing defiled myselfe therewith.

Medit.

Meditat. VI.   *Conteyning a Repetition of the former Meditations.*

IN this meditation the repetitions are to be made, that our Holy Father S. Ignatius putteth down in his exercises of the first week, and the points of the precedent meditations are to be pondered, in which a man hath felt any consolation or desolation: Wherein three Colloquies are to be made touching the same. The first to the B. Virgin, as to our Advocatress, that she may obtaine for vs a knowledge and horrour of our sinnes, and the grace of God for our amendment, and forsaking of the worlds vanities. The second to our Blessed Sauiour, and our only Soueraigne Mediatour, beseeching him to obtaine vs the same fauours of his eternall Father. The third to God the Father, that he would please to graunt vs the three thinges aforesaid.

Meditat. VII.   *Of Death, and of the properties thereof.*

TO consider, that death is most assured & certaine, & how God hath determined the yeare, moneth, day, and houre, & that impossible it is to alter this finall decree. For as I came into the world the time and day that God chose for my natiuity, so shall I go forth of it againe at the time he hath appointed for

B 2   my

my paſſage, which is altogeather vncertaine.
Of this I will draw a firme reſolution to liue
euer prepared for my death, ſeeing I know
neither when, nor how I ſhall dye. For the day
will come as a thiefe &c. I will call to mind,
that God hath pleaſed to leaue me in this incer-
titude, expreſly thereby to bind me to ſtand
continually vpon my guard and be watchfull,
that by pennance of my ſinnes, and by good
workes I may preuent the ſeuerity of Iudgement, that attendeth me at my paſſage out of
this life, whereof our Sauiour hath made often
mention in the holy Ghoſpell. I will thinke,
that all the vnexpected and ſodaine deaths, that
haue happened and doe euery day happen to
men, be as ſo many admonitions and warnings
giuen to me, to be in readynes, ſith I am not
more priuiledged then be others, & the mortall ſinnes beſides, whereof I am culpable, de-
ſerue that I ſhould expect a rigorous intreat-
ment at that houre.

2. I will conſider, that death cometh but
once, and thereof I will conclude, that the
hurt and domage which a bad death bringeth
with it, beſides that it is the greateſt euill of all,
is alſo wholy irremediable: and that in like
manner the good of an happy death abideth
for euer, as the Wiſeman ſaith *Eccl.* 11. *VVhere
the tree faileth, there it ſhall be.* Herehence I will
take occaſion carefully to examine my confcience, and to doe condigne fruits of pennance,
to the end that in the fall of my body, my ſoule
may be found on the right ſide of glory. For
concluſi-

conclusion I will breake forth into an admiration of this, that notwithstanding I belieue all the aforesaid thinges so certainly as I doe, yet I liue the meane time in so great negligéce, and with so little a care of my soules good.

Medit.t. VIII. Of the thinges that cause griefe and affliction to them, who are neere vnto their death.

TO consider the inexplicable heauines, which the remembrance of all my passed pleasures shall cause, of the sensualities, carnall delights, ryots, surfettings, ambitions, reuenges, and the rest of the sinnes which I haue committed. The remembrance of my slouthfull coldnes in Gods seruice, mine omissions & negligences will assaile me on all sides, and will compasse me round, like vnto enraged beasts, to deuoure me, in so much as in such and so pressing an agony I shall find that more bitter then vvorme-vvood, vvhich I vvas wont to swallow downe as hony. To thinke, what cruell a paine it will be to me to remember the time lost, which was giuen me for the negotiating of an affaire & busines of such importance, as is myne eternall saluation. How much I shall be afflicted to thinke, that I haue let so many good occasions passe, which God sent me to make my profit of. Then I shall desire to haue but one only day of so many which now I loose, and I shall repent my selfe perad-

B 3   uenture

uenture in vaine, that I haue not obeied so many diuine and holy inspirations, that I haue not lead a good religious life, and finally that I haue not answered the infinite fauours, which I haue receiued from heauen.

2. To consider, that the houre of death when it approacheth will make me iudg much otherwise of the thinges of this world, then I doe now. For then I shall esteeme of them, as they are of themselues in effect and verity, & now I esteeme them as they are in apparence & shew. And of this I will make a resolution, and firme purpose, from hence forwards to loose no more time, nor to suffer any occasion to ouerslip me that may make to my profit, following heerin the counsaile, that the holy Ghost hath giuen me in these words: *Depriue not thy selfe of one good day.* I will resolue also not to permit my selfe to be carryed away with the vanity of thinges, that vnder a faire pretext & apparence inuite & sollicite me to sin.

3. To consider the sorrowful pangs of the soule in forsaking these thinges present, as honours, liuings, pleasures &c. but aboue all in it seperation from the body, a deare part of therof, so louing an host, & good friend, wherunto God had vnited it by so strait a band, without carrying any thing away with it, all thinges beeing then conuerted into bitternes, and into an vnspeakable disgust, when necessity shall seperate it from parents, and friends, and from all the world. This will be a very grieuous farewell, that it must bid to all visible

sible creatures, leauing them for euer, as though the same had neuer been made for the seruice of man : & the more the affection shall adhere vnto them, the more painefull and af-flictiue will be the griefe of that separation. And of this I wil endeauour to diuert & with-draw myne affection from the lesse rectified loue of creatures, that I may not feele the trouble of leauing them at the houre of death. I will also consider, how great folly, or rather grieuous sinne it is to forsake God for so vaine thinges. Moreouer I will represent to my selfe, that whether I will or no, I must one day leaue them, and therefore I will take an occasion to reioyce and be glad, that I haue already aban-doned them for the loue of my Sauiour, and I will beware for the tyme to come not to fasten mine affection too much vpon any creature whatsoeuer.

3. To consider the perplexity, feare, & deadly anxiety, in which I shall find my selfe in this last houre, when I am to render an ac-compt to my God of my passed life. For the euill, that threatneth me, is greater, then I am able to apprehend : the definitiue sentence without appeale, without repeale or reuocati-on, ineuitable, & such as is indispensable; to be put in execution that very instant; my bu-sines doubtfull, & withall most dangerous. For I know I haue committed many sinnes, & I know not, whether they haue been pardo-ned me. And therefore my feare will be most great, and inexplicable, the craft of the malig-

nant

nant spirit increasing the same by his tentatiõs. For in this laſt conflict he will doe his vttermoſt, labouring to put me into despayre, by the consideration of my bad life, and of the seuerity of Gods iuſtice: and therefore I will now, whiles my labour may ſtand me inſteed, enter into a seuere accompt with my selfe.

Meditat. IX.   Of the particular Iudgement, that paſſeth at the inſtant-of our death.

TO consider, how my soule ſhall, in that laſt moment be presented before the throne of God, to giue accompt of the good & euill it hath done, where nothing ſhal accompany it, but my workes good and bad, where it ſhall behold on the one ſide, the Diuells in an hideous and dreadfull forme, & on the other ſide the soueraigne Iudge with terrible countenance, who will demaund an accompt of the graces and benefits I haue receiued; and being vpright and withall moſt wise, he cannot be circumuented, nor deceiued. Thẽ will I represent to my selfe the moſt ſtrong accusation, that the malignant spirits ſhall preſſe me with, by aggrauating my ſinnes. And vpon this consideration I will make a good purpose to liue well for the time to come, ſith in that laſt houre I ſhall not haue any other defence, and protection, besides a good conscience.

2.   To consider, that the time, wherein
the

the iudgment is to be made, is the very inftant
my foule leaueth my body, an inftant, that I
ought euer to haue before the eyes of my
mind, faying often, *O moment, O inftant, wheron dependeth my Eternity*! The place of this
Iudgement is the place, where death fhall
feize vpon me, be it vpon the earth, or fea.
Wherby I will conceiue a great feare of offending God in any place of the world, remembring *Loths* wife, who had no fooner turned
her head to looke backe, then that fhe was
conuerted into a ftatua of Salt, & many haue
been furprized by death in the very action of
their finne.

3. To imagine the order & proceffe of this
iudgement, and confider that my accufers fhal
be the Diuells, the mortall & capitall enemies
of men : my owne confcience, that fhall for it
owne part preffe much, fhall ferue in fome fort
for a witnes againft me : my good Angell fhall
alfo be my accufer of the often rebellions and
refiftances, that I fhall haue made againft his
good counfailes : whence I will learne not to
contemne, or reiect diuine infpirations. To
thinke alfo ; that in this rigorous Iudgement I
fhall be examined of all my thoughts, wordes,
workes, omiffions, negligences, ingratitudes,
yea of not acknowledgements of both generall and particular benefits : That this examen
fhall be moft euident, and cleare, in fuch fort,
as the finnefull foule fhall be conuinced of her
crimes, God (by a certaine light concurring)
difcouering all the finnes to the eye, as alfo all
the

the good workes of a pious soule, her thoghts, wordes, her obedience, her pennance, mortifications &c. A thing that will exceedingly reioice the good, & in like manner infinitely afflict the bad.

4. To confider, that as our Lord fhall by his iuft fentence fpoyle the bad of the graces & fupernaturall gifts, that remained vnto them after their falling into finne, by degrading them (as doth a Bifhop a Prieft conuicted of a crime & condemned to dye) for their deliuery ouer to the Diuells, who fhall precipitate them into eternall flames, depriuing them of faith, hope, Charity & all the other graces & gifts, fo as the foule fhall remaine naked & defpoyled of all good, clad a new with confufion, reproach, & ignominy, & condemned to row for euer, as a miferable bondflaue, in the gallyes of hell. To thinke, how the fentence being once pronoũced againft the finfull foule, our Sauiour Iefus fhall driue the fame from his company, & the Angell guardian fhall forfake it faying: Seeing thou neglectedft and refufedft to follow my admonitions & coũfayles, & to obey myne infpirations, goe thou with him, that is, the Diuell, whome thou haft preferred before me: who fhall fodainly feize vpon that vnhappy foule, attended vpon with an infernall band, & fhall precipitate it into the euerlafting flames. And all this fhall be done in a moment, fo as the moft vnfortunate finner fhall paffe from the pleafurs of a fhort continuance, to torments & paines, that fhall endure for euer.

5. To

5. To confider the fentence, that is giuen in fauour of a iuft foule, our Sauiour faying vnto it : Come, thou bleffed of my Father, to the Kingdome, I haue prepared for thee, enter into the glory of thy Lord . Then fhall the Diuell with confufion and defpayre withdraw himfelfe, & the good Angell with many other in company, fhall take the foule, & conduct it ftraight to heauen, if there be not any thing remayning in it to be purifyed, and cleanfed in Purgatory . I may heere make a comparifon of the different conditions of the good & the bad, thereby to excite my felfe to liue well, fith it is the way and meanes to dye well and vertuoufly .

Meditat. X.   *Of what befalleth to the body after death, & buriall of the fame.*

TH I s meditation hath very great effect to moue a foule to the mortification of her own paffiōs, & to the contemning of the world, for that both in regard of what we haue already fayd, and of what we are to fay afterwards, it difcouereth the very end, where the vanity of it endeth .

1. To confider the ftate, wherein the body remaineth after the feparation of the foule from it, how it forgoeth the vfe of the fenfes, and the mouing of the members, without feeing, hearing, vnderftanding the thinges of this world, no more then if they were not at all.

It

It becometh pale, foule, ftincking, fearefull to fee, and as chaunged into corruption, and rottennes. It remaineth alone, none able to endure to fee it, the friendes leaue it, and will not come neere it, thofe of the houfe fly and runne from it, all do with impatience attend & expe&t the houre, when it is to be carryed to the graue. Whereupon I will learne, how I ought to handle my body, knowing what the condition of it is.

2.   To confider, what manner of cloathing is beftowed vpon it, and to fee that commonly it is the worft that is to be found in the houfe, a poore fheete that is lent it, a poore and ftrait pit or graue is prepared for the lodging of it: for the bed to lye on, it fhall haue from thenceforth the cold and hard earth: the bones of the dead fhall ferue for the pillow to lay the head on, the wormes fhall intertaine it, & the toads bid it welcome. Hereby I will acknowledge the worlds deceit, and if I be relígious I will animate my felfe to pouerty, & to the contempt of vanities.

3.   To confider the fhort iourney, the body maketh from out of the mothers wombe to the buriall, whither it is carryed by others, fome finging, & others weeping: how it is let downe into the graue, how it is couered with earth, trodden vpon with the feete, preffed downe with an heauy and weighty ftone, forgotten of all, and abandoned and left to the wormes. And this is the beft, & happyeft condition, it can expe&t: for how many haue
                                        there

there byn which the wild beasts haue deuoured, the fowles of the ayre, and the fishes of the sea haue buryed vp within their bellies? O piteous state of all corruptible flesh, thou teachest me, wherein endeth the glory of mortall meu.

Meditat. XI. *Of the dust and ashes, whereinto we are to be dissolued & brought.*

TO consider these vvordes: Remember man, that dust thou art, and to dust thou must returne. This was that, which God said to our first Parent Adam presently after he had sinned, giuing him to vnderstand, what he was, and what we are. His diuine Maiesty pleased to make our bodyes of a vile and grosse matter, such as is the slyme of the earth, to the end by the remembrance of our origine, euer continuing in the soule, we should pull in the wings of our pride, humble our selues lowly, & thinke, that if we should be trodden vpon, as earth, we haue not any cause of complayning: to the end also we should wonder at the power & wisdom of our maker, who knew how, of so abiect and vile a matter, to compose so excellent a worke.

2. To consider, that God condemned Adam to death for his pride, and sentenced him to returne to dust, to notify how detestable a thing sinne is: to the end also the remembrance of our future conuersion into dust may serue for a soueraigne medicine for our pride, & that the feare of this punishment might serue for a spur

C

and

& incitement of our coldnes to pênance , & for a bridle to our vnruly and difordred paſſions,& ſo in the houſe of aſhes (as ſaith Micheas) I will couer my ſelfe with duſt . Vpon this I will ponder , that if I couet , and follow earthly thinges with ſo great an heate and affeÆtion, it is becauſe I am made of earth : and I will confider, that all, that I can haue heere on earth , is nothing but durt , and filth , to the end the vanity of the world bewitch me not with the apparent glittering,& faire ſhew therof .

3 .   To imagine, that God euer and a none inculcateth theſe wordes vnto vs , Remember, that thou art duſt , & to duſt thou ſhalt returne . To ruminate ofté in mind the words,that *Eccleſiaſticus* ſayth in the perſon of one , that is dead : *Remember my iudgment, for thyne ſhall be the ſame: yeſterday for me, to day for thee.* The dead bodies, the bones & ſculls of the dead muſt imprint in my ſoule this conceipt , and I muſt oftentymes weigh and ponder this word (to day) to the end I may not differre and put of mine amendment, till another day .

Medit. XII.   Of the deceits, and hurts , which the forgetfulnes of Death cauſeth .

TO meditate that parable, which our Sauior propoſeth of a certayne couetous rich man, who hauing gathered abundance of riches togeather, flattered & deceyued himſelfe, in promiſing himſelfe long life . Vpon which I will

will confider, that the firft deceit of the Diuell, is
Hope which is giuen of long life, and it may be
that a man may liue a leffe while, then there is
apparence. The fecond is the affurance, that a
man conceiueth to be alwaies in good health, to
haue forces of body, & the cōtentment of mind
by meanes of the goods he poffeffeth, and yet
all dependeth on the goodnes of God. The third
is a forgetfulnes and negligence of preparing
our felfe to death, as though we expected not an
other life. And for this reafon this rich man is
called a foole, a name & tytle, that they all merit who become followers of him.

2. To confider the inexplicable infelicity,
that in death befalleth vnto them, who during
their life doe flatter their fenfuality with vaine
hopes : alfo the irreparable hurts they incurre,
the firft wherof is to dye in their blindnes without knowledge of their miferyes, but when they
be irremediable, and too late to diuert them.
The fecond is to dye fodainly in the middeft of
fo many finnes, pleafurs and contentments. The
third is to dye a violent and forced death, becaufe it is not voluntary, God bereauing them of
life, whether they will or no.

3. To thinke, what afflictiue payne they
feele, who are forced to leaue their goods, wherunto their affection was fo faft tyed, not hauing
the time to difpofe of them, as it hapned vnto
this rich man. The goods, that thou haft coue-
toufly heaped togeather, whofe fhall they be?
An interrogation, that euery one may make to
himfelfe, and fay : This foule, that now lodgeth

C3   in

in my body, what shall become of it, and whither shall it goe? And to this purpose I will consider, what holy Writ recordeth of King *Baltazar*, who being in a magnificall banquet, eating & drinking, & making good cheere, perceiued vpon a suddaine the fingars of an hand, that wrote vpon the wall of his pallace: God hath numbred thy Kingdome, & hath finished it: he hath weighed thee in his equall ballance, and thou art found to light: he hath deuided thine Empire, & hath giuen it to thine enemies. Which is as much to say, as God hath made a separation of thy body & soule, giuing one to the wormes to consume it, & the other to the Diuells, to be tormented for euer. And this sentence was executed forthwith, whiles the King was in the very middest of his pleasurs.

Meditat. XIII.   *Of the generall Iudgement, & of the signes that goe before the same.*

TO consider the reasons, wherefore God would, that there should be a generall, & publike Iudgement. The first is for confirming the setence giuen in the particular Iudgment, & to notify vnto the world, how equitable and iust it is, to render vnto the body eyther a compensation for it trauailes and paynes, or a punishment for it demeritts. The second is, for that the diuine maiesty hath an intent to discouer & lay open the honour of the iust, vniustly oppressed, & taken from them in
this

this life, to manifest the iustice and right, that himself hath to the gouermēt of the vniuerse, & wherfore he permitteth vertue to be persecuted. The third, to the end the glory of Iesus Christ might become manifest not only in heauen to the good, but vpon earth also to the bad, and that they, who had seene his humility, might see and behold his exaltation, and that this sight of him might fill the wicked with confusion and sorrow.

2. To contemplate the prodigious & wonderfull signs, that shall goe before this finall, & vniuersall Iudgement, the horrour, & variety thereof: that all creatures shall rise in armes against the sinner for the punishing of him, because he abused their seruice: that the Moone shall put on the colour of bloud: that the Stars shall fall downe from heauen: that the celestiall spheres & orbes, being neere the ending of their course, shall make a dreadfull noyse: that the sea shall roare and rage to the astonishment of all: and in few words, that all creatures shall begin to make a commotion against men, who in this affright and terrour shall not know what to resolue, or what to doe, shall wyther and dry vp, and become deformed for very distresse, especially the wicked, whome their owne conscience shall a thousand wayes gnaw, and then shall begin their torments & gnashing with their teeth. Heere I will craue of God, that he would please to bridle, and restraine the motions of my soule with the bridle of his holy feare.

3. To meditate, that fire seat from the foure

C 3. quarters

quarters of the world, shall burne & consume to
ashes all thinges vpon earth : vpon which I will
consider, what is the end of the worlds glory.
This fire shall be most cruell & raging against
the bad, that shall be then found aliue, but nothing so seuere against the good, to whome it
shall serue insteed of purgatory, and increase
their merit, and their crowne of glory. This conflagration of fire shall continue, vntill the Iudgment be finished, and the fire shall purify and
purge the bodyes of the iust, and shall torment
those of the reprobate, with whom after the definitiue sentence it shall goe downe into hell.

4 .   To consider, that the latter day of Iudgment is hidden among other the secrets of the
diuinity, and therefore it will come vpon mortall men at vnawares, & vpon the sodaine, when
they shall least thinke of it, and which is more,
when they shall be in the middest of their pleasurs, as it hapened in the time of the great floud,
& of the conflagration of Sodome .

*Meditat . XIIII.   Of the generall Resurrection
of the dead , & of the comming of the Iudge.*

TO consider, how all thinges being brought
and consumed into ashes vpon the face of
the earth, there shall be vpon the sudaine
heard the fearefull voyce of an Angell from the
foure quarters of the world, saying, Arise yee
dead, and come to Iudgement • A voyce of such
efficacy, as in that very instant the sea, and the
earth shall giue vp the bodyes, that they haue
                                            kept

kept from the beginning of the world, at what time euery one of them shall without delay be reunited to their soule. To consider, how foule, vgly, & heauy the bodyes of the reprobate shall be, and what bitternes of sorrow the miserable soules shall feele to see themselues imprisoned within that fowle and stincking prison, vvhat cursinges they vvill vse the one to the other, accusing one the other of that common disaster, and imputing one to the other the cause thereof. To imagine that, when the soule shall enter againe into it owne body, it shall begin to burne, & to cast forth smoke, like a furnace set on fire: & that on the contrary the bodyes of the blessed shall rise agayne lightly, immortall & impassible, compassed with a splendour & light, & that their beautifull soules shall with pleasure & contentment reunite themselues vnto them, giuing them thankes for hauing been faythfull and loyall vnto them, during the time of this mortall life. I will thinke heere, vpon the different condition of the one and the other, for the stirring vp of my selfe to the following & imbracing of vertue.

2.   To consider, with what Maiesty our Sauiour will come, his glorious attendance, his Royall standard, his Crosse, his throne of Maiesty: what his countenance will be, his innumerable troups of Angells: those who shall sit in Iudgement with him, and the rest of his company. How he shall come, powring forth a torrent of fire for the consuming of the wicked, who shall behold the most holy stadard of the Crosse

to appeare on high to their extreme confusion,
& to the exceeding comfort of the good. To
meditate, how our Sauiour shall sit vpon a most
wonderfull throne, composed of a bright shining cloud, shewing a coūtenance most benigne
to the good, and most terrible to the bad.
That out of his sacred wounds shall come beams
of light for the one, and fearefull flashes of light-
ning for the other. That by his side shall be placed another throne of glory for his holy and
blessed Mother, not that she shall carry herselfe
for an aduocatresse in that place, or that she shold
craue mercy, as now she doth, but to confound
the sinners, who haue neglected oportunities
to make recourse to her protection, & to reioice
the assembly of the iust, to whome the consideration of the honour she shall receiue of the
whole world, will cause contentment. That the
Apostles also shall sit, euery one in his throne,
to iudge the twelue tribes of Israel, by their
workes & holy life. I may meditate here, what
the holy Doctours say, that such as shall haue
professed voluntary pouerty, to wit, the Religious imitatours of the Apostles, shall sit e-
uery one in his seate: wherein I will represent
to myselfe the difference, that is now betweene
poore Religious persons and the monarches of
the earth, & that far more which shall then be
betweene them there. For many of the great po-
tentates of the world shall in that place be foūd
among the most miserable of all: and thereof I
will learne to hold myne owne condition more
happy, then those of the worldlings, and I will
yield

yield God thankes for the honour, that he hath done me in calling me vnto it.

3.   To contemplate, how the Iudge will commaund a separation to be made of the good from the bad, placing the good on the right hand, the bad on the left, though we see them now intermixt in the world, & that the peruerse be ordinarily more honored, then the good: but then this confusion shall cease & be taken away, the good graine shall be separated frō the chaffe, the wheate from the drosse, & the lambes frō the scabbed sheepe. Hereupon I may represent to my selfe the rage and fury of the reprobate, whē they shall see themselues so contemned, & banished from the society of the elect; & contrarywise the contentment of the good, beholding themselues chosen, and drawne from out of the company of that rabble. How happy shall they esteeme themselues to be for exercising obedience, humility, pennance, &c. And how will they blesse the trauailes & paines, that they shall haue endured in this mortall & short life.

4.   To consider, that the consciences of all men shall be laid open, in so much as euery one shall see, what ech other hath euer done: that there shall appeare before the whole world the most secret thoughts: there they shall see the abbominable sinnes, that haue been committed in darknes, & in hidden places, euen those that shall haue been concealed in confession, so as the sinner, because he would not endure a little, light, & secret confusion, shal suffer that publike, eternall, & continuall confusion in the face of the whole

whole world. There shall come to light all the bad works, that shall haue been cloked vnder the pretence of holines, nothing shall remayne hidden, all shall be reuealed, both good & bad. There the sinnes shall appeare in their own deformity, and there vertue shall shew it selfe in it owne naturall beauty : wherehence I will endeauour to moue my selfe to loue & imbrace vertue now, & to shun vice.

5. To consider, of how strange crymes the wicked shall be accused, as well on the part of the malignant spirits, who will charge them to haue yielded consent to their suggestions, without hauing profited them any whit, as on the part of God himselfe, who will reproach them of his benefitts generall & particular, of his holy inspirations, of his Sacraments, & of the helps he hath giuen them to draw them out of their vices and sinnes, and to incite them to vertue. Their good Angells will vpbraide them for the obstinate rebellion against good counsayles: the Iust will come in accusation against them, for hauing set naught by their good examples : finally their owne conscience, conuicted by the truth, will be the strongest accuser of them for their eternall reprobation.

Meditat. XV. Of the sentence in fauour of the Elect : and of that of the Reprobate.

TO consider, that our Sauiour, turning himselfe graciously towardes the good, will with a sweet & pleasing cheere say vnto them;

them ; Come yee blessed of my Father, come to take possession of the Kingdome, that hath been prepared for you from the beginning of the world : for I was hungry , and you gaue me to eate , &c. I will weigh euery word by it selfe , to stir my soule vp to follow vertue, that it may in this latter day be participant of these diuine benedictions , and enioy the heauenly Kingdome, that God in his prescience, & eternal predestinatiō, hath prepared for the elect. I wil cōsider also, what these works of mercy be, that giue right to this Kingdome, & set open the gates of heauen , & I wil put on a resolution to exercise them for the tyme to come , rendring thanks to the infinite liberality and goodnes of God , for hauing promised for so few thinges the inestimable inheritance of his glory . I will also ponder , what our Sauiour shall say to euery one of the iust in particular, & as it were thanking them for what they shall haue done for loue of him : to the religious , for hauing contemned the world for his sake : to the chast , for hauing preserued , and kept their chastity, &c.

2. To consider , that after this , turning himselfe towards the bad, he will pronounce the sentence against them with an angry & terrible countenance , saying: Goe yee accursed , into fire euerlasting, which is prepared for the diuell, & his Angells : for I was hungry, and you gaue me not to eate &c. Away , separate your selues from me , who am your God and benefactour , & had beene your Redeemer if you would haue accepted of me, vpon whom I haue so oft called,

and

and you stopped your eares, that you might not heare my voyce. Away from me, who will haue no more friendship with you for euer: you shall haue no part in my Kingdome, nor in my company, nor in the company of my Mother, and my Saints. Away, Away, yee accursed, into fire euerlasting, vnquenchable, and endles, that shall without mitigation torment you for euer with the Diuells, to whome you haue voluntarily subiected your free will. Heere I will examine the cause of this dreadfull malediction, and the subiect of this banishment, and I shall find it, that it was for not hauing exercised the workes of mercy towards our neighbour, which our Sauiour accepted, as done to his owne person. I will further consider, that the damned, hauing heard the fearefull sound of these thundering words, will be seized with a deadly and most fore heauines, seeing themselues banished from the company of God for euer, without hope of recouery, and condemned for eternity to row in the gallies of hell, vnder the mercyles cruelty of the Diuells.

3. To thinke that the sentence is no sooner pronounced, then that it is instantly executed, the earth opening it selfe vnder their feete, and swallowing vp all that infamous multitude, as it were so many vncleane swine whom the Diuells their swin-heards, shall throw downe headlong into the bottomles gulfe of hell, whereinto they are no sooner receiued, then that the earth shall close againe vpon them, & they shall abide shut vp in that infernall close prison for eternity, ne-

uer

uer to come out any more.

4. To meditate the griefe, fury, & despaire of these most vnhappy wretches, and their deadly enuy, most sensible in their harts, seeing the glory and felicity of the iust, from whose company they shal behold themselues so shamfully seuered. O alas, experience will giue them then to vnderstand, how bitter & vnhappy a thing it was for them to haue been in this life separated from their creatour, & to haue contemned his commaundements, and shaken of the yoke of his diuine feare. O that they shall well vnderstand, but ouer late, the vanity of the thinges, for which they haue lost & forgone inestimable goods. Hereupon I may meditate the ioy of the iust, when they shall see the seuerity of the diuine iustice, though they behold their owne parents amongst the damned: iust reason on the part of God giuing them satisfaction, and ministring them matter of that their ioy. I may also ponder, how the chosen shall raise themselues vp in the ayre, following their grand captaine Iesus Christ, the King of Kings, to whome they shall sing a thousand songs of praise, and particularly the versicle of the Psalme: *Blessed be the Sauiour*, *Who had deliuered vs from our enemyes teeth*. And so carryed in the ayre on high, they shall penetrate all the heauens, they shall tread the Sunne, the Moone, & the stars vnder foot, & shall passe all the celestiall spheres to the heauen Empyreū, where being arriued they shall be placed in thrones of glory, and therein repose for eternity. O happy labours, most happy obedience,

D

dience, most fruitfull humility &c. Finally to
consider, that this world is an house of proba-
tion, wherein such, as obey not the commaun-
ments, and inspirations of God, are cast out for
euer: & on the contrary, those who obey God,
and voluntarily subiect themselues to his lawes,
heare his voice, follow his instincts, and performe his commaundements, shall be admitted
into the Society of those of heauen, and shall enioy God, and that felicity, which consisteth in the
fruition of his diuine essence, for euer.

*Meditat. XVI.   Of Hell, and of the Eternity
of the Paynes, and dreadfull horrour of the
place.*

TO consider, that hell is a perpetuall prison
full of fire, and most grieuous torments
for the torturing of them for euer, whome
death shall take away in mortall sinne. That it is
a state of an eternall continuance, in which the
sinners are to abide without end, depriued of all
the goods, that they might haue desired for their
felicity, and shall suffer all the euills, that they
might apprehend for their torment: in so much
as in this disastrous place there is nothing but a
priuation of all good temporall and eternall, &
the affliction of all euills both of this life and of
the other, which are so great and so extreme,
as the cruellest and greatest euills that can be i-
magined vpon earth, be but painted euills in
comparison of those of hell.

2.   To

2. To confider, that whatfoeuer is in hell, is of côtinuance without end; that they who out of a raging fury defire their finall confumation, do in vaine defire that which is impoffible for thê to obtaine. That the prifon, the fire euer burning & not confuming, the gnawing worme of confcience, & Gods ineuitable decree be eternall. For in hell there is no redemption, nor ranfome, nor returne thêce : the precious bloud of the Son of God penetrateth not thither, not euer fhall, for that at the tyme, when it was fhed, the diuine vertue and efficacy of it paffed not fo far, as to come to that place fo vnhappy. That there is not any true fatisfation, nor pennance to effeçt there. That the finners fhal there be depriued of faith, hope, and of all ouer vertues, as vnworthy therof : that (to fay in one word) their infelicity fhall continue & abide ineuitable and eternall, becaufe the fault alfo, which hath precipitated them into that place, is eternall.

3. To confider, that the perpetuall continuance of fo extreme paines, which fhal not giue any moment of mitigation or eafe, and fhall neuer diminifh in their bitternes (as may be feene by the example of the rich glutton) fhall not be fuch, as is in this life, where cuftome eafeth the paine, and the pricking thereof becometh with time leffe grieuous, but on the contrary, that the reiteration therof fhall euery day renew & increafe the torments. And if one troublefome night be fo long to a man preffed with an eafy ficknes, and with a tolerable paine, what will it be with that night of euerlafting darknes?

D 2   4. To

4. To consider, that hell being seated in the center of the earth, is darke, depriued of all light, that the fire burneth, and giueth no light: that it is most strait, and that the damned shall be therein, as be the brickes within a burning furnace, without possibility of mouing. That it is a place most intemperate; where no ayre, nor breath of wind can haue place to asswage the excessiue heate, and withall most vncleane and stincking, the sweat and other filth of the damned yielding an infectious, pestilent, and intollerable bad smell. Finally that these miserable creatures shut vp on all sides, can neuer get out thence either by force, or any other whatsoeuer skill.

5. To consider the inexplicable misery, infelicity, and disaster of the inhabitants of this wretched place, where they shall lay imprecations and maledictions one vpon another, without respect of sonne to the father, or of seruant to the maister: where they shall be replenished with rage, fury, and cruelty one against another, especially those, who shall haue been companions in mischiefs, and shall haue committed some sinne in company togeather. And this fury shall increase by the consideration of this, that whether they will or no, they shall be forced to continue eternally tormented togeather, and shall not be able eyther to kill themselues, or to seperate themselues one from another, or to come to reconciliation, or to get away, but transported with Diuellish rage, some shall roare as do the Lyons, and others shall howle as do

the

the hungry wolues &c.

6. To confider the dreadfull figures and fhapes of the infernall furies, that fhall torment them. For befides that euery one of the damned fhall be the tormentour of all, and all of euery one, the Diuells fhall yet torment them in particular, & fhall difcharge vpon them the hatred and malice, they haue conceiued againft God, and Iefus Chrift. And more then this, the neuer-dying worme of confcience fhall cruelly torment them, reprefenting vnto them the great and good occafions, they had of fauing their foules in this life; the helpes, that God from time to time fent them for the withdrawing of themfelues from finne, & the auoyding of thofe torments they novv endure: finally the inuincible, and heauy hand of Almighty God fhall exercife his reuenging ire vpon their facrilegious heades. And they on the contrary part, who fhall not be ignorant, that his wrath and anger is the caufe of their punifhment, will vtter againft his diuine Maiefty all forts of blafphemies, wifhing that he neither had bin, nor were of power. But all this fhall be conuerted into their torment: and heereupon I wil thinke, how heauy and fearefull a thing it is to fall into the hands of God, when he is angry.

D 3   *Media.*

Meditat. XVII. *Of the payne of the Senses, and of the inward Powers, togeather with the paine of Losse, that the damned suffer.*

TO consider, that euery one of the damned is punished by the very same thinges, by which he hath offended, and where the sin entred in by the gates of the senses, by them shall the payne enter also, in such sort as the sight shall be tormented by the visions of horrible shapes, and it shall not be in the power of the damned to shut his eyes, that he may not see them: the hearing shall be tormented with the fearefull blasphemyies and maledictions against God, & so of the rest of the senses, euery one of them beeing punished withall that, which may giue them torment. And this shall stir me vp to doe pennance for my sinnes in time, which I haue committed by my senses.

2.   To consider the insupportable sharpnes and viuacity of hell fire, in comparison whereof our terrestrial and elementary fire is nothing but a painted fire: and a fire, that shall cleaue so fast to the miserable damned, as it shall neuer be in their power to free themselues from it, but they shall be tormented with it, some more, some lesse, some with more seuerity in one part, some in another: the murmurers, and blasphemers in their tongue: the gluttons, and drunkards in their tast. This fire wanteth light, which might giue some ease to their misery, and casteth

forth

forth a thicke and blacke smoke, that tormenteth, and killeth not. And if we be so far from enduring our fire heere, what wil it be to liue euer a middest those deuouring flames?

3.   To meditate the paine of the invvard povvers of the soule : as of the Fancy, that shall be tormented vvith horrible imaginations : the memory with a continuall remembrance of thinges past that vve haue possessed, of thinges present, & those, that may happen after for all eternity : the vnderstanding, that shall be filled with darkenes, errors, and falsities, and shall not haue the power to discourse nor comprehéd any thing, that may cause any pleasure, but iudging with a temerarious conceyte, that God wrongeth them, they shall say, that he is vninst, and wicked in handling them in such sort. The will, that shall be obstinate in the sinnes, and in an irreconciliable hatred towards God, and his Saints, shall neuer yield, nor chaunge, nor repent it selfe. Finally to thinke, that the damned shall be like vnto a deep sea of bitternes, whercinto all the torrents of miseries & of punishments do disgorge, & empty themselues.

4.   To consider, the paine that they call of Losse, which consisteth in the priuation of the supreme good for euer, and of the eternall fountaine and source of diuine pleasurs, seeing themselues for euer banished from heauen, and debarred of the end, for which they were created. The greatnes of this inexplicable payne, yea and the greatest of all others, cannot be any

way expressed, by the similitude or proportion, that may be drawne from thinges of this world. As if we imagine some person of quality, who hauing right to succession in a Kingdome, where he might be in hope to enioy the pleasues, honors, and riches therof, should see himselfe depriued, by his owne fault, of his both right, & hope, and should find himselfe ouerthrowne and ruined by euills, and miseries, contrary to that his hope, expectation &c. Heere I will goe downe in thought into those darke dens of hell, and making a turne through the vnhappy habitations of the damned, I will demaund the cause, wherefore some doe burne amiddest the flames of fire, and others be plunged in most extreme colds, &c. for the conceiuing of a great feare in my soule for offending, and of a more feruent desire to doe pennance for my sinnes for the time to come, saying with Saint Augustine: Burne me heere, and cut me agayne and againe, my Lord and Sauiour, in this world, that thou mayst pardon me for euer in the next.

Meditat. XVIII.   *Of Purgatory, a pregnant and strong motiue for the styrring vs vp to pennance.*

TO consider, how none can enter into heauen, soyled with the very least stayne of sinne eyther of fault, or of paine, & therfore God hath assigned a place vnder the earth, which we call Purgatory, whither the soules of

the

the iust are to goe, if there remaine any thing to be purged after the passage from this life, to the end they may make satisfaction, if any be due, to the diuine iustice: which appeareth wonderfully in this, that it may not endure any fault without paine, any offence without a punishment, any cryme without satisfying for it: and yet God euer of his benignity intermingleth the sweetnes of his mercy with the seuerity and rigour of his chastisements, changing the paine that should be eternall, into temporall, which, if during this mortality, it be not throughly satisfyed, and fully paied by the sinner after the remission of the fault, the soule when it goeth out of this world, is to pay to the full in Purgatory, if any satisfaction remaine then further to be made: for as much as the Purity diuine admitteth not any thing into its presence, that is not cleare, as is the light • Here will I wonder at the naughtynes of the nature of sinne, considering that if it were but one veniall sinne, though the soule should be otherwise iust and holy, yet can it not enter into heauen, when it goeth out of this life, vntill it be first purged in the fire of Purgatory. I will also wonder at the grieuousnes of veniall sinne, that of it owne weyght precipitateth a soule into this deep gulfe, hindreth it from mounting vp presently to heauen, and depriueth it of the vision, and presence of God for the tyme.

2.   To consider the extreme griefe, that those soules haue now, & our owne shall haue, when they shall see themselues confined to the

obscurity

obfcurity & darknes of that hard prifon, where they may not enioy the felicity they defire. For faith, that giueth them an affurance of the beauty of God, is ftill very liuely in them, and is vnto them as a ftrong and fharpe goade, putting them forwards with a certaine paffionate defire of feeing, and enioying their laft end, and confequently the dilation of this fruition afflicteth them exceedingly. And more then this, the loue of their Lord continueth liuely imprinted in them, in fuch fort, as the holy foule longeth with a burning defire to fee the obiect of the loue of its owne beatitude, and to be moft ftraitly & infeparably vnited vnto it, And if holy mē, during the exile of this miferable life, endure with their fo great griefe, the differred and prolonged feparation from the glorious vifion of God; how much more, thinke you, fhall thefe holy foules be pierced with griefe to fee thēfelues for a time detained frō the fame vifion after death? Finally, the incertainty that holdeth them in fufpēce, not knowing how long the time of their combersome imprifonment fhall continue, much afflicteth them, though otherwife they euer conforme themfelues to the diuine will, confidering that, that paine hath the origine from their own default, & negligence of not fatisfying for their finnes in the time of this prefent life. The priuation of the vifion of our Sauiour, his glorious Mother, and of other thinges there to be feene, which they belieue for certaine, giueth them exceeding great occafion of griefe: As we may be perfwaded, that fome perfon of quality fhould should be afflicted, if depriued of all that, which might bring him contentment, he should see himselfe thrust into some darke, & loathsome prison.

3. The soules are tormented by that fearefull fire, that is like to that of hell, and burneth them in a wonderfull manner, as Gods instrument, & minister of his ire, for the punishment of their sinnes. And as we see, that our fire here melteth siluer for the purifying of it, euen so doth that fire punish the soules for the cleansing of them. So affirme the holy Doctours, that the paines of Purgatory do far exceed those of this present life, euen those, that the holy Martyrs haue euer suffered, yea & of our grand Captaine also, our Sauiour Christ Iesus. By this I may come to vnderstand and to imprint in my soule the conceit of Gods iustice, & a feare of his rigorous punishments, considering he punisheth the soules that loue him, seuerely for their light faults. I will make a firme purpose to satisfy for my sinnes in this life, receiuing and admitting willingly the pennances and afflictions, that shall be enioined, and imposed vpon me: sith besides that, that they be satisfactory, they be meritorious also; a priuiledge not to be found in Purgatory, though the paines be so great there as they are. I will further endeauour to beware of committing veniall sinnes, as neere as I possibly may. For one to suffer himselfe to fall easily into them, is no other thing, then to heape & put wood continually togeather to cause the fire longer to burne in Purgatory.

4. To

4.   To confider that the foules of Purgatory doe make an entiere refignation of their will to that of God, touching the feuerity and continuance of their paines, fuffering them with great patience, & in not being fory, that God exerciseth his iuftice in chaftizing them: that they be in extreme follicitude and care, defiring to be holpen by the fuffrages, facrifices, almes, & other fatisfactory workes of the faithfull. To thinke, how much we our felues would defire to be affifted and holpen, if we were in the fame paines, and that it is now in our power to fuccour them, to their good, & our owne. For certaine it is, that beeing afterwardes in heauen, they will not be ingrate to their benefactors.

¶   Our B. Father S. *Ignatius* putteth not this meditation in the booke of his Exercifes, & yet it feemeth to good purpofe to put it downe in this place for the purifying of the confcience, beeing the principall fcope, whereunto the firft Weeke aymeth. And to the fame end alfo we fhal here propofe the meditations that concerne the feauen mortall finnes with their contrary vertues: and thofe alfo, that appertaine to the ten Commandements, the fiue Senfes of the body, and inward Powers of the foule, which is one of the three manners of meditating, which our fayd B. Father putteth downe in his Exercifes, towardes the end of the fourth Weeke, in manner following.

Three

Three wayes to Meditate.

1. The first way is about the mortall sinns, set down heere following, & that for those, who exercise themselues in the purgatiue way.

2. The second manner hath for the subiect some wordes or other taken eytber of some versicle of a psaime, or of some sentence or saying of our Sauiour, of a prayer, hymne, or Antiphone of the Church, in ruminating euery word by it selfe, and endeauouring out of it to draw some good motion, or holy desire. The manner to meditate them is, to consider, who is he, vvho sayth such a vvord; to vvhom it is addressed; to vvhat end; and with vvhat spirit, or intention it vvas vttered; vvhat it signifieth. This manner of meditating is for them, who exercise themselues in the illuminatiue way, & desire to procure the vnderstanding of the truth that fayth teacheth vs, for our profiting in deuotion. It is also proposed among the meditations of the second weeke, vpon the *Aue Maria*, *Magnificat*, & *Pater noster*.

3. The third is made by aspirations, desires, & affections, that correspond to the respirations of the body, by endeauouring to do it so, as betweene one respiration and another, our soule rayse it selfe vp by some pious motion, casting forth some spirituall groane, some inflamed sigh of the loue of God, or some short iaculatory prayer. Which is an easy manner of prayer,

E   much

much vfed among the Saints and holy men in former tymes, and may be done with the more attention and feruour: & which is more, is very effectuall to the obtaining of that, which is defired of God. This third manner of meditating is moft proper for them, who are in the Vnitiue way, fighing & longing to come to an actuall vnion with God, and feeke to conioyne them-felues with him in as inward, and as inceffant a manner, as their frailty will permit. For as the life of the body is intertained by meanes of the refpiration, euen fo the fpirituall life is conferued by the meanes of thefe holy infpirations, & de-uout affections.

Meditat. XIX.   Of Pride, & Vayne glory.

TO confider, how pride is an inordinate appetite of Excellency, and to appeare more and greater then others, founded ey-ther vpon the temporall goods, honours, great-nes, nobility of birth, &c. Or vpon fpirituall goods, fuch as be knowledge, vertues, graces, &c. And is deuided into foure heades. The firft is to attribute to ones felfe, that which appertai-neth to God. The 2. to afcribe to his own merits and deferuings, what cometh from the only grace and mercy of God. The third is to thinke, that himfelfe is better, or hath more goodnes, or graces, then he hath. The fourth is to per-fwade himfelfe, that he is more excellent, and better deferueth, then all others. This Pride produceth many other finnes, as vaine glory, **which**

which is an inordinate appetite to be praysed, &
esteemed of men, vaunting, ambition, presumption, hypocrisy, obstinacy and pertinacy in
maintayning ones owne opinions, contempt of
another, euen to the contemning of God himselfe. Of euery one of these sinnes, consider in
which of them he hath committed any fault, &
amend himselfe.

2. To consider the punishments of God
exercised and done vpon the proud, according
to that, which is written: He that shall exalt himselfe, shall be humbled, meaning that he shall
be spoiled of the excellency he hath; that which
he desireth to haue, shall be denyed him; and in
place thereof there shall be giuen him confusion
which he feareth, as may be seene by the exāples
of the Angells, of Nabuchodonosor, and of many others. Pride causeth an aridity or drynes in
the soule, & an insensibility and disgust of heauenly thinges, God permitting the proud to fall
into many sinnes in this life, and that in the o-
ther they be despised of the whole world, and
filled with shame, reproches, & confusion.

3. To consider the great good, that shall
come to a man, if he seeke to mortify his pride,
& to imbrace humility. For he that humbleth
himselfe, shall be exalted : That is, the humble
shall be deliuered from their miseries, towardes
which their infirmity shall haue caryed them,
God will in them conserue & increase his graces,
which they haue already receyued from his li-
beral hand, & more then that, will honour them
with other greater excellencyes, & fauours: and

therfore a man muſt ſeeke to poſſeſſe himſelfe of this vertue, & ſhunne the contrary vice: for God hateth this ſinne aboue all other.

Meditat. XX.   *Of Gluttony, and of the vertue of Temperance.*

TO conſider, that Gluttony is an inordinate appetite of eating and drinking, eyther of meates, by the Church prohibited, or when he eateth or drinketh ouer much, and that the exceſſe hurteth the health of body, or endomageth the ſpirit; or when he maketh o-ouer much good cheere, in eating & drinking more oft then he ſhould; or when he eateth with ouer much pleaſure in the taſt. And a man muſt examine himſelfe, if he hath committed any fault in any of theſe, & do pennance for it.

2.   To conſider the puniſhments of this vice. Firſt gluttony is a puniſhment to it ſelfe, carrying with it the ſcourge, & the payne of it owne exceſſe: for it ſurchargeth the body, it taketh a-way the health, it haſtneth death, it dulleth the vnderſtanding, taking away the viuacity, and weakning the ſubtility of it; and in one word, it maketh the ſoule altogeather incapable of thinges appertaining to God. It hath alſo in for-mer tymes been ſeuerely puniſhed, as were our firſt parents for eating of the forbidden fruit, & as were the children of Iſrael, who had a deſire to eate meates, and others the like. In the other world the gluttons ſhall ſuffer moſt ſore, & moſt

ſeuere

seuere torments, as the history of the euill Rich man teacheth vs, who could not haue a little drop of water graunted him for the cooling of the heate of his tongue. I must thinke, that they shall be tormented there with an enraged fierce hungar &c.

3. To consider the good, that Temperance bringeth vs. It conserueth the health, it prolongeth the life, it disposeth the soule to prayer, & to heauenly consolations, which God communicateth in plenty to those, who for loue of him depriue themselues of earthly fauours which he doth them in this life. For in the other he honoreth them with much richer giftes, and feasteth them more magnifically & royally, causing thē to sit downe at his table, & giuing them to eate of the meate, wherof he feedeth himselfe, which is nothing els, then the diuinity it selfe.

Meditat. XXI. Of the sinne of Luxury, & the vertue of Chastity.

TO consider, that Luxury is an inordinate appetite of carnall and sensuall pleasure against, and contrary to the order that God hath limited therein. This sinne is committed in thought, when a man voluntarily consenteth to a lingring delectatiō: which is also done in work and word.

2. To consider the seuere chastizements of this vice, which be so many, as they cannot be numbred, no more then can the miseryes, and

E 3   shame-

shamefull and abominable diseases, that it causeth, togeather with the losse of goods, of health, of contentment and quiet of mind, and of life it selfe. This vnhappy sinne was the cause, that God long ago did drown the world, consumed Sodome, and other the bordering Cittyes, with fire from heauen; and exercised many other iust, and most seuere punishments in reuenge of this sinne, as the Scriptures beare witnesse. To consider, that the luxurious & carnall shall be tormented in hell after a wonderfull manner: that they shall be plunged into a poole of fire and brimstone, where euery one of their members, by which they haue offended, shall haue their particular paine.

3: To consider the beauty of the Angelicall vertue of chastity, and the fauours and prerogatiues, that God hath imparted to the chast. The acts of it doe cause the conseruing and keeping of the eyes, and eares in purity, remouing far from the senses euery obiect, that might giue matter to any dishonest thought. They further teach a man to vse precaution, and cleannes in vse of those thinges, that minister pleasure to the tast, smelling, and touching: to obserue a decency, and honesty in words, in the actions, in the conuersation, in the talke, in the laughter, and in the gesture: to carry ones selfe purely in friendship, to treate and conuerse sincerely with all persons, and in all occurrents: to shunne the occasions of defiling the soule in the very least thing, eyther inwardly, or outwardly: to restraine the thoughts of the hart, or to cause, that

they

they goe euer accompayned with purity : to bridle and keep vnder the sensuall commotions & rebellions of the flesh, keeping thē still vnder the subiection of the spirit.

4 . To consider, the fauours, that God doth to the chast, in sending them Angells to be their assistants, and helpers in the warre they haue against the vices of the flesh, and of dishonesty. So gaue he ayde to the three yong men in the furnace of Babylon, in the middest whereof was to be seene an Angell, who did hinder the burning of the fire, and suspended the quality of it. For the Angells carry a singular loue to the chast, because of the neerenes, that is betweene them, and God : yea they keepe a watch ouer them, and protest them particularly. And therefore when any such tentation beginneth to assayle our soule, we must make our recourse to God, inuocating his assistance, & imploring the ayde of the holy Angells, who haue a particular care of keeping and protecting the louers of Chastity. And more then this, God maketh an alliance with the chast, and pure soules : he sendeth them spirituall consolations, which doe without all comparison exceed the carnall pleasurs in sweetnes and contentment, & giueth them abundantly of his graee, that in the exercise of good works they may multiply meritts, and become the spirituall children of that holy mariage. To consider moreouer the priuiledges and prerogatiues, that the chast, and the Virgins haue beyond others, as may be seene in the Virgin our B. Lady, in Saint Iohn the Euangelist, and

E 4   in

in others, of whome mention is made in holy
writ, as of Elias, Elizæus, &c. That in heauen
they haue this singular priuiledge to follow the
Lambe, whersoeuer he goeth, as they followed
him on earth, being imitators of his purity. Of
this I will make a collection, what an esteeme I
ought to make of chastity, and what a desire I
ought to haue to procure, & keep it &c.

Meditat. X X I I.   *Of the sinne of Auarice, or
   Couetousnes.*

TO consider, that Auarice is an inordinate
coueting of temporall goods, and riches. It
is committed by thought, when a man defireth to spoyle another of his goods: it is per-
petrated by worke, when he taketh them away
by fact, or when he will not restore them after
he hath taken them away, if he can, and be of
ability to do it. The Religious fall into this vice,
when they take without leaue of Superiours
that, which is not giuen them, sith they must not
appropriate it vnto themselues without consent,
nor alienate or hide what is giuen them; neyther
so much as set their affection vpon any thing for
the vsing of it, as if it particularly appertained
vnto them. Such must examine themselues, if
they haue fallen into such defaults, or other the
like.

2.   To consider the punishments, that God
hath exercised vpon men for their Auarice: for
there haue euer punishments followed it, and
                                                    the

the same very fore, as beeing the root, & cause of them, & hath precipitated the couetous into perplexities, and extremities. It is a fnare, by means whereof the Diuell feizeth vpon their foules, & draweth them through the pricking thornes of a thoufand tentations, renteth them with a thoufand cares, and in conclufion conducteth and leadeth them to the vnhappy gibbet of defpaire, as he did Iudas, whome he left hanging in the ayre, in fo much as he hangeth the miferable couetous perfons, and hindreth them from the enioying the goods of the earth, & depriueth them of thofe of heauen. The fcriptures reprefent vnto vs the feuere punifhment of this vice in Acan, Nabal, Iezabel, Giezi, Iudas, Ananias and Saphyra his wife, and others. But aboue all vve muft confider the punifhments, that attend thē in the other world, and prefent vnto the eyes of our mind the torments of the bad Rich man.

3. To confider the great good, that the perfect mortification of this finne bringeth vs, fith fpirituall pouerty, that is oppofite vnto it, hath for the reward & recompence the Kingdome of heauen in the other life, & iuftice, peace, & ioy of the holy Ghoft in this, God fhewing himfelfe moft liberall towardes them, who depart with fome of their goods to the poore, & much more towards them, who haue abandoned & quite left their goods, & haue imbraced Euangelicall pouerty, to whom he will in the day of Iudgment giue a throne of glory to iudg the twelue Tribes of Ifrael.

Medita-

Meditat. XXIII.   Of the sinne of Anger.

TO consider, that Anger is an inordinate appetite of reuenging iniuries done a man, or an inordinate heate, and commotion of mind for that, which succeedeth cōtrary to what he desireth. A sinne is by this committed in thought, word, and worke. Impatience goeth euer in company with anger, when a man is vexed & troubled beyond measure for that, which hapneth contrary to his will, & is much afflicted for it. And herehence arise many sinnes against God, against our neighbour, and against our selues.

2. To consider the euills, that Anger causeth, which be a dissimilitude with God, who is peace it selfe, disquiet and trouble to the conscience: it abates and extinguishes the spirit of deuotion. For anger is a short folly, and a briefe fury and madnes, & as a voluntary Diuel, that seizes vpon our soule, wherein he causeth commotions as ill beseeming and ill pleasing, as the diuers writhings of the countenance be ill fauoured, & vnpleasant to behold. And more then this a man must ponder, how great an enemy God is to this vice by the example of *Cain*, and *Lameth Gen.* 4. & by that, which our Sauiour saith in S. *Matth.* 5. *He that is angry agaynst his brother, shall be guilty of Iudgement &c.* Hence will I learne to shun al commotion of Anger, & to suppresse it quickly, before it get increase in my soule.

3. To consider the good, that is gotten by
the

the mortifying of anger, by the meanes of patience and meeknes. For thefe diuine vertues giue vs an abfolute dominion and commaund ouer our felues, making vs amiable, and beloued of God and men, man being made participant of Gods patience & benignity by his fweetnes and manfuetude, thereby difpofing himfelfe to the receauing of greater fauours from heauen, and making himfelfe to be admired vpon earth by meanes of his magnanimity, and courage, that he difcouereth in bearing iniuries patiently.

Meditat. XXIIII. *Of the finne of Enuy.*

TO confider, that Enuy is an inordinate fadnes, a man hath at his neighbours good, in as much as it exceedeth or obfcureth his. This vice proceedeth of pride, and is accompanied with anger. It taketh place in al forts, of good, both fpirituall and temporall, of grace & of nature, as appeareth by the enuy of the bad Angell againft man.

2.   To confider the great euills of fault, and of paine, that haue their origine from this fin, a moft cruell enemy to thofe that intertaine it. That it is the hiffing of that infernall ferpent, that thrufteth men forwards to the committing of moft great and moft grieuous finnes, making the foule obdurate, hurting the rigour of the body, and much more the vertues of the mind. That it conuerteth all thinges to its owne hurt. For the goods of others are as fo many euills to it, in fo much as this euil is in a mâner incurable; the

the cruell effects wherof are to be seene in Cain, in the brethren of Ioseph, in Dathan & Abiron, in Saul, and in the Iewes, who transported with a most execrable Enuy, bereaued our Saulour of his life. That the torments, which the enuyous suffer in hell be inexplicable. It is inough to thinke, that they be enraged, and transported with a fury, & enuy against themselues.

3. To consider the singular priuiledges, that be comprized in the perfect mortification of enuy, and in the exercise of fraternall charity, when we make resistance to the motions of sadnes, & griefe that we haue of our neighbours good, & prosperity: & that on the contrary we reioyce, & be glad, as if they were ours, desiring that many other had the same fauours, and graces that we haue, and greater also, if it might stand with the more glory of God, which we ought simply to seeke, and ayme at in all thinges. By this meanes I shall make my neighbours good myne owne, and shall begin on earth to tast of that happynes and felicity, which they enioy who are in heauen, where euery one esteemeth those to be his owne goods, which all possesse.

Meditat. XXV.   Of the sinne of Slouth.

TO consider that slouth is an inordinate heauynes, and a disgust of vertuous and pious exercises. The Actions of it be an exceeding great feare of taking of paynes, and of the asperity of vertue, pusillanimity or wanting of courage for the vndertaking of paynefull & difficult

difficult things for the seruice of God ; a remisse-
nes & langour in the accomplishing of the commaundements of God, and of the constitutions,
and rules of ones profession ; an inconstancy in
pursuying and prosecuting the actions of vertues
a diffidence of hart , and distrust of attaining the
vertues , which he vndertaketh to follow; an
animosity or a disgust against spirituall persons;
an idle disposition to loose and trifle the time;
an excessiue drowsines of continuance in time of
his spirituall exercises ; distractions in diuerse
vnlawfull and superfluous thinges; curiosity in
his senses ; and in few words all sinnes of omis-
sion and negligence in that, which concerneth
the seruing of God .

2 . To consider the domages of Slouth,
which is the very shaddow of death , next vnto
hell : that it depriueth the soule of diuine consolations, and disposeth it to be a receptacle of bad
spirits : that it is the pestilent canker of vertues ,
the moath of good works , and the wormewood
of the conscience . Finally that it tormenteth the
hart it possesseth : that it taketh much paines,
and yet goeth not forwards : & that in hell the
slouthfull shall be most rigorously handled .

3. To consider the spirituall ioy & contentment those haue , who will not haue any thing
to do with slouth and heauynes, and be seruent
in the actions of vertue, which they find within
a while very easy vnto them . That in a short
time they gayne much, as did those , who came
the last howre of the day to worke in the vineyard : that God taketh a singular pleasure to be

F   serued

serued with feruour, and prompt alacrity of spirit , and that on the contrary the slouthfull prouoke him to a vomit, & loathing of them.

Meditat. XXVI.   How to ouercome any parti-
    culer vice, when a man will make a particu-
    lar examen thereof.

HE may take the points of the precedent
meditations that he is to meditate , for
the roting out of some vice: wherein he is
first to consider, what the vice is, what the foulenes of it is , how vnbeseeming it is to a vertuous
soule, how vnpleasing to God, & how bad an example it giueth to the neighbour. Secondly, how
oft he hath fallen into it , with the causes & occasions of such fall . Thirdly , of what remedies
he hath serued himselffor his rising againe; what
documents he hath read , or heard to be good
for the compassing of that he seeketh , & ouercoming of the vice, to the end he may vse them.
Fourthly , what domage and hurt it hath caused
him , that he hath learned and found by experience in himselfe, or in another: the punishments,
that God hath exercised vpon them , who haue
suffered themselues to be supplanted by that
vice . Finally to consider the beauty & excellency of the contrary vertue; how much it hath
beene recommended by our Sauiour himselfe
both by words, and by example: how it is esteemed of men , and what and how great tranquility and peace of mind it bringeth . A man may
                            meditate

meditate in the same manner some points in particular, when he would get the practise and habit of some vertue.

Meditat. XXVII. *Vpon the ten Commaundements of the law of God.*

TO meditate the ten commaundements according as they ought to keep them who haue a desire to rayse themselues to greater perfection, is not to content himself with the shunning of mortall and veniall sinnes, but further to desire to auoyd that which is lesse perfect: to examine himselfe conformably to his owne state and profession, obseruing what he transgresseth, and wherein he fayleth, & crauing pardon of God for the same.

2. To consider the maledictions, that God thundreth out against the infringers and breakes of his law, & the seuere punishments, he threatneth them with, in this life, as is to be seen in Deteronomy cap. 27. & 28. To thinke, what and how seuere punishments shall be inflicted vpon the Religious, who make profession of a more perfect life, if they keep not the commaundments in a more perfect manner, then do others, as their profession bindeth them thereunto.

3. To consider the benedictions both spirituall and corporall, that God bestoweth vpon the obseruers of his law, as appeareth by the 28. chapter of Deuteronomy, and the 118.

Psalme.

Pſalme. Whereupon I will conclude, that God requireth at our hands, we ſhould make a moſt high eſteeme of his lawes, and that therefore reaſon it is, that I reuerence, & imbrace them with all my hart, ſeeing they are iuſt and holy, for the auoyding of the maledictions & puniſhments, that be ordayned for the preuaricatours of them, and the obtayning of the benedictions, that be promiſed to the obſeruers of them. I will thinke alſo, that it is more then reaſonable, that ſuch lavves ſhould be obſerued for the reſpect, that vve ovve to the Lavv-maker, vvho is God, & who became man, and obſerued them moſt perfectly himſelfe: and finally for the fidelity thereof tovvardes them, vvho keepe them. For I know by myne ovvne experience, what a contentment I feele in my ſoule, when I baue done myne endeauour, and vvhat trouble, and diſquiet of mind, vvhen I haue not done my duty in any thing: & I côſider, that at the houre of my death nothing will cauſe my greater conſolation, then to remember, that I haue kept them, nor greater griefe, then that I haue broken them. To conſider, & poiſe theſe words of *Eccl. c. vlt.* Feare God, & keepe his commaundments: for this is euery man. That is to ſay, In this conſiſteth all the beeing, & the perfection of a man, if he keep Gods commaúdments.

Meditat.

Meditat. XXVIII. *Vpon the fiue Senses, and outward Powers.*

TO remember & ruminate the sinnes, committed by the fiue Senses, making a discourse ouer them all, and from one to another, and thereunto adding the sinnes of the tongue, and those which a man shall haue committed by any immodesty in the vse of any member. For all which sinnes he shall procure a confusion in himselfe, and shall craue pardon of God.

,. To consider the great hurts, that our soule hath receyued by our senses: for they are the gates, and windowes, by which death findeth entrance for the ruyning of our soule, and spoyling it of the life of grace. By them there enter into our mind the images, representations, and figures of visible things, that molest, and trouble the imagination and memory by a thousand sorts of distractions, stirring vp and causing disquiet, & a disorder of the appetites, & passions of the mind By these parts our soule doth, as another Dyna, goe forth to sport it selfe all the world ouer, causing the spirit of deuotion to goe out also in company with it, in so much as by occasion of the concourse & multitude of distractions it remayneth dry, without gust, or feeling of spirituall sweetnes, & cannot afterwards returne home into it selfe, when it would. And therefore the holy Ghost in many places of

F 3 holy

holy vvrit admonisheth vs to haue a carefull eye, and keep a vvatchfull guard ouer our senses.

3. To consider the great good, that the mortifications of the senses bringe vs. For besides, that by those meanes we avoyd the aforesaid euills, we open vnto our spirit the port of prayer and deuotion, and bring it in, into our soule. For God taketh a pleasure to dwell with soules mortified, and enclosed, as pleasant gardens, on all sides, vvhen the senses, so mortifyed, giue entrance to that only, which may excite and stirre vp the soule. This outward mortification is a certaine signe of the inward vertue, and therewith it greatly edifyeth the neighbour, & giueth credit, & esteeme to religiō, euen as a statly Portall honoreth & setteth forth the house, and putteth into them, who passe by, a desire also to goe in to see the rest. And this was it, as I thinke, wherefore the Apostle saith to the Philippians cap. 4. Let your modesty be knowne to all men. A man must conclude this meditation vvith a colloquie to our Sauiour, pondering the mortification that he had, & vsed in his fiue senses; beseeching him, that he would please to giue vs it also, that we may auoyd the euills, which immodesty & neglect of keeping the senses causeth, and may finally enioy those goods and priuiledges, which this mortification bringeth.

Meditat.

Meditat. XXIX. *Of the inward Powers of the Soule.*

TO consider the vices, and sinnes, that take their beginning of the Vnderstanding, & the hurts they cause : the ignorance of the thinges, that a man is bound to know ; imprudency, precipitation, and want of consideration in thinges that he is bound to doe, and to say : the temerity in iudging and censuring the wordes, speaches, and actions of another; the inconstancy in the good, that he hath purposed to doe ; the obstinacy and stiffnes in his owne Iudgement ; the warynes, and wylines according to the flesh; the subtiltyes and shiftes in his owne affayres; the vayne curiosity to know that which nothing concerneth him. If a man examine himselfe according to these seauen heades, he shall find, that he hath committed many sins, for which he must aske forgiuenes in accusing, & confounding himselfe.

To thinke vpon the sinnes, that proceed from ones owne will, and the domages, that befall him for following the same. For the proper will is that, which seeketh only its owne particular pleasure, leauing that of God, & of the neighbour. From it, as frō their proper roote, grovv all the sinnes, that are committed in the world. Of it cometh disobedience to all that, vvhich God commaundeth, eyther by himselfe, or by his ministers, peruerting the

F 4   intenti-

intention in good thinges, appropriating to it selfe vvhatsoeuer it can, without consideration of the wrong, that is done to another: and heerehence spring forth an infinite number of kindes of iniustice, by reason vvhereof Saint Bernard sayd greatly to purpose: Let proper vvill cease, and there vvill be no hell. Vpon this I vvill call to mind, hovv disorderly I haue hitherto liued, by follovving myne ovvne vvill, & appetite, & how great reason I haue to aske God pardon.

3. To consider the sinnes, committed by the povver of imagination, vvhich is like an house paynted vvith many images, and figures, some fovvle, some profane, some ridiculous, some monstruous, &c The povvers of desire be as a troubled and tempestuous sea, tossed vvith the vvindes of passions, the surges, and vvaues of diuerse appetites encountring one another, as loue and hatred; the desire and refusing of some thing; ioy and sadnes or sorrow; hope and despaire; boldnes and covvardise, and these commotions are for the most part, and more commonly, imployed in bad thinges, vvith great disorder, trouble and confusion. For a man loueth that, vvhich he should hate, &c. These passions be the armes and vveapons, & snares, which the Diuell vseth, by meanes vvherof he maketh vvarre vpon vs, and thrusteth vs into most grieuous faults, in so much as vve doe our selues minister vnto our enemy his chiefest weapons, vvhervvith he intertayneth his vvarre agaynst vs. Moreouer

they

they be as the executioners of our foule, vvhich
is continually afflicted vvith the inceſſant and
reſtleſſe aſſaultes, they giue vnto it. And therefore we may with reaſon lament and be-
vvayle our condition, and ſay vvith
the Apoſtle : O vnhappy man that
I am, vvho ſhall deliuer me from
the body of this death? Hereupon I vvill make a firme
purpoſe to mortify theſe
paſſions, & aboue all,
the will, & proper
Iudgement.

MEDITA.

MEDITATIONS
OF THE SECOND
WEEKE.

IN this weeke the 2. 6. 7. and a part of the 10. Addition, which are to be found in the begining of this Booke muſt be chaunged. The ſecond thus. Preſently after our vpriſing we muſt call to mind the pointes of the meditation, ſtirring vp in our ſoul-s an earneſt deſire to vnderſtand more perfectly the Incarnation of our Sauior, to the end that through a better knowledge of the infinite loue he carryeth towards vs, we may diſpoſe our ſelues to ſerue him the more affectuouſly. The ſixt. To call to our remembrance the miſteries of our Sauiours life from the Incarnation till the miſtery we come then to meditate. The ſeauenth. To vſe the light, or darkenes, as we ſhall find the one,

one, or the other expedient for the attaining of that, which we seeke, & desire. The tenth. To vse pennance more or lesse, according to the mistery we meditate. For there be those, who obserue diuers and different wayes in exciting others to pennance, some more, some lesse, wherpon it followeth, that vse must be made of the ten Additions with much discretion.

2.   The Repetitions must be also made in some meditations, as our B. Father teacheth in his booke of Exercises before mentioned. For example. After we haue made two meditations, the third we make must be a repetition of the former two, marking the points, wherein we shall haue felt more consolation, or sorrow, or some other motion, making also the three colloques, which our B. Father putteth downe in his first weeke: we must also exercise the manner of prayer, that our B. Father putteth downe in the second weeke of his Exercises, to wit, by Application of the senses. In which manner of prayer we forme fiue spirituall senses conformably to the corporall, as to see spiritually &c.

3.   As touching the manner to meditate the mysteries of this second weeke, and those also of the third, and fourth, we are diligently to obserue foure thinges. The persons, of whome mention is made in the mysteries, and to represent them vnto himselfe, & togeather with the, first the excellencies, and inward affections, that be in them. Secondly to weigh and ponder their words one by one, and their manner of deliuering

ring them. Thirdly to confider their workes, and the vertues, that be difcouered in them. Fourthly, to confider what they doe, or what they fuffer, with other the circumftances. As for example, to be hold the thing, that is done; him, who doth it; for what end; at what tyme; in what place. Who it is that fuffereth, of whom, for whome, what, how, in what place, at what time he fuffreth. And fo of other circumftances. And out of this I will alwaies make my profit, by ftirring vp my felfe to doe that, which may be imitated: and in the end, or middeft of my prayer, when I fhall feele my felfe moued, I will make one or more colloquies with God, or with the facred Virgin.

Meditat. I.   Of the Kingdome of our Lord Iefus Chrift.

THE Prayer Preparatory is to be made after the accuftomed manner, with the compofition of the place &c. then you muft reprefent to your felfe, as though you did fee our Sauiour goe preaching from one City, Caftle, and Village to another &c. The prayer fhall be to demaund grace of God to vnderftand, and to obey his voyce, who calleth vs.

    1.   To confider the infinite charity of the eternall Father for giuing vs the beft, and abfoluteft King he could beftow vpon vs, his beloued Sonne, caufing him to take our nature, to the end he might treat vs with all fweetnes and compa-

compassion : and that beeing his only Sonne, & God Almighty, as himselfe, he was of ability to remedy and redresse our euills by his infinite power.

2.   To consider the excellency and worth of this great King, his infinite wisdome & knowledge, by meanes wherof he knew our miseries and our necessities: his mercy, that mooued him to take compassion of them : his omnipotency, that could remedy them : his goodnes & charity, that inclined him to doe it : his prouidence, meeknes, and most fauourable proceeding towardes vs, whome he treateth as his brethren : his liberality, and Royall magnificence in communicating his diuine riches to vs poore and needy, giuing himselfe, to his very bloud, & his owne body : his iustice, prudence and equity, & finally the eternity, which shall neuer haue end.

3.   To compare this omnipotent and most good King with the other petty Kings here beneath, who impose tributs vpon their vassalls & subiects, impouerishing them for the enriching of themselues : who commit a thousand errors in their gouernement by ignorance, passion, or malice; who bind their subiectes to lawes both hard, combersome, & vniust, and in the meane time they exempt themselues from obseruation of them, That their Kingdomes, be they neuer so great, must come one day to an end, & that they shall leaue their greatnes, that is but of short continuance, and their life also. That on the contrary our diuine and celestiall King redeemeth

G

deemeth

deemeth his subiects from tribute, and from the seruitude of the Tyranny of this world, paying and quitting their debtes with the price of his owne most precious bloud : he impouerisheth himselfe for the enriching of his : he is infinitely wise, & his Kingdome togeather with the greatnes of it, is no waies subiect to the lawes of alteration, or change.

4. To consider, that our Sauiour is come into this world to destroy the works of the malignant spirit, of death and of sinne, and inuiteth men vnto him for the animating of them to ouercome, as himselfe hath done, and ouerthrow the Kingdome of darkenes. To consider the sweet speeches, wherewith he inuiteth all men to follow him : the greatnes and maiesty of this most noble King, who calleth vs : who is our most liberall benefactour, and hath a thousand wayes bound vs vnto himselfe : the difficulty and excellency of the enterprize so auaylable to vs, whereunto he prouoketh vs by his owne example, marching before vs to excite vs to doe, as he hath done, to come to the marke he aymed at. To confound our selues, and to be ashamed for not hauing followed him for the tyme past, & to resolue to follow him for the tyme to come, vnder hope of a certaine & glorious victory.

5. To thinke, how great an offence it is, that men, who are affected to the loue of this world, will not follow so good a King, but out of an obstinate ingratitude towardes him, doe stop their ears, that they may not heare his voice.

6. To

6. To confider, how there be many, who would follow our Sauiour, and yet would euer liue in their pleafurs, as would that yong man in the Ghofpell, who was fad and grieued for this, that our Sauiour faid vnto him, that to be perfect, and follow him, he fhould fell his goods, and giue them to the poore. As there be others, who offer manfully to follow this King for to imitate him in all, by keeping his commaundements, and his counfayles, and confecrating themfelues to his feruice by the vowes of obedience, pouerty, and chaftity, in which they follow our Sauior in the excellenteft manner he may be followed. Such be the true Religious, who fhould euer and anone fay, and repeate thefe words of the pfalme 107. My hart, Lord, is ready, my hart is ready: making this oblation of a good will, moft pleafing to the diuine maiefty.

7. To confider, that there be fome againe, that offer themfelues to this King to ferue him, as inftruments, for drawing and gayning of others to ferue him, and this is an Apoftolicall office. For that is to take a care not only for the fauing of himfelfe, but alfo to procure the fauing of the foules of others. And for this we haue caufe to giue God particular thankes for hauing called vs to this charge, faying with the prophet Efay c. 6. Behold heere I am, fend me: though hungar & thirft: trauailes and daungers be prefented vs, & we were to goe into far remoued countreys, &c.

G2   *Medi-*

Meditat. II.   *Of the decree of the most Blessed Trinity, that the second Person should be incarnate, & take flesh for the saluation of Man.*

I Must represent vnto my selfe God, in Trinity of persons, sitting in the throne of his glory, and in another place all men, & my selfe amongst them, spoyled of all good, loaden with all euills and miseries, all ouer wounded, and halfe dead, as was the man that fell into the hands of theeues, as he was going from Hierusalem to Iericho. To imagine, that these three diuine persons regard vs with compassion of our myseries, and deliberate about the succouring of vs. The petition shall be to aske grace of God with all humility of spirit, that he would please to giue me to vnderstand in some sort the depth of this councell, that I may make my profit of it.

1.   To consider, that where both the Angells and men had sinned, God laid his seuere hand vpon the one by precipitating them from heauen into hell, without giuing them eyther tyme or place to doe pennance, and layd open to the other the endles treasurs of his mercy, remedying the fault by a meanes so wonderfull & so full of infinite charity, as is to become man for obtayning pardon to men, for which we remayne bound to an exceeding great acknowledgment, which we must endeauour to render him.   2. To

2. To confider the caufes, that moued the diuine goodnes to vfe fo great mercy towardes vs. The firft is, for that the children & offspring of Adam did not incurre the euills of finne by any actuall, or perfonall will of theirs, but only by that of their firft parent, which was, and was held interpretatiuely for their fin. And therefore the infinite goodnes would not endure, that fo many fhould be damned for the fault of one, nor that the vifible world fhould abide fruftrated of its end, feruing ftill to the vfe of finnefull man. And therfore we muft in fpirit prefent our felues before the face of the Maiefty diuine, & fay with the Royall prophet *Dauid: Lord, I was conceyued in finne, and in mifery*. And againe: *O God, defpife not the works of thy hands*. The fecond caufe is, for that the malignant fpirit made man to finne, by enuy tempting him, to the end he might reuenge bimfelfe by the Creator vpon the creature, whome he had made to his owne Image and likenes, and therefore God tooke vpon nimfelfe the caufe of man: & for this I ought to be affured, that his fauour will fteed me in all tentations.

3. To confider, that God chofe the beft meanes, that could poffibly be, which was the Incarnation of his moft beloued Sonne, which was an act of moft fingular honour; and profit to man, and of furpaffing humility, trauayle, payne, & defatigation for the Son of God, who became man to deify vs, by affumpting our nature in the hipoftatical vnity of his perfon. This confideration ought to caufe vs to wonder; and

to excite vs to yield him thankes for so singular a benefit, and to put an earnest desire into vs to serue him with all our hart.

4. To consider the infinite perfections of God, that shew themselues in the worke of the Incarnation: his goodnes, in communicating himselfe as much as he could, and in giuing his personall Being to the nature of man: his charity, in vniting vnto himselfe the same nature by a strait band of loue. His mercy, in marrying it with his iustice after a wonderfull manner, sith there cannot be greater iustice, then to see God himselfe to pay our debts euen to the giuing of his bloud, and of his life; nor greater mercy, then to consider, that he himselfe cometh in his own person to redresse our miseries: his wisdome, in composing thinges of so great distance, and difference, as is man and God, the passible and impassible, &c. His omnipotency in doing all for vs, that was in his power, for the honouring and enriching of vs: His holines, and concourse of his vertues, which he communicated to his Sonne, and imprinted in him, when he tooke flesh, that he might be a liuely paterne of all perfection, for the exciting & encouraging of vs to follow his example. And out of all this we must draw a most affectuous acknowledgment of this benefit.

Meditat.

Meditat. I I I.   *Of Gods infinite Charity, shewed vnto man, in the mystery of the Incarnation.*

TO consider these words of our Sauiour Iesus Christ to Nicodemus : God so loued the world, as he gaue his only Sonne, that euery man, who shall belieue in him, perish not, but may haue life euerlasting.

1. To consider the immensity, and infinite greatnes of the person, that hath loued vs, and the basenes of the creature, that is loued, comparing one with the other. To thinke, that God hath done vs this incomprehensible good, out of his goodnes alone, not for any need, he had of vs, nor for any profit, that might accrew vnto himselfe by it : and that the person so loued, which is man, was most vnworthy of his loue, by reason of his innumerable sinns & offences, and of his ingratitude for so many benefitts, he hath receyued. To consider, how much God loueth man, vvho hateth him, in so much as his maiesty intermitteth not to bestow benefitts vpon him : and therefore of this I will take an occasion to wonder deeply at Gods goodnes, & to be greatly confounded at myne owne naughtynes.

2. To consider the infinite greatnes and worth of the gift, that God hath presented to the world, which is his only Sonne, altogeather equall to the Father, and to the holy Ghost. Such

G 4   was

was Gods loue to man , such the honour, and esteeme, he made of him, as he pleased to make him so great , to enrich , defend , exalt and glorify him by his owne grace alone . To thinke , what man ought to doe in acknowledgement of so great benefitts : to acknowledge that he oweth vnto him both what he is, & what he hath, and that on the contrary he offendeth him with all that he is , or is in him .

3 . To consider , that the end, wherefore God meant to bestow his only Sonne vpon vs , was to saue the world, and to deliuer it from the seruitude and tyranny of the Diuell , from the euerlasting prison of hell, and to free vs from the miseries , that be annexed to sinne , and to restore vs to life, and to grace, togeather with all vertues , that accompany it . Hence will I draw and conceyue the honour , reuerence, and loue, that I owe to my Lord , & Sauiour .

Meditat. IIII.   Of the diuine Decree and reso
lution , that Christ should be borne of a wo
man : and of the election of the most glorious
Virgin to be his Mother .

TO meditate , how God determined to become incarnate , & though he might haue taken a body in the age of a perfect man , as was Adam , yet he would not , but humbled himselfe so far , as to be borne of a woman , as he had before promised , Gen. 3. for the honoring and raysing of man to the infinite dignity
of

of the Sonne of God, and of a woman to the excellency and prerogatiue of the mother of God, wherein he shewed his incomprehensible liberality. For as our first disaster hapned vnto vs by one man, and one woman, so vouchsafed he agayne that the first good of our redemption should come vnto vs by another man, and an other woman, to whome we might make our recourse in our necessities. Finally he pleased to become a little babe for loue of vs, and to haue a mother on earth, whome he obeyed, thereby giuing vs an example of perfect humility, and obedience.

2. To consider the election of the sacred Virgin, chosen by particular grace, among all other women, to be the mother of the eternall word incarnate, the same Words assistent in the work of our Redemption, the Aduocate of men, and such as is God himselfe, in as much as being man he obeyed her : the great esteeme, that the holy Virgin euer made of this singular fauour, knowing that God might and could haue chosen another. Whereof I will take an occasion to reioyce with her, for her so singular a priuiledge of dignity.

3. To consider, that the most pure Virgin was chosen, as a most excellent vessell, whereinto God powreth those treasurs of grace, and of glory, that sorted with the mother of such a Sonne, the greatest fauours, that in a pure creature may be imagined, in regard whereof she is called, Elect & Chosen as the Sunne. For she was elected to be holy in all kind of sanctity, & of

of vertue, that may be giuen to the reſt of creatures, ſurpaſſing all in perfection. She was choſen to be pure, and without ſtaine to the higheſt
dignity, that may be, to the end the mother
might in ſome ſort reſemble the Father. She
was choſen to be holy and immaculate, not after
a ſort, but before the face of God, that is, that
the maieſty of God pleaſed himſelfe in her, as
his moſt faithfull daughter, and true mother,
who was to beare, and ſerue his Sonne in this
world. I will reioyce much, and be glad, that
the ſacred Virgin was choſen to ſo noble an end,
giuing thankes to the moſt Bleſſed Trinity for
this fauourable election, ſo honorable to her, &
ſo profitable for vs.

*Meditat: V.   Of the tyme, that God chooſe for
the diſcouering, and executing of the myſtery
of the Incarnation.*

TO conſider, that inſtantly after our firſt
parents had ſinned, God reuealed vnto
them the miſtery of the Incarnation, that
ſhould ſerue for a remedy to their offence, and
to the paynes, whereunto they were bound.
That when he came vnto them, to cauſe thē to
giue him an accompt of the diſobeying his commaundments, & pronoūced againſt thē the ſentence of death for the ſame, he added, as a moſt
mercifull Father, a promiſe to become himſelfe
man, & to dye for the loue of thē: in ſo much as
at the very time whē he thruſt them out of paradiſe, & ſent them into ſeruitude, he promiſed thē
their

their deliuerer: when he layeth maledictions vpon them for their faults, he graciously offereth them the authour of all benedictions: and seeing them supplanted and beguiled by Sathan, he assureth them of the victory that shall be had afterwardes ouer him, to giue them a testimony of his infinite loue, to the end none may despaire of obtaining pardon for his sinnes, sith instantly after the offence committed against his maiesty, he promiseth a remedy for redressing, and repayring the same.

2.   To consider, how fit the tyme was, that he pleased to choose for the sauing of man, by discourse running ouer their thoughts, and workes, and obseruing the great disorder, and confusion, that then was: euen as on the contrary Gods thoughts, and resolutions were far different in another kinde, sith all tended to the good of men. That the three Persons in Trinity sayd, Let vs redeeme man, whome we haue created: let vs repayre the Image, which we haue giuen him: and they reioyced to see the tyme approach, that was ordayned for the accomplishment & performance of their promise. On the contrary, to represent vnto our selues, that the world was at that time as a deluge of sins, in such sort, as when God prepared to do it infinite fauours, it imployed it selfe in multiplying incredible sinnes, and yet that did not stay his bounty and goodnes, nor quench the flams of his diuine loue. And this shall giue me occasion to weigh the greatnes of his loue to man, & I will endeauour to answere it by a certaine acknow-

knowledgement, as farre as I am able.

3.   To consider the reasons, for which
our Sauiour differred, for so many thousands
of yeares, his comming into the vvorld. The 1.
vvas, to the end men might in so long a tyme
vnderstand by experience their owne myseries,
and long vvith a greater desire after him, vvho
might ease them thereof : and by knovving
their ovvne maladies, they might vvith the
more care, and affection seeke after their heauenly Phisitian : vvho further curing them by
his infinite vvisdome, and by his omnipotency, might discouer and make knovvne the diuine attributes of his essence, and many other
that manifest themselues diuinely in his vvorks,
We must apply all this to our selues. The second reason is, to the end that delay might
make them to conceyue the better of Gods
gifts, and that the patience and hope of the iust,
to vvhome he had made this promise, might
be the more tried. For God maketh high esteem
of that confidence, that is reposed in him in
tyme of tribulation, and tentation.

Meditat. VI. Of the comming of the Angell Ga-
    briel to the B. Virgin, when he announced to
    her the mystery of the Incarnation.

TO Consider, who it is, that sendeth
    this Embassy, and further what the most
    sacred Trinity is, that is desirous and sol-
licitous of the good of man. To whome: that
                                                    is,

is, to the most Blessed Virgin, chosen, & preferred before all that, which is most beautifull, and most excellent in the world, and yet a poore mayde, marryed to a tradef-man, who liued by the labour of his hands. An Angell Embassadour, who hath the name of Gabriell, that is, The strength of God. The designe is, to demaud of the Virgin her consent to be the mother of God, who will not vse the seruice of his reasonable creatures without their owne consent, be the same in neuer so great matters. Heere I must thinke, how great care God hath to send Embassages downe from heauen into earth, giuing him due thankes for this his paternall prouidence, and conceyuing a confusion of my selfe for myne owne negligence, in not shewing my selfe correspondent therunto.

2. To consider the Angells graue and humble modesty, when he entred in and presented himselfe before the sacred Virgin, wherby vve may learne, vvhat respect and reuerence, we ought to carry towardes God, and his mother. The wordes of the salutation, dictated by the most Blessed Trinity. The first is, All bayle : that is, God saue you, as if he sayd, Peace be with you, reioyce, and be glad, for the newes, and tydings I bring you, is full of ioy, and of comfort. Full of grace : that is, full of faith, hope, and charity, full of the holy Ghost, adorned with vertues : thy memory is full of holy thoughts, thy vnderstanding of great and diuine illustrations, thy wil replenished with feruent affections of loue, and inflamed desires of

H the

the increasing of Gods glory, & of the saluation of men. Thou art full of grace in thy workes by occasion of the most singular purity of their intention: and in few words, thou art full of perfection, and holines. Of this I will draw my profit, and I will haue the most Blessed Virgin in singular esteeme, and be glad of the graces, & fauours, that God hath bestowed vpon her, and done vnto her. To examine these other words, Our Lord is with thee. Which our Lady reioiced to heare, knowing and vnderstanding therby, that God fauoured her, both touching body and soule, with a particular protection, in conseruing by his grace all her powers both corporall and spirituall, and directing them to his honour and glory, in so much as she might say better then any creature of the world, that, which is written in the Psalme 11. Our Lord gouerneth me, and I shall want nothing. Blessed be thou among all women. As if he had sayd, God hath powred all manner of benedictions vpon thee, none excepted: for thou shalt be a mother, and yet still remaine a Virgin: both Angells & men, the iust, and the sinners will giue thee a thousand benedictions, for that all shall reape profit by the fruit of thy wombe.

3.   To consider the feare, and virginall bashfulnes, that surprized this holy Virgin, at the hearing of this the Angells salutation, wherin she discouered foure singular vertues. The first is chastity, in being troubled at the sight of the Angell in the forme of a man, not hauing been accustomed to see any, because she liued in

a continuall retirement . The second is humility , in hauing a poore esteeme of herselfe : for it
is peculiar to the humble to be troubled , when
they heare their owne prayses. The third is prudence , in forbearing to be precipitant, and haste in answering. The fourth is silence , answering with an humble , and bashefull demeanour
& carriage. Eue demeaned her selfe much otherwise with the serpent , and we imitate her in the
leuity of our words, in curiosity, in imprudēcy ,
in facility of belieuing . Thesse we must obserue,
and marke for the confounding of our selues.

4 . To consider , how the Angell appeased
the trouble , that had surprized the B. Virgin ,
it being the office of the good Angell to appease
the agitations and troubles of the mind . To
ponder these wordes , Thou hast found grace
before God : and to see , wherin the greatest felicity of a soule consisteth . For if the world deemeth them happy, who are in credit , & fauour
with Kinges and Princes (an happynes , which
most commōly as we see , is turned into smoke)
how much greater esteeme should we make of
this , that we be in the grace and fauour of God,
for as much as thence proceed all goods, & gifts
of heauen , and all besides that may and ought
to satiate , and content our desires . This is that,
which we ought to wish , this is that, which our
affections ought to ayme at , endeauouring a-
boue all thinges to procure and haue humility ,
by which the B Virgin became pleasing to God.
By what hath been said , I will learne, to reuerence and respect this sacred Virgin more and

more, reioycing my selfe at her perfections.

Meditat. V I I.   Of the manner how the Angell declared vnto the B. Virgin, the mystery of the Incarnation.

TO consider the greatnes, and excellencyes of her Sonne, whereof the Angell maketh a promise to the Virgin. The first, that he shall be named Iesus, which is to say, the Sauiour of the world. The second, that he shall be great in all thinges, great in his diuinity, great in his humanity, great in office, great in power, &c. The third, that notwithstanding he should be her Sonne, yet should he be God also. The fourth, that his Father should giue him the throne, and supreme commaund ouer all his E-lect. The fifth, that his Empire should be euer-lasting. To thinke, that these excellencies, and priuiledges were founded vpon the most pro-found humility, that was in the Sonne of God, for that he vouchsafed to cōtinue nyne months within his mothers wombe, an abiection, that gaue beginning to his future greatnes, Of this I will learne to loue humility, because it is the be-ginning of all celestiall goods.

2.   To consider these wordes of the Vir-gin: How shall this be done, because I know not man? As if she had sayd, I make no doubt at all of the puissance and power of God, nor of your promise, but I would be well informed, how this may be compassed and done, and of the

the manner, that I am to obserue for the obeying of Gods will, sith I haue made a vow of Virginity. In which wordes the Virgins prudence meruailonsly sheweth it selfe, because they be both necessary, and few, but yet very important, and vttered with a surpassing humility, accōpanyed with a wonderfull silence also. I will learne to loue chastity, and reuerence silence in imitation of the most B. Virgin.

3. To consider the Angells replication, when he sayd: The holy Ghost shall come vpon thee, & the power of the Highest shall ouershadow thee: note the three excellencies heere promised to the Virgin. The first, that this Conception should not be effected by the worke of man, but by the operation of the holy Ghost, that should come downe vpon her with store of graces. The second, that the power of the Highest should ouershadow her, preseruing her from all sensuall pleasure in her conceyuing him, and forming the body of our Sauiour of her most pure bloud. The third, that he, whome she should conceyue, should be the naturall Sonne of God, by reason of the hypostaticall vnion of nature humane, with the nature diuine. Heere I will reioyce togeather with the Virgin for so excellent fauours, beseeching the holy Ghost to ouershadow my soule that it may conceiue holy desires.

4. To consider the ensuing words of the Angell: Thy Cosin Elizabeth hath conceyued in her old age. Which gaue much contentment to the B. Virgin, who reioyced at her neighbers

H 3 good

good, and confirmed her in the Angells promise, shewing that which he sayd, was a thing possible. For as a woman, arriued almost to decrepite old age, had conceyued: euen so might a yong maide haue a Sonne, and be a mother without losse of her Virginity , because nothing is impossible to God . Hereby I will learne alwayes to haue a good confidence in God , when I shall see my selfe assayled with tentations, by putting my hope in him, who is of power to deliuer me.

Meditat. VIII.   *Of the Answere, which the B. Virgin made vnto the Angell*.

TO meditate, what a longing desire the Angell had to vnderstand the B. Virgins answere, & the delight that the most sacred Trinity had to see her giue consent to the mystery of the Incarnation , which was effected instantly . The fayth of this holy Virgin giuing credit to the Angells words: her most profound humility amiddest so great prerogatiues, when she sayd : Behold the handmayd of our Lord, be it done to me according to thy word. Words giuing testimony, that she did put herselfe in the lowest degree of all, reputing herselfe vnworthy to be the mother of God, and testifying her prompt obedience, and absolute resignation to the diuine will, saying : Behold : a significant word for the expressing of this promptitude of obedience.

    1.   To consider, what honour it is to be
                                     Gods

Gods handmayde. For the handmayde is not to
herselfe, but to her maistresse, whose will she
doth, and not her owne. A bondman is alwais
deuoted to the seruice of him who oweth and
possesseth him: a faythfull bondman is neuer
his owne mayster: he continually remayneth
attentiue and ready to execute, what he is commaunded: he serueth not for hire, or wages,
for he expecteth none, but is bound to do others
seruice: he doth nothing for himselfe, but all for
his maister: he doth not his seruice to his Lord
& mayster alone, but to all those of the house &
family also. He troubleth not himselfe, though
he be worse handled then all the rest, but taketh
all in good part, though they treate him as a
slaue. This is that, which the B. Virgin did, and
I haue much more iust reason to imitate it, by
exercising my selfe therein in what I can, sith
there is so great an obligation imposed vpon me
to doe it.

2.   To examine these words: Be it done to
me according to thy word. The Virgin shewed
by these words (Be it done) that the mystery of
the Incarnation was a worke, that depended on
the omnipotency of God, as did the first creation of the world. She also presented her selfe to
beare part in the trauayles and paynes, that her
Sonne was to suffer: wherein she gaue testimony of her absolute resignation, presenting her
selfe to suffer as an handmayde, & not to be serued as a Lady & maistresse. To thinke what māner of fayth, and obedience was that of the holy
Virgin, as witnesseth that which she sayd: Be

it done to me according to thy word : obedient not only to God, but to the Angell also, who spake vnto her on the part of God.

3. To consider the Angells ioy, when he had so happily performed his Embassage : how he admired the Virgins singular prudence, and great vertue : and that so he returned instantly to Heauen, where we may imagine, he extolled the holy Virgins woderfull perfections. Whence I will learne to retyre my selfe into my chamber presently after I shall haue done the worke of obedience commaunded me, and how I must publish and make knowne to others the vertues of this holy Virgin.

Meditat. IX.   *Of the accomplishment of the Incarnation: and of other circumstances thereunto belonging.*

TO Meditate, at the very instant, that the B. Virgin had giuen her consent, the holy Ghost formed of her most pure bloud a most perfect body, & created a most excellent reasonable soule, vniting it with the person of the eternall Word, God yet continuing, made man, and man made God, and consequently the Virgin eleuated to the dignity of the mother of God.

1. To consider the contentment, the most sacred Trinity had, seeing the accomplishment of their promise, how the eternall Father reioyced for hauing giuen his most beloued Sonne,

who

who was more deere to him, then all creatures put togeather: the Sonne, to see himselfe made man, for that respect tēdring all men in generall, as his owne parents: the holy Ghost, for hauing done a worke of the greatest charity and loue, that could be. The iov of the holy Humanity of the Word, seeing it selfe raysed to so high a dignity, and eleuated from the deep gulfe of nothing, to that eminēcy, that is to the diuinity it selfe. The exultation of the Blessed Virgin at the instant of the Incarnation, by occasion of the extraordinary light, that God communicated vnto her, that she might see the wonderfull manner of the mistery, that was wrought in her immaculate wombe, considering her selfe to be both a Virgin, and a mother of such a Sonne, who as a bright shining Sunne, communicated most singular graces vnto her. Heere I will reioyce & be glad in company with al these most holy persons, representing vnto my selfe the allyance that is now between God & me, for which I will conceiue in my hart a generous resolution not to doe any thing vnworthy of such a parent, & allye, as is God himselfe.

2. To consider the infinite charity of God for hauing pleased to take a passible and mortall body: seeing that if he would haue become incarnate, an impassible and immortall body had more beseemed his greatnes, for that he was exempt from all fault both originall, & actuall, not by priuiledge, but by right, as being the naturall Sonne of God. That further he was conceyued by the operation of the holy

Ghost,

Ghoſt, not by the vvorke of man, and finally
that his ſoule vvas Glorious and Bleſſed from
the very inſtant of his conception, and ſo by
all right his body ſhould haue beene impaſ-
ſible and immortall. But his ſurpaſſing charity inuited and moued him to depriue himſelfe
thereof for our good, to the end I may learne,
that I ought to depriue my ſelfe of the enioying
of myne appetites, for the regard of him, and
for his ſake.

3.   To conſider the cauſes, for which it
pleaſed God to become an infant, and to be
conceyued in the vvombe of a vvoman. Firſt
to make himſelfe in all thinges like vnto vs
his brethren, to the end he might by that occaſion bind vs to loue him the more affectiu-
ouſly: for little children doe cauſe a tender affection in mens harts tovvardes them. Secondly, to giue vs an example of humility, &
to make vs louers thereof. Thirdly to teach vs
patience, & perfect mortification, becauſe he ſuffered a ſtraite and obſcure impriſonment the
ſpace of nyne moneths in a womans wombe,
where the infants be very ſtraitly lodged, without being able to ſtir, nor turne themſelues, nor
to moue hand or foot. And this was in our moſt
B. Ieſus a proofe of moſt ſingular loue, becauſe
he had then the perfect vſe of reaſon.

Meditat.

Meditat. X.   Of the Excellencyes of our Saui-
ours soule : and of the heroicall acts of vertue,
which he exercised from the first instant of
his Incarnation.

TO consider the graces and excellencies of
our Sauiour, as he was man, and to see
that they were illimited & infinite in him.
For as S. Iohn sayth: *God gaue him not the spirit*
by measure, as he did to the rest of the Saints.
And in his first chapter he sayth: *VVe haue seene*
his glory, glory as it were of the only begotten of the
Father, full of grace and verity. This beseemed
the personall being, that was communicated vnto him. All these graces may be reduced to seauen. The first is purity, in so much as he neuer
sinned nor could sinne, nor erre, nor haue any
the least imperfection. The second was the grace
of sanctity, which surpassed without all comparison that of all Angells and men togeather. The
third, to be happy and blessed from the very instant of his creation, and of his essence diuine.
The fourth, to haue the fulnes of the knowledge
& wisdome of God, in knowing all thinges created, past, present, and to come, without exception, as he, who was to be the Iudge of all.
The fifth, power to doe & worke miracles. The
sixt, the power of excellency to pardon sinnes,
to chaunge the harts and wills of men, to institute Sacraments, and distribute graces to men.
The seauenth, to be the head of men and of Angells,

gells, as well in the Church militant, as in the triumphant, our Sauiour being the first, and the chiefest of all the predestinated, in regard of whō God hath predestinated all the others. Out of the consideration of these excellencies I vvill draw diuers motions & affections of deuotion, in praysing, extolling, and thanking the Eternall Father, and in being glad of the goods, & perfections, that shined in our Lord, and Sauiniour.

6.   To consider the heroicall actes, of vertue, that his most holy soule exercised in this first instant, seeing himselfe so highly honored, and adorned with so great graces. For it produced an act of most burning loue: a most perfect acknowledgement of all prerogatiues: a most profound humility before the diuine maiesty, seing the nothing, out of which it was drawne a most prompt oblation, and presentation to obey God in all, that he should please to commaund, desiring that the occasion might present it selfe, that it might by effect testify its own good will. I must also endeauour to conceyue all the same affections in my soule. To thinke what, and how sweet conferences the soule of our Sauiour held and intertayned with the three diuine Persons, and principally with that of the Word, vvhereunto it vvas hypostatically vnited.

3.   To consider the great sorrow of his soule, seeing the eternall Father, whome it so perfectly loued, iniured and offended with such enormity of sinnes, the tyranny of the Diuell, & the

the losse of mens soules, whome it euen then regarded, & beheld as its brethren. And this was the greatest sorrow vnto it, that euer was, & euer shall be. To consider that our Sauior knowing that very instant, that it was the will of his Father, that he should saue men, in lieu of so many benefits receyued, as he was man, loued vs with the same loue, that he loued his Father, and offered himselfe volutarily to dye for the sauing of our souls, reioycing that the occasion was presented him to shew the loue, that he caryed to God and men, saying these words, as the Apostle obserueth, Hebr. 10, taken out of the 39. Psalme: Behold I am come to execute in this, & in all things els, thy holy will, putting thy lawes in the middest of my hart. For this I must be gratefull, render him thankes, and endeauour to trace his steps. To meditate the magnanimity and great charity of our Sauiour, who seeing before his eyes the trauailes, and the torments, he was to suffer, as present to him as they were at the very time of his passion, did euen then voluntarily offer himselfe to endure them, and so he carryed his Crosse all his life long. The generosity of his courage, that was ready and willing to endure much more, if his Father would so haue commaunded him, & if it had been necessary for our saluation. To ponder, that in that very instant he had in his vnderstanding presented vnto him all men in generall, & me also among the rest, & that he offered himselfe for euery one of them, yea & for me, as if there had been none other besides me alone.

I   *Meditat.*

Meditat. XI.   Of the Iourney, that the Eternall Word tooke presently after he was incarnate in his Mothers wombe, to sanctify S. Iohn Baptist.

TO Meditate, that our Sauiour delayed no tyme to enter into the exercise of his charge, and to take possession of the office of Redeemer. For presently after his conception he vouchsafed to goe to cleanse S. Iohn of originall sinne, and to sanctify him in his mothers wombe. To consider the great desire, our Sauiour had of our saluation: the care he hath of the good of his elect: how vigilant and ready he is to exercise his office of the Messias: how great an euill sinne is, and how displeasing a thing it is to God to see any stay and continue therin, but for a very little time.

2.   To consider, that though our Sauiour might and could haue sanctifyed Saint Iohn without stirring from Nazareth, yet he pleased to goe in person to the house of S. Elizabeth, to giue vnto vs an example of humility and charity, in that, which he, who was the greater, went to visit his inferiour. And of this example his holy mother made her vse in like maner in the work, that he went to doe, seruing her selfe thereof as an instrument of that first sanctification that he euer exercised in the world, to giue vs to vnderstand, that this most sacred Lady & Virgin is the mediatresse betweene God, and men. To thinke,

that

that our Sauiour was no sooner entred into the most pure wombe of his mother, then that he moued and incited her to make that voyage vp to the hills. And so entring into a soule by his grace, he moueth it, and putteth it forwards to produce the manyfold and diuers actes of vertue.

3. To meditate the B. Virgins perfect Obedience, who tooke her iourney presently vvithout expecting any more expresse commaundment. For her intention was most pure, tending only to the glory of God, and to the accomplishing of his holy will. And this obedience of hers went accompanyed with a singular charity, patience, and humility, sith she would not stay to consider, that the greater went to visit the lesser, or that she, the mother of God, went to the mother of one, that was but man. To consider the B. Virgins rare modesty vpon the way without diuerting of her mind, & thoughts, euer thinking still vpon her sweet Sonne, in whome was all her pleasure and contentment in her iourney. Out of the aforesayd I will seeke to draw some profit for my soule, by stirring my selfe vp to the loue of these vertues.

Meditat. XII. *Of what passed in the Blessed Virgins Visitation of S. Elizabeth.*

TO Consider the benefitts, and diuine fauours, that entred with the Blessed Virgin into that fortunate house; for by the meanes of her voyce God clensed S. Iohn of ori-

ginall sinne, iustified him, replenished him with
the holy Ghost, hastned the vse of reason in him,
made him his Prophet, gaue him to vnderstand
the mystery of the Incarnation, and finally mul-
tiplyed his graces vpon him, and put ioy into
into him, as he testified by the leaping that he
made within his mothers wombe. To consider
Gods omnipotency, who produced so great effects in an instant: the efficacy of the Blessed Virgins words, by meanes whereof these meruailes
were wrought, this holy fruit coming to maturity before the tyme.

2. To consider, how S. Elizabeth was
filled with the holy Ghost, and receiued a diuine
light, that did put into her the knowledge of the
Incarnation: how she in like sort receiued the
gift of prophesy, by meanes whereof she cryed
out, moued by diuine inspiration, such as the
presence and visitation of God is wont to cause
in the soule, raysing vp her voyce in the prayse
of the diuine maiesty, and of his holy mother,
saying: Blessed art thou &c. And then with a
most low and humble reuerence she prosecuted
her speech, and sayd: And whence is this to me,
that the mother of my Lord cometh to me? And
further witnessing her singular acknowledgement, she forthwith added: For behold, as the
voyce of thy salutation sounded in myne eares,
&c. Such happy motions, I will endeauour to
haue, when God shall vouchsafe fauourably to
visit my soule.

3. To consider, how S. Elizabeth confirmed the Virgin in her beliefe, & in her holy &
pious

pious refolutions, faying : And bleffed art thou,
tnat haft belieued &c. I will learne of this, that
it is an holy thing to animate, and confirme the
neighbour in good workes, and heauenly defires.

4. To examine all the wordes of the Canticle Magnificat, which the B. Virgin deliuered
in the prayfe of God, being replenifhed with
illuftrations diuine, & tranfpored with a feruour of loue towards him, proceeding from a
foule fet on fire with charity, as a teftimony of the outward fire, that burned within. Of
this i will draw affections of praysing God,
and a ioy & contentment at the vertues, & perfections of this moft worthy Lady.

5. To confider, how the Virgin made
well neere three monethes aboad in the houfe
of S. Elizabeth, bleffing and enriching that holy habitation with the example of her admirable
vertues, & of her moft fweet & diuin difcourfes.
And that if at her firft entring, in fhe caufed and
wrought fo wonderfull effects, what might fhe
then doe in fo long a tyme of her continuance
there after that? And if God in fauour of the
Arke of Couenant beftowed manifold benedictions vpon the houfe of Obededon, in fo much
as Dauid defired to tranfport it from thence to
his owne houfe, what did not the diuine maiefty doe in fauour of this holy Virgin &c. Of
what I haue faid, I wil learne to be more & more
affected to the feruice of the mother of God.

Meditat. X I I I. *Of the Natiuity of S.* Iohn *Baptist.*

TO confider, how before the Conception of this holy Infant, God would honour him for his Precurfour, caufing him to be miraculoufly borne of barren & holy parents, by meanes of deuout prayers, and holy defires. He would alfo, that the fame Angell Gabriel, who announced the Natiuity of our Sauiour fhould notify alfo that wonderfull Conception of Saint Iohn. To examine the meruailes, and perfections, that the Angell foretold of S Iohn, declaring his name, that fignifyeth Grace. He added further, that he fhould be great before God both in vertues, and in other gifts that he fhould receiue from heauen: that he fhould be moft temperate, fhould forbeare the drinking of wine, or ficer, & of all that, which might inebriate or make drunke, as a Nazarean, wholy deuoted to the feruice of God: that he fhould be replenifhed with the holy Ghoft, euen in his mothers wôbe, that he fhould goe before the face of our Lord, as his Precurfour, conuerting many foules to God with an inflamed zeale, and the fpirit of Elias. To confider, that this child was perfect towardes God, towards himfelfe, & towardes his neighbour. Towards God, for being moft fingularly enriched with abundant grace: towardes himfelfe, in being moft auftere in the rigour of his owne mortification, and pennance:

towards

tovvards his neighbour, in burning vvith a most feruent zeale to conduct him in the way of saluation. I must follow this most excellent paterne of perfection, & haue it euer before the eyes of my soule to imitate, as I am able.

2. To consider the fauours, that our Sauiour did to this holy and Blessed babe. For whiles he was yet in his mothers belly, he sanctifyed him, in so much as he was the first Saint, that God sanctifyed after he became incarnate: he gaue him the vse of reason before the ordinary time: he illumined his vnderstanding, & inflamed his will with holy affections. The vse of reason was neuer taken from him, because God giueth his gifts without repentance. And so our Sauiour Iesus, being a little Infant, did help him to increase in ver̄ue, as the B. Virgin did the same also towardes S. Elizabeth. To thinke, that in fauour of S. Iohn our Sauiour did many fauours and communicated many graces to his mother, filling her with the holy Ghost, & honouring her with the gift of prophesy. By this I will learne, how much it profiteth to keep company with the iust, sith God doth so many & so great fauours to others for their sake.

3. To consider what hapned in S. Iohns Natiuity. First his Name, vvhich signifyeth Grace, was giuen him, a signe that God would impart his graces abundantly vnto him for the discharg of the office, wherwith he honored him. Secondly, his Father, who had contynued mute for a tyme, recouered his speech, was replenished with the holy Ghost, & receyued the gift

of

of prophesy, by occasion whereof he composed
the Canticle *Benedictus*, full of excellent wordes
and sentences, which I must diligently weigh.
Thirdly, all those, who tooke notice of S. Iohns
Natiuity, reioyced thereat exceedingly, a most
euident testimony, that God carryed a particular respect of honour to him, & fauoured him
by this present priuiledge with an assurance,
that he would guide & direct him in all his actions for the tyme to come.

*Meditat. XIIII.   Of the great perplexity, that
S. Ioseph was in : and of the reuelation of the
Angell.*

TO consider, how God had bestowed vpon
this holy personage a most singular sanctity, & many heroical vertues, to the end he
might be worthy to haue his B. Mother in mariage, and to be his foster-Father : yea so, as he
was reputed & held to be his owne Father, giuing him grace, correspondent to the dignity &
worthynes of such an office. That his fayth, &
obedience was more perfect, then was that of
Abraham : his patience and suffrance of trauayles greater, then that of Iacob : his chastity
most singular, as also his familiar conuersation
with God, his charity, his humility, his meeknes. These vertues and the like increased euery
day in him, by occasion of his ordinary & daily
communication with the B Virgin his spouse,
both of them endeauouring, whether should
                                        excell

excell the other in louing God, and in producing the acts of that most inflamed loue : and from hence proceeded his perfect chastity , without being troubled , or feeling in himselfe any immoderate motion, & this by a particular fauour from heauen .

2 . To thinke, how much he was afflicted to see his spouse with child, without knowing the cause thereof. That the secret iudgments of God should afflict two persons so holy, without any their fault, his will being that the diuine mistery accomplished in the B. Virgins wombe , should be concealed. Wherhence I will learne to be alwayes ready to receyue the tribulations, that God shall please to send me, & with humility to reuerence his secret & profound iudgments .

3 . To consider S. Iosephs eminent patience and prudence in suffering , without complaint, the iniury that he thought was done him , neyther murmuring , nor defaming his Spouse, but thinking long time with himselfe , what he were best to doe. Here I will examine the vertues, that appeared in the B. Virgin in this busines , that I may imitate them ; as her most singular humility, her deepe silence, her most assured confidence in the diuine prouidence, her continuall prayer, putting her cause into the hands of God .

4 . To consider, how God doth neuer abandon, or forsake any in necessity, as he did neyther abandon S. Ioseph , but sent vnto him an Angell to declare vnto him the mistery , that lay hid within the B. Virgins wombe , conuerting

ting his teares into pleasure, & his heauines into ioy. To ponder the words of the Gospell (Ioseph, the Sonne of Dauid, feare not) and to
thinke, what a ioy it was to him to see himselfe
deliuered from the iealosy and suspition, that
tormented him in his soule, and what thankes
he vvas to yield vnto God for hauing giuen
him so holy a spouse, and made him as the
Father of his only Sonne, and that the time
of the redemption of the vvorld vvas then
come. The Virgins ioy, in seing her Spouse free
from his trouble, and considering Gods paternall prouidence, vvho had exempted him
from that payne. Out of this I will draw a motiue of putting my trust in God, when I am in
the middest of my afflictions. The singular ioy
& contentment of these two terrestriall Cherubims, their holy conferences and discourses, the
purity of their loue, their more then Angelicall
life, the conformity of their wills, the submission and respect our Lady did beare to Saint
Ioseph, as to her head: how she recounted vnto him, vvhat had passed vvith her in the Annunciation, and vvhat in the house of Zachary, because it vvas then tyme to make report of
those thinges.

Meditat,

Meditat. XV. *Of the expectation of the B. Virgins deliuery: and of the preparation for the Natiuity of the Sauiour of the world.*

TO consider the surpassing desire, our Sauiour had to bring the worke of Redemption, already begon, to a conclusion, wishing to come speedily to hand-blowes with the enemy of Nature, and to be baptized in the water of trauayles and paynes, in so much as he was with a vehement desire, to come to the encounter; yet would he not be borne, till the nyne moneths were expired, because he would be conformable to that of other little children, and submit himselfe thereinto the ordinary law of nature, taking that tyme as a certayne retyre, and premeditation for the affayre and busines, he was to vndergoe.

2. To consider the most affectionate desire, the Virgin had to see with her eyes him, who was her owne Sonne, and Gods togeather; to adore, serue, and cherish him, saying these words of the Canticles: Who shall graunt me, O my Son, that I may see thee out of my wombe, to serue thee &c. and to the end the world might enioy the good, whereof she was then possessed alone: for she would not keepe and reserue him to her selfe alone, but for all in generall: Euen so must I set myne owne desires on fire with the fewell and matter of such affections, crauing of God by frequent & iaculatory prayers, that it would

would pleafe him to be borne in my foule.

3.   To confider, that the B. Virgin held her felfe moft affured, that her Virginity fhould not be any way hurt, by her deliuery of child, whiles fhe euer and a none reprefented to her mind thefe words of the Prophet Efay : Behold, a Virgin fhall conceyue, and bring forth a Sonne &c . Then fhe fayd : whence cometh this good fortune to me, that I am this Wonderfull Virgin ? And therefore fhe had no other care, but to prepare her foule, and to adorne and fet it forth with excellent vertues. And this muft I alfo doe, that my Sauiour may vouchfafe to be borne in me. To meditate the great defire, that holy Iofeph had to ferue God incarnate, in acknowledgement of the fingular benefit and fauour, he had done him, in chofing him for his fofter-Father.

Meditat. XVI.   Of the Iourney, which the B. Virgin made to Bethleem.

TO Meditate, how the word incarnate, being yet within his mothers wombe, abandoning all that the world loueth and feeketh, fought what the world refufeth and abborreth, leauing vnto vs a manifeft proofe therof, in that he left Nazareth, where he might haue foud fome little comodity in his birth in his mothers poore houfe, as S. Iohn Baptift had done. In which fact of his he teacheth vs, how much he loueth pouerty, and how much he auerfeth delicacy,

licacy, and therefore I will by this confound my selfe, seeing I desire the quite contrary, & conforme my selfe to the proceeding of the world.

2.   To consider, that the cause, for which our Sauiour went from Nazareth to Bethleem, was to obey the Emperors Edict. Here I must thinke, how far and different Gods thoughts be from those of men. The Emperour had none but terrene thoughts, of pride, vanity, and auarice, seeking that the whole world should reuerence him, whiles our Sauiour thought of nothing, but humility, pouerty, subiection, and contempt of riches, and vanities. And though this Edict proceeded of pride, yet it was Gods will, that it should be obeyed, to giue to vnderstand how much obedience pleased him, though it be done to Superiours that commaund for their owne interest. He would also be borne at Behleem, because it was the wil of his eternall Father, whom he desired to obey in his Natiuity, as he obeyed him in his death.

3.   To consider the iourney the B. Virgin made, and the manner of it, the vertues she exercised on the way, the discourses, and sweet conferences she had with her Sonne, and holy Ioseph, all her actions being diuine. To thinke vpon her wearisomnes vpon the way, whereof I will make my profit.

4.   To consider the Virgins arriuall to Bethleem, where she found not one, who would affoard her lodging, in so much as she was driuen to retire herselfe into a stable; God so disposing it for the making of his entry into the

world, poore, and necessitous, hauing chosen
for himselfe whatsoeuer was worst amongst me.
To consider, who this Lord is that seeketh out
a place to be lodged in and findeth none, all being taken vp, and filled with men, at whose
blindnes I am to meruayle for not acknowledging him, nor offring him an house, as also the
good, whereof they depriue themselues. Of all
this I must draw tender motions, and affections
of compassion. To consider, how the men of
the world doe giue entrance and intertainment
to ryoting, and to the pleasures of the world,
which they refuse to giue to God: to examine
also the great patience, humility, and spirituall
ioy, wherewith the B. Virgin, and holy Ioseph
receiued this incommodity, and constantly endured the repulse and bad handling and entreat-
ment of them, who reiected them agayne and a-
gayne, because they were poore, though they
were most rich in spirituall goods.

Meditat. XVII.   Of our Sauiours Natiuity.

TO meditate, how the nine moneths ended,
God for vs, made a little babe, was borne
vpon earth, and began to runne the
course of his trauayles with great feruour, as the
Prophet Dauid sayd psal. 18. He reioyced as a
Giant to runne the way. Who in compensation
of the retrayte, that his mother had prouided
him, enriched her at the tyme of his Natiuity
with the inestimable gifts of most high contem-
plations, & of extraordinary ioyes, & comforts,
when

when as other women in that tyme of their deliuery of child are wont to feele most great dolors
and paynes Of this I will learne , what good
our Sauiour bringeth to a soule , that receyueth
him in the Sacrament , if he receyue good intertainment at the soules hand . That he came out
of the immaculate wombe of his mother without the preiudice or hurt of her Virginall purity, in this also requiting the good in treaty & intertainment , she had giuen him.

2. To consider the contentment , and spiritual iubilation the B. Virgin had in time of her
deliuery, how being there gone aside into a corner of that poore and straite stable , and her
thoughts fixed in most high contemplation , she
brought furth , and was deliuered of her most
beloued Sonne, the only Sonne of God. To consider the ioy and comfort she had to take him
into her armes : the motions & affections of her
mind in holding him in her lap : the thankes she
yielded him for so singular a benefit , the most
sweet speeches she vsed vnto him . How swad-
ling him in poore and cleane cloathes , she layed
him , being the King both of heauen & earth , in
the manger, esteeming her selfe vnworthy to imbrace him in her armes, and kneeling before him
adored him as her God and Lord . That good
Ioseph did the same , and I will also doe the like
with them, yielding him all possible thankes, &
offring him both my soule & body with the best
affection I can .

3. To consider the wonderfull greatnes of
this little poore infant , layd in the manger , re-

presenting him to my selfe, as my God, and such,
as I owe vnto him all manner of respect, seruice,
intertainment, and duty. To thinke, that though
he had been but man, it was too contemptible a
thinge to lay him in a manger of beastes, much
more he being the Creatour of lights : to behold
him bound both hands and feete, is a thing prodigious and most strange, him I say, who is the
glory, and eternall splendour of his omnipotent
Father. To thinke, what thoughts it was likely
he might haue in this piteous estate; the speechs,
he framed to vs in his mind; the teares, that fell
from his eyes; the incommodities he suffered
in his body; for whome, and how he endured
them; and the heroycall vertues he exercised.
And therfore I wil ruminate these rare examples
againe and againe. I will endeauour to conceiue
the tender affections of loue, of admiration, and
of gratitude, with a feruent desire to imitate him,
remembring what S. Bernard sayth : I will loue
thee so much the more, the more I consider thee
contemptible for loue of me.

Meditat. XVIII.   Of the Ioy of the Angells at our Sauiours Natiuity.

TO consider the Angells ioy, and their admiration, when they saw God himselfe,
infinite in essence and in power, pressed to
shrowd himselfe in a corner of a poore stable,
vnknowne, and contemned of men; how the
eternall Father sent al the Hierarchies of heauen,

com-

commaunding them to honour, and reuerence his Sonne, and to acknowledge him for their King and foueraygne Lord, as witneffeth the Apoftle, when he fayth Hebr. 1. When he bringeth the firft begotten into the world, he fayth, Let the Angells adore him. And fo we muft belieue, that they aksed leaue of the eternall Father to come downe to the earth to publifh the news of the power of God made man, to the end the whole world might acknowledge him.

2. To confider, how God fent an Angell to the Sheepheardes, who watched & kept their fheep, & what the Angell fayd vnto them, whofe wordes are thefe: Behold, I Euangelize to you great ioy &c. That this newes and good tydings was not brought to the wife, or to the noble, or to the rich of this world, but to the poore fheepheardes, becaufe our Sauiour came particularly for the poore and humble. To examine thefe wordes: for you is borne a Sauiour. In fo much as he is not borne for the Angells, but chiefly for me, and for finners fuch as I am, that he may communicate the riches, that he hath brought from heauen, to vs, by publifhing a generall Iubily, and a plenary Indulgence of all our finnes. To ruminate thefe wordes: you fhall find the Infant fwadled in cloathes, & layd in a manger. Wordes, that teach vs, how God is willingly in poore houfes, or keepeth company with the poore, & the innocent &c.

3. To confider, how there was fodainly heard a multitude of Angells, melodioufly finging: Glory in the higheft to God, and in earth

K 3.   peace

peace to men of good will . To confider , who fent thefe Angells, and to fee that it was the E-ternall Father , for the honoring of his Sonne fo abafed , and anihilated for loue of him : for this was the end , for which God fent them , by this example to teach vs what we ought to doe . To ponder thefe wordes : Glory in the higheft to God, &c. And to feeke to make our profit ther-of . To thinke , how the Angells, before their returne to heauen-came to adore this little one , lying in the manger , to doe him homage, & to fing him a moft melodious fonnet of their hea-uenly muficke, which was only heard & vnder-ftood of him , of his holy mother, & of good S. Iofeph , and caufed vnto them a thoufand good affections of loue, deuotion & reuerence .

Meditat. XIX. Of the sheepheardes adoring Chrift ; and of what paffed in the ftable at Bethleem.

TO confider the fheepheardes promptitude and readynes in obeying the Angells com-mandement , exhorting and encouraging one another to the place of the Natiuity. Wher-in they witneffed their great obedience , though they had not receiued an expreffe commaunde-ment to goe to Bethleem , and their much fer-uour and deuotion , as we are giuen to vnder-ftand by that which is fayd in the Ghofpell, that the Sheepheardes went with great diligence and fpeede , and therefore they were alfo worthy to
                                                          find

find him, whome they sought for.

2.   To consider, how from the face of this blessed child I E S V S there proceeded a diuine light, that penetrated the Sheepheardes vnderstanding, & discouered vnto them by a liuely fayth, that he, whome they beheld with their eyes, was God & man, the Messias so much promised in the law, and expected of the world. The B. Virgins ioy, and sweet countenance, who humbly accepted the seruice, by them done to her Sonne, in so much as the Pastors remayned astonished at the rare modesty, and singular sanctity, that appeared outwardly in our B. Lady. How they fell vpon their knees, & with inflamed affections of loue adored the little I E= s v s with great humility, and reuerence, presenting vnto him their seruice, with wordes of deuotion, & further presenting him vvith some gift, or other, according to their poore abi= lity.

3.   To consider, hovv the sheepheards, after they had done their deuotion, returned to their charge, reporting euery vvhere the vvonders they had seene. That the holy Virgin kept all these thinges, & conferred them in her hart: teaching vs, hovv vve ought to keep, & esteem of things, that come from God. To ponder this, that there be foure sorts of persons; some, vvho vvould not moue their foot to goe to the stable, though they heard, vvhat the sheepheardes re= ported: others, vvho vvent indeed, but yet tooke no notice eyther of the little child, or of his mother, and vvere there present in body

K 4   only:

only; some, moued of a diuine instinct, entred in, as did the Pastors, & adored the little Iesus by a liuely fayth, vpon the sodaine inspired into them, and thereby returned with great profit of spirit. Finally others, as the B. Virgin, and S. Ioseph stayed continually by, in the stable, and were assistant to our Sauiour, and serued him with great affeection. And these must I imitate, or if I cannot doe that, I will at least imitate the Sheepheardes.

Meditat. XX. *Of the Circumcision of Christ.*

TO consider the B. Virgins, and S. Iosephs perfect obedience in that, which concerned the Circumcision, though they were not ignorant, that the execution of that legall commaundment would become vnto them burdensome and much more paynefull to the little Iesus, vpon whome that piteous sacrifice was to be accomplished. To consider the obedience of the holy Virgin, which was so deere vnto her, as if neede had been, she would her selfe haue taken the knife to do it, though she should haue dyed afterwardes of pitty, & sorrow for it. To consider, how she would be present at this dolefull spectacle, because she would not leaue her Son, but bind vp the woud of his Circucision, gather vp the little peece of flesh, that was be to taken away from him, and the precious bloud, that he was then to shed, knowing that the one & the other were diuine. To imagine what talke, full of motions of affection she had with her Sonne,

in

in so much as she might call him her spouse of bloud; and with euery other person of the Trinity.

2. To consider the heroicall vertues, that our Sauiour exercised in his Circumcision. The first was his obedience, and that most perfect, though a commaundement had not bound him, witnessing by that action, that he kept and obserued all the old law. The second, his humility: for though he neyther was, nor could be a sinner, yet would he be esteemed such, because Circumcision was the badge of sin. The third, his patience: for seeing he had the perfect vse of reason, and was of a most delicate complexion, he could not but by his natural inclination haue a feeling of the wound, that the knife made. The fourth, his most burning charity in shedding this little quantity of bloud, with a desire to powre out all the rest, if it had been at that tyme necessary for the sauing of man.

3. To consider, how in lieu of this corporall Circumcision God requireth of me a spirituall, to wit, the cutting off of all inordinate pleasures, of vanities, and of other carnall and sensuall works, & the mortification of vices, and of all that, which hath contradiction with God. Heere I will resolue willingly to endure to be mortified for the helping of my selfe to circucise whatsoeuer is out of order in me.

Meditat.

Meditat. XXI.   Of the Name of IESVS.

TO Meditate, how it was the eternall Father, who imposed vpon him this sacred Name of IESVS, because of the excellency and worthynes of this little child, which was such, as the Father alone, who knew his greatnes, could giue him a fitt Name. That IESVS, which is as much as Sauiour, because he deliuereth vs from all sorts of euills both of fault of payne, communicateth vnto vs all sortes of goods of grace in this world, such as be vertues, and the gifts of the holy Ghost in this life, and glory in the next: & for the manner, by which he hath saued vs. Therefore this most sweet Name could not consort with God alone, nor with man alone, but with him, who being God and man both, hath in the rigour of iustice set vs free by his infinite meritts. To thinke, with how spirituall a pleasure the holy Virgin, and S. Ioseph pronounced this Blessed Name of IESVS, saying: IESVS shall his Name be, at the vttering whereof all had their part of a most sweet smell, and with how singular a promptitude the most benigne infant accepted the name & office of Sauiour, because it redounded to the honour of his eternall Father, & to the good of mortall men.

2.   To consider, how this name was giuen our Redeemer publikely in his Circumcision, to the end it may appeare, that what tyme he tooke vpon him the forme and shape of a sinner, his

eternall

eternall Father gaue him this Name of honour
& glory, which in maiesty and dignity surpasseth all other Names : to the end also it may be
vnderstood, that the Name & office of Sauiour
should cost nim his bloud, insinuating and sig-
nifying the price, that he was to pay afterwards
for the accomplithment of the totall Redemption, though the bloud, which he did euen then
shed, was more then inough to ransome a thousand worlds.

3. To consider the meruayles of this most
sweet Name, and the vtilities, that it bringeth
vs, and to craue of the eternall Father, that he
vouchsafe to graunt vnto vs to vnderstand it
better. For this Name of I ESVS is as an a-
bridgement of all the graces, & excellencyes,
that are to be found in our Sauiour, as to be infinitly good, infinitely wise, holy, mercifull,
&c. That if he be I ESVS, he is surpassingly
humble, sweet, meeke, patient, magnanimous,
modest, obedient, charitable. If he be I ESVS,
he is our Phisitian, our Maister, our Father,
Iudge, Pastour, & Aduocate : for all this and
much more is comprehended vnder the name
& office of Sauior. To thinke, that in this name
be comprized & contained all the other names,
and tytles, which the prophets haue giuen him,
namely Esay c. 2. where he calleth him God,
strong, Admirable, Consaylour, Father of the
world to come, Prince of peace. And these
words I must examine and ponder one by one,
and draw by consideration of them vnto myne
owne vse & profit, the great fruits that are contayned

tayned in this sacred Name IESVS. A Name,
that I will alwayes haue in reuerence, which I
will imprint and engraue in my hart, & which I
will euer haue in my mouth, saving: IESVS
meus, & omnia. O sweet IESV, be thou to me
IESVS for euer. Amen.

Meditat. XXII.   *Of the comming of the three*
Kings from the East, to adore the child Iesus.

TO consider, at what tyme the Starre appeared, in what place, to what end, and
what effects it wroght in these three Kings
of the East. That as the Eternall Father had sent
an Angell to the Sheepheards of Iury, so vouchsafing that his Sonne should be knowne to all,
he also sent a Starre to the Pagans, to the end
the one, and the other should come to adore
him, and to doe him homage, because he came
equally for all. That many, seeing this Starre,
wondred at the beauty of it, and yet eyther for
slouth, or because they would not take a little
paynes, or because they would not leaue their
pleasures, they would not follow it, in so much
as of so many of the world there were to be found
but three, who had the will to doe it. And in
this I am to admire the efficacious calling of
these three Kings, and to make my profit of it,
thinking, how by this is accomplished, & veri-
fied that which S. Matthew sayth: Many are called, & but few be chosen.

2.   To consider the meruaylous fayth of
                                    these

these three Kinges, which moued them to cast themselues into the armes of the diuine proui-dence, leauing themselues to be conducted & lead by a Starre, staying where it stood still, & euer following the conduct of it. To thinke how, when they arriued neere to Hierusalem, they sodainly lost the sight of it, as well for the prouing of their fidelity, as also to the end that, whiles that direction from heauen was taken from them, they might recurre to those Starrs that God had appointed on earth, who be the Superiours, and the holy Scriptures. And of this I must learne to do the same.

3. To consider these wordes: Where is he, who is the King of the Iewes. In which they gaue testimony of a singular fayth in belieuing so certainly that, which they had not yet seene, & an excellent magnanimity, and great cou-rage, whiles they apprehended not the perills, whereunto they expoſed themselues, in seeking a King in a strange countrey. By which I must learne to ouercome the difficulties in the pur-ſuite of vertue. To thinke, how the King & all the people, and especially the Iewes, were trou-bled, who had all indeed most iust cause to re-ioyce, and be glad, & that yet for the pleasing of the King, and because they were piteously in-gulfed in all sorts of vices, they were troubled with him. See, how domageable the company and amity of the bad is.

4. To consider, how King Herod called his Councell togeather vpon the demaund and question of these forraine Kinges, and how the
L   wiser

wiser of them answered him, that the Kinge whome they sought, was to be borne in Bethleem. Here I am to thinke, how God serueth himselfe of the wicked for the seruice of the good, & how he discouereth the truth of the holy Scriptures vnto them, who desire to know it, to make their profit of it, by the meanes of his ministers, though they be otherwise bad, and vitious. To consider, that the Kings were come thither from remote countreyes to their great paynes, & being wearyed, for the finding out of Iesus Christ, & that the Iewes, among whome he was borne, who had for a long tyme expected his coming, and read it euery day in the Scripture, would not moue a foot to seeke him out, differring to doe it, till the returne of the Wise-men, and so they lost the occasion they might haue had.

Meditat. XXIII.   Of the departure of the three Kings from Hierusalem, and of their comming to Bethleem.

TO consider, how the Wise-men, after they had had the Kings answere, went forwards on their iourney very ioyfully, whiles their ioy was also redoubled, by new apparition of the Starre vnto them agayne after their departure from the Citty. To consider further the care of the three Kings to hold on their way, without staying any where, whiles they shuned the knowledge, & the trouble of the bad. Here I am to consider the wonderfull prouidence of God,

God, and the great fidelity, that he obserueth in rewarding thofe, who feeke him. For though the three Kings might haue gone to Bethleem without the conduct of the ftarre, yet he vouchfafed to comfort them with the fight of it, by that ioy recompenfing the payne, and trouble, they had in Hierufalem.

2. To confider, how the ftarre made a ftand right ouer the place, where this little child was newly borne into the world: how they wondred to fee the ftar ftay without moouing ouer fo poore a place as was that, becaufe their conceyt was, they fhould find him in fome royall pallace, by which they might learne, that that King made no efteeme of the pompes & vanities of this world. To weigh thefe wordes: you fhall find the child with Mary his mother: to giue to vnderftand, that Iefus is not ordinarily found without his mother. To confider further, that at the tyme, that the Wife-men faw the little child, a celeftiall beame of light, proceeding from his face, penetrated their harts, & made them fee, that he was both God and man, and caufed in their foules a fingular ioy, & contentment for hauing found him, vvhome they fought.

3. To confider, how the Kinges proftrated themfelues vpon earth with foueraigne reuerence, and adored the child Iefus with that adoration, that appertaineth to God alone, fpeaking vnto him, and yielding him thankes for the grace and fauour he had done them, in conducting them thither by a ftarre, offring him ab-

folutly

solutely their seruice , & protesting that they would be his Maiesties vassalls. To consider the presents, that they gaue him in testimony of their submission, and of the homage, they did vnto him; and how inwardly they offered him in spirit the Gold of their loue , the Incense of their deuotion , & the Myrrhe of their mortification. How acceptable this oblation was vnto the little I E S V S. For he , who reiecteth not little things , despiseth not the great, nor yet the affection, wherewith they are presented, as he gaue them to vnderstand by his gracious countenance , in speaking vnto them not by outward wordes, but by inwards motions, and instincts, by meanes wherof he gaue them more precious gifts, then were theirs to him, and gaue them to returne into their countrey more rich, then they were when they came thence . I must in imitation of these Kinges endure all sorts of trauayles & paynes to find out Iesus Christ, & to offer my selfe all, that I am, to his seruice .

4.	To consider the sweet discourses and talke , the Kings had with the B. Virgin , whose beauty, grace, modesty, and sanctity astonished them : how they related vnto her, what had befallen them by the way , & in Hierusalem : the Virgins gracious answers, who thanked them for the paines they had taken in their long iourney, assuring them of the faythfull correspondence , that they should find at her Sonnes hands towardes them . Finally , how they being admonished , that it was Gods will , they should not make their returne by Hierusalem , but by ano-

ther

ther way into their Countrey, obeyed thereunto vvith all promptitude, choosing rather to breake their word to men, then to fayle in obedience to God. Wherin I will wonder at Gods prouidence, deliuering not only the child I E-s·v·s out of Herodes handes, but also the three Kings from the mischiefe, that he had prepared for them at home in his house.

Meditat. XXIIII. .Of the Purification of our Blessed Lady: and of the Presentation of Iesus in the Temple.

T O Consider, hovv the B. Virgin would present herselfe in the Temple for the accomplishing of the commaundement of Purification, which no way bound her: exercising therein the heroicall acts of obedience, and of most profound humility, & of singular deuotion & reuerence, beseeching the Priest to be pleased to pray for her, & further testifying the affection, that she had to the purity of hart, sith being most pure, and immaculate, as she was, she notwithstanding desired a greater purity in her selfe.

2. To consider the holy motions, and affectiõs, that this B. Virg might baue in doing this action, & the singular deuotion, wherwith she offred her Sonne to the eternall Father in the behalfe of all man-kind, & to thinke vvhat, & hovv affectuous words &speeches she was likely to vse. As also those, that the little I E·s·v·s

L₃   might

might speake, in presenting himselfe in our behalfe to his heauenly Father, hovv he besought
him to moderate and forbeare his iust anger a-
gainst men. That this sacrifice was offered to the
diuine maiesty about the morning, at what time
the custome vvas to offer the ordinary host of
the Lambe, to the end the figure might be correspondent to that vvhich vvas figured.

3.   To consider, hovv the B. Virgin bought
her Sonne out of the Priests hands vvith fiue
peeces of siluer. Whereupon vve are to examine, vvho sold this little child; vvho bought
him againe; at vvhat price? for vvhome?
and vvhat Good ariseth of this action?
He, that selleth him, is the eternall Father,
vvhome yet he giueth a second tyme to the
vvorld : the Virgin bought him, that she might
nourish and bring him vp for vs : the price for
him is most vile, and very little : the end is to
make him as it vvere a slaue, & seruant to men,
and to the end he might euery vvay procure our
good: the fruit & profit, that resulteth thereof,
be the liuely, and efficacious examples, that he
hath giuen vs, and the great merits he hath purchased vs. Of this I vvill learne, that I ought to
buy Iesus Christ vvith the mortification of my
fiue senses.

Medi-

Meditat. X X V.   *Of what happened in the pre-*
sentation touching old Simeon, and Anna the
Prophetesse.

TO confider, hovv God brought thefe tvvo
Holy fouls to the Temple, that they might
acknovvledge the Sauiour I E S V S, and
make report of him. Heere you muft meditate
the vertues of Simeon, vvho vvas iuft, and one
that feared God, that is to fay, vvho obferued
the Lavv exactly, and had a moft great hope,
and a moft earneft defire of the comming of the
Meffias, fpending his tyme in continuall, and
feruent prayers, and crauing of God, that it
vvould pleafe him to graunt ynto him to fee the
Redeemers comming into the vvorld. That the
Holy Ghoft, the comforter, gaue him the effect
of his defires, and fauoured him in that, which
he craued. Whereby vve are to learne, hovv
great an efficacy there is of prayer, and of perfeuerance therein, & vve muft excite, & ftir vp
our felues to the imitation of the vertues of this
holy old man.

2.   To confider, that the Holy Ghoft gaue
ynto Holy Simeon more then he afked, permitting him to take the Sauiour into his armes,
to kiffe and adore him. That there were at that
tyme in the Temple many perfons of diuers e-
ftates & conditions, Doctours, Priefts, &c. a-
mong vvhom God opened but the eyes of Saint
Simeon, & Saint Anne the Prophetefie, making
      L 4   him-

himselfe knowne to them alone in fauor of their good & vertuous life : a distinction, that the diuine maiesty hath euer, & still vseth till this very day. The ioy of this good old man in seing & imbracing the sweet child IESVS : how he held himselfe most contented, and satisfied, & most abundantly recompensed for all his passed trauayles & paines, & care of so long expectation : how not being able to dissemble, or containe his ioy any longer, he began to prayse God, & to say that he was euen then contented to leaue this mortall life, hauing receiued that diuine fauour. To weight euery word of the Canticle : Now thou dismissest &c. And to consider, how holy soules sigh with S. Simeon after Eternall felicity, and groane to see themselues held imprisoned in their bodyes, hauing an eye to life with a griefe and paine, & to death with desire. What thinke we, should the ioy of the glorious Virgin be, in seeing her Sonne knowne, reuerenced, & honored, & in hearing the meruaylous thinges that were spoken?

3. To consider, the thinges, that S. Simeon Prophesied touching the little child IESVS, saying to the Virgin, That her soule should be transpierced which the sword of sorrow. Wherupon we are to consider, how God intermixeth sweet alwaies with the sowre, insinuating that the B. Virgin should liue all her life long in a Crosse, whereunto she willingly offered herselfe. How Simeon further said, That this little child was come for the Resurrection of many, that is, that many soules should by grace rise againe

from

from the death of sinne to the life, and perfection of Holynes; and for the ruyne of many o-
thers, who would not make their profit of his
comming. That it should be a new, and prodigious signe of contradiction, foretelling the
fury of the Iewes, and of the persecutours of
the Church. And for this we must conceyue a
sorrow, in seeing so many sinnes committed a-
gainst the diuine maiesty, and so many soules to
be damned, & become supliants to God that
he vouchsafe, that our Sauiours comming may
be for our soules good, and resurrection to life
for euer.

4. To consider the vertues, that shewed
themselues in Saint Anne, as her restles prayer,
her fasting, her obseruing of Gods law, her deuotion to his seruice, and her perseuerance
therein.

Meditat. X X V I.   *Of the flight of Iesus into*
Ægypt.

TO consider, how our Sauiour was no sooner borne, but that there was an ambitious Herod to persecuted him, hauing the
Iewes who flattered him, for his companiuns
& assistants, and aboue all being instigated by
the Diuell, who feared, that this little, but yet
wonderfull child, was come to make warre v-
pon him, and to depose him frō the dominion
he then had. How the eternall Father would,
that his only Sonne should haue his part of the

paynes, & incomodityes of a laborious & long
iourney in his tender infancy, for the inuring
him to trauayles in tyme, & to giue vs withall
to vnderstand, that vertue is persecuted the very instant, that it beginneth to shew it self: conformably to that, which the Apostle saith 2.
Cor. 3. All that will liue piously in Iesus Christ,
shall suffer persecution. To consider, wherefore
our Sauior would saue himselfe by flying away,
as being a testimony of imbecility, sith he might
haue made himselfe inuisible: and to consider,
that this was to depriue himselfe of the commodities, that he might haue found among his parents, & therefore he would not goe into the
countreys of the three Sages, where he might
haue been knowne & serued, but into the land
of Ægypt among strangers, & enemies, to the
end he might so doe good in going to that countrey, blinded with Idolatry, and so he accomplished that, which Esay saith c. 16. Behold our
Lord will ascend vpon a swift cloud, and will
enter into Ægypt, & the Idols of Ægypt shal be
moued at his presence. And this happened then,
when he layd the foundation of that eminent perfection, that was afterwardes followed, & practised by the Religious men of Ægypt.

2.   To consider, how an Angell admo-
nished good Ioseph in his sleep, saying vnto him,
that he should fly into Ægipt with the yong child
and his mother, and that he should abide there,
vntill he should receiue other commaundement
from him, to the end, by that going aside he
might decline & auoyd the fury of King Herod,
who

who fought to make away, and to till our Sauiour. Heere we muſt meditate, who it is, that giueth this commaundement, & to thinke, that it
is the Eternall Father, to ſhew the prouidence,&
paternall care he had of his Sonne. Who caryeth the meſſage. It is an Angell, to giue vs to
vnderſtand, that he muſt obey the miniſters of
God. To whome? To Saint Ioſeph, who was
the head of the Bleſſed Virgin, leauing her ſelfe
to be gouerned by him, as by her Spouſe. To
conſider the very wordes of this commaundement ſo exact and preciſe: and the moſt prompt
obedience, like vnto that of the Partriarke A-
braham, when the Angell willed him to goe to
ſacrifice his Sonne. How it was by night, when
Ioſeph was at reſt, and a ſleepe, who obeyed
without allegation of any excuſe. How being
willed to take the little child, and his mother,&
to goe inty Ægypt, he inſtantly departed without other company, without carrying any mo-
ueables, or baggage, or any other thing, that
might hinder him in the way. And this is worthy the conſidering, becauſe the Countrey, whither he was to goe, was inhabited of a people
barbarous, and enemyes to the Iewes. How
the Angell left Ioſeph in ſuſpence touching the
tyme of his aboade in Ægypt; for as much as
Gods will is, that we ſhould haue our eyes alwaies lifted vp to heauen, and that we ſhould
put our truſt and confidence in his diuine prouidence, & not in our ſelues. Of all this we muſt
make our profit, in applying it to our ſelues.

2. To conſider the prompt obedience of

S. Ioseph, who submitted his owne iudgement to the reuelation of the Angell, without replieation, or allegation of any reason, or excuse whatsoeuer. In which he gaue a testimony of the promptitude of his will in a matter of it selfe so difficult and hard, such as was to leaue his countrey, & his friendes, going away naked, & deuoid of all commodities, as though he had been banished out of Palestine. He obeyed most exactly, rising vp the very instant, and entring into his iourney, during which he receiued spirituall consolations, that eased his paines and sorrowes, because he had in his cõpany the God of consolation, & the mother of mercy, I E S V S & Mary, with whome whiles he treated in time of that his laborious iourney, by occasion therof he found but little difficulty in the way.

3. To consider, how this Holy family aboade seauen yeares in Ægypt, where they liued most poorly among a people, that were enemies vnto their Nation, intertayning themselues with the labour of their hands: with vvhat a quiet, tranquility & peace of mind they liued, assured of the prouidence of God, vvithout desiring or vvishing Herods death. To consider the griefe, apprehension & feeling, that the multitude and enormity of the sinnes caused vnto them, vvhich they savv continually to be committed against the diuine maiesty, of vvhose honor they vvere zealous in a most high degree: a griefe far greater, then was that of Lot, in seing the Sodomites: as sayth S. Peter 2. Epist. c. 2.

Meditat.

Meditat. XXVII. *Of the cruell death of the Innocents, & returne of the child Iesus out of Ægypt.*

TO consider, how Herod caused all the little children vnder the age of two yeares to be massacred & killed within the countrey of Bethleem. Where we are to weigh, how Diuellish the fury of Ambition is, and how proper it is to the ambitious to be fearfull, & suspitious. What was the feeling and affection of the sweet little child IESVS, seeing and beholding from Ægypt the death of all those little Innocents, which were massacred for him: how exceeding was his griefe of minde, when the Tyrants sword was thrust into their bodies, though on the other side, he was glad of the spirituall profit and good, that fell vnto them by that temporall losse, by occasion wherof they were consecrated to God, as being the glorious & first fruits of martyrdome, endured and suffered for the name of Iesus Christ.

2. To consider, how Herod being dead, an Angell appeared vnto S. Ioseph in Ægypt, willing him to returne into the land of Israel with the yong child, & his mother. Where we are to meditate, how that vnfortunate King dyed a most vnhappy death, both for body and soule, and how his proud ambition, & damnable designes serued him not for other end, but to draw vpon himselfe the vengeance of God, who

M   notwith-

notwithstanding he diſſembled for a time, made
the miſerable and impious King in fine to feele
the rigour of his iudgements. To conſider the
prouidence of God, how he ſendeth his good
Angell preſently after that Herod was dead, to
put an end to the baniſhment, that afflicted the
little IESVS, his holy mother, & good Ioſeph.
Of this I will take courage in my afflictions, and
I will put my truſt wholy in the diuine prouidence. And by the way I muſt obſerue, that the
Angell ſaid not to Ioſeph, take the little one, &
thy Spouſe, but the little one, and his mother,
to giue to vnderſtand, that it is a more glorious
tytle of our Bleſſed Lady, to be the mother of
God.

3.   To conſider, how this holy man o-
beyed with promptitude, and returned to Nazareth, by occaſion whereof our Sauiour was
called a Nazarean, that is, a Saint flouriſhing: for
he is the Saint of Saints, and the flower of all
Sanctity. To thinke how thoſe, who had frequented company, and had, had conuerſation
with IESVS, and his mother in Ægypt, were
full ſory for their departure, & for the loſſe of
their ſweet conuerſation.

*Meditat. XXVIII.   How our Sauiour ſtayed
behind in the Temple.   Luc. 2.*

TO meditate, how the holy Virgin, & her
ſpouſe Saint Ioſeph were wont to go euery yeare vp to the Temple of Hieruſalem
with

with the yong Iesus; Ioseph being by obedience
bound vnto the law; the Virgin by deuotion, to
honour & glorify God in that solemnity; & the
sweet Iesus by humility, and obedience, that he
yielded as well to his eternall Father, as to his
temporall mother a perpetuall Virgin, and to
the other his reputed Father. Here I must think,
with how great reuerence, and deuotion they
demeaned themselues in the temple, as in the
house of prayer, repayring thither neyther of
obligation nor for custome sake, as men doe
now a dayes. And of this I will endeauour to
make my profit.

    3.   To consider, how the child I E S V S
stayed in the Temple, being then but twelue
yeares old: to teach vs, that we must exercise &
imbrace vertue betimes, & to giue vs to vnderstand, that he would willingly haue always continued in the house of his Father of heauen, to
serue him in a much more perf. & manner, then
did Samuel, when he was yong. How in this he
asked not leaue of his parents, testifying that flesh
and bloud had not in that respect any power o-
uer him: to the end we may learne to comtemne
such terrene respects, and not to make accompt
of our carnall parents, though they weepe and
lament neuer so much, and oppose themselues
against our spirituall profit. For it is written: He
that loueth his Father, or his mother more then
me, is not worthy of me. Matth. 10.

    3.   To consider the wonderfull modesty,
humility, discretion, and zeale of Gods honour,
whereof our Sauiour gaue a testimony, in ma-

        king

king novv the first proofe of the diuine vvif-
dome and grace, vvhereof he vvas full; of modesty in his countenance, grauity in his speech,
humility in his demaundes, discretion in his
vvonderfull ansvvers, zeale in referring all his
vvorkes to the glory of God, & not to his ovyne
particular prayse.

4.   To meditate, hovv this diuine and
most Holy child spent the tyme, that during
those three dayes, vvas left him after dispu-
ting, in prayer to God his Father for the saluation of mankind, hauing nothing to lye v-
pon, but the cold, and hard ground, and for
his intertainment nothing but the almes of some
vvho came into the Temple, vvhere seeing the
irreuerence, and sinnes, that vvere committed therein, he vvas extremely afflicted by reason of the burning zeale, he carryed tovvardes
the honour of his Heauenly Father, as is recorded in Saint Iohn, cap. 2. The zeale of thy
house hath eaten me. Out of this I vvill dravv
Holy motions, and good purposes of imitation.

Meditat. XXIX.   Of the missing of Iesus,
and his finding in the Temple.

TO consider the wonderfull secrets of God
in afflicting the sacred Virgin, & holy Ioseph in a thing that might afflict the most
of al, though it were without any fault of theirs.
How sorrowfull and heauy the desolate Virgin
was

was all that time, who ceased not to pray, nor gaue ouer seeking: whereby we must learne to to seek after God diligently by prayers & good workes, and to admire at the vertues, that the Holy Virgin, & S. Ioseph practised in this their seeking for their Sonne: their patience, without being troubled in so hard a case: their humility, in being afraid, that there was some default on their part, esteeming themselues vnworthy of the company of such an one: their diligence in seeking him with all possible care: their earnest and most harty prayers to God the Father. We must further consider the causes, wherefore God is wont to absent himselfe from a soule: sometimes by occasion of mortall, or of veniall sinne, or for some tryall of his, to exercise them to the practising of the vertue of humility, or for the inordinate imployments and occupations, wherunto the soule attendeth, wandring & distracted in outward thinges. When therefore God shall absent himselfe from vs, we must practise the vertues aforesayd.

2. To consider, in what place the child I E S V S was found: namely in the Temple, being Gods house consecrated to prayer, & not amongst his friendes, & parents, though they sought for him among them. That he was in company of the Doctours, to teach vs, that God is infallibly found, when we follow the doctrine of the Doctours of the Church. The ioy, that possessed the Virgin, when she saw her Sonne, a ioy, that was vnto her as a resurrection after three dayes of mortall anguish and affliction of

M 3   minde,

minde , much like vnto that she felt in his refurrection after his dolefull passion : remembring
the sollicitude of the poore afflicted mother of
Toby for the abfence of her Sonne , and the
great comfort and contentment , she receyued
agayne by his returne ; The modesty , whereby
the Virgin difcretly tempred her ioy , and the
admiration that she conceyued to fee him a-
mong the Doctours of the Law , reuerencing in
her hart the fecrecy of this hidden mystery. Of
this I must make my profit .

    3.   To confider and weigh these wordes :
Sonne , why haft thou done fo to vs ? My Son ,
wherefore haft thou delt fo with vs ? By which
wordes she witnessed the affection of her mind ,
& difcouered a certaine manner of praier , that is
very ordinary with the Saints .To ponder these
wordes (Thy Father & I) wherein there is to
be feene the B· Virgins profound humility , preferring Iofeph before herselfe , and naming him
Father of her Sonne Iefus , which she did out of
her humility , and for the concealing of the incomprehenfible mystery , that the Holy Ghoft
had wroght in her. We forrowing did feek thee.
This is a document , that we muft feeke God
with forrow , proceeding of loue which ordinarily caufeth abundance of teares for the abfence
of the thing beloued ; with a purity of intention
in feeking it ; with diligence to vfe the meanes
to find it, & with perfeuerance til it be found. Finally to confider how few words the Virgin v-
fed , & the force of this word (fo) wherin she
recommendeth filence.

                           4. To

4. To confider our Sauiours anfwere : What is it that you fought me? Which feemeth in fhew fomewhat harfh , & yet it is not fo . For by thefe wordes he gaue her to vnderftand, that he was more then man , & therewithall he gaue the B. Virgin an occafion of exercifing her patience, modefty, & humility . This is alfo an inftruction to Superiours to proue their inferiors otherwhiles, and to mortify them, though they be blamelefle, for the exercifing of them in vertue. Did you not know , that I muft be about thofe thinges , which are my Fathers? wherein he teacheth vs , that all our imployments ought to be addreffed to the feruice of God, & that we are to lay afide all that , which may caufe any impediment thereunto, be the fame otherwife neuer fo ferious , deare vnto vs , or precious.

5. To confider, how the child I E S V S returned with his mother , & S. Iofeph to Nazareth . And credible it is , that he did by the way recout vnto the B. Virgin, what had hapned vnto him , & had paffed for thofe three dayes , all which fhe reflected vpon, & ruminated in her mind . That from that tyme forth , fhe had a more watchfull & carefull eye ouer her Sonne that fhe might not loofe him, taking occafion by what was paft to be more follicitous for the time to come.

M 4

*Meditat. XXX.   Of the life, and aboade of Ie-
sus at Nazareth, vntill he was thirty years old.
Luc.* 2.

TO Meditate these words: And Iesus proceeded in wisdome, and age, and grace
with God, and men. Where we are to
consider, that though our Sauiour were replenished with wisdome, and holynes from the
very instant of his conception, in so much as
more he could not haue, yet his perfections
still increased, as touching the exercising of
them : Euen as we say, that the Sunne being alwaies the same, beginneth to giue light in the
morning, & goeth on succeshuely increasing in
the light vntill midday. This must we imitate,
and not giue ouer, but contrariwise renew and
proceed on with our feruour in the purchasing
of vertues.

2.   To consider, how he increased and
grew before God, and men : because the one
& the other is necessary, that is to say, to please
God, & to be exemplare to men. He increased
in wisdome and grace, in commending, & esteeming things spirituall & eternall, & in contemning thinges temporall, & transitory ; He pro-
profited in grace, which sheweth it selfe in the
exercise of vertues, which make vs esteemed, &
holy before God, & amiable to men. And such
be the loue of God, a burning zeale of his glory,
contrition and deep sorrow for the sinnes, and
conti-

continual praier. He was in the grace & fauor of men for his good examples of humility, mode-sty, patience, mansuetude submission &c. ver-tues, which we ought to imitate, as did the sa-cred Virgin.

3. To consider, how he was subiect to his mother, & to holy Ioseph. Vpon which I must Meditate, that he, who obeyed, was God of infinite maiesty, and those, to whome he was in subiection, were the Virgin, and a poore Ar-tizan, the Creatour to his creatures, the Lord to his vassaills. In what he obeyed: euen in all thinges, that ordinarily passe in the house of a poore Carpenter, seruing him, as doe the chil-dren their poore parents. Of which I must make my profit, in admiring at so profound humility, & obedience.

4. To meditate, how our Sauiour ex-ercised the Carpenters trade, as S. Marke recor-deth cap. 6. saying: Is not this the Carpenter, the Sonne of MARY? He did this office for the shunning of idlenes, and because he should earne his meate and drinke with the sweet of his browes, subiecting himselfe of his owne volun-tary will to the malediction, that he had layd v-pon Adam, for the exercising of humility, sith he tooke paynes for the getting of his liuing. but yet whiles he trauayled with body, he neuer in-termitted to pray.

5. To consider, how though our Sauiour were Wisdome it selfe, endued with so ex-cellent graces, & perfections, yet would he con-ceale the same for the space of thirty yeares, during

ring which time he was reputed for an Idiote, &
simple person. By which we learne humility, &
silence in imitation of this our supreme Lord.

**Meditat. XXXI.   *Of the miraculous life, and
preaching of Saint Iohn Baptist. Matth. 3.
Mar. 1. and Luc. 3.***

TO consider, how Saint Iohn, being a very
child, left his parents, and retired himselfe into the desert, where he exercised
himselfe in all sorts of pennance, did eate but
Locusts, and wild hony, and had for his gar-
met a cilice of Camels haire, for his bed the hard
ground to lye on, and a caue vnder ground for
his place to retyre. The pennance that he did,
was not for any sinns of his owne, but to the
end he might not commit the very least sinne,
he mortifyed his flesh, and disposed and prepared himselfe for the receiuing of gifts & graces
from heauen. And in this vve must imitate him.
Hovv he spent his time in continuall prayer, and
meditation, hauing the holy Ghost for his mayster, & directour, vvho in that his solitude imparted vnto him sundry cõsolations of the temporall goods he had abandoned, and forsaken,
and for the easing of his austerity of life, and rigorous pennance, of which togeather vvith his
solitude this contemplatiue, and penitent Saint
serued himselfe, as of a meanes proper for the
enioying of God after a more singular manner.
Heerehence vve must take hart and courage to
do

doe something, that goeth accompanyed with difficulty for our Lord, who repayeth his seruants in so liberall a manner. Euen as Saint Iohn exercised himselfe a long time in the desert, and purchased a constant habit of vertue, perseuering so many yeares in the austerity of a penitents life, during which credible it is, that he had many encouters with Sathan, & was by him assayled with many tentations, laying before the eyes of his mind the weaknes of his tender age, the pleasurs & dainty fare of his Fathers house, &c. For doubtles he, who spared not our Sauiour himselfe, would not forbeare S. Iohn his Precursour, who notwithstanding all that the enemy could doe against him, went forwardes, exercising himselfe in continuall prayer, & keeping himselfe from committing the least sin, as witnesseth S. Luke c. 1. Where he saith : And the child grew, & strengthned in spirit.

2.   To consider, how Saint Iohn, beeing come to some more maturity of age, left the desert, and went forth to preach pennance and to baptize, whereunto the holy Ghost, who had been his conductour, & directour in the wildernes, at that time moued him, in so much as it was the same holy spirit, that led him into the wildernes, and that brought him out of it: a most excellent example to teach vs to leaue our selues to the conduct of obedience. How the spirit, and feruour, wherewith S Iohn preached, was full of zeale, & of terrour, as was the spirit of Elias, and this against the Pharisies. who were more hard-harted, then the rest, i

so much as he called them a Generation of vipers . But he was besides that, mercifull and pittifull, receiuing and imbracing the vulgar sort with compassion, without reiecting of any. How the more ordinary subiect & matter of his preaching was to exhort to pennance , and to giue an hope of the Kingdome of heauen togeather with the threatning of the paynes of hell . And whiles he thus preached both by worke and by word , he wrought most great good , the world making an high esteeme of his conuersation & manner of life, and admiring it , as a continuall miracle .

3 .   To consider, how he demeaned himselfe , in so much as he became of such reputation,and to be of so great authority, as many held him for their promised Messias , an opinion , which he most constantly reiected with most profound humility , being neuer awhit proud of the gifts , that God had giuen him, nor of the applause of men , but sincerely confessing & acknovvledging before all his ovvne littlenes , & greatnes of Iesus Christ , the latchet of vvhose shoes he sayd he vvas vnworthy to vnloose . He also affirmed meanely touching his ovvne Baptisme, saying: That it was of water only, & could not forgiue sins, & extolled that of our Sauiour Iesus, that vvas of force to remit sins, & to communicate the holy Ghost. We must imitate this humility .

Meditat.

Meditat. XXXII. *Of the demaundes made to S. Iohn, to know who he was.*

TO confider, how whiles the comon report increafed from day to day among the people, that S. Iohn was the Meffias, he was by the Priefts, and the Leuites of Hierufalem afked, if he were the Meffias, or not? How he promptly denyed, and faid with a lowd & cleare voice: I am not Chrift. Wherin he gaue a moft noble teftimony of his profound humility, yielding honour to him, to whome it appertained, not doing as did Lucifer, who attributed it to himfelfe, and therefore was precipitated from heauen into hell. How this offer was a moft fore tentation of the Diuell to caufe S. Iohn to fall, & becaufe he could not ouercome him by other weapons, he would fet vpon him with this, becaufe he had ouerthrowne many therewith.

2. To confider the fame humility of this great Saint, vvhich he manifefted, vvhen he anfwered, that he was neyther Elias, nor a prophet, though he might truly haue faid, that he was Elias in fpirit, and more then a Prophet. But he denyed it in the fenfe, that he ment it, in fevv & refolute vvords.

3. To confider, hovv this humility of Saint Iohn appeared the more, vvhen being afked vvho he vvas, he anfvvered, that he vvas the voyce of him vvho cryed in the defert, meaning to fay, that he was in a manner one, not to be regarded.

N

garded. For as the voyce is not of permanent
being of it selfe, but depēdeth of him who speaketh, euen so did S. Iohn esteeme of himselfe,
as not being, nor being able to doe any thing.
He did not vaunt himselfe for being the Sonne
of Zachary of the rribe of Priests, but only he
gloried in this, that he was the voyce of Iesus
Christ, making a far greater esteeme to be a seruant of his, then of all the nobility of the world.
We must here obserue, that he said, he was the
voice of him who cryeth : Prepare yee the way
of our Lord:for as much as his life, his doctrine,
his exercises were as many voyces diuine, that
gaue to vnderstand the maiesty of God : for all
that which S. Iohn did or said, gaue a testimony
of nothing, but of sanctity, & perfection: Of this
we must draw instructions for our owne profit.

4. To consider these wordes: I baptize
in water. In which he declared the profundity
of his humility, esteeming himselfe vnvvorthy
to vnloose the latchet of our Sauiours shoe, &
excused not himselfe being wrongfully reproued by the Iewes, but confessed who was Iesus
Christ, to the end all the world might honour
him, and what himselfe was, that he might be
contemned of all.

Meditat. XXXIII. *Of the Baptizing of Iesus by S. Iohn Baptist. Matth.* 3. *Mar.* 2.

TO confider, how our Sauiour, being arriued to the 30. yeare of his age, feparated himfelfe from his moft holy mother, declaring vnto her, that the time was then come of manifefting himfelfe to the world, whereof the B. Virgin reioyced much for the great defire fhe had of the faluation of men. How he then went to the riuer of Iordan to receaue Baptifme amongft the Publicans, and finners, by that giuing vs a moft notable example of humility, for that he taking vpon him the forme and likenes of a finner, being the fupreme Creatour and Lord of all, fubiected himfelfe to his creature, and vaffaile. How by this action he would alfo honour the baptifme of his forerunner, euen as he had approued the Circumcifion in fubmitting himfelfe vnto it, thereby manifefting himfelfe for an exact accomplifher, and obferuer of the law.

1. To confider, how our Sauiour afked of S. Iohn to baptize him, which S. Iohn refufed to doe, knowing well, who he was. Heere I am to meditate the great fpirituall ioy, that this glorious Precurfour felt in his foule, when he knew his Sauiour: for the ioy, that he had being ftill in his mothers wombe, was renewed in his hart. His profound reuerence, and humility, in refufing to baptize the Meffias, to whome he

N 2   fayd:

said : Comeſt thou to me to be baptized? words,
which we are to ruminate well, eſpecially when
we prepare our ſelues to the holy Communion.
To ponder our Sauiours anſwere : So it becometh vs to fulfill all Iuſtice : that is to ſay, all holines, & perfection : I in humbling my ſelfe, and
thou in obeying. In which two things conſiſteth
the abbridgement of all ſanctity , that is , for a
man to humble himſelfe before God , and men,
and to obey the diuine maieſty , & his miniſters
alſo , by practizing the three degrees of obedience , the firſt being to ſubmit ones ſelues to his
ſuperiours, the ſecond of more perfection, to his
equalls , eſteeming them as his ſuperiours , the
third , and that of moſt perfection , euen to his
inferiours , as our Sauiour did to S. Iohn in his
baptiſme . The prompt obedience of S. Iohn ,
executing what our Sauiour commaunded him
without further contradiction , ſubmitting his
owne iudgment to his will, with profound humility, & reuerence .

3 . To conſider , how the eternall Father
ſeing his only Sonne ſo humbled , meant to honour him, for the performing of that , which he
ſaid afterwards : He, that ſhall humble himſelfe,
ſhall be exalted . For the heauens opened , and
the holy Ghoſt came downe in the likenes of a
doue , ſignifying the plenitude of the diuine
graces, that our Sauiour had in himſelfe, his innocency, purity , ſweetnes , and mercy , & that
the deluge of ſinnes ſhould ceaſe in the world :
that he ſhould not be barraine , but that he
ſhould haue many children gathered togeather
in

in the congregation of the Church. To thinke how great a ioy that was of S. Iohn, when he heard the eternall Father pronoûce these words: Loe my beloued Sonne, in whome I am well pleased : We muſt weigh and ponder theſe words one by one, & thereof make our profit . That on that day was reuealed to the world the miſtery of the moſt holy Trinity by the voice of the eternall Father, who called Ieſus Chriſt his Sonne, & by the doue, that repreſented the perſon of the holy Ghoſt.

4. To conſider, that in this action of the baptiſme of our Sauiour, the diuine maieſty inſtituted the Sacrament of baptiſme, communicating vnto it the power to open the gates of heauen, to impart the gifts of the holy Ghoſt, and to make them, who be baptized, the adopted children of God, in ſo much as if they ſhould then dye, they ſhould goe ſtraight to heauen. And for this we muſt yield thankes to God. Then our Sauiour himſelfe baptized S. Iohn the ſame time alſo, according to that, which he craued, ſaying : I ought to be baptized of thee : & he multiplied his heauenly graces, & gifts vpon him, for which he became more thankefull to God, and more affectioned to the ſeruice of our Sauiour, all his life after : whereof I am to make my profit.

5. To conſider, how all this happened, when our Redeemer was in prayer, as S. Luke recordeth. Wherby is to be ſeene of what force prayer is, ſith by it the gates of heauen are opened, the fulnes of the holy Ghoſt is giuen, in-

ſpirations

spirations are communicated from heauen, and mortall men are honored with the title & dignity of Gods adopted children, & this then most of all, when prayer is accompanyed with humility, as it is written Eccl. 5. The prayer of him, who humbleth himselfe, penetrateth the clouds. That our Sauiour ioineth prayer with baptisme, to teach vs, that deuotion & prayer ought to go in company with all other workes, with the vse of the Sacraments. He prayed also to giue vs an example to pray incessantly, in regard of our great necessities, to yield thankes to our eternall Father for the graces, & fauours, he hath done vs, & for them, that were present to receiue their baptisme. Out of all this we must draw a feruent affection to prayer.

Meditat. XXXIIII. Of Chrifts going into the desert, and of his fourty dayes fasting there. Matth. 4.

TO consider, how our Sauiour, replenished with the Holy Ghost, retyred himselfe into the desert. Wherein our Sauiour exercised an act of humility, in shunning the praises of men, that he might haue had of the people, to giue to vnderstand also, that a soule, replenished with the holy Ghost, must shunne the tumult, and trouble of the world, that it may vnite it selfe the more inwardly with God.

2. To consider, that our Sauiour was inspired of the Holy Ghost, & conducted into the

the defert by him, giuing vs to vnderftand, that
we ought alwaies in all our workes to follow
the motions, and infpirations, that come from
heauen, & not thofe, vvhich Vanity fuggefteth
vnto vs by flying from pride, & whatfoeuer o-
ther finifter affection. That the diuine fpirit carried our Sauiour with a great fwiftnes into the
defert, and yet with a fweetneffe, fith it is he
that tempreth all thinges : making thereby manifeft, that he is an enemy of delaies, and of the
langour of the will, as alfo of manifeft repugnance. We muft alfo obferue, that the fame holy Ghoft incited our Sauiour IESVS to make
his aboade in thofe folitary places, to the end he
might liue among the fauage beaftes, for the
time, and that fo he might practife humility in
the defert, as he had done it before in the manger, & fhould exercife it ftill in peñnance, prayer, & mortification, in watching much, in fleeping little, in lying vpon the hard ground, and
in fafting after fo rigorous & auftere a manner.
Out of all this I muft draw an example for my
felfe.

3.   To côfider, that our Sauior wold faft 40.
dayes, & 40 nights for the fatisfying of the finne
of furfetting & gluttony, which our firft parents
committed: a finne, that was caufe of their owne
hurt, and ours : as alfo for the fatisfying of all
the gluttonies, ryotings, diforders, and ex-
ceffes of all mortal men; teaching vs by his own
example, that vve muft faft for the mortifying
& maiftering of the vnruly defirs of our fleth,
and the bringing of it in fubiection to the fpirit.

That

That this our Sauiours fast vvas most seuere &
straite, yea and miraculous, to teach vs to order our ovvne fastings, and to moderate them,
not expecting that God should vvorke miracles
by vs, adding as much perfection, as vve can,
to our fastings, taking in the meane tyme vvhat
may seeme to be iust and necessary for our intertainment. The continuance of this holy fast
of 40. dayes teacheth vs the perseuerance, that
vve ought to obserue in the exercises of pennance. That the effects of fasting be satisfaction
for our sinnes : an acknovvledgement of benefitts receiued: an impetration of those vertues,
that vve vvant ; a disposition to the glory of resurrection. That this first, notvvithstanding the
austerity of it, vvas accompanyed vvith the diuine sweetnes of contemplation, vvhich is wont
to sweeten, moderate, & qualify the paynes, &
difficulties of this present life. Of all this I must
make my profit, by drawing out the motions
of deuotion.

*Meditat. XXXV. Of the Tentations, that
Christ endured in the desert. Mar. 1. Luc. 4.*

TO consider, how the Holy Ghost lead
our Sauiour into the desert, to be tempted
of Sathan, as it is ordinary with the same
spirit of God to expose perfect men to the assaults of the enemy, permitting thē to be tempted, to cause them to see the efficacy of his holy
grace, vvhich appeareth in the victory, that they
go

go away with. That the defert is a place, where the Diuell taketh occasion to tempt: and vnhappy is he, who is alone, faith the Holy Ghoft. Whereby we are to learne, that it importeth much to liue in company, & to lay open the cõfcience to our fpiritual Father. That at the very inftant a man beginneth to attend to the feruice of God, Sathan beginneth alfo to caufe war againft him, to hinder him, that he proceed not: a thing, that a man ought to confider, to the end he be not aftonifhed at the matter, nor loofe courage, nor hope amiddeft fuch tentations, but fortify himfelfe by the meanes & help of praier, & pennance.

2. To meditate, that the firft tentation, wherewith Sathan affalted our Sauiour, was of gluttony, when he faid: If thou be the Sonne of God. Here we muft thinke vpon diuers manners, that the enemy obferueth in tempting. For to fome he prefenteth the pleafure of meates, that they may exceed and tranfgreffe the law by God appointed: to others he propofeth their neceffities, inciting them to remedy the fame by vnlawfull meanes: fometimes by open, fometimes againe by fecret wayes, craftily pretending fuppofed neceffities, or counterfaiting fome reuelation, or hiding himfelfe vnder a fhadow of piety &c. To confider the humble anfwere, our Sauiour made him, faying, That not in bread alone fhall man liue, but in euery word, that proceedeth out of Gods mouth. In which he teacheth vs the way, how to ouercome the tentations, that are founded vpon temporall neceffities

sities , by putting our confidence, & trust in the
diuine prouidence .

3 . To consider , that the second tentation
was of vanity , and of ouermuch confidence, accompanyed with presumption , and temerity ,
when he did set our Sauiour vpon the pinnacle,
of the temple , perswading him to cast himselfe
downe . Vpon which we must meditate , how
Sathan seeketh to vndermyne, & find out the
particular, and proper inclinations of euery one,
not the bad alone , but the good also , for the
better applying of his tentations afterwards . Of
this we may learne, that we can neuer be assured
in that, which seemeth vnto vs good at the first
represe̅tation, but we must examine it at leasure.
That the holy Ghost conducted our Sauiour into the desert , to cause him to shunne the vaine
prayses of the world , and the malignant spirit
carryed him to the top of the temple, suggesting
vnto him , vnder supposed pretenses ; to seeke
the glory of God before men . To consider the
meeknes , & humility of our sweet Lord , who
permitted Sathan to cary him, that he might not
be knowne of him to be the Sonne of God. Here
we are to meditate the way , how our Sauiour
ouercame this tentation in saying : It is written,
thou shalt not tempt thy Lord God . As though
he had said . I must not worke miracles out of
vanity, or presumption, & sith I may goe down
from hence by the stayers , I haue no reason to
tempt God , nor to cast my selfe downe headlong . An answere full of discretion, and of most
singular sweetnes , which be vertues of most
singu-

singular force for the ouercomming of the enemies tentations.

3. To confider, how the Diuell tooke
our Sauiour, & brought him into an high mou-
taine, where he shewed him all the riches & honours of the world, & said to him, that he would
giue them all to him, if he would fall downe
before him, & adore him. Here we are to confider the most extreme hunger, the Diuell hath
of the perdition of foules, sith after so many o-
uerthrowes he ceaseth not, nor giueth ouer to
seeke out new waies & deuises for the beguil-
ing and ruyning of them. To thinke, that the
cruell enemy maketh so great a reckoning of the
perdition of but one foule, that if the whole
world were his, he would giue it me, to cause
me to commit but one mortall sinne against the
diuine Maiesty. Wherof I will gather how high
an esteeme I am to make of my foule, and how
carefull I ought to be not to doe any thing, that
may be cause of the perdition of it, for all that
which is most precious in the world, still remembring that, which our Sauiour saith in S. Matthew cap. 6. What will it profit a man to haue
gained the whole world, if in the meane tyme
he loose his foule? To confider, that it is proper
to the Father of lying, to deceiue vnder false
promise of that, which is not in him to performe
& which he cannot giue. How grieuous a sinne
is that of auarice, and of ambition, sith it is nothing els, but to adore Sathan with knee to
the ground. How finally our Sauiour remained
victorious ouer Sathan, & his tentations, after

a commaunding manner saying vnto him: A-
uant Sathan: for it is written, Thou shalt adore
the Lord thy God, & him only shalt thou serue.
By which wordes he hath taught vs, what zeale
we ought to haue of Gods honour, and with
how resolute a courage we are to withstand the
Diuells tentations, euer puting our trust in his diuine maiesty.

    5.   To consider, how after that our Sa-
uiour had ouercome Sathan, the Angells of heauen came to serue him: God the Father sending
them vnto him for the honoring of the victory
he had gotten, & giuing vs to vnderstand, with
hovv attentiue an eye he regardeth them, who
fight for the loue of him. By this we may in like
manner learne, that the holy Angells be inuisi-
bly preset to them that fight, for the assisting of
them, and when they haue gotten the victory,
they reioice with them for it. In the last place
we are to consider, how necessary patience is in
time of tentations, how sore, or of what continuance soeuer they may be, being assured, that
God will put the malignant spirit to flight, when
need shall require: in the meane tyme it behoo-
ueth vs to stand well vpon our guarde so long, as
we shall liue here on earth.

                                Meditat.

Meditat. X X X V I. *Of the Election of the A-*
postles. *Matth.* 4.

TO confider the quality & condition of the
Apoftles according to Nature, that they
were men, poore, abiect, contemptible,
& ignorant, and being poore tradef-men in diuers kindes, and yet it pleafed our Sauiour to
choofe them, as poore and miferable as they
were, leauing the noble, rich, great, and learned, and wife of the world. To meditate the
caufes of this election. The firft is, that as God
humbled himfelfe, making himfelfe man to
teach vs humility : euen fo would he practife it
in ioining humble and lowly perfons in company with him, in whofe conuerfation he pleafed
himfelfe. The fecond is, for that he defired,
that his difciples fhould be huble of hart indeed,
to the end they might not attribute vnto themfelues the gifts and graces he meant to beftow
vpon them, nor the wonderfull thinges, that he
intended to worke by their meanes: wherehence
we muft learne to exercife the vertue of humility with feruour, & earneft affection. The third
is, to the end vve might not afcribe the conuerfion of the vvorld to the induftry, or power of
men, but only to the vertue diuine.

2. To confider the quality of the Apoftles
in as much as concerneth manners, that is, touching their vertues, or vices, and their propen-
fions afvvell good, as bad. Here vve may confi-

O   der

fider Gods vocation, who calleth vs, proceeding from the only bounty and goodnes of God, and the merits of our Sauiour, wherunto we ought to referre all our good. That it pleased him to tak fome of his difciples out of S. Iohns fchoole for the honouring of his Precurfours doctrine, among whome was S. Andrew, in whome there concurred two excellent thinges, that difpofed him thereunto. The former vvas a great defire he had to become perfect, and to follovv that vvhich vvas beft. The latter, a feruent zeale to make his brother to haue part in the fame good, & for that caufe he inuited him to follovv him. This vve muft apply to our felues. That our Sauiour called others, vvho vvere vertuous, vvell borne, and qualifyed, for the more honoring of vertue, fuch vvere Saint Peter, Saint Iames, and Saint Iohn, vvho exercifed themfelues in all abiect, and painefull vvorkes, and particularly affected one another. Wherein vve muft imitate them, to the end God may regard vs vvith a cōpaffionate eye. That our Sauiour againe called others, vvho vvere great finners, ill habituated, and of ill complexion, as Saint Matthevv, and Saint Paul, men exceedingly affected to the tranfitory things of this vvorld, to fhevv the powerfull effect of his grace, & the greatnes of his mercy, to the end no finner might hold himfelfe debarred from it.

5.   To confider the fweet force and vertue of our Sauiors words, by which he called his Apoftles, as is to be feene in the calling of Saint Peter, and Saint Andrevv, of the Sonnes of Zebedy,

bedy, and of S. Matthevv, vvho vvas as it vvere perforce dravvne from his infamous Office, vvhich he exercised, by a pleasing constraint & force of our Sauiours svveet vvords. To thinke, that the very same is done tovvasdes vs by an infinite number of holy inspirations, that God puteth into vs. And therfore we must examime our selues, if vve haue ansvvered the same.

4. To consider the excellent & perfect obedience of the Apostles, when euery one of them at the instant, that they vvere called, left of their trade and manner of life, thereby putting in practise the three manners of obedience, that is, of the vnderstanding, of the vvill, and of prompt execution. And this must vve imitate. The fauours, that our Sauiour did them for their obedience. For he conferred vpon them the most soueraigne dignity, that is in his Church, to wit, the Apostleship: he alwaies had them for his companions: he communicated vnto them his secrets, & treated with them, as with his friends. He conferred vpon them greater graces then he euer did vpon any other of the Saints, both of the old, & new Testament, & gaue vnto them the primicies of Gods spirit. Finally he promised vnto them, that he would cause them in the day of Iudgement to sit vpon twelue seates, to iudge the twelue Tribes of Israel, for that they had obeyed his voice, & had forsaken all to follow him. All this is proposed for our imitation.

Medi-

Meditat. XXXVII.   *Of the generall vocation of all men, whome* Christ *dayly calieth to the renouncing of themselues, & to the carrying of their Crosse.*

TO consider, how Lucifer, the Prince of this world, sitting in a throne of the infernall fire, enuironed round with an infinite multitude of wicked spirits, sendeth his Angells all the world ouer to persecute, and make warre vpon the soules, by concupiscence of the eyes, and the pride of life. To represent to our selues, how the Diuells goe roaring, & raging vp and downe the world, seeking whome they may deuoure. To lament the losse, perdition, and infelicity of so many millions of poore souls, which this cruell tyranny treadeth vnder foote : to take compassion on them, and to procure to help them by prayers.

2.   To consider our sweet Iesus, sitting in a low place, with an amiable and gracious coûtenance, compassed round with his poore Apostles, and other simple persons, and saying : if any will come after me, he must renounce himselfe, take vp his Crosse, and follow me. Where we must ponder these words, renounce himself, & oppose the same against the three tentations, vvherewith the Diuell assayleth vs. To consider hovv reasonable the condition of this vocation is, sith it requireth, that we fly from all, that may any vvay endomage vs, such as is our ovvne

concu-

concupiscence : & that vve take vp our Crosse, & follovv our graund Captaine Iesus Christ.

3 . To consider , that the diuine maiesty persvvadeth vs this by three most pregnant reasons . The first is , He, that vvill saue his soule , shall loose it : and he , that shall loose it for loue of me, shall find it . The second is : What will it profit a man to gaine the whole world , and to loose his soule for eternity. Or what compensation shall a man be able to giue, in place of his soule? As if he should say, all thinges must be cōtemned for the sauing the soule . The third is : For the Sonne of man shall come in the glory of his Father, with his Angells, and shall render vnto euery one according to his works. To make a comparison of these two vocations the one with the other , by considering the diuersity of their effects, and by meditating whether of them being at the article of death I should haue followed in my life time , to the end without further procrastination I may dispose my selfe to follow the same from this very instant.

4 . To consider, hovv heauy the yoke is, that the Diuell putteth vpon the shoulders of them, who follow his voice, though he seemeth in the beginning to giue them their cōtentments in their pleasurs, delicacies, honours, riches, liberty , and quiet : but in conclusion his yoke is found most heauy and hard to beare, and in that kind increaseth euer more and more; where as on the contrary that of our Sauior is sweet, light & easy , intermixed with a thousand helpes of sweetnes, which giue vs encouragement & hart

to

to beare it, as our Sauiour himselfe teacheth vs in Saint Matthew, cap. 11. When he saith: Come to me all yee, who labour, and are burdened, & I will refresh you. Take vp my yoke vpon you, for my yoke is sweet, & my burden light. See this exercise in the 2. week of our B. Father. &c.

Meditat. XXXVIII. *Of resignation, necessary to obey the Vocation of Christ, and to renounce all things for his seruice.*

TO consider, that many persons there be, who desire their owne saluation, without laying hand on the meanes of working it, by reason of the difficulty they find in practising the same. Such persons haue a disposition cleane contrary to the vocation diuine, & the commaundement that God hath made touching the renunciation of all thinges. Here I must make a reflection vpon my selfe, by considering whether I be not seized with this very malady, and whether I haue a desire to come to humility, without taking of paines, or disposing my selfe to the purchasing, & getting of it.

2. To consider, that there be others, who desire their finall saluation, & do vse the meanes to come to it, but they would take the same as it pleaseth themselues best, and not according to the will of God, whose voice they inwardly vnderstand right well, that counsaileth them to forsake their riches, but yet they haue not a will to put any thing in execution, but they afflict themselues,

felues, are fad, and make a ftand, as did the yong
man of the Ghofpell: like vnto the ficke, who
haue a will to be cured by the medicines, that
their owne appetites fuggeft vnto them, and not
by fuch, as the Phifitian ordayneth for them.
Such men haue a mind to force God to condef-
cend to their owne will, and not contrariwife.
We muft here make a reflection vpõ our felues,
to vnderftand, if there be any the like thing in
our foule &c.

3. Others there be, who defire the end of
their faluation, and to procure the perfection of
vertues, refigning themfelues wholy into the
hands of the diuine will, not hauing a will, or
inclination to any thing, but what God willeth
in all thinges, that be prefented, euen when the
fame fhould be repugnant to their fenfuality.
Thefe fay with the Apoftle: Lord, what wilt
thou haue me to doe? We muft endeauour to
procure this wonderfull difpofition of mind for
the receiuing of diuine illuftrations, abfolutely
refigning our felues into the hands of God.

4. There be yet many others more perfect, who abafe themfelues for the loue of God,
& defire, in what they are able, to be poore, cõ-
temned, & afflicted, keeping themfelues euer in
an indifferency to take, or leaue that, which it
fhall pleafe God to fend them. Perfections, that
we ought to wifh, & procure with all our forces,
conformably to that which the Apoftle faith
Gal. 6. I glory not in any other thing, but in the
Croffe of our Sauiour Iefus &c. See this meditation alfo in the Exercifes of our B. Father.

Medita-

Meditat. XXXIX.   Of the miracle, wrought at the marriage of Cana in Galilee. Ioan. 2.

TO confider the fweetnes & facility of our Sauiour in vouchfafing his prefence at this feaft, the purity, modefty, and grauity he held at the table, whiles others were pleafant & merry, whereof we muft make our profit. The compaffion and great care of the B. Virgin, who feing that there was want of wine, was fory for the confufion, that might follow, and was fo moued with pitty, as fhe prayed her Sonne with a certaine and amiable confidence, proceeding of the knowledge fhe had of his compaffionate benignity, to remedy that neceffity, faying vnto him only, They haue no wine. By this I will learne to haue my recourfe to the facred Virgin in all my neceffities, vfing the fame manner of prayer, that is made in fimply reprefenting the neceffity, that preffeth me, or others.

2.   To confider our Sauiours anfwere: What is it to me, and thee woman? my houre is not yet come. To weigh what might be the caufes of fuch an anfwere. The firft, for our Sauiour being both God and man, it was in him to worke miracles, when, and as it pleafed him: whereby we are to learne to refigne our felues entierly into the hands of the diuine prouidēce. The fecond was, to declare and manifeft, how far he was from carnall and terrene loue and affection to parents: and therefore he vvould

not

not call the Virgin, his mother, but he named her Womā simply, both now, & whē he was on the Crosse, and vpon many occasions besides. Of this I am to learne to reiect all carnall affection, and to rid my selfe of the loue of creatures, that I may adhere to God, and vnite my selfe with him. The third was to exercise the B. Virgin in the vertue of humilitv, patience, and confidence, as she herselfe testified by the effect, being neither offended, nor moued at the answere, that seemed otherwise so harsh.

3.   To consider, how the sacred Virgin willed them, that serued at the table, to do what her Sonne should say vnto them: wherein we are to wonder at the vertues, she exercised in this action, to wit, a most heroicall confidence, a most singular light in vnderstanding our Sauiours benignity, and a perfect obedience, whereunto she aduised them, who serued at the table, willing them to doe what her Sonne should say vnto them, and teaching vs thereby, that obedience is a singular, and a most ready disposition for the receiuing of Gods gifts, and finally a silence full of mystery, sith in a matter so importing she would vse but three words.

4.   To consider, how the sweet Iesus willed, that the potts should be filled with water, which was changed into most excellent vvine, whereof he caused some to be giuen him, who was the chiefe man of the feast. Vpon this I am to consider the prompt obedience of them, who wayted, so well instructed, and prepared by the counsayle of the B. Virgin, doing simply what
she

she willed them, without eyther delay, or dispute about the matter. To confider the omnipotency of our Sauiour in changing the water into wine by the only act of his will: whereof I muft take an occafion to be glad, and to affure myfelfe that his goodnes can eafily change the icy coldnes of my hart into the burning heat of the loue of God; and of proud, as I am, make me humbly and fimple: a thing, that I ought to craue inftantly at his hands &c To thinke, how liberall God is in requiting the feruice, that is done him; fith for one poore glaffe of bad wine, that might perhaps be giuen him, he rendred fix great potts of excellent wine. This ought to animate vs to doe much for God, & for our neighbour. To meditate, how the diuine maiefty, bringeth in the foules, which by the meanes of prayer doe folemnize with him their fpirituall weddings, into the cellars of his moft delicious wyne, and he inebriateth them with fweet Nectar, whereof the inhabitants of the heauenly Countrey haue their fill.

5.   To confider the B. Virgins ioy, when fhe faw this miracle wrought; and how effectuall her prayers and petitions be, fith they may feeme to haue haftened the determined time of our Sauiours working of miracles. That as the fame our Sauiour vfed his holy mother for the inftrument of the firft fanctification of his Precurfour Saint Iohn, fo would he in like manner worke his firft miracle by her meanes, thereby to teach vs, that this foueraigne Lady muft be our mediatreffe and aduocate to God. Therfore

we

we haue iuſt cauſe to reioyce, that we haue ſo
worthy a mother, ſo ſollicitous to craue & aſke
what is good for vs, & ſo powerfull to obtaine it
for vs. That the diſciples remained wonderfully
confirmed in their fayth, at the ſight of this miracle, and were right glad to be in ſo good company, being aſſured, that ſo long as they ſhould
continue in it, they ſhould not haue want of any
thing. That the admiration of the chiefe ſteward
muſt needes be great, when he taſted of this miraculous wine: wherehence we are to learne to
make an eſteeme of the vvorks of God, & humbly to reuerence them, thinking that the diuine
maieſty neuer communicateth ſpirituall pleaſures, vntill vve ſhall haue throughly mortified
the carnall. Euen as he neyther rayned the heauenly Manna in the deſert, vntill the meale of
Ægypt vvas all conſumed, & ſpent.

Meditat. X L . *Of the driuing the buyers, and*
ſellers out of the Temple. Ioan. 2.

T O conſider the ſingular zeale, our Sauiour had of Gods honour and glory, and of
the Temples purity. For zeale is nothing
but a very earneſt deſire to remoue, and take a-
vvay all that, which is contrary to the thinges
vve loue: and as our Sauiour loued his heauen-
uenly Father in a moſt perfect manner, and con-
ſequently his houſe on earth, ſo he moſt earneſtly affected vvhatſoeuer he did affect alſo. And
this for that it is ſaid in the 6. Pſalme: The zeale

of thy houfe did eate me: giuing to vnderſtand,
that he vvas ſo farre moued in that behalfe, as in
concluſion he vvas brought to his Croſſe for the
maintayning of Gods honour, the zeale of him
poſſeſſing him, and tranſporting him as it vvere
out of himſelfe, in ſo much as all his thoughts,
his vvords, & vvorkes gaue a moſt manifeſt teſtimony of that his moſt affectuous, & burning
zeale. To conſider the magnanimity of our Sauiour, in making head againſt ſo great a multitude, hauing for his weapōs nothing but a poore
vvhip in his hand, to driue ſo great a company
out of the Temple.

2. To conſider, hovv the Ievves hauing
demaunded the ſignes, and reaſons to prooue
the authority that he exerciſed, he anſvvered
them: Deſtroy this Temple, and I vvill build
it againe in three dayes. By which wordes
he permitted them to deſtroy the Temple of his
body by the cruelty of the blowes of whipps, of
the prickings of thornes &c. ſo great a deſire
had his infinite goodnes to ſuffer for men: inſi-
nuating alſo by the ſame wordes his Reſurreti-
on, which was an effect of his omnipotency.

3. To conſider, how our Sauiour at an
other time alſo, being neere to his paſſion, droue
the buyars and ſellers againe out of the Temple,
ſaying: my houſe is an houſe of prayer for all:
& you haue made it a denne of theeues. Where
we are to conſider, that the ſecond time, he droue
them out, he vſed not the whip, reſeruing it for
the inſtrument to torment him in his paſſion,
but only forcible words, and the ſame moſt miraculous.

raculous . Here we may learne, how God draweth the soules vnto him, somtimes by loue, somtimes by feare . To thinke , that the Temple of
God is an house of prayer , by applying all to
our soules , and how in it we ought not to haue
any cogitation eyther profane , or terrene . For ,
as saith Saint Augustine : The purity of the hart
doth by a certaine tranquility, and spiritual ioy,
that it causeth , of it selfe prouoke, incite, & induce to prayers in as much as it doth inwardly
mollify the soule , and moueth it to recurre by
prayer vnto God, and therefore we must vndergoe the paines to get it .

Meditat. **XLI**.   *Of the Sermon made on the*
mountayne , and of the eight Beatitudes .
Matth. 5 . *Luc.* 6 .

A F T E R the composition made of the place ,
by representing vnto our mind Iesus Christ
vpon an high hill, set lowly vpon a tufte
of earth , or Mole-hill , with his disciples, and a
great multitude of people about him , we must
meditate, how in this action he exerciseth the office of a maister , teaching , and discouering the
most high misteries of our faith , as being the e-
ternall wisdome: and withall the office of a law-
giuer , communicating his holy law , exempted
and free from errors , which the malice of men
would haue corrupted . He executeth also the
office of a cousaylour , teaching vs the highest
counsayles, that may possibly be conceiued , &
P   therefore

therefore he is called the Angell. To thinke, that he exercised not these offices only, as other men do, but as God omnipotent, giuing grace to doe what he taught. That euen now he still doth the same thinges inwardly in the soules, that aspire to perfection.

2.   To consider, that he drew out of the treasury of his infinite wisdome, eight wonderfull vertues, which be as it were the compendium and abridgement of all Euangelicall perfection, which he pleased to call the Beatitudes, in regard of their spirituall sweetnes, though they be otherwise full of much bitternes to the flesh: wherein he testifyed the zeale he had of Gods honour, raysing vp so diuine vertues againe, that were in a manner depressed, trodden vnder foote, and driuen out of the world: & entitling them in generall, and in particular with honorable and glorious names. To thinke, that these eight beatitudes be as eight ladders, wherwith to mount vp to heauen, by holding on in the way of holines of life, vntill we come to a perfect vnion with God: which ought to be vnto vs a most great inducement and motiue to practise them. To ponder the actions of euery one of them and the example that our Sauiour himselfe hath giuen vs, togeather with the recompēce, he promiseth on the one side, to those, who exercise them, & the punishment on the other to them, who contemne them.

3.   To consider the first of them, which is Pouerty of spirit, whereunto is promised the Kingdome of heauen. The acts of it. The first
                                                           whereof

whereof is with a prompt will to renounce
thinges temporall. The second of more perfection, to leaue all that we possesse with an affection, for the loue of God. The third, to clense our
soule of al vanity, by côtening, as much may be,
all the worlds pomps. The fourth to depriue our
selues of our owne will, and to subiect our own
iudgement, by forcing it to a conformity with
the diuine will. The fifth & the perfectest of all,
to contemne our selues, by acknowledging our
selues to be so miserable, as we be not able to do
any good at all of our selues. To consider the
rare and wonderfull examples, that our Sauiour hath giuen vs of this vertue, during the
whole course of his life, vpon which we must
discourse, and reflect seriously: and the singular
compensation he promiseth to them, who shall
practise it: as also the castigation, that attendeth
the contemners of it, & the disobedient, saying:
Woe be to you, rich men, who haue your consolation in this world. Luc. 6.

4. To consider the second Beatitude,
which is Mansuetude or meeknes, wherof we
must meditate the acts. The first whereof is to
represse and restraine the motions of anger, both
inward and outward. The second is to be af-
fable to all. The third, not to requite one euill
with another, neither to make violent resistance
to them, who wrong vs. To consider the most
excellent examples, left vnto vs by our Sauiour,
especially by his words, and speeches: Learne of
me, that I am meeke, and lowly of hart. To côsider the reward promised to this vertue, name-

ly, the possession of the earth, of our hart, the cō-
maund and dominion ouer our passions, and
power ouer anothers will. For the benigne and
meeke gaineth the loue of all, who frequent his
company: and finally the possession of the land
of the liuing.

5. To consider the third Beatitude, to
wit; Blessed be those, that mourne, because they
shalbe comforted. To examine the acts of this
vertue. The first whereof is to refrayne much
laughter, sportings, and disorders. The second
to bewayle our owne sinnes, especially for this,
that they offend the diuine maiesty, as Dauid,
and S. Peter wept for theirs. The third is to lament the sinnes of others for the same reason.
The fourth to be sory for the prolongation of
our owne miserable exile, sighing for the absence of our heauenly countrey, and for that we
see our selues confined into this vale of miseries
amongst the brute sauage beasts: and aboue all,
to be sory and weepe for this, that we cannot
weepe, and that we are ouermuch affected to
thirgs terrene, and to the vanities of this world.
To consider, that we no where read, that our
Sauiour euer laughed, but that he often wept.
That the teares, that are to the worlds seeming
signes of misery, be before God testimonies of
happynes, and to them he promiseth an eternity of ioy. That our Sauiour finally sayth: Woe
be to you, who laugh now, because the tyme
will come, that you shall weep.

6. Happy be those, who hungar and thirst
after iustice, because they shall haue their fill.
                                                        To

To consider the acts of this beatitude, the first whereof is to satisfy all that, whereunto our ability, and iustice binds vs towardes God, and towardes men without omitting any thing. The second, to desire to perfect our selues in vertue more and more. The third, to haue an hunger and thirst, that iustice raigne in the world, that is, to haue a most earnest desire, that it would so do. The fourth to haue a most vehement desire to receiue the body of the Sonne of God spiritually or Sacramentally, as also the celestiall gifts, and graces. The fift, with a most great affection to long after the crowne of Iustice, sighing after the vision of God in glory. In this hunger and thirst consisteth the feruour of spirit. To consider the hunger and thirst, that our Sauiour had of Iustice, as he testifyed himselfe, when he said: my meate is to doe the will of my Father: & by the most burning desire he had to drinke the bitter Chalice of his dolorous Passion, as he gaue to vnderstand, when crying vpon the Crosse, he sayd: I am a thirst. That such, as haue such a manner of hunger and thirst, are blessed, because they shall haue their fill of spirituall fauours, & graces, God communicating himselfe vnto them in this life, and in the other giuing himselfe by the cleere vision of his glory. That this is a terrible threate: Wo be to you, who haue your fill heere, because you shall endure hunger. He calleth them filled, who in their affection are full of transitory thinges of this vvorld, and those, who are full of the vvind of pride, for that such shall haue their part of hunger in the other life.

7.   Blessed be the mercifull : for they shall obtaine mercy . To consider, how this beatitude comprehendeth the 14. workes , that we call of mercy; a vertue that must extend it selfe towards all our neighbors, by remedying all their necessities temporall, and spirituall, and must be exercised with an inward compassion of anothers misery, by esteeming it as our owne, & by putting to our hand for the helping of it , only for the loue of God , without hope of any other recompence . That our Sauiour was most mercifull in the supreme degree, and did good to all, without difference of persons , with most great loue, and in all occasions. And therefore Saint Matth. cap. 9. sayth : Learne , what is mercy. That the recompence of the mercyfull is , to obtaine mercy at Gods handes againe , which we must thinke will be infinitly greater without cōparisō then that, which we shall exercise towards our neighbour. For it will cause and procure our exemption & deliuery in part frō the corporall, and spirituall euills of this life, and make vs perfectly happy afterwardes in the other . That he , who refuseth and neglecteth to doe mercy , is most miserable , because he may assure himselfe not to find any mercy with God , as he shall find by experience to be most true, in the day of Iudgement.

8.   Blessed be the cleane of hart: for they shall see God . To consider the first condition of this vertue of purity, which is to cleanse the hart from all sinne . The second is an holynes , and cleannes of conscience , hauing the soule filled
with

with holy and pure cogitations. The third is a
simplicity of treating with God, and with men.
It is called Purity of hart, for that this purity is
from the hart deriued into the body, and into all
the outward works. To consider the surpassing
purity of our Sauiour, who neuer sinned, neyther could sione, but accompanyed his innocent life with the purity of his works, and of his
holy speeches and words. To consider, that the
reward of this purity, is the essentiall beatitude
of the Saints, as well in this life by contemplation, as in the other by cleere vision of the diuine
essence. And therefore Dauid, after he had demaunded: Who is he, who shall ascend vp to
the mountaine of our Lord, made this answere.
The innocent handes, and the pure of hart.
Psal. 23.

9. Blessed be the Peace makers: for they
shall be called the children of God. To consider
the first degree of this vertue, which consisteth
in the mortification of the flesh, bringing it in
subiection to the spirit: for by this meanes a man
pacifieth himselfe. The second is, to intertayne
concord, peace and amity with all, and to continue in that vnion without breaking it. The
third is to pacify others, & to make them to accord and agree. The fourth and most perfect is,
to reconcile the soules to God. We must pray
hartily to God, that we may accomplish all these
degrees. To consider, that our Sauiour is called
The pacificall King by excellency, for that by
bringing peace downe from heauen into the
earth, he hath made a peace betweene God his

heauenly Father, and men; an action wherwith he would honour himselfe, greeting his Apostles after his Resurrection with the salutation of peace; & it was the Angells song also at his Natiuity. That it is the reward of the peace-makers to be aboue al others called the children of God, that is, that they shall be loued particularly of his diuine maiesty, who will take them vnder his paternall protection, as his deerest children, and inheritors of his glory.

10. To consider the last Beatitude, to wit: Blessed are those, who suffer persecution for Iustice: for theirs is the Kingdome of heauen. To consider, that vnder the name of persecution be comprehended all sorts of afflictions, and iniuries, in honours, in goods, in contentments and pleasurs, in the health, and in the life, by the instigation of the Diuell, the enemy of vertue, & by bad men. That the lawfull causes of a meritorious persecution be not the particular faults of them, who suffer it, but the conseruation of the faith, and of religion, or for the performing of ones duty, conformably to the office euery one beareth, or to the profession he is off: and then also he must suffer iniuries with patience, and spirituall ioy, holding it for a great fauour, that he may suffer any thing for the loue of God. To consider the most excellent examples, that our Sauiour hath left vs of this vertue, especially during the three latter yeares of his life, receiuing all manner of outrages, and iniuries for the promulgating of his holy law, & bearing them patiently. To consider the recompence
                                                            promised

promifed to them, who endure perfecution, namely, the Kingdome of heauen : and in this world a fpirituall ioy that comforteth them a-middeft their afflictiós, enioying a quiet repofe, and contentment of mind in all their outward troubles. And therefore our Sauiour faid : Be glad, and reioyce : for your reward is very great in heauen. On the contrary to thinke, of how great and excellent goods they depriue them-felues, who will not fuffer any thing for the loue of God.

Meditat. X L I I. *Of that which our Sauiour recommended vnto his Apoſtles, in his Sermon vpon the mauntayne. Matth.* 5.

TO confider thefe words : You are the falt of the earth &c. In which is briefly mani-fefted the fummary of the office of Apo-ſtolicall men, which is, to feafon the harts of men, and to giue them the falt of their good life and doctrine, in preaching by exemplar works, and edificatiue wordes, to the end other men may by the acrimony of this facred falt be pur-ged of their bad humors, and that in imitation of them they may feele pénance vnto théfelues taftfull. But they muft in the firſt place feafon themfelues, and make themfelues proper for the taft of the diuine maiefty, that they may be found worthy of his holy table, &c. To confi-der that our Sauiour did performe this office of falt in a moft perfect manner, anihilating and
humbling

humbling himselfe for vs , that we might find vertue lesse bitter, proposing himselfe for a most perfect Example of all sanctity . We must endeauour to haue the purity of salt, that we may not be cast forth into the dunghill of this world for reprobates .

2.   To consider these words : You are the light of the world &c. By which is meant the office of Apostles , and of the Religious their imitators , who imploy themselues about the gayning of soules . For they ought to be as starrs of the Church, to giue light by exemplare life and holy doctrine,and to driue away darkenes from the harts of the men of the world . Herehence will I learne , what purity of life there is required in me for the worthy exercising and performance of this office . To consider,how great an errour and pusillanimity it is for a man to hide the light , and talent , he hath receiued at Gods hands , by obscuring his doctrine and learning by a sinister intention of vanity, or of temporall gaine . How grieuous is his sinne, who being by office bound to be the light of the world , & to serue for a looking-glasse for men, giueth not any light at all, either by worke , or by doctrine , but filleth all with darkenesse : he (I say) who should by his good life honour God , and illumine soules ; which is all, that we ought to pretend , and to propose vnto our selues in all our works.

3 .   To consider these wordes : A Citty seated vpon a mountaine , cannot be hidden. Where is insinuated the height of perfectiō, that Aposto-

Apostolicall persons ought to haue , & the great
charity, whereunto they are bound in regard of
them , who make their recourse vnto them for
the auoyding of the captiuity of their infernall
enemy ,

Meditat. X L I I I. *Of the Euangelicall law,*
which our Sauiour promulgated vpon the moun-
taine. Matth. 5.

TO meditate, how our Sauiour came down
from heauen into the earth , for the strait
obseruation of the law , and to giue vnto
his disciples a perfect example of the obseruing
of it, as he himselfe said: I am not come to break
the law, but to fulfill it : words, that I ought to
haue oft in my mouth , saying : I am not come
to breake the rule, and the statuts of my religion , but to keep and fulfill them . He came to
accomplish the promises of the law , and thereunto to adioyne the perfection, that it wanted ,
by explaning his precepts after a more sound
manner , by adding of wonderfull counsayles ,
and imparting grace for the obseruing of them.
2 .   To meditate these wordes : He, that
shall breake one of the least commaundments ,
and shall so teach men, shall be called the least in
the Kingdome of heauen : that is to say, shall be
contemned, & excluded from the Kingdome of
heauen, as one vnworthy to enter in . If the cō-
maundment bind no further then to venial sin,
he that doth vvittingly transgresse it , shall
also

also be little in vertue : for he , that maketh no
reckoning of little faults, shall also fal into grosse
ones , because there is nothing little , that God
commaundeth : and he , who breaketh but one
commaundement , and induceth others to doe
the same, eyther by his owne bad example , or
by expresse wordes, shalbe called the least in the
Kingdome of heauen . But he, that shall doe and
teach, shall be great in the Kingdome of heauen.
That is, he who by his good example induceth
others to the obseruation of Gods commaundements , shall be great &c.

3.   To meditate these words : Be ye perfect , as also your heauenly Father is perfect .
This perfection consisteth in an exemption fró
all fault , and in the execution of all vertues , by
endeauouring to haue euery one of them in the
highest degree of perfection . For to say vnto vs
that we should be perfect , as is his Father , is to
insinuate vnto vs, that we must not content our
selues with any degree of perfection, and to stay
therein : And therfore we must resolue to seuer
our selues wholy from all sinne , and to pursue
vertue to our vttermost ability , and in the highest degree , that we can possibly arriue vnto.

4.   To consider , that Euangelicall perfection forbiddeth al manner of sinne, great or little,
commaundeth to render good for ill , counsay-
leth all vertues, both Theologicall, and Morall,
and euery one of them in the highest degree of
perfection , that may be . Therefore we must
yield thanks to God , for that he hath pleased to
                                                                   giue

giue vs a law so holy, and so perfect, encouraging and animating one another to an exact observation of the same.

Meditat. X L I I I I. *Of our Lords Prayer, called the Pater Noster.*

THis prayer is of all others most perfect, because our Sauiour himselfe did dictate it at the request of his Apostles, and is to be said publiquely and particularly with great reuerence, & attention.

1. To consider the first word (Father) & to thinke, that God would be so called, because he hath giuen the Naturall being to men, in creating them to his owne Image and liknes, and the Supernaturall being of grace, which he imparteth dayly vnto the iust, adopting them for his childrē, as often as they haue lost it, he giueth it them againe & againe, & conuerteth them vnto himselfe: an adoption, that cost our Sauiour deerly vpon the tree of the Crosse. How perfectly God exerciseth the office of a Father towardes vs, and how far therein he goeth beyond the Fathers of this world, whome in regard of himselfe he will not haue vs call our Fathers, neither doe they indeed in that sense merit so to be called. In saying that he is my Father, he giueth vnto me withall the dignity of his Sonne, which ought to be an inducement vnto me to loue, honour, and obey him in all thinges, as a good Sonne ought to do in regard of so good a Father.

Q That

That he would be called Father, to the end he might reuiue in our harts loue, and confidence, giuing vs to vnderstand, that he deserueth to be of vs serued with the affection of children, & to the end we may addresse vnto him our petitions and prayers with an hope to obtaine the same, beginning our prayers with the praises we owe him, & yield him that title, which pleaseth him so much.

2.   To consider the other word (our) by which is discouered his infinite charity, who notwithstanding he hath one naturall Sonne, would yet haue many adopted children to communicate his riches vnto: to the end also we may vnderstand, that we are all brethren, and children of the same Father, which should be a motiue vnto vs to loue one another. And this very word giueth vnto vs new matter & occasion of exercising the greater reuerence towardes God, &c.

3.   Which art in heauen.) Though God be euery where, yet he saith that he is particularly in heauen, to imprint in our harts the respect we owe him, by considering that our Father is Lord of heauen and earth, that we may raise vp our mindes to thinges aboue, and empty them quite of thinges heer beneath, especially in our prayers, knowing that from heauen must al our help come, and to make vs to passe ouer this mortall life as pilgrims and strangers on earth, & to sigh after life of immortality. To consider, that the iust are called the heauens, because God dwelleth in them by his grace: and therefore I must

must seeke to conserue in my selfe a great purity, to the end the diuine maiesty may settle his
habitation, and seate in my soule.

4. Thy name be hallowed.) That is to say,
that it be knowne, praised, glorifyed, and held
for most holy of all creatures, both visible & inuisible, present and to come, and honoured of
both Christians and infidells, glorifying God at
all times and euery where, by thoughts, wordes,
and workes, without offending him in the very
least. We must exercise our selues in these affections oftentimes, saying with the Seraphims
Holy Holy Holy, Lord God of hosts. And with
the Prophet Dauid: Not to vs, Lord, not to vs,
but to thy name giue glory. We must further
ponder these wordes: Thy Kingdome come,
By which we craue of God, that he may raigne
peaceably in vs by his grace, as he raigneth in his
iust ones. Wee craue also the Kingdome of e-
uerlasting glory, where his maiesty raigneth in
peace with the blessed, and we wish that the
Kingdome of sinne, and of the malignant spirit
should haue an end, and that of our Sauiour be exalted, as it ought to be. We must heere
awake in our soules the desire of our heauenly
Countrey, sighing & groaning, that the time
of our banishment is protracted, saying: Alas
that my seiouring heere is prolonged, in which
meane time I passe my life in company of them,
who dwell in darkenes.

5. Thy will be done in earth, as it is in
heauen.) By which wordes we craue, that Gods
will be accomplished in all his Creatures, and
that

Q 3.

that men doe it with as forward an affection on earth, as the Angells doe it in heauen, that is, that they cary themselues with a purity of hart, and a sincere intention to doe the will of God alone, and to pleafe the diuine maiefty with promptitude, and without repugnance, with conftancy and perfeuerance in the execution of his commaundements, and with loue and feruour, in imitation of our Sauiour, who faid : my meate is to doe the will of my Father. Heere I muft refolue frō this time forwards not to do my owne will any more being my greateft & heauyeft enemy, by cōfidering the euils & domages it hath wrought me in following it for the time paft.

6. Giue vs this day our dayly bread.) To confider, how we afke heere the moft holy, and moft excellent bread of the holy Sacrament of the Altar, and the fupernaturall refection of our foule, as grace, the Sacraments, holy and diuine infpirations &c. We further demaund bread, and the nutryment neceffary for the conferuation of our body, and life, whereof Gods pleafure is we fhould haue a moderate care. To ponder this word (our) for we call this bread, that we afke, our, becaufe it is vnto vs neceffary, and becaufe our Sauiors hath bought it for vs with the price of his owne bloud, and becaufe he promifed it vs. Againe we call it quotidiane, or daily bread, to infinuate that we haue our continuall dependance on the diuine prouidence, that there is not a moment, wherein we haue not need of Gods help, & that for that very caufe we ought to afke of him whatfoeuer is vnto vs neceffary

for foule, and body. And in faying, giue it vs this day, we exercife an act of charity, praying for all men in generall, as being all brethren.

7. Forgiue vs our trefpaffes, as we for-giue them, who haue trefpaffed againft vs.) To confider, that heere we craue, that it would pleafe God to pardon vs our both mortall & ve-niall finnes, togeather with the paines, where-to we remaine obnoxious for them. And none there is exempted, or excufed from making this prayer, fith there is not any fo iuft, or fo holy, who falleth not into veniall finnes, more or leffe. The offences, that we are to forgiue vnto our neighbours, be the iniuries, that haue been done vs, how great foeuer they haue been, neyther defiring reuenge, nor keeping them in mind, but forgetting all, neuer to thinke vpon them any more, and rendring good vnto them, who haue wronged vs, to the end God may pardon vs our offences alfo.

8. And fuffer vs not to fall into tentati-tion) To thinke, that we fuppofe heere, that God permitteth vs to endure tentations, & that we be now and then affayled for our fpirituall profit, and on our part we muft ftill be difpofed and prepared thereunto : yet his will is, that we fhould demaund grace and forces, that we may not be ouercome. And in this we confeffe our owne fragility, and his power to affift vs. And we adde: But deliuer vs from euill.) Where we pray, that we may be deliuered, and preferued from all euills paft, prefent, and to come : e-ternall & temporall, both of foule and of body,
saying:

saying: Deliuer vs, Lord, from all sinne, from
all inordinate passions, from wrath, vengeance,
from ill will, fornication, &c. To conclude, by
the word (Amen) which is as much, as So be it,
is intended, that we must vtter it with great feruour, and most affectuous desire, that it would
please God to yield vnto vs our petitions, and
with a firme hope of obtaining what we craue,
sith we require no more, nor other thing, then
what our Sauiour hath commaunded himselfe.

*Meditat. X L V.   Of sending, the Apostles and
disciples forth to preach. Matth. 9. & 10.*

TO consider, how our Sauiour, when he
sent forth his Apostles to preach the Gospell, vsed these wordes vnto them: (The
haruest is great, but the workemen be few: pray
therefore the Lord of the haruest, that he send
forth workmen into his haruest.) That is to say,
That the chosen, and those, who attend and expect the ayd and help of Euangelicall Pastors, be
in great number: whereas on the other side very
few they be, who dispose and prepare themselues to assist them, all men being naturally e-
nemies of trauaile, and friendes of ease, and idlenes. And therfore prayer is instantly to be made
to God that it would please him to send so many
and such workemen, as shall be needfull to
draw the poore soules out of darkenes, who are
on earth depriued of the knowledge of the true
God, and to conduct them into the way of saluation.

wation.

2. To confider, how our Sauiour fent his Difciples two and two in company togeather, that the one might comfort and help the other, that they might exercife themfelues in charity, that they might be two witneffes of one only truth, and might giue examples of edification vnto fuch, as repayred vnto fuch, as repaired vnto them. To confider further in how liberall a manner he communicated vnto them the auctority and power of working miracles, greater then thofe, he had wrought in his owne perfon, for the auctorizing and confirming of his holy doctrine thereby, admonifhing them freely to giue, what they had freely receiued, which is as much to fay, as that they fhould not doe any thing for their particular intereft, but only to procure them to admit & receiue the verity of his heauenly doctrine.

3. To confider the vertues, our Sauiour recommended vnto them, as the meekenes of Lambes, not doing ill vnto any, though they fhould receiue ill at the hands of all : patience to beare all outrages and difgraces, charity in giuing themfelues, euen as the fheepe giue themfelues all that they are : a confidence and fteadfaft hope in their foueraigne Paftour : the prudence of Serpents, and difcretion to obferue and take the time, place, and occafion proper & fit to preach with profit : Finally the fimplicity of doues, without bitternes or gall, with a pure and right intention : perfections, which preachers of the Gofpell ought to feeke for, and haue.

Q 4   4. To

4. To consider the manner, that they were to vse in going vp & downe the world, commaunded by our Sauiour, when he sayd: doe not possesse gold, nor siluer, nor money in your purses. That is, that they should cut off all superfluities in thinges temporall, and content themselues with what was precisely necessary, without charging themselues in such sort, as their iourney might not be hindred therby: that they should not take ouermuch care about their intertainment, but should cast their care & put their hope in the diuine prouidence, and assure themselues that God would prouide them of all, that should be for them necessary: and that going vp and downe they should shunne conuersations, company keeping and discourses, that profited not, as also profane salutations, & shold inuite all sorts & conditions of persons to the receiuing of the peace of the Gospell.

5. To consider the excellent subiect and matter, he gaue them to preach vpon, saying: The Kingdome of heauen is at hand: doe yee pennance. Where I am to learne, that holy pennance, the extirpation of vices, the exercise of of vertues, & the contempt of things terrene be the true & sure meanes for the gayning of saluation: & that the Kingdome of heauen ought to be the motiue to all this, which is now most easy to compasse, since God being made man, abundantly communicateth his grace to euery one, who hath any disposition to receiue & accept it.

Meditat.

Meditat. X L V I. *Of the glorious Martyrdome of S.* Iohn *Baptist.* Matth. 14. Marc. 6.

TO confider the conftancy , ftability , and feruent zeale of this new Elias , with fuch magnanimity and courage reprehending King Herod of adultery, that he committed with Herodias, his brothers wife, notwithftanding he were nothing ignorant of the cruelty of them both, and knew well inough that he fhould loofe his life, notwithftanding the fauour and refpect, that Herod vfed towardes him . Conftancy I fay , for our imitation in fhaking of all humane feare, when the truth is in queftion , & to be defended.

2 . To confider , that God permitted this imprifoning and death of S. Iohn, to the end he might paffe by the fame way, that auncient Prophets before him had paffed firft , and which way the iuft , and the fauoured of God doe ordinarily paffe : and for this alfo, that by giuing a teftimony of the rare and wonderfull vertues of his foule amiddeft aduerfities , as he had made them to appeare and fhine to the world in time of profperity, whe all thinges fucceeded to him well, and as he defired, he might be refined the more in the fornace of tribulation . To confider with what patience, refignation to Gods will, & fpirituall ioy and alacrity this glorious Precurfour of our Sauiour permitted himfelfe to be apprehended, laid hand on, and to be loaden with

greas

great weight of irons, which credible it is he kissed euer and a none, as the most deere pledges of the amity, and loue our Sauiour did beare him, making of his prison an Oratory, as he had done before of the desert, not ceasing to preach to his disciples, whome he sent vnto our Sauiour as to the true maister and instructour of soules. And as he had done the office of Precursour in this world, he had now a desire to be deliuered frō the bandes of his body, that he might goe to exercise the same office in Limbo, where the old holy Fathers were.

3. To consider, how Sathan leuied a great army and troupe of vices to encounter & fight against the rare vertues of this glorious Saint, as gluttony against his temperance: the vaine leuity of a foolish girle against his modesty, and grauity: excessiue mirth against his mortificati-on: prodigality against his Euangelicall pouer-ty: Finally cruelty against his sweetnes, and meeknes. Where I am to take notice of Sathans policy, and guilefull proceeding against vertue, and such, as exercise it. To consider of what power, dishonestie the infamous vice of loxury is, sith it carieth men on headlong to the infringing & transgressing of all lawes diuine and humane: and therefore we must conceiue an implacable hatred against such a foule, vgly and detestable monster.

4. To consider the spirituall alacrity and ioy, wherewith this holy Precursour receiued the sentence of death, giuen vpon so vnworthy an occasion, which credible it is he receiued,

when

when he was vpon his knees, praying for his e-
nemies, & for his poore afflicted disciples. The
Angells ioy, when they receiued his pure soule,
which much exceeded that, which they had,
when they receiued the soule of Lazarus: and as
they were many, who were glad, when he was
borne into the world, so many more, namely
the holy Fathers of Lymbo, reioiced in his precious death. The most excellent glory, that he
now possesseth in heauen, where he sitteth in a
most high eleuated throne with three prerogatiues, in quality of a Virgin, Doctour, & Martyr, yea and of double Martyrdome through a
perpetuall will, he had to suffer Martirdome, liuing in continuall chastity, pouerty, and mortification: and by the effusion of his bloud in dying a violent death.

5. To consider, how Herod, Herodias, &
their vnhappy daughter, though they trium-
phed, and were merry that day for the cutting
off the head, and death of this glorious Saint,
had not any long continuance in that their ioy.
For all three by the iust and seuere iudgement
of God came within a while after to distastrous
ends, and perished miserably: and such commonly is the end of the wicked.

Meditat.

Meditat. X L V I I.   *Of the miracle wrought by the fiue little loaues, wherwith Christ fed fiue thousand Persons.* Ioan. 6.

TO consider the great deuotion , wherwith this great multitude followed our Sauior , drawne by the sweetnes of his doctrine , that they forgot themselues , so much wrought his sweet presence in their wills . The compassion and pitty the Apostles tooke off the poore multitude , though their desires were indeed short , weeke, & not of power inough . How they intreated our Sauiour to giue them leaue to goe their way, to get them meate to eate : and the great mercy of our Sauiour himselfe, accompanied with ability in that desert place to prouide refection for the body , who yet first proued the faith of S. Philip , and of other the Apostles when he asked of them, where they wold find bread inough to feede such a great number of people .

2.   To consider, how there were brought to our Sauiour fiue little loaues , which was all the prouision for that multitude . Wherein is to be seene the precise obedience, and the wonderfull charity of the Apostles : for hauing but that small prouision of bread for their owne refection, they did neuertheles offer it with a good will at the very first : taking it , as I may say , out of their owne mouthes , to giue it to their neighboure, that they also might haue their part in
this

this charitable worke.

3. To consider, how our Sauiour willed the people to sit downe, that he might the better see the great number, which was of fiue thousand men besides women and children, to the end euery one might sit in his rancke, and the greatnes of the miracle might the more appeare. How our Sauiour tooke the fiue loaues into his most blessed hands, lifted his eies vp to heauen, gaue thanks to his heauenly Father, blessed the loaues, and by such his benediction multiplied them in so great abundance, as all that multitude had their fill, and yet a great deale remained besides, and the bread, which was of it selfe without tast before, was then most sauorous, toothsome, & nutritiue. To consider the paternall prouidence of God towardes his, for vvhome he prouideth all thinges necessary, & that in miraculous manner also, when there is need. And therefore vve must stir vp our selues to serue him, and by this learne, hovv a religious person, and euery good Christian ought to cary himselfe, vvhen he is to take his refection, that is to say, vvith orderl, issting his eyes and hart vp to heauen giuing God thankes, and making some reflection, or short meditation, that the soule may not fast, vvhiles the body is fed, & blessing meates before the going to the table. In this meruailous feast is represêted that which our Sauior doth euery day to the faithfull in the holy Sacrament of the Altar.

4. To consider, hovv the fragments of the bread being gathered together, there vvere

tvvelue

tvvelue basketts filled therevvith, giuing vs to vnderstand thereby, hovv God vvith a liberall hand recompenseth the almes, that be giuen for the loue of him, & rendreth with vsury & gains in the other life that, vvhich vve haue lent him in this life. How all the multitude much astonished at the greatnes of the miracle, tooke a resolution to make our Sauiour King: but he who was not come to seeke after honours, and dignities of this world, preuented that designe of theirs by absenting himselfe, flying all alone into the most secret part of the desert.

Meditat. XLVIII. Of ceasing the Tempest at sea. Matth. 8. Mar. 5.

TO consider, how the sleeping of our Sauiour in the ship, was to giue to vnderstand, that as he was man, he needed to take some refreshment and repose after his trauailes. And yet he tooke it with great precaution, being alwaies watchfull and awake in mind, & interrupting it at the intreaty of his Apostles, who saw themselues in the middest of eminent danger. Whereby we are to learne, what our sleep ought to be, and how we ought to order it: how neere at hand God is to them, who be in affliction, though he may seeme sometimes to sleep for the trying, and confirming of our faith, for the exciting of our confidence and trust in him: for the increasing of humility in vs, & the stirring vs vp to prayer, and the exercising of
other

other vertues. Herehence I will learne to conceiue a good and firme refolution to endure fomething for the loue of God, when occafion fhall prefent it felfe.

2. To confider, how, when the tempeft was at the greateft, the poore difciples recurred to their maifter, faying vnto him: Lord, faue vs, for we perifh. At another time they faid vnto him: maifter, haft thou no care of vs to fee vs perifh? Of this I will learne to make my recourfe to God in my neceffities. To ponder the fweet and gentle reprehenfion, that our fweet Iefus gaue them in thefe wordes: wherefore are you afraid, O yee of little fayth? As if he had faid, As long as I fhall be with you, what iuft caufe haue you to feare?

3. To confider, how our Sauiour commaunded the fea, and the vvind to be ftill, and to ceafe, and they vvere obedient to his vvord: vvherein appeared the povver of God, and the obedience of his creatures: making me glad to fee his maiefty fo povverfull, and confounding my felfe for my difobedience to his commaundments. When I fhall find myfelfe at any tyme troubled vvith diuers thoughts, I vvill recurre to my fvveet Iefus, and pray him to calme and appeafe the furges, and vvaues, that turmoyle and toffe me.

*Meditat. X L I X.   Of our Sauiours miracu-
lous walking vpon the water .   Matth.* 14.
Mar. 6.

TO confider, hovv our Sauiour vvas giuen
much to prayer , in fo much as he fpent
vvhole nights in it , as he did at this time ,
vvhen he vvithdrevv himfelfe from his difciples
to pray . The obedience of the Apoftles , vvho
vvere feparated from their good maifter perforce and againft their wills, and went vpon the
fea , where there arofe a great ftorme about the
very time, that the day began to breake.

  2 .   To confider, how the Apoftles laboured
in all they could to withftand the wind, and
the fea: to teach vs the firft thing that we ought
to doe in all our tribulations . The great loue &
affection, that our Sauiour did beare to his , to
whofe affiftace he came in the extremity of their
affliction, walking vpon the waues in teftimony
of his omnipotency, & the efficacy of the prayer , that he had made vpon the mountaine ,
whence the iuft are wont to come , prouided &
armed to tread all tribulations vnder foot . The
feare , that the Apoftles were in , when they faw
our Sauiour goe vpon the water , and the conceite they had , that it was a fpirit , in fo much as
they began therefore to cry out for feare . By
this we may difcouer the diuerfe manners of il-
lufions , and fraudes , that they fuffer who frequent prayer for pride, or vanity . For fometims
                                                    they

they take Iesus Chrift for him who he is not , &
when it is he indeed , they take him for a fanfy
or fpirit, and therefore the difcretion of fpirits ,
and the rectitude of good counfaile is vnto fuch
perfons moft neceffary .

3.   To confider , hovv our Sauiour
fpake vnto his Apoftles , vvhen they vvere
moft afravd and comforted them , faying :
It is I , feare yee not. At the found of vvhich
vvordes , they tooke hart , knovving that it
was their maifters voyce. Where we are to confider, how our Sauiour is prefent at all the tribulations of the iuft , & how they know his diuine
voyce.

4   To confider , how Saint Peter knowing his maifter by the wordes he vfed , faid vnto
him : Lord , if it be thou , bid me come to thee
vpon the water . Wordes in truth, well worthy
Saint Peter, wherin he difcouereth the true figns
of true feruour of fpirit, which be, to haue a great
light for the vnderftanding and efteeming of the
miracles of our Sauiour: to defire with great
affection , that God commaund vs fomething ,
whereby we may witneffe the loue , we beare
him : to wifh from our hart to be vnited with
our beft beloued : to offer our felues manfully
to doe fomethings , that feeme to exceede our
forces , and yet not with precipitation, but with
commaundement , leaue , or particular infpirations of God .

5.   To confider , how our Sauiour gaue
leaue to Saint Peter to come vnto him , not reprehending him in his action for his feruour, as at
other

other times he did, because it proceeded of a sincere & perfect loue, & great resignation of himselfe, with no lesse assurance of his diuine power, to the end the other disciples might by experience see, how assured those be, who put their trust in him, and in his words, by seing a weighty body walke miraculously vpon the liquid, & thin waters.

5.   To consider with what speed S. Peter leapt into the sea, to walke vpon the water in testimony of his prompt obedience, & how beginning to be afrayd, he began therewith also to sincke, which our Sauiour permitted for the humbling of him, and to giue him the more & better vnderstanding of the imperfection of his faith. To thinke, that whosoeuer putteth himselfe in daunger, & exposeth himselfe thereunto by commaundement of our Sauiour, & vnder the caution of his holy word, cannot possibly perish. For he shall no sooner implore his aide, then that he will giue him his hand to deliuer him out of his necessities. Finally to consider, how so soone as our Sauiour entred into the ship, the wind forthwith ceased: which giueth vs to vnderstand, that the tentations, which our enemy thrusteth vpon vs in his absence, doe vanish into the ayre, and are dispersed by his comming, and that vnder the protection of his holy preséce our ship saileth happily in this sea of the world, & arriueth finally safe at the port of saluation in the land of the liuing.

Meditat.

Meditat. L. Of the Confession that Saint Peter made, touching the diuinity of Christ. Matth. 16.

TO consider, that the demaund, which our Sauiour made to his Apostles (What is it that men say that I am?) was after his coming from his prayer: to giue vs to vnderstand, that the light, that S. Peter receiued for the confessing of our Sauiour, was the fruit of his prayer going before, and for the taking an occasion thereby to make himselfe better knowne to his disciples, and withall for the instructing of vs to make inquisition about that, which is said of vs, not for vanity sake, but for the correcting and amending of that, which we shall find to be reported of vs. Heere we must consider the humility of the Sonne of God, who called himselfe the Sonne of man, a name to him contemptible and base, in whose power it was to take other names so noble.

2. To consider the prudence of the Apostles in answering, and saying what seemed most honorable among the qualityes, that men gaue vnto our Sauiour, iudiciously concealing & saying nothing of the iniurious and ignominious names, that the Scribes and Pharisies maliciously gaue him. To consider, how man of his own nature is subiect to errour in the knowledge of our Sauiour, eyther by passion, that blindeth and troubleth in him the light of reason; or by weaknes of his vnderstanding, that would mea-

R 4.   sure

sure God by his owne reach or capacity. How there be many Chriſtians, who by their bad life doe outwardly confirmne and witnes the erroneous opinions they haue of the diuiniey, being deſperatly abandoned and giuen ouer to all manner of ſinnes, and temerariouſly preſuming of Gods mercy, which they abuſe, to the end they may become the more ſtiffe, & obſtinate in their iniquities.

3.   To conſider, how our Sauiour hauing vnderſtood of his Apoſtles, what was the opinion of the vulgar ſort of him, demaunded of the, what their opinion was touching his perſon. Whereof I will make my profit, aſking of my ſelfe, what opinion I haue of the diuine maieſty. That S. Peter made anſwere in the name of all the Apoſtles, though the queſtion were addreſſed and propoſed indifferently to all, as being the more feruent and forward in that, which concerned the ſeruice of Ieſus Chriſt: in which kind he euer ſhewed himſelfe more affeƈtioned then the reſt: for this alſo, for that the diuine maieſty hauing ſeene him diſpoſed & apt to receiue his graces, illumined him inwardly with an extraordinary light, to the end he might vnderſtand his greatnes, and what he was, and ſo he tooke vpon him to ſay: (Thou art Chriſt, the Sonne of the liuing God) words moſt ponderous, & worthy moſt due conſideration.

4.   To conſider, that this notable confeſſion very much pleaſed our Lord Ieſus Chriſt, who therefore called S. Peter (bleſſed) for herewith began his happynes: and our Sauiour named

med him Simon the Sonne of Iohn, which signifyeth Grace, or Iona, which signifieth a Doue:
adding further, that neyther flesh, nor bloud
had reuealed this mistery vnto him, because
their boundes are ouer strayte, & short to reach
so high, but that it was the eternall Father to
vvhome alone it appertayned to reueale such
thi·ges for the increase of his glory, of that of his
Sonne, & for the saluation of men.

5. To consider the great and magnificall
promisses, that our Sauiour made to S. Peter,
manifesting thereby, how liberall he is in recom-
pensing the seruices, that are done him, and the
zeale, that is caryed towardes him. He called him
Peter, making him therein like vnto himselfe,
who is the Churches fundamentall stone both in
constancy, & in immoueable stability. He made
him in effect as a precious stone, singular for
many excellent vertues it hath, vpon which,
like a wise Architecte, he was to set the foundations of his Church, making S. Peter the vniuersall head of it, & he assured him of an inuincible
perseuerance till the very end, against which
though the infernall powers should raise themselues, yet should they neuer preuayle. He
gaue him the charge of the keyes of heauen,
that he might both open and shut the gates of it
to men: he gaue him the key of knowledge for
the manifesting and declaring of the truth, hidden vnder the difficult and hard places of Scripture, to the profit of the vniuersall Church in generall, and of euery one in particular. And for
this I am to yield him thankes, and to be glad,

and

and euer haue this holy and blessed Apostle in
great honour , and reuerence for the great prerogatiues and priuiledges , he hath receiued at
the liberall hand of our Lord,& Sauiour.

Meditat. LI.   Of the Transfiguration of our Lord . Matth. 17. Marc. 19.

TO consider, that wheras our Sauior would
be transfigured, and shew himselfe glorious to his Apostles,and in their persons to
the whole world, he did it to giue some testimony of the glory, that he kept concealed , and
hidden vnder the veyle of his mortall humanity , and of that which those are to haue , who
shall serue him sincerely, when they shall raigne
in company with him in heauen . To teach vs
also , that God giueth often euen in this life a
tast of the pleasures of the other , though for a
very short time , to animate and encourage vs to
his seruice .

2 .   To consider, that he transfigured himselfe, after he had exhorted them to the carying
of his Crosse , ceasing the weight of it by the
consideration of the recompense , they were to
haue for carying it . That this transfiguration
was vpon a mountaine apart , to teach vs that
God is found in the solitary retire of a deuout
soule,& not in the middest of tumultuous troubles .

3 .   To consider , that he chose three of
his most feruent disciples , to animate vs to
a feruour of spirit , and to cause vs to see , that
he

he giueth fauour where, & to whome it seemeth
to him best. That the three Apostles represent
three vertues, that must goe in company with
feruent prayer, liuely fayth in Saint Peter, hope
piously founded in Saint Iames, and burning
charity in Saint Iohn, our Sauiour euer marching before: out of vvhich I will draw a good
affection to the exercise of prayer, since vve see
God by meanes of it, and the soule to be transfigured from a terrene to a celestiall, and from
an humane to a diuine loue. To consider, how
our Sauiour by transfiguring himselfe did nothing, but take away the barre, that kept in the
glory of the soule, and permit it to redound v-
pon the body, whereunto it appertained, and
was vnto it due: and yet he was voluntarily depriued therof, to the end he might suffer it to dye
for the redemption of man. And for this we
must render immortall thankes to the diuine
goodnes, desiring to depriue our selues of our
pleasurs for the loue of God, sith for the loue
of vs he depriued himselfe of his owne glory,
that it vvas due to his precious body.

Meditat. L I I. *Of that which happened, du-*
ring our Sauiours Transfiguration.

TO consider, how our Sauiour would, that
Moyses, & Elias shold accompany him in his
Träsfiguratió, & how they were with him,
& appeared in great maiesty, as so singular an a-
ction required. How these two were particularly
chosen,

chosen, becaufe they were better known among
the Ifraelites , and were the moft zealous in the
obferuation of their law : and for that the one &
the other had fafted fourty dayes , and as many
nights , as had done our Sauiour . To confider,
that the fubiect of their difcourfe , was our Sauiours exceffe , that he was to make in Hierufalem, which was an exceffe of paynes forrow, and
ignominy, correfpondent to the exceffe of that
loue , he did beare to men . Vpon which I am
to confider, that our fweet Iefus would neuer
yield vnto himfelfe the very leaft relaxation fo
long as he liued , for as much as this very fhort
repofe, that he gaue to his body, was intermixed
with a dolorous , and bitter difcourfe of his paffion , to teach vs , that we are not to feeke after
an abfolute repofe and quiet, fo long as we lead a
mortall life .

2. To confider , how our Sauiour being in
prayer , and transfigured vpon the mountaine ,
the three Apoftles began to fall a fleepe inftead
of compofing themfelues to prayer in company
with their maifter , fhewing in that their weaknes , and the difference of one that is deuout ,
and feruent in his prayer , & of him who is re-
miffe , dull , and negligent in it . To confider,
how S. Peter remained aftonifhed with admira-
tió, in feing our Sauiors body transfigured , and
the glory of it . And if but one little drop of this
diuine liquour gaue fo great fatisfaction vnto S.
Peter, as he faid, it was very wel with him there,
and that it was good for him to be in that place;
what will that then be of the endles fea of the e-
ternall

eternall glory? To thinke, that Saint Peter, made dronke vvith this present contentment and pleasure, and troubled togeather vvith the feare of our Sauiours future Passion and death, knevv not vvhat he said, desiring to make his continuall aboad vpon the mountaine; That vve are not to vse this mortall life to take our pleasure therin, but to suffer.

3. To consider, hovv the eternall Father, and the Holy Ghost, appearing in forme of a cloud, pleased to honour our Sauiour with their presence in this action: The Father vsing these vvordes: Loe, this is my deere Sonne, in vvhome I am vvell pleased: heare yee him. And this are we to ponder and consider vvell.

4. To consider, hovv the Apostles hauing heard and vnderstood these magnificall vvordes, fell sodainly dovvne vpon their face, and being after a vvhile come agayne to themselues, they looked about them, and savv nobody but Iesus there all alone: vvhome vve also must only seeke for, because he is more worth to vs, then all. That he willed them not to say any thing touching vvhat they had seene, vntill he should be risen from death againe: wherein he haue a singular testimony of his most great humility.

S   *Medita-*

Meditat. LIII.   Of the demaund, that the Sonnes of Zebedy made. Matth. 20. Mar. 10.

TO consider, how S. Iames, and Iohn, being yet imperfect, and hauing heard our Sauiour say, that he should rise againe, & raigne, discouered their ambitious affections, and demaunded of him the first places in his Kingdome, saying: mayster, we will, that what thinges soeuer we shall aske, thou doe it to vs: manifesting thereby, that they were full of selfe will, and were most far from a resignation of themselues into the hands of their Sauiour, and that they were further presumptuous in an high degree, because they suffered themselues to be carryed away to this ambitious passion, not remembring any more, that our Sauiour was to dye vpon the Crosse. How both the Brethren conspired in making this petition: for flesh and bloud are wont to make ioynt compacts for the obtaining of what is pretended touching worldly honour.

2.   To consider our Sauiours wonderfull prouidence, who notwithstanding he knew the brethrens will, did yet aske of them what their petition was, to the end they might themselues cast forth by their owne mouth the enuious venine, that troubled them in their mindes, & the discontentment they had, that S. Peter was preferred before them. By this we must conceiue

aa

an horror of this accurſed ſin of ambition, which had ſo deepe roote euen in the harts of the diſciples of our Sauior . To conſider our Sauiors anſwere , who told them , that they knew not what they aſked . Wherein he manifeſteth the cauſes, wherefore our praiers be not oftentimes heard , becauſe we craue ſome temporal thing without reſigning our ſelues into the hands of Gods or ſome ſpirituall thing, without parity & ſincerity of intention ; or with ſuch conditions , as it exceedeth our deſeruings; or for that we haue a deſire to obtaine it by our prayers only without accompanying it with meritorious workes; or we aſke that, which is giuen in recompenſe to thoſe , who fight , and ouercome , without putting hand to mortification . By all this I muſt learne to pray to God, as I ought, that I may be heard .

3. To conſider , how our Sauiour aſked of them, if they could drinke his chalice, and be baptized with his baptiſme ? Where he inſtructeth and teacheth them to aſke what is good , diſcouering his great charity and infinite goodnes in this, that he ſweetly inuiteth his Apoſtles, by wordes and examples , to accept of trauailes willingly and to take part with him in his Paſſion , teaching them by the ſame meanes , what was the way of the right hand , and what of the left, the way that he was firſt of all to goe himſelfe. To ponder and examine the weight, poiſe, and meruailous ſenſe & meaning of theſe words, that our Sauior vſeth, in calling his Paſſion, Chalice & Baptiſme, & the other wordes, that he ad-

S 2   ded,

ded, saying (That I drink) giuing to vnderstand, that he did drinke it continually by desire, & inward representation. And of this I must take an occasió to desire to suffer for the loue of this my sweet Sauiour, & to imagine with my selfe, that he asketh of me, if I haue the hart & courage to drinke his Chalice; & to examine my selfe about the same.

4. To consider the Apostles answere, who sayd, We can. An answere, that might proceed of ambition, presuming more, then their forces would permit, or of a blind, and vnexperienced feruour, that did put them forwardes to offer themselues to suffer, without considering what they said. It might also proceed from an holy instinct of God, who inspireth vnto his such desires, as is this, which we are to belieue was giuen them by the holy Ghost. That our Sauiour doth a great fauour vnto them, whome he causeth to drinke of his Chalice, as those his two beloued Apostles did, that they might come one day by that meanes to those seates, which they demaunded.

5. To consider, how the rest of the Apostles were moued with indignation against those two, in regard of this their pretension, thinking that they sought to haue a superiority ouer them. Where is to be seene the euill, that bad example causeth, and the disorders and confusions, that ambition bringeth vnto all communities. To admire the sweetnes and meeknes of our Sauiour, and his wonderfull doctrine, wherby he expressed this their ambition, teaching
ough

them, that such, as would be imitators of him, ought to place their greatnes in doing seruice to the whole world, as he had done, who being their mayster, and soueraigne Lord, was come to serue them, and not to be serued: and that such ought their intention to be, who had a mind to follow him. Where on the contrary it is the humour of the children of Adam, insatiably to seeke after the greatnes, that perisheth, and passeth away, and to haue a commaund ouer all.

Meditat. LIIII.   *Of* Lazarus, *and the Rich* Glutton. *Luc.* 16.

TO consider the patience of poore Lazarus, which he made shew of, in enduring the sore paines of his vlcers and sores, whereof he was full from head to foote, suffering extreme pouerty, hunger, and nakednes, in so much as his misery spake lowd inough by the mouth of his vlcers, though he said nothing at all, patiently bearing the contempt of all sorts of persons, who abandoned him cleane, none at all succouring him, in so much as he neither could obtaine any of the little crums of bread, that fel from the eductous rich mans table. Finally the miseries, he endured, were so great, as he could not so much as driue away the dogges from him, that came to like his sorts, being exposed moreouer to the cold and frost &c. To consider, how by meanes of these his miseries he arriued to such sanctity, as he merited to haue our Sauiour to commend the memory of him, and his life, to

S 3   posterity

posterity, which in paines & trauailes was much like to the life of our Sauiour himselfe. The happy conclusion of Lazarus life, whose soule was by the holy Angells carryed into Abrahams bosome, God honouring him in his death, whome men had cōtemned in his life time, & crowning him with glory of immortality, for the paines that he had constantly suffered; which glory he now enioyeth in heauen in compensation of the miseries and paines, he suffered on earth. Of this we are to learne, how liberally God rewardeth the trauailes and paines, that are patiently suffered for loue of him.

2. To consider, that the diuine goodnes did not content it selfe to honour this poore beggar in the other life, but would doe him also honour in this, by manifesting his name, that was in obliuion, and forgotten amongst men, and leauing it recorded in his holy Ghospell, that the poore may vnderstand, that God forgetteth them not: and canonizing him for a Saint in heauen, to the end the Church may honor him for such, & dedicate Altars & churches on earth to his honour.

3. To consider the vices of the naughty Rich man, namely, his pride, auarice, royotous manner of liuing, loue of himselfe, and hardnes of hart towardes his neighbour, which precipitated him into a thousand wickednesses besides. And more then that, our Sauior vouchsafed not to deliuer his prophane name by his holy mouth, as being raced out of the booke of life. Of this we may inferre, how different

Gods

Gods iudgements be from thofe of men, whiles
they honour the vicious rich ones, and reiect &
contemne the vertuous poore ones, God ob-
feruing a contrary courfe.

4. To confider the auaricious Rich mans
vnfortunate, and vnhappy death, whofe foule
was buryed in hell, togeather with life, leauing
his riches, vanities, pleafures, gluttony, & all
wherein he was fo deeply plunged, and beginning his torments, and miferies, that fhould neuer end, conformably to that faying of holy Iob.
cap. 21. They lead their dayes in wealth (and
pleafures) and in a moment they goe downe into hell. To reflect vpon the torments, that this
vnfortunate foule fuffereth there, where he was
couered ouer with flams of fire from top to toe,
inftead of the purple, wherewith he was clad in
this world, where his tongue, that had been the
inftrument of a thoufand wicked blafphemies,
was punifhed with an incredible heate and burning, his gluttonous ftomacke tormented with
a moft raging hunger, and a moft burning thirft,
his foule tormented alfo with a Diuellifh enuy in
feeing the happy ftate of Lazarus, and himfelfe
abandoned of the whole world, without finding
any one to pitty him in his paines, as he had
himfelfe beene vvithout pitty tovvardes Lazarus.

5. To confider the hard anfwere, that
Abraham gaue him, faying: That he had receiued good thinges in his life time, and Lazarus
likewife euill, and that therefore their conditions being different, reafon there was, that feing
he

he had been giuen to his pleasures, and had ill vsed the goods that God had giuen him, in this life, he should now be tormented after death for eternity, as it also was meete, that poore Lazarus, who had with patience endured his afflictions in this world, should enioy the reward, he had deserued, in the other. Let vs learne by this, how different the states of the good and bad be after this life: and that impossible it is to goe from hell to heauen, against the immutable decree of Almighty God.

Meditat. LV. Of the Conuersion of S. Mary Magdalen. Luc. 7.

TO consider the qualities of this poore abandoned woman, which are comprehended vnder this name of sinner, out of whome, as Saint Marke saith, Iesus Christ our Sauiour did cast seauen Diuells, that is to say, many most great, and most deeply rooted sinnes in her soule, by occasion whereof the malignant spiritts had found in her a most quiet habitation and aboad for themselues. Of this I must learne to be diffident in my selfe, and to be confident in the goodnes of God. To consider, that one motiue of this womans conuersion, was a Sermon, that she heard our Sauiour make, and the sweetnes, wherewith she saw him to receiue penitent sinners. But the principall motiue was an effectuall inspiration from heauen, which touched her hart at the quicke, and gaue her to vnderstand, derftand, how deeply fhe was bound to loue God, and for that caufe hauing a defire to fatisfy this obligation, fhe omitted not the time with diligence to feeke out our Sauiour. We muft imitate this diligence of hers, when we feele any good defires enkindled in our foules.

2. To confider, what this holy finner did, when fhe went firft to caft her felfe downe at our Sauiour Iefus his feete: how fhe watered them with teares, wiped them with the haire of her head, annointed them with precious oyntment, and did all this, approching vnto him behind. In all which actions is difcouered her repentance perfectly accompayned with a liuely fayth, profound humility, moft bitter contrition and forrow, and moft burning loue, togeather with moft great motions of deuotion, & of prayer, which fhe demonftrated by outward fignes, by conuerting the vfe of the inftruments of her fault into a worke of fatisfaction, & imploying to Gods feruice her eyes, the hayre of her head, &c. with fuch an affection, as being wholy tranfported into God, fhe forgot herfelfe, and trod vnder her feete and contemned quite all confideration of humane refpects.

3. To confider the Pharifies murmuring, proceeding of their haughty pride, temerarioufly cenfuring our Sauiour for neither Prophet, for that he knew not the woman, as they thought: nor for an holy man, becaufe he fuffred her to touch him; whiles they alfo gaue rafh iudgements of Magdalen, thinking her then to be a finner indeed, without reflecting vpon the teftimonies

monies, that she gaue of her most true repentance. By this we are to learne, that the iudgements of men be as preiudiciall, as they be easy,
and rash.

4. To consider, how our Sauiour did
by his prudence, and diuine wisdome, represse
and reprehend the Pharisies testimony of iudg-
gement, performing the office of an Aduocate
for Magdalen, and honoring her before all the
company by a pretty similitude, which he allea-
ged in fauour of her, applying vnto her the Parable of a creditour, that had two debtors. How
God is wont to confound the arrogancy of thē,
who esteeme themselues iust in regard of them
who be great sinners, as is to be heere seene. Of
how great efficacy one action of feruour is, whē
as by it a great sinner mounteth oft tymes vp to
a far higher degree of perfection, and charity,
then a iust one, by many old, and languishing
acts: and how the loue of God is a wonderfull
meanes to the obtaining of remission, and pardon for sins past.

5. To consider, how Magdalen receiued
the absolution of both fault, and paine, as may
appeare by these our Sauiours sweet and fauourable wordes: Thy sinnes are pardoned thee.
Whereupon I will resolue to make many acts
of contrition for the obtayning of a plenary indulgence and remission of my sinnes. The great
modesty of our sweet Iesus, who seing that they
were scandalized, that he forgaue sinnes, would
not ascribe that pardon to his owne liberality,
but to the sinners faith. Finally, to consider,
how

how Magdalen did euer after this remayne exceedingly deuoted to the feete of our Sauiour, at which she had found the remission of her faults, and could not leaue them, because that was the place of refuge, which was the cause, that she was alwaies most affected vnto them. Of the aforesaid I am to learne to stir vp a desire of imitating the actions of this holy penitent, that I may obtaine Gods grace, and the absolution of my sinnes.

Meditat. LVI. *Of the conuersion of the Samamauitan Woman.* Ioan. 4.

TO consider the long iourneyes, and the great, and wearysome trauailes of our Sauiour for the gayning of soules, while he alvvaies vvent on foote in the excessiue great heates of sommer, burning inwardly with an infinite great heate of his eternall loue. How he sat vpon a Well, not so much to rest himselfe, and to take breath, as to take occasion of gayning a sinfull and sensuall soule, as that Samaritane was, who came to that Well for water, thinking on nothing lesse, thē of the great good, that befell her.

2. To consider, hovv our Sauiour demaunded of the womā to drinke, which she refused to giue him. Wherein is liuely expressed the ingratitude, and want of knowledge in man towardes God, and contrariwise the liberality, and prodigality (as I may say) of God to man. How

God

God ceaseth not still to inuite the soule to admit and receiue his graces, as may be liuely seene in this conference with this Samaritane, who being carnall, and sensuall, could not yet tast any thing of God, or of that which appertayned to him.

3.   To consider, how our Sauiour proceeded on by little and little, mouing her to desire the Eternall goods, and inuiting her in a sweet manner to take of him the liuing water of his grace, of which he made a counterposition of the one water with the other, of that (I say) with the dead and elementary water. For the properties of this liuing water be, to slacke the thirst, and cleane to extinguish and quench the desire of all other waters, that perish and passe avvay, vvhich as being earthly, satiate not at all, but doe alter the thirst and desire, and hurt it. It is also proper to this diuine liqsour to runne continually, for as much as the holy Ghost, the eternall source & spring of grace, is in the soule, that drinketh of it: and more then this, it is naturall to it to augment, and increase continually: moreouer this liuing water riseth and mounteth vpwardes with a certaine diuine and holy impetuosity and violence to heauen, inclining the soule, that tasteth of it, to the desire of celestiall thinges, whereunto the sweet violence and power it hath, carieth the soule, with a spirituall promptitude and ioy. And therefore our Sauiour sayd, that it mounted vp euen to life euerlasting, being a pledge of the inheritance of heauen, after which vve attend. To consider,

                                                                hovv

how the Samaritane, hearing this difcourfe, began to defire this wonderfull water; in imitation of whome we muft defire it alfo, and craue inftantly to haue our part in it, accompanying good workes with prayers, and faying: Lord giue me this water of life, that I may not thirft any more.

4. To confider the dexterity, cũning, and fkill of our Sauior, vfed for the difpofing of this foule, and taking from it all the impediments & obftacles of grace, making the woman to know and vnderftand the bad eftate, in which fhe liued, plunged in her iniquities. By meanes wherof beginning to open her eyes, and to feeke a remedy of her infenfible malady & ficknes, fhe addreffed her felfe to our fweet Sauiour, whome fhe acknowledge for a Prophet, praying him to apply a remedy and cure thereunto. To confider that, which our Sauiour faid vnto her, whem he notified vnto her, that God is to be adored in fpirit, and verity, that is, that he is to be adored al places, & principally in our foule, which is the fpirituall temple of the diuine maiefty, & that fuch adoration ought to proceed and come frõ the holy Ghofts infpiration, and of the truth it felfe, which is Iefus Chrift our Lord: not contenting it felfe with rendring him outward feruice and adoration alone, but with proceeding rather to the inward, which confifteth in the ornaments of vertues, fuch as be faith and beliefe in the diuine miracles, humility in the knowlege of our owne fragility, &c.

5. To confider, how our Sauiour difcoue-
T   red

red himselfe to this woman, saying vnto her, that himselfe was the promised Messias, illumining her vnderstanding with true beliefe. He gaue her the liuing water of his grace which she had asked of him, filled her with so much spirituall ioy, as she forgat her pitcher, and elementary water, and came in all haste to the City to make him knowne to her fellow Cittizens, and imprinted in her hart most profound humility, that she confessed herselfe a sinner: great prudence and wisdome, in so much as she seemed to preach Iesus Christ; and to be short, a great feruour of spirit, whereby she moued many of the people to goe to see our Sauiour.

6. To consider, how the Apostles meruayled much to see their maister to humble himselfe so far, as to talke with a poore woman, that came to the Well for water: as also to see him to treate with her alone, a thing rare and extraordinary in him, and wonderfull to them, who reuerenced all his actions. To consider these words: my meate is to do the will of him, who sent me, and to perfect his worke. Where he discouereth his great affection that he had to accomplish the will of his heauenly Father, which was to conuert soules and to put them againe into the way of saluation. To consider, how in the meane time the Samaritans came forth to our Sauiour, who benignely receaued them, and preached vnto them the Kingdome of God, & at their intreaty stayed two dayes in their City, where he imparted abundantly vnto them of his spirituall meate, & conuerted many sinners.

Medi-

Meditat. L V I I. *Of the Woman taken in adultery, whome our Sauiour delyuered from her accusers, and from her sinnes. Ioan. 8.*

TO consider the sweet benignity of our Sauiour in conuersing with poore sinners, and his great mercy and facility in pardoning, which was such, as his enemyes by that occasion sought to intrap him, making him Iudge touching that adulterous woman, and thinking his facility and benignity so great, as it would easily goe beyond the law of Moyses rather, then condemne her. And this is a tricke and subtility very familiar with the diuell, who tempteth the iust, in the vertue whereunto they be most disposed, that they may fall into the contrary vice by exceeding & going beyond the lymitts of vertue.

2 - To consider, how our Sauiour bowed downe, & wrote with his fingar in the dust, to giue to vnderstand, that he did not regard the question, that they had proposed vnto him, as not being willing to be a Iudge in such causes, as was that: & further to teach vs, that in great matters, wherein there is question of the life, & honour of our neighbour, a man must proceed without precipitation, & with maturity, & leasure, sith it is a very easy thing for men to be deceiued in their iudgments. He would also write vpon the ground for this, that he might giue vs to vnderstand, that it was he, who with his fingar

gar wrote the law of Moyſes vpon the tables of
ſtone, and that therefore he knew right well,
who were the tranſgreſſours of it. To imagine,
that it may be our Sauiour wrote the ſinnes of
this womans accuſers, that they might ſee the
duſt, that was in their owne eyes, and not con-
trole others for a fault, that was but ſmall in
regard of their owne abominable exceſſes.

3.   To conſider, how our Sauiour ſayd to
her accuſers, that the firſt amongſt them, that
found himſelfe exempt and free from ſinne,
ſhould take vp a ſtone to ſtone her. Wherin he
ſhewed his ſingular prudence. For without going againſt the law, he confounded the accuſers, to whome he gaue an occaſion of remembrance of their owne ſinnes, and of weeping
for them, and not of accuſing the poore woman. But thoſe obſtinate and willfull perſons,
after they had taken notice of their owne offences, went their way one after another, inſteed of confeſſing them humbly to our Sauior,
and of asking pardon of him for them. Wherehence we may inferre, how adominable a
thing ſinne is, ſeeing thoſe, who knew themſelues deſtayned therewith, might not endure
the light of our Sauiour. And therefore what
ſhall my confuſion be at the houre of my death
and iudgement, when the darkenes of my ſinns
ſhall be driuen avvay, and God ſhall bring my
workes to light, and lay them open to the eyes
of the whole world.

4.   To conſider, how our Sauiour rayſing himſelfe, beheld this poore woman with

a

a compassionate & mercyfull eye, & freed her
from her enemyes. For in that meane tyme she
was inwardly striken with compunction, and
sorrow for her offence, being ashamed that she
had committed it. Where we are to conceyue
with what eyes of pitty our Sauiour beheld the
humbled and contrite sinner, far different from
those, wherewith he considereth the rebellious
and obstinate ones, such as were the Pharises.
To ponder these words: Goe, & sinne no more.
I haue not pardoned thee thy sinnes, & deliuered thee from thine enemies, that thou shouldst
take an occasion to returne to thy passed sinnes
vnder the assurance of my present benignity, but
that thou amend, and become better for the
tyme to come, &c.

*Meditat. LVIII. Of the Conuersion of
Zachæus Prince of the Publicans. Luc. 19.*

TO consider the conuersion of this great
sinner (for the Publicans, or Customers
were esteemed and held for such in those
times) and to see that the motiue thereof was a
desire, that God did put into him, to see our Sauiour Iesus, and to know him, belieuing that
the only sight of him would profit him much, as
also it did, when he did put that his desire in ex-
cution, by contemning the points and respects
of worldly honour, and the reports of obtrecta-
tours, who might haue censured him for this,
that being a man rich, and qualifyed, he should

T 3   runne

runne like a little child, and mount vp vpon a tree. This must we imitate.

2. To confider, how our Sauiour inuited himfelfe to Zachæus his houfe, without being called of Zachæus, to whome he faid, That he fhould come downe quickly from the Sycomore tree, vpon which he was got, for that he meant that day to be a gueft in his houfe. For the defire, that God hath to iuftify foules, is fuch & fo great, as when he findeth an occafion, he differreth it not, his pleafure being to abide alwais in the foule into which he once entreth, as he manifefteth by thefe vvordes: This day I muft abide with thee.

3. To confider the precife and exact obedience of Zachæus to the voyce of our Sauiour, which he no fooner heard, but that he fhooke of all pufillanimity, vnprofitable fhame and bathfulnes, that had vvithheld him till then, confidering his ovvne vnvvorthines, and the excellency and greatnes of our Sauiour, againft vvhó the ignorant and malicious murmured, becaufe he frequented the company of finners, and did eate familiarly vvith them, not knovving the end, for vvhich he did it, vvhich vvas the iuftification of foules.

4. To confider the perfect converfion of this finner, occafioned by the moft holy converfation of our Sauiour Iefus Iefus, and the good houre, in vvhich he receyued fuch a good gueft into his houfe. The good & firme purpofe, that Zachæus made to reftore the goods that he had il gotten, and to giue great almes of that,

which

vvhich he lavvfully poſſſſed, by occaſion wherof he might morally geſſe, that he ſhould become poore, though in truth he was neuer ſo
rich, ſith his ſoule was iuſtified, and beautified
with Gods grace, and himſelfe well inſtructed
in all thinges of his maiſter, to whome he gaue
a ſtrait accompt of his life paſt, and of that
vvhich he intended for the time to come, to the
end that that, wherein he erred, might be a-
mended.

5. To conſider, hovv our Sauiour approued the good deſire of Zachæus, and ſanctifi-
ed him, and all his family, that had a will to follow their head, and to be conuerted by his example. A man may ſerue himſelfe with this meditation for the receiuing of the holy Communion, by conſidering his owne littlenes, and the
infinite greatnes of God, repreſenting vnto himſelfe, that his diuine maieſty willeth him to come
ſpeedily downe from the height of his vanities,
to prepare him a place and lodging in his ſoule:
which he muſt ſeriouſly reſolue to doe, by making firme purpoſes to ſerue him for the time to
come, &c.

Meditat. LIX. *Of the Woman of Cananea.*
Matth. 15.

TO conſider, how this Woman cryed a-
loud after our Sauiour, beſeeching him to
cure a daughter of hers, whome the Diuell
tormented cruelly, and calling him Sonne of
Dauid.

Dauid. In which manner of prayer she discouered her great fayth, hauing a most great opinion
of our Sauiour; her charity in reputing her
daughters euills her owne; her humility in attri-
buting her afflictions to her owne sinnes: her
profound and surpassing reuerence towardes
him; her affection and constancy, which she discouered in that reiteration, shewing herselfe in
her demaund importune by repeating it againe
and againe. So must we doe in our prayers.

2. To consider, how our Sauiour seemed to be deafe at the Cananeans voyce, and
more then that, he made a semblance, that he
meant to refuse & reiect what she craued, & he
further in shew called her dog vnworthy to obtayne the effect of her petition. But we must vnderstand, that our Sauiour did this to trye, humble, and dispose her the better. For he proued
her in patience, in humility, & in perseuerance:
patience in supporting wordes of bitternes our
Sauiour vsed, without being displeased, or sur-
ceasing from that which she required: humility
in confessing, that she was indeed a poor dog aba-
doned &cast off, vnworthy to eat the crums that
fell fro the table of the childre: perseuerace, cou-
nuing still in her petition till the end.

3. To consider, how being intituled by
the name of dog for her humility, she subtilly al-
leadged one reason for the obtayning of what
she craued, saying, that the whelps also did eate
of the crums, that fell from the table of their
maysters. That in conclusion she got that at our
Sauiours handes, that she sought for, who re-
commen-

commended her meruailous faith, taking a pleafure to fee her fo humble, patient, and faythfull.
Whence I will learne, how accepted to the diuine maiefty be thofe, who haue their part in
thefe excellent vertues .

Meditat. LX. *Of the Centurion, whofe feruant our Sauiour healed . Matth. 8.*

TO confider this Centurion his piety, vvho
was fo carefull of the health of his feruant:
how he was wont to doe good workes, in
difpenfing what he had, about the reparation of
the Synagogues, and in doing much good to the
Iewes, though he were otherwife a Gentill. How
he was a man eminent for his great humility,
holding himfelfe vnworthy to appeare before
our Sauiours face, and therefore he fent vnto
him to craue the cure of his feruaunt, by the mediation of the Auncients of the people, who
might reprefent vnto him the good workes, he
had done them. The liuely fayth, that he had,
in belieuing and confeffing, that our Sauiour
was of power inough to cure his feruant, though
he fhould not take the paines to goe home to his
houfe. Whereby we muft learne to treate with
God more by affection of hart, then by word of
mouth.

2. To confider, how our Sauiour receiued
this Embaffage moft willingly, faying, that he
would himfelfe come in perfon, and cure him.
Whereunto the Centurion returned this anfwere,

were, that he was not worthy, that his maiesty
should enter into his house, but that he would
please but only to say the word, and he would
belieue, that his seruant should be healed. Where
is to be seene also our Sauiours most singular
bounty, in doing more then was of him required, as also the fayth and humility of the Cen-
tuturion, by occasion of which vertues he merited to produce other actes of more excellency.

3.   To consider, how our Sauiour greatly
commended this Centurions fayth, that he had
not yet found so great fayth in all the people of
Israel, though he were a Gentill: giuing to vnderstand, that there be many thousands of
soules, that be out of the Church, & that are
to enter into it, to enioy the right of the Kingdome of heauen for all eternity. As on the contrary, those vvho thinke themselues the children of it, shall be shut out, and cast dovvne
into outvvard darkenes for their bad vvorkes.
Finally to meditate, hovv our Sauiour cured
the sicke person by only saying the word.

*Meditat. LXI.   Of the Woman, whome our
Sauiour cured of a bloudy fluxe.* Matth. 9.

TO consider, what was the misery of this
poore Woman, & hovv little help she
had found in the Phisitians, who had
made her spend al her goods without profit, besides the sore paynes she had endured for the
space

space of twelue yeares, God so permitting, that she might recurre to the Phisitian of heauen, in whose power alone it is to heale the incurable diseases. We must consider here, how our soule is spiritually sicke, as this poore Woman was corporally: to consider the great fayth she had, in beleeuing that if she could but only touch the hem of our Sauiours garment, she should be eased and rid of her fowle and incurable malady, as she was indeed in an instant, that coming secretly behind our Sauiour, she had toucht his garment: in which action togeather with her wonderfull fayth did also appeare her respect, and humility. By this we must learne, with what fayth and reuerence vve ought to come to the most B. Sacrament of the Altar, to the end that by touching the Sacramétal species, which be as it were our Sauiours garments, the fluxe of our bad propensions and inclinations may leaue vs in perfect health of soule.

2. To consider how our Sauiour, after he had wroght this miracle, would that it should be disse couered, & made known, who had cócealed many other miracles at other tymes. But this he did for our instruction in three respects. The first is, to giue vs to see & vnderstand the differéce, that is betweene them, who touch him in his Sacra-craments with reuerence, humility, and deuotion, and those who come vnto them without any of these. The second was for the remedy-ing and helping of the ignorance of this poore woman, who, though she were otherwise very deuout, thought neuertheles, that she might

touch

touch our Sauiour, and he perceiue it not : and therefore she touched him in the great thronge, and presse of the people. And this was the reason for which he asked, who had touched him, giuing to vnderstand, that nothing was to his eyes hidden. The third was, to take away from the poore woman the bad confusion and shame, that troubled her for her infirmity, thinking that because it was fowle and shamefull, all the world would shunne her, as one vncleane : and further to imprint in her hart the vertue of humility, and withall to teach vs not to suffer the confusion of our sinnes to hinder our coming to the Sacrament of pennance for the Confession of them.

3.   To consider, how this poore Woman, trembling for feare, least she had displeased our Sauiour, came and cast her selfe downe at his feete. How our Sauiour comforted her, calling her his daughter, and willing her to goe her way in peace. Whence I will learne, that God is more pleased, that I repayre vnto him by loue, then that I forbeare to approach vnto him by feare.

Meditat. LXII.   Of the sicke man, healed by our Sauiour, at the pond of Probatica. Ioan. 5.

TO consider, how this Pond of water receyued the bloud of the beasts, that were sacrificed in the Temple, about which there
                                                were

were many ficke and difeafed perfons, that one of them might be cured at the tyme, that an Angell came downe, and it was a figure of the Sacraments, which our Sauiour was to inſtitute in his Church, in communicating vnto them vertue by the effufion of his bloud. That the miracle of the curing of the firſt ficke perfon, that entred and went downe into the Pond, contayned three things. The firſt, that it perfectly cured all maladyes of the body: the fecond, that an Angell defcended for that effect from heauen: The third, that it healed but one euery time, that is, the firſt that entred in, in recompenfe of his diligence. That this Pond was particularly a figure of the Sacraments of Baptifme, and Pennance, which haue the fame fpirituall effect in a moſt high degree of perfection without comparifon, meafure, or limitation, by meanes of the coming downe of the Angell of great Counfell, our Sauiour, & Redeemer Iefus Chriſt, curing, and cleanfing all ſtaynes at all tymes, and in all forts of perfons.

2. To confider our Sauiours moſt fingular humanity and benignity in entring into this hofpitall, that was filled with thofe, that were fick of incurable maladies, where he afked of one of thẽ, who had cõtinued ficke the fpace of 38. years, if he defired to be cured; for that to the iuſtifying of a finner there muſt cõcurre two wills, the one of God, the other our owne. The ficke mans anfwere, declaring his will, & what was in his power, faying, That he had not a man to help him, nor force in himfelfe to goe into the

V　　　　water:

water: where we are to obserue, how the vnderstāding of our own weaknes is vnto vs necessary
towards the receiuing of graces & fauors at Gods
hands. The perseuerance of the same patient in
expecting for 38. yeares, and attending still his
cure without vexing himselfe therefore, or murmuring against any. By this I must learne to
persist in prayer, though it be long, before I obtayne what I craue.

3. To consider, how our Sauiour willed
this poore man to take vp his bed, and goe his
way, after his perfect cure, manifesting in this
his omnipotent power, that in an instant gaue
perfect health to this poore sicke person, abandoned of the whole world, an effect, which he
produceth daily in the spirituall curing of souls.
This man also gaue a testimony of perfect obedience, by taking vp, and carying away of his
bed, without further consideration of the Saboth
day, on which it was forbiddē, that none should
cary any burden, and by answering them, who
found fault with him, that he, who had healed
him, willed him so to doe, and that therfore it
was simply permitted him. Wherein we haue
an excellent example to submit our iudgement
perfectly to that of God.

4. To consider, how this man seing himselfe whole, went presently to the temple to giue
God thanks for his recouery, where our Sauiour
finding him, sayd vnto him: Behold thou art
made whole; sinne no more, least some worse
thing chaunce vnto thee. In which words he
giueth him three admonitions, and those most
importing.

importing. The first, that maladyes happen, for the more part, as a punishment for the sinnes. The second, that the sinner must make a firme purpose neuer (with the help of Gods grace) to offend God any more. The third, that the relapse is much worse, then is the first fall, by reason of ingratitude. To consider, how this man, where euer he went, made it with great feruour euery where knowne, that it was Iesus, who had cured him, declaring by his example that, which they ought to doe, who receiue any fauour at Gods hands, that is, to render him thanks, and desire, that all haue knowledge of his diuine bounty.

Meditat. LXIII. Of the Leaper, whome our Sauiour cleanfed, and fent to the Priestes. Matth. 8.

TO confider, the humble petition of this poore Leaper, made to our Sauiour, who humbly cast himfelfe downe at his feete, & said vnto him: Lord, if thou wilt, thou canst make me cleane. Where he manifested much reuerence both inward and outward, togeather with a liuely fayth, and perfect refignation, wherewith we ought also to prefent our felues before God, &c.

2. To confider, how our Sauiour ftretching forth his hand, touched, and healed him, faying: I will. Be thou made cleane: fhewing thereby his great compaffion, and infinite

V 2   bounty.

bouutv. For without conceyuing any horrour at his fowlenes, which made the man hideous and fearefull to fee, he benignely touched him to cure him. And it is expreſſely ſayd, That he ſtretched forth his hand to make him cleane, whereby he gaue to vnderſtand, that he ſhould bring perfect health & cure to the World, whē he ſhould ſtretch his holy hands on the tree of the Croſſe.

3.   To conſider, how our Sauiour willed the Leaper to preſent himſelfe to the Prieſts, & to make his offring in the Temple: In which he ſhewed himſelfe a Zelatour, and obſeruer of the law: to the end alſo we may learne, that e-uery ſoule, ſtayned with the ſpirituall Leapro-ſy of ſinne, notwithſtanding it hath obtayned pardon by true contrition, muſt yet preſent it ſelfe to a Prieſt, and diſcouer vnto him the Lea-proſy in the Sacrament of Confeſſion, & then offer vnto God the ſacrifice of an humbled and contrite ſpirit, & finally humbly receiue the ſen-tence of abſolution.

4.   To conſider, how, after our Sauiour had wrought this miracle, he expreſly forbad the Leaper to diuulge it, giuing vnto vs an ex-ample of humility; which he yet did, notwith-ſtanding ſuch prohibition, & made it euery where kuowne, moued, as it is credible, by an inſtinct of the holy Ghoſt, in teſtimony of his gratitude, & of an acknowledgement of the be-nefit receyued, to the end our Sauiour might be knowne to the whole world.

                                        Meditat.

Meditat. LXIIII.   *Of the ten Leapers,
whome our Sauiour cleansed, and sent to the
Priestes. Luc.* 17.

TO consider, how these ten Leapers made
their petition, lifting vp their voyce a far
off, and saying : Iesus, mayster haue pitty on vs. Wherein they testifyed their great humility and renerence, standing a loose, and not
daring to come neere, as also their hope, in vniting, and ioyning their consents, and voyces in
making their prayer togeather, wherby it is
made more acceptable.

2. To consider, how our Sauiour sent them
to the Priests, & how they, obedient to his commaundement, were miraculously healed on the
way, where we are to obserue that our Sauiour,
the author of this cure, and of all other our
happy euents, meant to proue the obedience of
these Leapers, in regard whereof, and of their
fayth towardes him, he wrought this miracle,
to teach vs to obey, and to submit our selues in
all humility to the Priestes and pastours of the
Church.

3. To consider, how one of these ten Leapers, who was a Samaritane, seeing himselfe
cured, returned to render our Sauiour thankes,
who had done him that good, whiles the other
nyne neglected to doe the same. Wherein is
seene liuely expressed the extreme ingratitude
of men, who receiue benefitts dayly at Gods

V 3   hands,

hands, and yet very few there be, that giue him thankes for them: a proceeding that greatly displeaseth him, as our Sauiour gaue to vnderstand himselfe, when sweetly complayning of the ingratitude of the other nyne Leapers, he sayd : were there not ten made cleane, & where are the nyne? This Samaritan alone hath giuen glory to God. And he spake very benignely also vnto him in compensation of his gratitude. Here we must consider, that this Samaritan liuely representeth that which oftentims bapneth to many great sinners, who shew themselues, more gratefull to God for the fauours receiued at his most magnificent hand, thē many other iust persons, who continue ful oftē very remisse, & cold.

Meditat. L X V.   Of the blind man to whome our Sauiour restored sight in the way to Hiericho. Mat. 10. *Luc.* 18.

TO consider, how this blind man, knowing that Iesus was to passe that way, where he sat begging, cryed with a lowd voyce, saying : Iesus, the Sonne of Dauid, haue mercy vpon me. And the more he was willed to hold his peace, the more he raised vp his voice, shewing therein a most great fayth, and stedfast hope in our Sauiour Iesus, togeather with a wonderfull feruour, and deuout affection, arising of the vnderstāding he had of his blindnes, perseuering also constantly in his petition, whiles all that other did, or could do, could not make him hold

his

his tongue. Wherin by a certayne force & violence he obtained thinges worthy the imitating.

2. To confider, how at the firſt our Sauiour made ſemblance not to heare him, for the
trying of his conſtancy, which after he knew,
he cauſed him to be brought before him, all the
multitude, that followed him, making a ſtand
to ſee the miracle, and aſked of him, what it was
he deſired of him. Where we are to obſerue, &
to imagine, that God asketh the very ſame of
vs, and we muſt make him the ſame anſwere,
that the blind-man did, & ſay: Lord, that I may
ſee: & much more deſire to heare our Sauiours
anſwere, which was: Do thou ſee.

3. To confider, the exceeding great ioy,
that the blind-man felt at the hart, when it was
told him, that Ieſus called him : for credible it
is, that he made towardes him with all the haſt
he could poſſibly make. How that after the recouery of his ſight he followed our Sauiour, e-
uery where, and to all perſons reporting the miracle, that our Sauiour had wrought vpon him.
And this we muſt vſe for our inſtruction, that
if it pleaſe God to beſtow fauours vpon vs, we
be not ingrate vnto him for the ſame.

Meditat. LXVI. Of the miracle, that our Sauior
wrought vpon him, who was borne blind. Ioan. 9.

TO confider, how our Sauiour paſſing by,
where there was one borne bling, looked
vpon him, much pitying the poore mans
caſe. Where we are to marke, that God caſteth

his

his eyes vpon the good in another manner, then
he doth vpon bad. How the afflictions, and infirmities of body be not alwayes for the chasti-
sing of the sinne of the soule, but are sometimes
sent for manifestation of Gods infinite power,
and wisdome, whiles he draweth good of such
euils, which be the subiect & argument of his glory. To examine & ponder our Sauiors words: I
must work the work of him, that sent me, whils
it is day: for the night will come, when none can
worke. As long as I am in the world, I am the
light of the world. Wordes, that be full of
matter of solidity, & ought diligently to be con-
sidered.

2.   To consider, how our Sauiour Iesus
taking clay and tempering it with his spittle,
layd it vpon the blindman-lyes, thereby manifesting his omnipotency, for that he restored the
sight by that, which was apt inough to take the
sight away. And this was also to teach vs, that
the way to recouer the sight of soule, and the
spirituall light of grace, is to lay before our eyes,
that we are clay, ashes, & dust, composed of our
Sauiours spittle, that is, made and formed by
his wisdome. To consider, how our Sauiour
willed this blind-man to goe to wash in the
Poole of Siloe, that is to say, (sent) meaning
figuratiuely the Sacraments of Baptisme, and
Pennance: And this blind-man, did with great
fayth, humility, and obedience, as he was willed, permitting the clay to be laid vpon his eyes,
without regarding that men might peraduenture mocke him, and laugh at him, as he should
                                        goe

goe a long in the ſtreets, of his owne ſimplici-
ty, and exactly obeying as our Sauiour had willed him.

3. To conſider the noble Confeſſion,
that this poore blind man made, who went vp
and downe, in teſtimony of the acknowledgement of the receyued benefit, euery where reporting, that Ieſus had healed him in his ſight,
without regard eyther of the Phariſies, or of
their rage and malice agaynſt our Sauiour, notwithſtanding they ſought to peruert him by all
the wayes, they poſſibly could : whiles he on
the contrary ſtill perſiſted conſtant in his confeſſion, in ſo much as he for it endured many
maledictions and imprecations at their hands,
and to be thruſt out of the Sinogogue for an ex-
communicated perſon.

4. To conſider, how our Sauiour Ieſus,
knowing what the blind-man had ſuffered for
loue of him, comforted him, and confirmed
him in his fayth, and increaſed in him an inward light of ſoule, by meanes whereof he
came to haue a knowledge of his diuine maieſty, adoring him proſtrate vpon the ground, as
the only Sonne of God.

Meditat. L X V I I.   Of him, that was both deafe and dumbe, whome our Sauiour cured with spittle. Mar. 7. Luc. 11.

TO consider, how by this man is represented the spirituall silence, and deafnes of the soule ; the one, a default of fayth and obedience, & the other of praier & of confessió. These two faults are wont to goe in company togeather, for as much as the enemy doth almost alwaies ioyne them in the soule of a sinner: we must apply this to our selues. To thinke, that this poore man would neuer of himselfe haue come to our Sauiour, if others had not intreated for him. And therefore we are to learne, how much the company of the prayers of the good auayleth.

2   To consider, how our Sauiour, taking this sicke person by the hand, tooke him a part, and put his fingars into his eares, and then with his spittle touched his tongue, cast his eyes vp to heauen, and groaned saying vnto him, Be thou opened. Where is to be obserued, how great a difficulty it is to cure the vices, that haue také roote in the soule by long custome, & that such, as be touched therewith, must retyre themselues from conuersation with the world if they desire their deliuery. Such soules, as those, doe cause our Sauiour to groane and to fetch deep sighes, who for the manifestation of the difficulty of the curing of them, would obserue

ferue all thefe ceremonies, though he could, if he
had pleafed, haue cured the malady with a
word.

3.   To confider, how this man was fodainly cured of all his infirmityes, and began to
fpeake very vvell. And though our Sauiour
forbad them, who were prefent, to diuulge the
miracle, yet they could not hould their tongues,
but made report of it with lowd voyce, faying:
He hath done all things well. He hath made the
deafe to heare, and the dumbe to fpeake. Of
thefe words I will make my profit, reflecting v-
pon this deuout peoples gratitude and acknowledgement, vvhoby their manner of reafoning
confefled that he, who had done fo many miracles & fo great, could yet vvorke other much
greater.

Meditat. L X V I I I.   *Of him, who had a
deafe and dumbe fpirit: which could not be
caft out by the Difciples. Matth.* 17. *Marc.*
9. *Luc.* 9.

T O confider, hovv one came to our Sauiour, and caft himfelfe dovvne at his feete,
craving help of him for his Sonne, vvho
vvas cruelly tormented by the Diuell. For fome-
tymes he cafteth him into the fire, at other times
into the vvater, maketh him gnafh vvith the
teeth, and to beate his head agaynft the vvalls.
Here vye may confider the povver, and cruelty
of the Diuell, vvhen God giueth him leaue to
                                        torment

torment men, whome he hateth to the death: and the great mischiefs he doth, & the fearefull effects he worketh vnto them, and in them, on whome he hath seized. To consider, how great his rage and fury shall be agaynst the damned, when he shall haue them vnder his power in hel in effect, as he already holdeth them here in hope, and how miserable a case it is to serue this cruell tyrant: and to contemplate by the way also the fowlenes, and enormity of mortall sinne.

2. To consider, how our Sauiour in this action cryed out agaynst the incredulous, who stood by, for whose incredulity this poore man could not be cured, but vvas tormented in the presence of our Sauiour in a more cruell manner then accustomed, our Sauiour so permitting it, to the end the fury and rage of the Diuell agaynst him, and all mankind might appeare. To obserue the wordes of the yong mans Father, saying to our Sauiour: If thou hast any power, help vs, and haue pity on our misery. Whose weake and wauering fayth he confirmed rather, then to doe any other thing, and so the man added, saying: I belieue, Lord, helpe my incredulity, meaning to say, I belieue as much as I can, and I pray thy goodnes to supply vvhat there is vvanting of fayth on my part.

3. To consider, how our Sauiour menaced the malignant spirit, and commaunded him to goe forth, and to enter into the yong man no more. Wherin he discouered his omnipotency, by

by forbidding him to returne, for as much as he knew very well, how fore and bitter a thing it was for the Diuell to abandone the foule, which he had long poffeffed, and what wayes, and deuifes he vfeth to returne to the poffeffion of it agayne. To confider, with what fweetnes our Sauiour tooke the poffeffed perfon by the hand. For it is proper to him to giue his hand to them, who lye vpon the ground to raife them vp: and he gaue the fonne to his Father, to fhew that he did good, *gratis*, without refpeſt of any his owne particular intereſt at all.

4. To confider, how our Sauiour blamed his Apoftles in fecret of their little faith, teaching them, that for the working of great miracles a man muſt haue a liuely fayth, like vnto a graine of muſtard, that is to fay, a vehement, ftrong & eff ſmall fayth in a little and low fubieſt, and he muſt withall ioyne prayer and fafting with the fame fayth, of which other vertues muſt take their beginning.

Medita. L X I X. *Of the Refufcitation of the daughter of the Prince of the Synagogue. Matth.* 9. *Marc.* 5.

T O confider, how death tooke away this poore yong mayde in the flower of her age, without regard had to her nobility, in the middeſt of her riches wherein is to be feene the little aſſurance, that is to be had in this miſerable life. How fhe being dead, fhe could not

X   come

come herselfe to pray our Sauiour to bring her to life agayne, but it was necessary that her Father should come to prostrate himselfe at our Sauiours feete, and to intreate that it might please him to take the paines to go to his house, to lay his omnipotent hand vpon his daughter: whereby we are to learne, how much the intercession of the iust profiteth, and is necessary.

2. To consider the sweet benignity of our Sauiour, who franckly offered to goe whither he was required, where he entred in company only of three of his disciples, to teach vs to shun ostentation and vayne glory, and in all thinges to seeke humility. For this was one of the greatest miracles, that he had hitherto wrought, because it stood vpon the resuscitation of one, that was dead, to life.

3. To consider, how he tooke the dead person by the hand, & with a lowd voyce said vnto her, Woman arise. And at that very instant she rose, and walked, and he willed that meate should be brought her to eate. Wherin our Sauiour gaue to vnderstand, how great efficacy there was in his wordes, & how they, who sinne of frailty, meant by this yong mayde, are easily raysed to life agayne by the fauourable hand of God, who assisteth and helpeth them in ouercoming their weaknes, commaunding them not to continue in idlenes for the tyme to come, but to exercise themselues in good workes, eating the celestiall bread, that confirmeth, & strengtheneth the hart, and this is the most B. Sacrament of the Altar.

Medi-

Meditat. L X X . *Of the death, and raysing to life the Sonne of the widow of Naim .*

TO confider, that there is neyther tyme, nor age, nor perfon, free from the affaults and expectation of death, and that this yong man, departed this life, is a liuely repreſentation and figure of a finner, fpiritually dead by mortall finne, whofe foule is in the body, as a corps vpon the beere, caryed ftreight to hell by foure violent paffions, to wit, luxury, vanity or ambition of honour, auarice, & wrath, paffions that cary the miferable finner into the bottóleffe gulfe of all wickednes, therby to preæipitate him finally into hell. The great charity of our Sauiour, who came purpofely to the Citty of Naim to meete the dead corps at the gate therof, for we muft not thinke, that it hapned by chaunce .

2 . To confider, how our Sauiour would refufcitate this dead corps in publike, out of his compaffion to the poore widdow, whofe only fonne he was. How fhe vfed no words, but fpake only by her teares, which was the thing that fo moued our Sauiour, as he touched the beere with his hand, and forthwith ravfed the yong man to life. Here we learne the efficacy & great force of teares, and of diuine infpirations for our rayfing from death to life.

3 . To confider, how this yong man being refufcitated, he rayfed himfelfe vp vpon the

X a   Beere,

Beere, and began to speake, representing therby, that sinners, long tyme accustomed to sinne, are cured by little and little, by confession of their faults. How our Sauiour restored the sonne liuing to his mother the good widdow, comforting her, and easing her of her affliction.

Meditat. L X X I.   Of the Resuscitation of Lazarus. *Ioan. 11.*

T O consider, how Lazarus being fallé sicke, his sisters Martha and Mary gaue our Sauiour to vnderstand thereof by a short letter, conceiued in these wordes: Lord, behold, he, whome thou louest, is sicke. Where we are taught an admirable manner of addressing our petitions and prayers, by representing in few wordes our necessities to the diuine Maiesty, & saying: O Lord God, he, whome thou louest, is heauy, afflicted, and desolate, drye, & cold in deuotion: A petition, that must be made with a confidence in the diuine goodnes, with an assurance of his loue, and with a great resignation of our own will vnto his.

2.   To consider the answere our Sauiour made, which was: This sicknes is not to death. By which wordes his meaning was to comfort those two deuout sisters, and by the same means to make an experiment of their fayth, hope, patience, resignation, & other vertues.

3.   To consider, how two dayes expired, our Sauiour deliberated to goe into Iury, notwithstanding

standing the difficulties his disciples represented
vnto him , and the passed daungers , for the encouraging of them to doe the like , saying vnto
them : That there were twelue houres in a day,
and that they , who walked by day in the light,
could not stumble , because they saw the light :
teaching vs by this , with how great a sollicitude
and care we ought to liue , and take paynes, before the light and day of grace passeth away, especially being so short , as there be but twelue
houres at the most , during which , the variable
and inconstant will of ours may chaunge, and of
good become bad . How our Sauiour discouered
vnto his Apostles the death of Lazarus vnder
the name of sleepe , giuing them to vnderstand ,
that it was to him as easy a matter to resuscitate
him from death , as it was to awake him from
sleepe : & he told them plainly afterwards , that
he was dead, to take from them the repugnance
and ill will, they had to goe into Iury . By occasion whereof S. Thomas began couragiously to
say : Let vs also goe, and dye with him : therby
shewing his feruour , and giuing good example
to the rest of his companions .

4 . To consider , how , when our Sauiour approached , and was come neere to the
castle of Bethania , Martha came forth to meete
him, and weeping sayd vnto him : Lord, if thou
hadst been heere , my Brother had not dyed.
Whereby we are giuen to vnderstand, how miserable be the effects , that arise to Gods absence
from our soules . To consider the conference,
that passed between our Sauiour, & this deuout

X₃   Woman,

Woman, whome he enformed and confirmed
by degrees in the fayth, vntill in conclusion she
came to confesse, that it was in his power to restore her deceased brother to life agayne.

5. To consider, how Martha called her Si-
ster Mary to come forth to our Sauiour, who
arose presently, to shew her great obedience,
and resp ̃ & she caried towards him, went forth,
and cast her selfe downe at his feete, certainely
belieuing, that he would resuscitate her brother
Lazarus. To consider, that by these two sisters
be represented two manners of life, the actiue
and the contemplatiue, which must goe togeather in the resuscitation of a sinner, that is, prayer must go in company with preaching: because
prayer commonly is of more force then it.

6. To consider the teares, that our Sauiour
did sheed, before he raysed Lazarus, as well
of compassion, weeping with those that wept,
as also by occasion of sinne, that brought death
to the world: and for the obstinacy of the incredulous and vnbelieuing Pharisies, who were
present. To consider, how hauing caused the
stone to be taken away, that was vpon the sepulcher, he lifted his eyes vp to heauen, & gaue
thankes to his Eternall Father, for that he alwais
heard him. By which I must learne to rayse my
hart vp to God, before I begin any thing, especially if it be such, as goeth accompanyed with
difficulty.

7. To consider, how our Sauiour cryed
with a lowd voyce, saying: Lazarus, come forth:
& how that very instant the dead body rose vp
with

with his face bound vp in a napkin , to giue the
more ample proofe of the miracle . For this I
will reioyce and be glad . Seeing that God is of
power to doe so wonderfull thinges : and I will
learne how miserable the state of a sinner is, who
dyeth obstinate in his iniquities , sith he causeth
our sweet Iesus to shed teares , who is Ioy Eternall : crauing most affectuously of God , that he
would please to call me with his efficacious
voice, that I may rise out of the sepulcher of my
sinnes , miseries, and tepidities , to myne owne
particular good , and to doe him seruice : making besides a firme resolutiō to resigne my selfe
into the hands of my Superiours, that they may
vnloose me , and take from me the most heauy
and fatall bands of my passions , and disordered
affections , as the Apostles did vnloose Lazarus
in his sepulcher.

*Meditat. L X X I I.   Of the Councell , that the
Pharisies held agaynst our Sauiour. Ioan.* 11.

TO consider , how execrable a sinne that is
of Wrath, Malice , and Enuy ,sith he who
is seized therewith , draweth his infelicity
from that , whence he should haue his felicity ,
and conuerteth his medicine into poyson, as did
the Iewes , who , insteed of making their profit
of the resuscitation of Lazarus , and of taking
occasion therby to acknowlege our Sauiour for
true God , did for the same conceiue the greater
hatred , malice , & ill will agaynst him . To con-

sider, how the malignant did concurre in great diligence to that pernicious Councell, carryed thereunto by their passions, and Diuellish fury.

2. To consider, how Caiphas pronouced the setence of death against the innocet Iesus, adding wordes of disgrace agaynst others of the Councell, whome he called Ignorant, saying, That they knew nothing, for that it was expedient, that one should dye for the people, that the others might not perish. Vpon which we must obserue, that it was the holy Ghost; and not Cayphas, that did speake, for that God sometimes serueth himselfe of the tongue of wicked persons for the manifesting of his diuine will, as he did now manifest it by the mouth of this vnfortunate man, that the death of our Sauiour Iesus was most necessary, to the end the whole world might not perish.

3. To consider, how this sentence of his vvas receyued and confirmed vvith great applause of the whole Councell, where I am to wöder at our Sauiours patience, who caryed himselfe; as if he had knowne nothing of all that, which had passed: & the fidelity of his disciples, who did not abandone or forsake their mayster and Lord in so manifest a daunger, but kept cöpany with him in his retraite, for as much as he then retyred himselfe, and went aside, vntill the tyme of his passion should come. To consider, what motions, that compassionate & diuine hart of his felt within it selfe, when he saw, that he was euen then sentenced, and condemned to

death

death by thofe, who were fo deeply bound to
honour him.

*Meditat. LXXIII. Of the Wife-man, who
   built his houfe vpon a rocke : and of the Foole
   that founded his vpon the fand . Matth.* 7.
   Luc. 6.

TO Confider, that of fo many, as heare
      the word of God, and his holy doctrine,
   fome keep it, and practife it, and fuch be
called wife, becaufe they build vpon a rocke, &
do as they belieue : others heare it indeed, but
yet liue in a far different máner from that which
fayth teacheth them, and thefe are worthily called fooles. To confider, that the confciences,
which be the houfes of the one and the other, be
contiqually beaten with the windes of many
tentations; which yet the wife heare and refift,
and are not ouercome or ouerthrown by them,
where, on the contrary the fooles are caryed a-
way by thofe windes, by reafon of their negligence.

   4.   To confider, how the houfe, that is,
the confcience of a foole is borne down with the
leaft wind of tentation, that beateth vpon it, becaufe it is founded vpon the vnftable fand of fole
fayth without good workes, or vpon fayth that
is intermixed with terreftriall affections, as of
honours, goods, pleafures, &c. or becaufe it is
founded vpon Selfe-will, and proper Iudgement, which be things mutable, and inconftant.
                                                    a§

as is the sand. And herehence followeth the fall, and ouerthrow of the conscience, by occasion of the often reiterated sinnes. Such soules be like vnto Nabuchodonosors statue, which was huge and great, and stood vpon feete of brittle earth.

3. To consider, how the conscience of the good is sure, constant, and stable amiddest tentations, because the foundation of it is layd vpon a liuely faith; receyuing life from charity, vpon the mortification and abnegation of himselfe, vpon a firme resolution & purpose of doing all that is by God commaunded, rayfing the foundation of his workes vpon fayth, and the meritts of our Sauiour, the fundamentall, and immoueable stone of the faythfull.

Meditat. L X X I I I I.   Of the Parable of the Sower of seed. Math. 13. Luc. 8.

TO consider, how this seed is the word of God, as well that which is receiued by the outward eare, as that which God casteth into our soules by good inspirations. The sower is God, who scattereth his diuine seed eyther immediatly by himselfe, or by his seruaunts, or by other meanes, that he pleaseth to choose. The earth is the soule, with the powers threof: for in the Memory he soweth good thoughts: in the Vnderstanding diuine illustrations, and good cousailes: in the Will holy affections, & healthfull desires. And God casteth this seede, not for
any

any profit, he hopeth for himselfe, but for the soule, to make it better then it was, and a more fertill and fruit-bearing ground, of a bad and barrayne, as it was before, and therefore he cultiuateth, & manureth it continually, and soweth it from day to day. For this we must yield his diuine Maiesty thankes, and conceiue an earnest desire to vnderstand his holy word so, as we may effectually practise it.

2. To consider, that though this seede be precious, yet three parts of it be lost. One, because it falleth vpon the way, that is, vpon an hart, soyled, and todden on with all manner of terrene thoughts, in which the Diuells doe make hauocke of the good seede. Another, for that it is cast vpon a stony soyle, which putteth forth some blades, but it is soone parched, & easily withereth away. By which be meant those, who hauing some naturall sweetnes, doe heare the word of God with some little tast, yet the Diuell no sooner tempteth them, then that they forthwith forget that word, and their good purposes dye, and vanish away by occasion of their inconstancy, and mutable disposition, & because they are nothing well founded in humility. The third falleth among thornes, which grow, and choke the good seed. And these be the soules, that dreame, and thinke vpon nothing, but riches, and the pleasures of the flesh, and of the world. And we must obserue, that riches, pricking cares, and sensuall pleasures, be called thornes in the schoole of our Sauiour Iesus himselfe.

3. To consider, that the seede, that fell v-

pon

pon the good ground, yielded forth great abundance of fruit : and those be they, who willingly
heare , and receyue the vvord of God . All this
confidered, I vvill refolue to take paynes & procure , that this good and diuine feed fructify in
my foule thirty-fold , and threefcore-fold, or an
hundred-fold, accordingly as my religious pro-
feßion requireth .

*Meditat . L X X V .   Of the Parable of the
Cockle. Matth. 13.*

TO confider the vvordes of this parable , in
which our Sauiour teacheth, that it is himfelfe , vvho fovveth the good feed in the
foule of the iuft ones , vvho by their example &
inftruction produce other iuft ones, as be themfelues. That the enemy of nature foweth Cockle,
that is, bad men , vvhome he exciteth to offend
God, and they are very properly reprefented &
meant by this feede: for as much , as vvhen it is
little in the blade, it is like vnto the vvheat , but
vvhen it becometh great in the eare , it is eafily
knovvne and difcouered by the blackenes, Euen
fo the bad , liuing intermixed vvith the good ,
are not alvvayes knovvne for fuch ; but vvhen
they come to the point of death , then they giue
to vnderftand , hovv blacke they are, touching
their manner , and courfe of life paft . That the
enemy fovveth this Cockle, vvhiles men are a
fleepe , that is , he peruerteth the good, and maketh them bad , vvhen they fleepe negligently
in

in flouth, and coldnes of deuotion, and this he
doth by time and leyfure, and in secret, that he
may not be difcouered, cafting a ftone, as the
faving is, and hiding the hand, that caft it.
Whence I muft learne to be watchfull, and to
liue with follicitude, care, and due circumfpe-
ction.

2. To confider, how the feruants of the
goodman of the houfe, faid vnto him: Sir,
did you not fow good feede in your field?
Whence then hath it Cockle? As though they
had faid, how is it poffible, that there fhould be
wicked men on the earth, feeing there be fo many celeftiall rofes in the Sacraments! fo many
good infpirations, that touch them from tyme
to tyme, and fo many benefitts, and continuall
fauours beftowed on them! The anfwere of the
maifter of the houfe was this. The enemy, man,
hath done this; infinuating thereby, that he had
himfelfe for his part fowen good feede, but the
diuell had ouerfowed Cockle, out of the hatred
and malice, he carryeth to God and men, and
therefore is he called the fower of the Cockle of
tentations in our harts. Moreouer a man, who
hath the liberty of his owne freewill, may be
conuerted into Cockle, if he fuffer himfelfe to
be ouercome of the flefhes defires, and may become an enemy to himfelfe, and to his faluation.

3. To confider, how the feruants afked
leaue of the mayfter of the family to pull the
Cockle vp by the roots, but he would not permit them, for feare they might pull vp the good
Y   corne

corne togeather with it . Wherein is infinuated the exceffiue zeale, wherwith the iuft are fome-tymes carryed away, who feeing fo much ini-quity in the world, would pull all vp togeather at once, and deftroy all the Cockle of the bad at one tyme, and would preuent the tyme, that the eternall prouidence hath prefixed, and confider not the daunger, that might be of pulling vp the good corne, that is the good and vertuous, with them, tranfported more with a fpirit of Anger & indignation, then of compaffion . To confider the infinit charity of our good God, which ap-peareth in the mayfter of the families anfwere, who thogh he did at once pull vp all the Cockle of the bad Angells in heauen, and precipitated them downe from thence, would not yet vfe the like rigour and feuerity towards men, but gaue them tyme of doing pennance . His charity is further to be feene in this, that for loue of the good corne, he will not haue the Cockle pulled vp, fuffering the bad for refpect of the good, as he teftifyed in the punifhment of the Sodomits, in whofe Citty if he had found but ten iuft men, he would haue pardoned all the reft; and yet he faued the corne, that is to fay, Lot .

4. To confider the anfwere of the good man of the houfe in thefe wordes : Suffer the one and the other to grow, till the tyme of har-ueft, and then the Cockle fhall be feuered from the good corne. That is to fay, vntill the end of the world there will alwayes be good & bad, the one growing in holines, the other in wickednes, and when the harueft of Iudgement fhall be

come,

come , the corne fhall be referued and kept for
the granaries of heauen , and the Cockle fhall be
caſt into hell-fire by heapes . For as the wicked
doe confpire and confent togeather to doe miſ-
chiefe in this life : fo fhall they be put togeather,
& broyle togeather for eternity in the other.

Medĭtat . L X X V I . *Of the Parable of the*
Muſtard-feed. Matth. 13.

TO confider, hovv our Sauiour is reprefented by this grayne, which for bignes is very little , yea the very leaſt of all other
feedes , vile for outward apparence, and without colour, & yet the efficacy of it is very great,
which then moſt appeareth , when it is grownd
and eaten . Euen fo our Sauiour, as touching his
exteriour humanity was little, as other men be ,
and but as a little graine : yet in as much as
concerned his foule , and much more his diuinitv hidden, he had an infinite efficacy and vertue,
which then appeareth moſt , when we more inwardly confider his myfteries, efpecially that of
the B Sacrament. Moreouer this little grayne
reprefenteth the iuſt , the Cittizens of heauen ,
who both in the opinion of the world , and in
their owne , be little , who yet before God be
moſt great in refpect of their vertue, which they
make knowne in perfecution. The muſtard-feed
alfo fignifieth the vertues , by meanes whereof
men come to be poffeffed of the Kingdome of
heauen . For they carry not any outward appa-

rence

rence of greatnes, or loftynes, and vet be they efficacious, and of power in their effects, as is to be seene in the eight Beatitudes.

2. To confider, that neceffary it is for the caufing of this grayne to fructify, and to be profitable, that it be firft of all fowne, and caft into the ground, that it may take deepe roote firft, & after grow, and become a great tree. Euen fo our Sauiour Iefus, who made himfelfe man for loue of vs, and humbled himfelfe here on earth euen vnto death, became a great tree, yea fo great an one, as he doth now fuftaine & fupport the machines of both heauen and earth, & intertaineth with his Bleffed fruits both thofe inhabitants on high, and thefe pilgrimes beneath. To confider, how in imitation of our Sauiour the iuft, who are like vnto the little graynes of muftard, grow, and become great in holynes by meanes of mortification, pennance, and the abnegation of themfelues.

3. To confider, how this graine growing vp into a fayre tree, extendeth, and dilateth the braunches, that ferue for an harbour for the fowles of the ayre, both to neftle in, and to reft on. Euen fo our Sauior hath through the whole world extended the branches of his Sacraments, his good examples, vertues, & Saintlike works, on which the holy and humble foules do repofe, and receyue their comfort. There is it, whither they retyre themfelues, and finge Canticles of prayfe, and thankesgiuing, whiles they are there in their fpirituall quiet and retraite. In the very like manner the iuft extend the braunches

of

of their heroicall acts and vertues, with the light whereof they doe heere on earth diſſipate and driue away our darkenes , giue occaſion to thouſands to imitate them ; and in truth it impoſteth vs greatly to endeauour to follovv them .

Meditat. L X X V I I. Of the Parable of the Merchant , who ſought for precious ſtones . Matth. 18.

TO conſider, how all men generally doe naturally ſeeke for ſome good, or other , vvhiles ſome ſearch after the temporall , tranſitory , and ſuch as ſeeme to be good , and thoſe be riches , honors , & pleaſurs : others a- gavne ſeeke after the eternall , permanent , and ſuch as be true goods indeed , & thoſe by the meanes of vertue. We muſt endeauour to be of the number of theſe , that when we come to dye, we may not find our ſelues to be deceiued, thinking to be rich, when we ſhall be in extreme pouerty.

2.   To conſider , that the precious pearle we muſt ſeeke for , is Ieſus Chriſt, true God, & man, as alſo the vertues , which he teacheth vs , and this by the way of prayer and contemplati- on , of good deſires , and deuout affections , of frequentation of the Sacraments , and by other vertuous, & pious actions .

3.   To conſider, how, when the wiſe Mer- chant had found out one precious pearle , he

fold all that he had, & bought it : in imitation of
whome, hauing found God, we muſt abandone
and leaue all thinges terrene, mortify and ouercome our inordinate paſſions, and renounce all
that we poſſeſſe and haue, not in any cold manner, or to rid our ſelues of them, but with a feruour, not ſtaying vpon the ſearching & finding
out of precious ſtones, and of riches, that appeare
for ſuch, but of thoſe, that be ſuch indeed.

4.   To conſider, that this one precious
pearle ſignifyeth Euangelicall perfection, which
the Religious profeſſe in imitation of our Sauiour Ieſus, which is ſayd to be but one, becauſe
it doth in a moſt eminent and moſt perfect manner contayne all the precepts of the loue both of
God, and of our neighbour, & is of ſuch worth,
and ſo high a price, as when God diſcouereth the
valew of it to a man, he moſt willingly ſelleth all
that he poſſeſſeth for the buying therof, and leaueth the world, and all that it may pretend for
moſt excellent or moſt pleaſing, and both by
effect, and in affection diſburdeneth himſelfe of
all thinges terrene.

*Meditat . LXXVIII.   Of the good Paſtour,
who ſought for his ſtrayed sheepe. Ioan. 10.*

TO conſider, how this good Paſtour our Sauiour Ieſus Chriſt, who came down from
heauen to be the Paſtour of men, whome
he gouerneth with a wonderfull prudence, and
ſingular vigilancy, omitting nothing, that concerneth

cerneth the office of a good Paſtour. The hundred ſheep be all the faythfull of Gods Church
in generall, though in particular they be the iuſt
ones, who know their Paſtour, heare his voyce,
obey him, and imitate his vertues, receyue their
nouriture and intertainment from him, giue him
their wooll, and their milke, that is, conſecrate
vnto him all that they haue, and their pleaſure,
and ſacrifice themſelues for him, when need requireth, as he was himſelfe ſacrificed for them.
That the ſtrayed, and loſt ſheepe is the ſinner,
that leaueth the company of the iuſt, neither hearing nor obeying the voyce and call of his Paſtour, nor taking any pleaſure in the paſture of
the holy Sacraments, nor of the holy doctrine
and inſtructions, that be giuen him, but with
paſſion tracing the footſteps of the world, where
he drinketh the troubled, and taynted water of
the crazed ciſterns, and finally falleth into the
power of thoſe infernall wolues, who runne vp
and downe, enraged with an hunger to deuoure
the ſheepe of our Sauiour Ieſus Chriſts fold. To
conſider the infinit charity of this heauenly Paſtour, who leauing ninty nine ſheepe in the deſert, came to ſeeke that one that was gone aſtray,
and was not at quiet, vntill he had found it, and
caried it backe to the flocke. For this cauſe he
came downe from heauen vnto the earth, trauayled much, and tooke much paynes, and endured much more for the gayning of ſoules, and
of ſinners, euen to the ſpending of his moſt precious bloud to doe them good.

     e, To conſider, how our Sauiour alwayes
         Y 4   had

had this charitable care to feeke out the fheepe,
that was gone aftray, by inward infpirations
and motions, by his preachers, by pious
bookes, and by a thoufand wayes befides,
confirming thereby the great defire he had to
find it agayne: and when he had found it, he
did charitably take it vp vpon his owne fhoulders, without beating it with a ftaffe, or drawing it by the leggs. Thus doth our diuine Paftour deale with a finner, plunged in myre of
vices, if he ftrayeth not out of his holy prefence. Therefore we are to craue of him, that he
would pleafe to feeke vs out, as poore fheepe,
ftrayed from his field, & flocke.

3.   To confider, how glad our Sauiour
was after the finding of his ftrayed fheep, when
he inuited his holy Angells in heauen, & men
on earth to reioyce with him. Wherehence it
followeth, that the holy Angells receiue a new
accidentall ioy, euery tyme, that a finner is
conuerted: euen as on the contrary they are fory, and the Diuells iocund and glad, when the
iuft fall into finne.

Meditat. L X X I X.   Of the Prodigall
Sonne. Luc . 15 .

TO confider, how by the Father of thefe two
Sonns is meant God: by the elder Son be
fignifyed the good & vertuous, & by the
yõger who was difobediét & prodigal, be figured
the bad & wicked. For difobedience goeth euer
accompanied with imprudency, pride, & vanity,
in

in so much as it seemeth to them, who are touched with this vice, that the diuine maiesty is bound to them. On the contrary the good, and humble, who acknowledge, that all which they be, or haue, commeth from God, haue also the good fortune to abide alwayes in the house of their heauenly Father vnder the shaddow of his wings, and in his particular protection: as the bad be vnhappy to goe out of it, to gouerne themselues after their owne lust, and proper will, estranging themselues from God by sinne, giuing themselues ouer to the loue of creatures, and in the pursuite thereof consuming and wasting all their goods, as well the supernaturall of soule, as the naturall of body, which they profane, and lauish a thousand wayes. Here a man must reflect vpon himselfe, as one like vnto this ryotous yong man. To consider Gods infinite liberality, and endles bounty in distribution of his gifts to the good and bad, giuing to the one, & to the other liberty to vse them according to their free will, without restraint, or compulsion.

2. To consider, how after that this foolish yong Man, had miserably and foolishly wasted his goods, he fell finally into so extreme misery, as he was forced to vndertake the keeping of swine, and was pressed with so excessiue hunger, as he did eate the leauings of those vncleane beasts, and yet could not haue his fill. Circumstances, that doe in a most liuely manner discouer the infelicity of a sinner, who depriueth himselfe of Gods grace, suffereth hunger, and for want of spirituall refection maketh

keth himselfe a slaue to the Diuell , and serueth him, as his mayster , in thinges most infamous, and most vnworthy the generosity of a man . For what more abiect, and contemptible thing is is there , then to feed and keep swyne? What is more beast-like, then to blindfold ones iudgement, and to giue the raynes to his senses, to run after carnall pleasures, whereof a man, by experience, findeth himselfe neuer to haue his fill, nor to be satisfyed ? This is proper to brute-beastes: for such meates cannot take away mans hunger, who is created to a far more noble end .

3 .   To consider , how this affliction and misery made the poore yong man to open his eyes , and to be sory that he had left his Fathers house , whither he resolued to returne , though he should be receyued , but for an hireling into it . Where is to be seene, that the beginning of a sinners conuersion dependeth of Gods inspiration, and that he must first returne into himselfe, and acknowledge his miseryes . For it importeth much , that a sinner compare his necessity with the happy state of the iust , who serue God , that by vnderstanding and apprehending the difference of his condition and state from theirs, he may conceiue some good desire to get himselfe out of his misery . It importeth vs no lesse also to make a firme resolution of our conuersion to God, by considering our owne indignity , and his infinite goodnes and mercy , and we must not delay to put such a resolution in execution , least in tyme it come to be cold . An example wherof we haue in this prodigall child,

who

who delayed not his good purpose, but began
his iourney that very inſtant, with intent to returne to his father.

4. To conſider, how his compaſſionate Father, ſeeing him a-far off comming, was
much moued with pitty, and commaunded
that prouiſion of new apparell ſhould be made
him, and that a feaſt and good cheere ſhould be
made for his comming. Where is liuely diſcouered and layd open the ſurpaſſing bounty, and
mercy of our good God, ſeeing he is ſo eaſily
appeaſed, when he ſeeth an humbled and contrite ſinner, to whome out of his exceſſiue goodnes he reſtoreth that, which he had loſt by his
exceſſe of malice, commaunding, and giuing order, that he ſhould be forthwith reueſted with
his heauenly graces, with ſo great a precaution,
as though his diuine maieſty had been greatly
intereſſed therein, and receiuing him for his
Sonne, who thought himſelfe vnworthy to be a
poore hireling.

5. To conſider, how the Elder Sonne had indignation heerat, & was angry. Wherby we are
taught, that there are found ſome imperfect
perſons, whome God hath preſerued from grieuous ſinnes, that enuy the greater ſinners, when
they ſee God ſometimes to fauour them, and to
confer greater graces vpon them, then they haue
receiued themſelues. This further manifeſteth,
that Gods mercy, which he doth to ſinners, is ſo
great, as being conſidered in it ſelfe, it ſeemeth
to miniſter vnto the iuſt matter of complaint,
thogh indeed there is no enuy at all in the ſouls,
that

that be full of charity, and vertue. Finally we muſt weigh and examine theſe words of the Father to his Elder Sonne, when he ſaid to him: Sonne, thou art alwayes with me, and all my goods be thine. Where is to be ſeene, how good, and liberall our Lord God is.

Meditat. L X X X.   Of him who fell into the hands of Theeues, and was ſaued by the Samaritan. Luc. 10.

TO conſider, how our Sauiour, to teach vs, who is our neighbour, and how we ought to loue him, propoſed this Parable of a man, who went downe from Hieruſalem to Iericho, by whome be meant all the children of our firſt, and terreſtriall parent Adam, who falling off from God, and affecting the thinges of this world, plunged themſelues moſt deeply therein, and in the meane tyme came Theeues, that is, the malignant ſpirits, who ſpoyled them of grace, of the gifts of heauen, and of vertues, and wounded them in the inward powers of their ſoule, cauſing ignorance in the Vnderſtanding, debility and weaknes in the Will, and obliuion and forgetfulnes in the Memory. In this eſtate muſt I repreſent myſelfe before Almighty God.

2.   To conſider, how a Prieſt, a Leuite, and a Samaritan paſſed a long the way, where this poore man lay wounded: the two former vouchſafed not ſo much as to make a ſtand to
ſee

fee him, but paffed on, & the third mã only took
pitty on him. Where is to be feene the little
compaffion, that men are wont to haue on the
miferies of another, though it be in them to remedy the fame. By this Samaritan is meant the
eternall Word, made Man, who came downe
from the heauenly Hierufalem into this inftable
world, where he was held for a Samaritan,
and for a finner, who came to reftore to finners their perfect health, which neyther the
Law of nature, nor the written Law could giue
them.

3. To confider, how this our great God, &
Lord, difdayned not to make himfelfe man for
the fauing of mankind, wounded to death, but
approached fo neere vnto him, as he vnited himfelfe to his nature, mercyfully bound vp his
woundes, by meanes of the vertues, which he
communicated vnto him for the ftaying of the
iffue of his vices, annointed him with the oyle
of mercy, comforted him vvith the vvine
that confirmeth & ftrengthneth the hart, tooke
vpon his owne moft precious body the heauy
burden of our finnes, fupported, and ftill doth
our frailty by the fuccour and help of his diuine
infpirations, and finally taking vp this poore
wounded perfon from out of the way, where he
iay, that is, drawing him from out of daunge-
rous occafions, and perill of offending. brought
him into an Inne, which is the Catholike
Church, where all neceffaryes are to be found
for the recouery of perfect health. This done he
recommended him to the Superiors therof, and

Z   willed

willed them to haue a care of him, and he gaue
them two pence, that is, vertue and doctrine for
the difcharge of their office. The diuine Maiefty
proceedeth yet further, and doth more fauour
to them, whom he draweth into the houfe of religion, for that there they may in a more perfect manner recouer their former health; becaufe
there is more care had of the fpirituall maladies.
Finally we muft confider, how by this Parable
our Sauiour would giue to vnderftand, who
was our neighbour, and who merited to goe a-
way with that name, concluding, that he was the
man, who exercifeth mercy to the neceffitous.

Meditat. L X X X I.   *Of the Seruant who*
ought ten thoufand Talents.   Matth. 18.

T O confider, how in this Parable is defcri-
bed Gods infinit mercy, and his exceffiue
fweetnes in pardoning offences, be they
neuer fo grieuous. And yet the diuine maiefty
caufeth men to giue vp their accompts, not only in the article of death, when all our recko-
nings are made vp, and determined, but he further alfo demaundeth to be payed and fatisfyed
by euery one of vs, and this by pennance. And
this he doth euery day by frequent infpirations,
and other meanes, fuch as be trauayles, pains-
taking, afflictions, &c. That the feruant, who
oweth the ten thoufand talents, is a finner, charged and loaden with mortall finnes, euery one
whereof is exceeding heauy, becaufe it is iniurious

iurious to God , bynding a man to so great a summe, as all the meanes he hath be not inough to satisfy for them ; by reason whereof he becometh a sloue to the Diuell, for hauing, by his sins sold vnto him his liberty for euer.

2 . To consider, that the seruant, hauing vnderstood the commaundement his Lord had giuen , that he should be sold , and all his family besides, came and prostrated himselfe at his feet, crauing time of satisfaction . Where is to be noted , that he denyed not the debt , but humbled himselfe before his Lord, besought him to doe him fauour, & had a good meaning to pay him . This must we also doe for obtayning of the remission of our sinnes . To consider the Princes great liberality in remitting vnto this his seruant his whole debt, and in graunting him more then he asked: a munificence, that most highly recommendeth Gods infinit mercy & goodnes .

3 . To consider, how this seruant was no sooner gone forth frō the presence of his Lord , & meeting one of his fellow seruants, but he began to lay hand vpon him , and to treate him ill for a little debt that he did owe him : an act in very deed, that did plainly declare the cruelty of the bad man, who would not vse the like curtesy , that he had receyued himselfe , towardes him , who with like humility required it : testifying thereby his precipitant fury , and his extreme ingratitude in regard of his Lord, whome he moued to indignation in behalfe of his other seruant .

4. To consider, how the iniuries, we do to our
Z 3   neigh-

neighbour, do offend God, Angells, & men, as is to be seene in this violent & hard dealing of the naughty seruāt with his fellow, who caused him to be iustly condemned for that present outrage, & in some sort for his passed debt also, for that his ingratitude did aggrauate his sin. Heere I must learne, how much I am bound to pardon my neighbour, sith God requireth, that we forgiue one another from our hart: & the reasons, that may be giuen for it, be, because God will haue it so, for as much as he is the common Father of all men, and particularly of Christians. That for this cause, and by this meanes euery one ought to merit by bearing, and that God doth pardon vs more liberally, and more franckly for our so doing. For how is it possible for him to obtayne pardon of God, who himselfe doth not pardom others?

Meditat. L X X X I I.   *Of the Parable of the* Steward, *who consumed, and spent the goods of his Lord.* Luc. 16.

TO consider, how this Lord, who caused the accompt to be made, is God, to whom appertaine all the treasurs and riches both of heauen, and of earth, as well corporall, as spirituall. His Bayliffe or steward is man, to who God giueth the gouernement and managing of his goods of nature, and of grace, which he wasteth, when he vseth them ill, as when he gouerneth not well his inward and outward senses, his

health

health of body, his commodities, &c. by occasion wherof he is before God reputed prodigall,
and lauish.

2. To consider, how this Lord called his
Bayliffe, to giue him vp an accompt of all the
goods he had put into his handes. Where is to
be seene, how straite the reckoning shall be,
that we shall render of the graces and goods, we
haue receiued, whē we shall least dreame therof,
& when our sinnes shall cry alowd before God,
and shall craue iustice agaynst vs, who commit them. To examine these wordes: Render
accompt of thy Bayliffeship; for now thou canst
not exercise that Office any longer: that is
to say, Giue vp a reckoning of all, that thou hast
receuued inwardly, & outwardly, & of all that I
haue donne & suffered for thee.

3. To consider the prudence and subtility of this Bayliffe, whome his Lord commended. Where is to be seene, how much more diligent the worldlings are in procuring their own
commodityes, and in the meanes of giuing order touching their affayres, then be the iust, who
often proceed in their busines with much coldnes. Here we must learne to preuent the time of
accompt, that we are to render vnto God, and to
endeauour to goe through it with our honour
and profit.

Medi.

Meditat. L X X X I I I.   *Of the Publican,
and Pharisy, who went vp to the Temple to
pray. Luc . 18.*

TO confider the effects of pride, which the
Pharify difcouered in his prayer. Firft, he
held himfelfe for an holy man, full of vertues, and meritts, and commended himfelfe infteed of prayfing God. Secondly, he preferred
himfelfe before all others, efteeming himfelfe
better then all. Thirdly, he made high efteeme
of his good workes, out of a certaine vanity, &
temerarious oftentation, comparing them with
the workes of another. Laftly, he contemned all
others, and efpecially this poore Publican by
name. We muft examine our felues, if there be
not fome like thing in vs : for prayer, that hath
any admixtion of pride, cannot be pleafing vnto
God.

2.   To confider the Publicans acts of humility, who knocking himfelfe vpon the breaft,
was not fo hardy, as to lift his eyes vp to heauen,
but fayd : God be mercifull to me, a poore finner. He thought himfelfe vnworthy to come
neere the place, where God was honored, neyther yet to approach to the place, where the
Pharify was. And therefore he tooke his ftanding in the very lower part of the Temple, and
knocking himfelfe on the breaft, craued pardon
of God for himfelfe alone, as though there had
been no other finner in the world befides him-
                                               felfe

felfe, put his confidence alfo in the mercy of God, and made his prayer in few wordes. We muft propofe this to our felues for imitation in our prayers.

3. To confider, how the Publican obtayned the effect of his petition and prayer by his humility, when on the contrary the Pharify went out of the Temple fruftrated of heauenly graces, as he came in. For God is not fo much pleafed with outward thinges, as with the inward, that proceed from an harty affection, and good will. To ponder thefe wordes Enery one, that exalteth himfelfe, fhall be humbled : & he that humbleth himfelfe, fhall be exalted. Wherhence I muft conceyue a fingular affection to the vertue of humility, and an hatred to the vice of pride, in regard of their diuers and different effects,

Meditat. *LXXXIIII.* *Of the Houfe-holder, who called workemen to labour in his vineyard.* *Matth.* 20.

TO cófider that God is meant by this houfholder: for he hath many families in heauē aboue, and heere beneath on earth, & he hath a care of the very leaft amongft them. That the faithfull be this vineyard, and the iuft aboue the reft, of whom God caryeth a particular care, and husbandeth them diligently. The workemen be all men in generall, to whome it appertayneth diligently to cultiuate and manure their

owne soules, and they must haue the hooke continually in hand to cut off and prune the superfluous branches that sproute out in them. In
like manner the preachers, and all such, as giue
good example, be called labourers in this vineyard, and those be they, whome God calleth in
the morning: for without his diuine inspiration
impossible it is for any to enter into this vineyard, neither to labour therin. To say, that they
are called in the morning, is to giue to vnderstād
that from the tyme, that a man hath the vse of
reason, God beginneth to call him, testifying by
that, the Fatherly care he hath of his saluation.
And this must giue me occasiō to make an high
esteeme of Gods prouidence, to render him
thankes for it, and to craue grace, that I may be
answerable to his holy vocation.

2.   To consider, how all the worke men
were called, when the euening was come, as well
those who came about the eleauenth houre, as
those, that came at the breake of day, and euery
one receyued his hire. The meaning is, that all
mans life is but one day, and that at the end of it
our Sauiour Iesus, to whome God his Father
hath committed the charge of rewarding his
faythfull, shall render to euery one according to
his workes. That his maiesty regardeth not so
much the tyme, that the labour and worke continueth, as the feruour, and forward will, wherwith they trauayle. And of this it hapned, that
those, who came last, receyued as much for their
paynes and trauayle, as did the first, by occasion of their greater alacrity and more feruent affection,

fection, wherewith they laboured. Herehence
I muſt learne to put my ſelfe forwardes, and to
take courage, though God hath called me to his
ſeruice, being elder & ſtroken more in yeares,
then many other.

3.   To conſider, how the firſt workemen murmured, ſeeing the laſt to receiue as
much for their hire, as did themſelues: whereby
is inſinuated the ſingular munificence of our Sauiour in rewarding the affectuous ſeruices, that
are done him: for ſuch and ſo great it is, that if
there could be any enuy among the bleſſed, it
may ſeeme to miniſter them matter thereunto.
That the defaults of them, who haue ſerued God
long in coldnes, be alſo deſcribed in this figure
of murmuration, of which may be gathered,
that their faults be, to preſume of their deſeruings, by occaſion of their authority, thinking
that becauſe they haue a long tyme caryed the
burden of the day, and of the heate, their workes
be more, and yet nothing is the cauſe of their
complayning, and that they make ſo great an
eſteeme of their trauayle, is nothing but their
owne lazineſſe, and tepidity. To be ſubiect to
their owne intereſt, which they ſeeke: to be enuious, and ſory, that God doth greater fauours
to the more feruent, then to them.

4.   To conſider theſe wordes: Many be
called, and but few choſen. Which is as much
to ſay, as that there be many in this life, whome
men eſteeme for perfect in holines, yet before
God they are held otherwiſe, yea moſt wicked.
And agayne, as there be many called to the light
of

of fayth, fo be there many more, who do re-
fiſt it, and therefore the number of thoſe, who
are called to a perfect life, is great inough, yet
be there very few, who truly diſpoſe themſelues
conſtantly to purſue perfection, whiles they
content themſelues with their ſlouthfull tepidity.

*Meditat. LXXXV.   Of the Parable of the
Vineyard. Math. 21.*

TO conſider the wonderfull prouidence of
God towardes the Church, his Vineyard,
in which he hath placed a bulwarke, and
hath compaſſed it round with a ſtrong wall, that
is, with the Protection of Angells, which guard
& keep it, and in particular with the protection
of God himſelfe, who ceaſeth not to ſend it the
ſuccour and ayde of continuall inſpirations. He
hath giuen it a preſſe, that is to ſay, the Sacraments, and namely that of the holy Altar, togeather with the law diuine, commaundements,
and counſayles, the end whereof is nothing but
the pure wyne of Charity. He hath built in it a
very high Tower, which is his particular prouidence, by meanes whereof he preuenteth future accidents. Moreouer the holy Temple,
the houſe of prayer, the multitude and great
numbers of Prelates, and Doctours, who keep
ſentinell, and the profound and ſoueraygne doctrine of holy Scripture, be as many Towers in
the Church, wherin are to be found all ſorts of
                                    armes

armes offenfiue, and defenfiue againft all manner of tentations . This vineyard God hath put
into the hāds of men to cultiuate, labor, & farme,
to the end that euery one may husbād the groūd
of his foule, and of thofe of others which he hath
in charge , that they may beare fruit of benediction , feeming as though he abfented himfelfe ,
and went a long iourney, before he fhould come
againe , to the end euery one worke according
ding to the liberty of his freewill , that he hath
giuen him . Where I muft learne, how carefull,
and diligent euery one ought to be about the
husbanding of his owne foule., & the perfecting
therof in the beft manner he can .

2 .   To confider that all the tyme of this
life is to procure the fructifying of our foules ,
and God fendeth the Prelates , and preachers to
gather vp the rents and reuenewes therof ari-
fing, as he fent in former tymes the Prophets, &
Patriarkes; and after that his owne moft deere
Sonne , our Sauiour himfelfe , for the like end ,
vvhome vve contemne , and crucify agayne
by our finnes as much as is in vs , & as the auncient farmers of this vineyard once did . We
muft yield the diuine maiefty thankes for the
continuall care , it hath to admonifh and aduife
vs by the meanes of his feruants , and to exhort
vs to the conferuing, & intertaynig of our fpirituall vineyard .

3 .   To confider , how the Scribes , and
Pharifies, to whome this Parable was addreffed,
or the crime of putting the heyre to death recorded in the third perfon, condemned themfelues
by

by their owne mouth . For finne is fo hatefull,as the very authors of it themfelues do blame , and condemne it in another. That our Sauiour Iefus threatned the Iewes , of a moft iuft punifhment to fall vpon them , faying , That the Kingdome of God fhould be taken from them , for their negle&t in rendring him the fruit,and reuenewes that they fhould haue done,of his vineyard,that is,the good works of the Church,bv cétemning the exhortations, and good inftru&tions it hath giuen .

Meditat. L X X X V I.   Of the Parables of thofe that were inuited to the mariage Feaft , and to the Supper.   Matth. 22.

TO confider,how the eternall Father vouch-fafed , that his only Sonne fhould marry with humane Nature , in vniting it vnto himfelfe by an hypoftaticall & perfonall vnion , and beautifying it with fo many and fo great ce-leftiall gifts and graces : it pleafed him alfo to marry him with the Church, which is the affem-bly , and Congregation of the faythfull, conioy-ned in the Society of the holy foules in the vni-on of charity. How the diuine maiefty calleth & inuiteth vnto this marriage all nations of the world , not excepting any.

2 .   To confider, how for the folemnizing, and honoring of the feaft of this mariage, there is made a magnificall and great banquet , where are ferued in the precious meates of heauenly

do&trine

drine for the refection of the Vnderstanding: holy precepts and wonderfull counsayles for the tast of the Will, that desireth the owne soules good: the Sacraments, full of vertue and efficacy in communicating of celestiall graces & fauours to holy soules, principally the B. Sacrament of the Altar. Happy are those, that be worthy to be called to such a feast by the Churches preachers, & by inspirations diuine.

3. To consider, how many of them, that were inuited, would not come, some excusing themselues by the pride of this life, and the curiosity of thinges, that are seene therin: some of their desire to temporall goods, and an inordinate appetite of ease, delicacy, and carnall pleasures, all which were excluded and kept out from the banquet in punishment of their rebellion, and the contemning of the voyce of so great a King, who had called them.

4. To consider, how this King was angry for this their inciuility, and therefore commaunded his seruants to goe forth, and to inuite the poore, blind, impotent, lame, and all those whome they should encounter and meete with on the way. Wherein is to be seene the singular bounty and mercy of God in calling to this his marriage all sorts of people, without excepting any. How the house, and table of God goeth through the world, & filleth it, for that it wanteth not meanes to draw them with sweetnes, whome he will haue to come to it.

5. To consider, how whiles the inuited guests were eating, the King entred in to see thē,

A a   and

and perceyuing one there in place, who had not a wedding garment, he commaunded, that he should be bound hand, and foote, and cast into vtter darkenes, where is weeping, and gnashing of teeth. Whereby is to be seene, that it is not inough to haue only faith, to be worthy to sit at Gods table, but a man must further haue charity of life, at the ending whereof our Sauiour is to come to examine all the inuited guests. And therefore we must present our selues with great purity to the B. Sacrament, that we may not be reiected & repelled as vnworthy, if we come vnto it fowly, and vndecently cloathed. To thinke on the rigour of the sentence pronounced agaynst him, who appeared in Gods sight in soyled cloathing, by occasion whereof he was condemned to perpetuall imprisonment, to an obstinacy of hart, to extreme misery, to darkenes of soule and of body, to weeping and gnashing of teeth without end, where he shall be tormented with the dolefull remembrance of this feast, whereunto he was called, and of the prouision of the meanes of his saluation, which he neglected to vse. For a conclusion I must ponder these wordes: Many be called, but few are chosen.

Meditat.

Meditat. L X X X V I I.   *Of the Parable of the* ten *Virgins. Matth.* 25.

TO confider, that in the Church there be both iuſt, and finners, and that the one & the other attend the comming of our Saiour Ieſus in Iudgement. How by the fiue fooliſh Virgins be meant finners, who côtent themſelues with fayth alone, without making reckoning of good workes, whereby they may pleaſe God : or if they haue any, they haue done them to pleaſe men, and theſe are thoſe that are ſayd, to haue lampes without oyle. By the fiue wiſe Virgins be ſignifyed the iuſt, who haue their lamps full of oyle, that is, of Fayth, and charity, of the light of the truth, vertue, and good works outward and inward, togeather with the purity both of body, and of ſpirit.

2.   To confider, how whiles the bridegrome did forbeare his comming, the one and the other ſlept, the good in veniall finnes, and the bad in mortall, promiſing vnto themſelues a long life, notwithſtanding it be ſo vncertayne. How at mid-night, that is to ſay, when men thinke leaſt of it, there was this cry heard : The bridegrome cometh, goe yee forth to meete him. And this is it, that ſhould induce vs to be vigilant, watchfull, and to ſtand diligently vpon our guard.

3.   To confider, how both good and bad muſt appeare before God in Iudgement, when
they

they are to dye, and euery one cary with him his lampe of good workes, if he haue any. How the fooles will then vnderstand and acknowledge their folly, when there shall be no more tyme, seeing themselues without oyle, and not knowing where to procure any, for that the tyme of getting it is then past, & so the gate shall be shut vp agaynst them, and they shall not haue any part or place in the eternall rest; where, on the contrary the good shall be receiued, and let in, for that as wise, and prouident they prouided & made ready their lamps in this life: & therefore they shall ioy for eternity, as the others shall weep & groane for euer. Of this I must learne, that it much importeth me to imitate these Virgins. To examine these words: Watch yee, because you know not the day, nor the houre: that is, watch in prayer, pennance, and the continuall exercise of good workes: for you know not, whether the houre present will be the last of your life, or not.

Meditat. LXXXVIII.   Of the Parables, of the Talents, and Pounds.   Matth. 26.

TO consider, that the name of Talent signifieth all the meanes, that God hath giuen vs for our soules good, such as be the giftes of nature, as well of the soule as of the body, the light of reason, the good parts acquired and procured by humane industry, honors, riches,

riches , &c. The supernaturall vertues common
to all the faythfull good and bad , fayth , hope ,
grace and charity , imparted to the good alone
togeather with the vertues,that accompany thē,
and the perfections , they haue receiued for the
edification of the Church , and for the good of
the neighbours soules. All these be among the
number of talents , that God bestoweth , & di-
stributeth , to one more, to another fewer, as he
pleaseth , & according to the capacity , that euery one is of , to doe that for which such talents
be giuen him,for as much as God euer regardeth
such proportion . That the end , for which such
talents be conferred vpon vs, is our owne saluation , and that of our neighbour , which we are
bound to procure and seeke according to the
measure of the talent , we haue receyued . And
therefore it is sayd by our Sauiour . Traffique
yee, till I come . That is to say , I bestow not my
talents vpon you , that they should abide idle ,
and vnprofitable , but that you should make
your gayne of them by imploying them. Where
we are to thinke,how iust cause we haue to feare
if we make not profit of the talents we haue receyued of God.

   2 .   To consider , how those, who receyued the fyue , and two talents , doubled them ,
whereby be meant those, who doe with feruous
cooperate to Gods grace,euen as the lukwarme:
cold , and negligent are insinuated by him , who
did hide the talent he receiued , whereof he
would not make his profit through slouth and
negligence.

3.　To confider, how God cometh vpon the fodayne, when we thinke not, to demaund an accompt of the gayne we fhall haue made of his tolents. Where we are to reprefent vnto our mind the ioy and comfort, wherewith thofe, who haue trafficked well, fhall appeare before God, with the profit and gayne of their good workes; & the reward of the feruent, whome he will honour with the name of faythfull & good feruants, faying vnto them, That fith they haue been faythfull ouer a few thinges, he will giue then much, caufing them to enter into the end-les abiffe of his diuine pleafures.

4.　To confider the ill excufe, that the fer-uant made him for the concealing of his flouth, faying, That he had hidden the talent in the earth: & the fharpe reprehenfion that was gi-uen him, in calling him, naughty & flouthfull feruant: & condemning him by his own mouth, and taking from him the talent he had, that is, fpoyling him of the goods of grace, and then ca-fting him into the eternal darknes of hel, where he is to weep, & wayle for euer. Finally to con-fider, that if he be punifhed in fo rigorous a mā-ner, who would not vfe the talent well, & with profit, that God gaue him; what fhall be done with him, who vfeth it ill, and ferueth himfelfe of the gifts and grace, receyued of God, to offend him therewith, to fcandalize the world, and to wrong his neighbour?

Diuers

*Diuers good affections with which we are to excite
and ftirre vp our felues in meditation : With
other eafy meanes , which may ferue to ad-
uance and further vs, befides the pointes of the
Meditations.*

FOR to excite in thee confufion, hauing put
thy felfe in the preféce of God, of the B. Virgin Mary, & thy Angell Guardian &c. make
reflection on thy negligence, and how thou haft
not cooperated to the diuine grace for the getting of vertue, wherby thou mighteft be moued
and ftirred vp to the abhorring and flying of all
vice . After confider, how Iefus Chrift hath giuen thee an Example of this vertue, which notwithftanding thou haft not practifed ; whereupon thou oughtft fharply to reprehend thy felfe.

2. For Griefe , weigh how many and great
goods thou haft loft, & into how many & great
euills thou art fallen by thy negligence. Wher-
upon thou mayft confider how much God is offended , who fo much abhorreth finne, that he
became man, and fubmitted himfelfe to death,
only to driue it out of the world .

3. For Feare, thinke ferioufly how thou art to
render accompt to God of the abouefayd negligences, and how thou wouldeft cooperate at the
houre of thy death, to one fuch a grace and benefit .

4. For Humility or felfe-diftruft which is
begotten by this feare ; imagine that thou art in
A a 4   the

the prefence of the diuine maiefty , whofe giftes and graces thou haft fo little efteemed.

5.   For Hope, put before thine eyes all that which God hath done for thee , without eyther thy paynes or merits &c. After caft the eyes of thy foule vpon the admirable merits of Iefus Chrift, alfo vpon the works of the B. Virgin Mary & all the Saints.

6.   For Thankef-giuing , make great e-fteeme of the grace which God hath heertofore giuen thee, and of that he is yet ready to beftow vpon thee. This affection will be much more excited , if meditating fome great miftery that our Sauiour hath wrought , thou thanke him for it withall thy heart & affection .

7.   For Loue, gratitude and the confidera-tion of benefits receaued , doth ferue , whereby the foule inflamed by fuch thoughts , defires to be vnited to fuch a goodnes , from whence proceed fo many and fingular gifts .

8.   For Imitation , giue thy felfe intierly to the precedent affection , for it is moft certayne that from thence it takes beginning , feing that we muft willingly imitate their actions whome we moft affect.

9.   For Mortification of thy appetites , after that thou haft vndertaken the imitation of fome one vertue, make a firme purpofe vvith all thy power, to ouercome by perfect mortification all thofe difordinate defires , which might hinder the conqueft of the fayd vertue : to which end the examples of the moft notable Saintes will much auayle thee .

10 .   For

10.   For Force and generosity of courage proposing to thy selfe the difficultyes vvhich are presented in obtayning of vertue, purpose with thy selfe to endure all payne and labour, rather then be hindered by them in the pursuit of any one vertue.

11.   For Resignation giue thy selfe wholly to the foresayd affections, and they vvill vvithout doubt, beget in thee an entire resignation of thy selfe, vnto the good will and pleasure of the diuine Maiesty.

FINIS.

THE SECOND PART

MEDITATIONS
OF THE THIRD
WEEKE.

IN this third Weeke, we must in part chaunge the second, and sixt additions. Touching the second, when we rise out of our bed, we must represent to our mind, what we goe to doe, and briefly reflect vpon the matter of the Meditation we are to make, according to the mistery, that shall occurre for the same, and whilest we are apparelling our selues, we must conceyue in hart a most great sorrow and

griefe

griefe to see, that our sweet Sauiour should endure so much. As touching the sixt, we must take
heed, that no thoughts of Ioy may find entrance
into our mind, though the same be pious and
holy, as of the Resurrection, or of the Euerlasting glory; insteed whereof, we must seeke, in
meditating the Passion, to feele some payne, anguish, and trouble of hart, by the frequent memory of that which our Sauiour suffered from
the first houre of his passion, till the very last instant of his mortall life.

§. I.

Before we come to put downe the Meditations of the dolorous passion of our Sauiour,
which appertayne to the third Weeke of the E-
xercises of our B. Father, we are to obserue some
points, that may serue for our profit in meditating the holy misteryes of the Passion. The first
is, that our Sauiour did corporally drinke vp
the bitter chalice of his passion, receyuing it
at the hands of the ministers, and executioners,
and spiritually by the continuall memory, he
had of the cruell torments, he was to suffer, the
memory whereof afflicted him sore for all his life
long, as he testifyed in the prayer he made in
the garden, where the only representation of the
pains he expected, caused him to sweet drops of
bloud. Of this we are to draw two endes, whereunto we must tend, in these meditations of the
Passion. The former, to vnite & conforme our
selues to our Sauiour, yea & to transforme our
selues as much as may be, into him, afflicted
throgh the liuely affectiōs of cōpassiō & sorrow,

aa

as the Apoſtle admoniſheth vs in theſe wordes : Haue yee feeling in your ſelues of that, which Ieſus Chriſt felt in himſelfe. For his compaſſion was ſuch, as the B. Virgin felt with a moſt affli-ſted mind, the deadly paynes of her moſt belo-ued Sonne, which was the ſword of ſorrow, that S. Simeon had foretold ſhould tranſperce her moſt tender hart. The latter is to drinke corporally, togeather with our Sauiour the cha-lice of his Paſſion, by conforming our ſelues vn-to him in his ſufferings, and by voluntarily v-ſing ſome paynefull mortification, ſuch as be fa-ſtings, diſciplynings, wearing of hayre, &c. (Carrying in our body the mortification of Ie-ſus Chriſt, and the impreſſions and markes of his woundes). And heereof followeth, that a third end, and that the principall of theſe medi-tations is, to conforme our ſelues to our Saui-our, and to imitate him in his heroycall vertues, which he hath manifeſted in his moſt affectuous loue towardes God and men, in his zeale of ſa-uing of ſoules, in purity of intention, in obedi-dence, pouerty, patience, & humility, and fi-nally in the contemning of all thinges of this world.

§. II.

We muſt come to meditate the paſſion of our Sauiour with exceeding great and good diſ-poſition, for which there is neceſſarily required great humility of hart, and confeſſion of the ſins, that haue been the cauſe of ſo great ſorrowes, & torments to our moſt ſweet Sauiour. We muſt alſo exerciſe our ſelues in workes of humility,

&

& repute our felues altogeather vnworthy but
to thinke of thefe diuine Myfteries , or to haue
any the leaft feeling of them . We muft further
come with a confidence and hope in the mercy
of our Sauiour : For feeing he hath pleafed to
fuffer fo much, and fo many euills for our good,
he will alfo vouchfafe to graunt vs the grace ,
that we may be fory in côpany with him , to the
end we may draw out of the meditation of his
pains, the profit they haue merited for vs.

A feruour and diligence is further required towardes this difpofition : for we muft labour to make our prayer with attention , recollection , and deuotion, by putting and dryuing
away all matter of diftraction , fith it fhould be
a foule fhame to thinke coldly on that , which
our Sauiour hath with fo inflamed charity endured for vs . The purity of hart is alfo moft neceffary, & our foule muft be preferued cleane from
all mortail finne; to the end the precious liquor
of compaffion, and a true feeling and apprehenfion of our Sauiours paines , may find entrance
into our foule, & be inftilled into it from aboue.

§. III.

There are diuerfe wayes to meditate the
Paffion : for fome there bê , who meditate it, as
intending their owne vtility and profit , and the
meditations thereunto : fome agayne are referred to our Sauiour, as penall, and paynefull vnto him . Befides thefe two manners, there be yet
two other worthy to be noted , and practifed .
The former, and more ordinary , is to meditate
euery myftery a part , examining in euery one

Bb   of

of them, vvhat is vvorthy the confidering, and yet following the courfe and order of the ftory, and namely the points, that our Bleffed Father putteth downe in the third Weeke of the fpirituall Exercife: which be, to confider the Perfons, that therein offer themfelues, and thereof to make our profit: to obferue and examine the wordes and fpeeches, and to doe the like: to ponder the actions, euer learning fomething of our Sauiour Iefus: to prefent to our mind the great defire he bad to fuffer, imitating him therein, yea the very manner of his fufferings, and to thinke, that the diuinity feemed in fome fort to hide it felfe at that tyme, to fuffer the humanity to endure fo exceffiue torments. To be fhort, to conclude that if our Sauiour hath fuffered fo great and fore thinges for our finnes, what ought we to doe for the loue of him. The latter manner to meditate thefe myfteries is, to take for the fubiect of the meditation fome fuffering of our Sauiour in particular, or fome vertue he exercifed, examing that, which is about that matter remarkable in all the proceffe of his Paffion. For example, if I would meditate on his humility, I muft ferue my felfe with all the places, and myfteries, wherin fuch his humility is difcouered. After two or three meditations, a man muft make repetition of them once or twice, as we haue mentioned before in the beginning of the fecond Weeke. Alfo after euery meditation he muft make an application of the fenfes, as is fayd in the fame place, & according to that which our B. Fa. teacheth.

§. IIII.

§. IIII.

Among the affections of deuotion, which we ought to seeke to draw in meditation of the Passion, the first is of confusion, as I haue sayd, which we are to craue with great instance, and desire with humility. The second is to consider, how detestable sinne is, seeing our Sauiour hath endured so much for the destroying of it. The third, to thinke of the ineffable goodnes, & infinite Wisdome of God, for finding out a meanes so conuenient and fitting for the remedying of our miseryes, and all at once for the gayning of our harts to the loue of him, as witnesseth the Apostle in these wordes: God hath shewed the greatnes of his charity towardes vs: for we being his enemies, he vouchsafed to dye to saue vs. The fourth is to confirme our hopes, as S. Augustine sayth: He, who pleased to giue vs what was more, namely, the bloud of his beloued Sonne, will not sticke also to giue vs what is lesse, to wit, the glory of heauen. The fift to enkindle in our harts the fire of the loue of God, through the consideration of his so excessiue goodnes. The sixt, to imitate in as perfect a manner, as we can, the life of our Sauiour, as S. Peter teacheth vs to doe, saying: Iesus Christ hath suffered for vs, leauing vnto you an example to follow his steps. The last, to conceyue a feruent desire of sauing the soules, which our Sauiour hath ransomed vvith the price of his bloud.

§. V.

For the finding out of the more abundant

matter

matter for meditation, we may in euery mistery confider the circumftances following. Firft, the perfon who fuffereth, his innocency & holynes, his omnipotency, liberality, and infinit charity, &c.

The fecond, the multitude, variety, and grieuoufnes of the torments, they did put him vnto in all manner poffible, in his goods, in his honour, in his body, in his moft holy mother, in all his friendes, as in his Apoftles, in all his fenfes inward and outward, in all the parts of his facred body, finally in his bleffed foule, the hidden and fecret paynes whereof were far more violent, then were thofe, that were feene to the eye, and yet in body he fuffered moft vnworthy iniuryes and outrages, become by his whipping & the cruell vfage of his enemies in it, not vnlik to a Leaper, wounded from head to foot. The perfecutors & his enemyes that tormented him, namely, the Iewes and the Pagans, the noble & ignoble, yea and the powers of hell themfelues, who did put fire to the fury of men, that they might without mercy, and with all cruelty, malice, and inhumanity perfecute and torment him vnto death, as they did, and proceeded euen to more then a moft barbarous handling of him, vfing all the wayes to obfcure his facred name, and to make it to be forgotten on earth. All thefe iniuryes, and infinit other befides, exceedingly increafed the paynes of our fweet Iefus, becaufe he had inwardly, incomparably a far greater & more perfect knowledge of his perfecutors fury towardes him, then he had outwardly : befides

sides that, he was tormented by the most contemptible sort of people, and the vnworthyest
refuse of the world, yea and by them, who were
bound vnto him for his infinit benefitts and fauours towardes them.

The third, the persons for whome he suffered, which be men of the tyme past, present, &
to come; for whose synnes he made satisfaction
with the price of his bloud, suffering also for
those his enemyes, which actually tormented
him, yea and for euery one of them particularly
& as expressely, as for all mankind in generall,
though those ingrate and thankelesse persons
should within a short tyme after forget those so
great paynes endured for the loue of them, and
make so little reckoning of so memorable benefitts.

The fourth, the tender loue and affection,
wherewith our sweet Sauiour suffered. For the
consideration of this tendernes of loue is the
sweetest and deuoutest affection, that may be
rayfed in meditating the Passion, if we represent
vnto our selues, that our Sauiour receyued all
his torments voluntarily, without constraint
or any necessity at all, moued only by the infinit
loue, he carryed to God his Father, and to the
nature humane. Vpon which we may inferre,
that he desired to endure much more, if it had
been necessary for his Fathers glory, & for the
saluation of mankind.

The fifth, the heroycall vertues, that our
Sauiour exercised in his Passion, teaching them
vnto vs as our mayster, & recommending them

vnto

vnto the world, where they were contemned
and held in a very bafe efteeme, that he might
leaue them vnto vs by his teftament & laft will,
fith by the meanes of them he hath for vs merited all vertues. Thofe, which he practifed, be
comprifed in the eight Beatitudes togeather with
charity, perfect obedience, & humility in a fupreme degree of perfection.

The fixt, the feauen ftations, that our Sauiour made, in company, for the more part, of
his tormentors, who compaffed him round as
hungry Lyons, that thirfted for his bloud : the
place, from whence he went, & whither he went:
the manner of his going towardes the place : for
his enemyes rage and malice towardes him,
made him to make more haft, then his decayed
forces might well permit, and yet his owne extreme loue preffed him to haft much more, in fo
much as what was in him, he made all poffible
fpeed to accomplifh the worke of the faluation of
mankind.

The feauenth, the loffe that the B. Virgin
had in the paffion of her moft deere Sonne : for
fhe fuffered with him, and participated of all his
paynes and torments by the exceffe of her moft
affectioned loue towardes him, as towardes her
naturall and only Sonne : as well for the reafon
aforefayd, as alfo for the great refemblance, that
was of the Sonne to the mother, who was moft
holy, and moft wife : befides that, he was
her benefactour, of whome fhe had receyued fo
many benefitts, and fingular priuiledges ; but
moft of all for this, that fhe knew him to be the
only

only Sonne of God, who deserued to be infinitly loued. Finally for this, that the holy Ghost had tyed the harts of the Sonne and the Mother fast togeather, with the band of most straite loue: so as it may be sayd, that her sorrow was measured by her loue, & therefore these wordes may be applyed vnto her: The bitternes of thy hart is as a deep sea.

The eight and last is, to meditate the principall vertues of our Blessed Lady, practised in the Passion, which be foure, in which be comprehended all the others, and these be: An entiere resignation into the handes of God in renouncing her owne will to conforme her selfe to that of God: most profound humility, in not flying from the contempt of the world, but contrary wise exposing herselfe to be contemned of it, and abiding constant at the foot of the Crosse: a great magnanimity, & constant resolution, accompanied with wonderfull patience, without vttering of any word of bitternes: a most burning charity towards men, euen those, who crucified her Sonne, pittying their blinded malice, & praying vnto God for them, in imitatiō of her Sonne. A man may meditate these nyne circumstances in euery mistery of the Passion for the finding out of more copious & ample matter in time of meditation.

MEDI-

MEDITATION I.

How our Sauiour went vp to Hierusalem.
Matth. 22 .

TO consider, how the time being now come, wherin our Sauiour had determined to dye for man, & knowing also, that the Iewes had resolued to spoyle him of his life, he departed from Ephrem, to vvhich Citty he vvas togeather with his Apostles retyred, to goe vp to Hierusalem, making such hast vpon the vvay, as his Apostles found much difficulty to follow him. Wherin he shewed his prompt obedience, and feruour of spirit, wherewith he went to offer himselfe to death, put forwardes with the heat of his diuine loue, that made him to hasten and runne to his torments, teaching vs, that in an occasion of suffering both inward, & outward paynes, he was the first of all in the world. He would also make hast in that sort, to prouoke the Apostles by his example, who also strayned themselues to follow him, in ouercoming their feare, and pusillanimity of courage, and stirring vp in themselues the exceeding loue they bare to him. We must imitate their constancy in this kind also.

2. To consider, how our Sauiour did in a more couert manner, then at other times, declare vnto his Apostles, that he was to dye, to giue them to vnderstand, that he had his Passion alwaies

alwaies before his eyes , & he spake often to the
the same purpose , as though such his discourses
had giuen him singular contentment: and more
then this, to continue in them the imagination of
his owne torments, and the iniuries, that were to
be done him ; a thing that vnto them was more
hard to belieue , then the meruayles they heard:
and finally to the end they might prepare themselues to suffer that assault with constancy and
courage.

3. To consider, how the Apostles, hearing
those speeches of his , did not vnderstand the
sense and meaning of them , which appertayned
to the Passion , the fruit and benefit whereof
they yet conceyued not, as there are also very
many now a dayes , who neyther vnderstand ,
nor penetrate into the mistery of our Sauiours
painefull death, though they heare the same read
agayne & agayne . This the Apostles ignorance
proceeded of the excessiue feare they had of the
ignominies and contempt of the world , as S.
Peter couertly testifyed, when he made answere
to his mayster, who spake of his owne Passion :
Let it be far from thee , Lord, that it should be
thy hap to endure this . But our Sauiour reprehended him , and bad him away, and called him
Sathan , and aduersary, saying vnto him . Thou
conceyuest not the thinges , as they be , but iud-
gest like a man , and basely, as those are wont to
doe, who comprehend nothing but what is terrene, and sensuall. And therfore we must learne
what an esteeme our Sauiour made of his Passion, and in what reuerence we ought to hold it,

and

and how also we are to deeme them for aduersaryes, who would separate vs from it.

Meditat. I I.   Of our Sauiours entry into Hierusalem in triumph with Palmes Matth. 21.

TO consider, how our Sauiour Iesus would make his entry with magnificence, & tryumph, fiue dayes before he was to dye, when he should eate the Paschall Lambe, appointed for sacrifice, to testify the desire he had to suffer, and with what a ioy he presented himselfe to the torments, that he was to endure, that he might obey the will of his Eternall Father, & satisfy for the sins of mankind. He wold also manifest, how great the fire of his loue was, which the affronts, Iniuries, & indignities, that had been offered him already in Hierusalem, could not extinguish &c. Moreouer his meaning was to teach vs, that to endure afflictions, and to be despised of the world for the accomplishing of Gods will, was a thing honorable and glorious, in the sight of the diuine maiesty, of the Angells, and Saints, who for that cause reioyced in their aduersityes. Finally our Sauiour made this honorable entry, to the end his disgrace and ignominy might be after it the greater, manifesting his buruing charity therin.

2. To consider, how for the making of his entry, he sent two of his disciples before, to bring him an asses colt, vpon which he mounted, his

his Apostles hauing first layd their poore garment vpon the beastes backe vnder him, and so he entred in tryumph; wherein he testified his pouerty, humility, and meeknes: markes, by which he was to be known,if the world had had eyes to know him. This was the tryumphant chariot, on which the King of Kings then apeared, who went euer before on foot, in disdayne of the worlds price & vanity, which we must learne to despise and contemne, as he did.

3. To consider, how an infinit multitude of people came forth to meete, and receyue him, moued by an inspiration diuine, some speading their garmēts in the way where he was to passe, some cutting boughes from the trees, others carrying Palmes in their handes in token of victory, and all in generall singing, Hosanna to the Sonne of Dauid, blessed is he, who cometh in the name of our Lord: where we may obserue the care the eternal Father had to honour his Sonne, to whome as he did honour in his natiuity by sending the Angells, his musitians of heauen, to sing his praises: euen so doth he now also inspires men to resound the glory of his victories in his death. And for this we must be glad, and reioyce. To ponder what manner of deuotion that of the people was, who honored our Sauiour in the best sort, they possibly could, in so much as they stripped themselues of their owne apparell, and layd it downe vpon the ground, that he might tread vpon it in the way, where he was to goe. By this we may obserue the efficacy and force of the inspiration diuine, that so powerful-

ly.

ly chaungeth mens mind. To confider what in the meane time was the blindnes of the Pharifies, who at fight of this were mad for enuy, & fayd to our Sauiour, that he fhold doe well to caufe the people to hold their peace. But he returned them this anfwere, that if men fhould hold their peace, he fhould caufe the very ftones to fpeake: for to him appertayned the glory, which their diuellifh paffion fought to obfcure.

Meditat. III. Of the teares, our Sauiour did fhed vpon Hierufalem. Luc. 19.

TO confider, how our Sauior did weep often, as in the cribbe, on the Croffe, at the refufcitation of Lazarus, and now, when the world did him fo great honour. Whereby he gaue to vnderftand, that his hart and affection tooke not much contentment in thefe exterious complements; and therewith alfo he manifefted his owne infinit Charity, reioycing for his owne part to fee himfelfe fo neere his tyme to dye for men, and vveeping on the other fide for the infelicity of them, vvho vvere to depriue him of his life. And fo I muft reprefent him to my mind, that he then vvept for my finnes, vvhich vvere to him then prefent in his diuine vnderftanding.

2. To confider thefe vvordes: If thou hadft knovvne, and that in this thy day, the thinges, that pertayne to thy peace: but novv they are hid from thyne eyes. Meaning to fay:
If

If thou kneweft what I know of thee, thou wouldft queftionles weepe, as I doe. If thou kneweft the good, that is this very day prefented at thy gates, thou wouldeft moft willingly receyue it: but thy finnes be the caufe, that this knowlege is hid, & not declared vnto thee. This is it, wherefore thou art obftinate in thy finnes, and weepeft not for thine owne loffe, neyther feekeft, nor receiueft what is for thy foules good. To confider, how he then prophecyed the ruyne & deftruction of that vnfortunate Citty, faying that it fhould be vtterly derftroyed fo, as there fhould not remayne one ftone of it ftanding vpon another, becaufe it would not know the tyme of its vifitation. I muft apply this to my felfe, and thinke, that if our Sauiour wept fo bitterly for the temporall ruyne of Hierufalem, with how much more feeling was he, thinke we, to weep for the eternall infelicity, that was to follow it in the other world.

3. To confider, how our Sauiour went ftraight to the Temple, to yield thankes to his Eternall Father, where he healed many ficke, blind, lame, impotent perfons, &c. in teftimony of the verity of his hidden diuinity, though the enuious Scribes and Pharifies ceafed not ftill to murmur, feeking to ftop the mouths of the little children, that fong his prayfes. How our Sauiour after this folemne receyuing, and continuing all the day in the Temple, there preaching, & working wonderfull thinges, found not a man, who vouchfafed to inuite him home to giue him to eate, whiles the whole world deeply apprehended

C c   hended

hended the fury of the Pharifies, in fo much as for that caufe he was forced to retyre himfelfe to Bethania two miles out of the Citty. By which is to be feene, how God carryeth himfelfe towardes men, and how they againe towards him.

Meditat. IIII.   *Of our Sauiours fupping in Bethania.*   *Matth.* 26.

TO confider, how our Sauiour fupping in the houfe of Saint Mary Magdalen, a while after the refufcitation of her brother Lazarus, fhe for an acknowledgement of fo great a benefit, tooke a certaine Precious oyntment, and powred it out vpon his feet, & then wept them, with the hayre of her head, as fhe had done before at her conuerfion. And after that agayne fhe annointed his head, in fo much as the whole houfe was filled with the fweet fmell of the oyntment. We muft imitate this pious and deuout action of hers, in breaking the flymy and fowle matter of our hart by true forrow, and contrition of our faults, in maiftering our fenfuall appetites, and in punifhing our body by feuerity of pennance, and mortification, that the houfe of our holy Religion may be perfumed, with the moft delectable fmell of vertues.

2.   To confider, how the difciples did of an ignorance condemne Magdalen, but Iudas moft of all out of a bad will, faying that fhe was

waftfull

waſtfull, and indiſcreet, and that it had been much better, if ſhe would haue imployed the value of that oyntment towardes the relieuing of the poore. Where this traytour did couertly blame his mayſter, our ſweet Ieſus: for he was a theefe, ſacrilegious, and a proprietary in holy Religion, whereunto he was called, and was the firſt, that gaue il exāple to others, filling, as it were in deſpight of that holy Woman, the whole houſe with the bad ſauour and ſent of his murmuration. Herehence I muſt learne not to iudge raſhly of any, nor ſiniſterly to interprete that, which may be taken in good part.

3. To conſider, how our Sauour tooke vpon him the defence of Magdalen, who was ſilent all the while her mayſter ſpake for her, and as an Aduocate pleaded her cauſe, manifeſted his fidelity towardes them, who ſerue him, taking their cauſe in hand: and his benignity to his diſciples, in ſweetly blaming them of the trouble and diſcontent, that the bad example of Iudas had put into their mindes. How our Sauiour tooke a very notable occaſion of honoring Magdalen for that, which by ſuch murmuring was intended for her reprehenſion, in promiſing that that pious action of hers ſhould be preached all the world ouer: giuing to vnderſtand, how he honoreth them, who honor him, & with how liberall an hand he requiteth the ſeruices, that are done him with loue, & deuotion.

Medi-

Meditat. V.   How Iudas sold our Sauiour for thirty Pence.   Matth. 26.

TO consider, who it is that is sold, and to thinke, that it is Iesus Christ our Sauiour, the soueraygne Prince of the Vniuerse, whose being and worth is impossible for any imagination to conceyue. He was treacherously sold, as if he had been a most cötemptible poore wretch of the world, and this to satisfy & make amends for that most ignominious and most iniurious outrage, that we doe to the diuine Maiesty in selling our soules by our so many sinnes vnto the Diuell: and to giue vs an example of humility, which could not descend lower, then put it selfe into the cödition of slaues, being sold for so poore & base a price.

2.   To consider, how this affront, and iniury is aggrauated by this circumstance, that he was sold by one of his owne, to whome he had done many fauours: how Iudas was this most vnfortunate traytour, who fell into this most horrible cryme by giuing entrance vnto auarice into his hart, that is the roote of all sinnes, by coueting money, and taking occasion of stealing and robbing, because he had the keeping & managing of the almes, that was giuen his mayster. How of this he came to the hight of all wickednes, vntill he sold our Sauiour Iesus to his enemies for so meane a price. Of this we must learne, that it is a very dangerous thing vnto a

Religi-

Religious perſon to tye his affection to propriety, and how further there is not a place in all the
world, wherin a man may or can be aſſured, ſith
Lucifer fell downe from heauen, Adam was
thruſt out of paradiſe, and Iudas of an Apoſtle
became an Apoſtata, and for this we haue iuſt
cauſe of great & continuall feare.

3. To conſider, how the Diuell perſwaded Iudas to commit this moſt heinous wickednes for the ruyning of his ſoule, which he
intrapped and caught with the netts of auarice,
and propriety, for the extreme hatred he did
beare to our Sauiour, whoſe life he practiſed to
take away, and to ſpoyle him of it by the hands
of one of his Apoſtles. And credible it is, that
this perfiſious architect of all villanies coloured
in ſuch ſort the reaſon wherewith he perſwaded
Iudas to the doing of this fact, with ſo faire pre-
texts of vtility and pleaſure (an ordinary tricke
of Sathan) as in fine he preuayled with him
therein.

4. To conſider the perſons, to whome
our Sauiour vvas ſould, togeather vvith the end
whereunto this moſt deteſtable bargaine tended
He vvas not ſold to his moſt ſweet mother, vvho
vvould haue ranſomed him vvith a thouſand
liues, or to his friendes, but to his cruell enemies, vvho thirſted his bloud, and vvere deſirous to extinguiſh his memory in the vvorld.
Circumſtances, that doe meruaylouſly aggrauate the outrage, that vvas exerciſed vpon our
Sauiour, as vvell on the part of Iudas, being one
of his diſciples, as of the reſt of the moſt vvicked

crevv,

crew, by occasion whereof credible it is, that this falsity coloured his treason , saying , that he was constrayned to goe out of the schoole of his mayster, who was a breaker of the law, to eate, & drinke, &c.

5. To consider the vility of the price, for which Ioseph also was sold by his brethren, and was the price that was ordinarily payed for the killing of a bond-man. But that , which yet increaseth the iniury more , was that the traytour demaunded not any determined price , but sayd only : what will you giue me , if I shall deliuer him to you ? As if he had sayd , Giue me for my labour , what you shall please : for the thing , I shall sell you , is so vile and contemptible as it deserueth no more , then what you haue a will franckly to giue me. Here we must consider , that we haue committed the very same treason, as oft as we haue offended God for a vile & contemptible thing .

6. To consider, hovv Iudas returned well contented and satisfyed , after he had concluded the bargayne, and from that time euer espyed and sought out the occasions of deliuering vp his mayster, that he might haue money of the Iewes. How notvvithstanding this he returned , and continued as before , in company of the rest of the Apostles, and conuersed among them , as a wolfe amongst a company of Lambes . How it is to be presuppo-sed , that our Sauiour recevued him louingly , though he knew all that passed , exercising ther-in many acts of patience , and charity towardes

that

that infernall monfter, that he might draw him
to repentance. How the Scribes and Pharifies
were very glad, feing that the tyme of the accomplifhment of their paffionate defires, & malicious defigne was at hand : for fuch is the condition of the wicked, to reioyce in doing ill.

Meditat. V I.   *Of the laſt Supper, in which
our Sauiour did eate the Pafchall Lambe: and
of his parting from his moſt holy Mother.
Matth.* 26.

TO confider, how our Sauiour in very precife, and exact manner, obeyed the precept of the law, in going to Hierufalem to
celebrate the Pafchall Lambe, though he knew
full well, it wold coſt him his life. How he tooke
the tyme, and gaue order about thinges neceffary for the accomplifhing of obedience, and fent
before two of his difciples to prepare all that
the folemnity required. To ponder the wordes
of the meffage, he fent to the mayfter of the
howfe, where he was to fuppe, faying : my time
is come : with thee doe I make my Pafch, togeather with my difciples. Wordes fo efficacious
with him, as he forthwith offered them the beſt
place in his houfe, and prepared it in the beſt
manner he poffibly could. And of this I muſt
make my profit.

1.   To confider, with what manner of
fweet words our Sauior tooke leaue of his moſt
deere mother, when he was now to depart, and

to goe to his death : and how peraduenture he related vnto her in particular all and euery the torments he was to suffer, and the dolefulll stations, he was to make, till he should come to the mount of Caluary, where he should be nayled to a Crosse, and giue vp his soule into the handes of his eternall Father. How he also prayed her to take a care of his poore flocke, which should remayne without a Pastour, as strayed sheep, and that for the three dayes, that his body should lye in the sepulcher, she would animate, encourage, and comfort his disciples. To consider, with what pinching panges of griefe the sweet Virgin heard these lamentable and pittifull discourses : how in all things she offered and resigned her selfe into the handes of the eternall Father, and of her most beloued Sonne, whome she intreated to permit her to beare him company to his torments, and to dye with him also, that she might not loose him, but with the losse of her owne life also.

3. To consider, how our Sauiour went ioyfully from Bethania to Hierusalem, being glad to see the tyme of his Passion come, though on the other side his Apostles went on sad & heauy for the feare they had of their good maysters death, who in the meane tyme sought to comfort them by sweet and encouraging speeches, whilest that Iudas followed behind all alone, deuising with himselfe, how he might find the cōmodity to deliuer him to his enemyes, that he might finger the money, that vvas promised him.

4. To

4. To confider thefe wordes: With defire I haue longed to eate this bread with you Which he vttered with an hart boyling with the heate of Charity, as he was fitting at the table with his difciples, to giue them to vnderftand, how affectuoufly he loued them, that he did eate in their company, not only that Pafchall Lambe, but alfo another much more precious, which was his body, and bloud.

4. To confider, how our Sauiour in the eating of the Lambe obferued all the ceremonier of the Law, reprefenting himfelfe, who was the true Lambe, that was to be roafted vpon the Croffe in the fire of his loue towardes God, & men, & was the Lambe, that was before figured. He did alfo eate bitter lettice, remembring the bitter gall, that fhold be giuen him to drinke in his paffion. Heere I muft confider, how our Sauiour offered then himfelfe to his heauenly Father, to fuffer all that was reprefented by thofe ceremonyes.

Meditat. VII.   *Of the washing of his difciples feete.*   Ioan. 13.

TO confider the moft affectionate loue, that our Sauiour manifefted to his poore Apoftles in this laft houre when he gaue them to vnderftand, and with their eyes to fee, that he loued them, as he did himfelfe. For as though he had forgotten all apprehenfion of his owne torments, he began to exercife acts of great kindnes

nes towardes them for the moderating of their
sorrow, and heauynes . He declared, that he ten-
dred them with a constant and excessiue affection, and that without limitation , as far as it was
in him possible to giue them a demonstration of
amity towardes them , by doing , and suffering
for them what it was possible for him to doe, &
to suffer . Finally, he testifyed, that his loue tended to their greatest good , and last end , which
is glory, after that they should in this mortall life
haue loued , serued, & honoured him : and that
he loued them , not to bestow riches, honours,
nor corporall pleasures vpon them, but to vnite
them vnto himselfe by the band of loue , which
is both the first beginning , and last end of all
thinges .

　2 .　To consider, how supper ended, our
Sauiour rose from the table , and putting of his
vpper garments , tooke a towell , and did put it
about him : he tooke a bason, and did put water
into it , and began to wash his Apostles feete, to
make them cleane, and wipe them . Heere I
must consider, who it is , who humbleth himselfe so lovv, as to doe the office of the meanest
vassayle, and to prostrate himselfe at the feete of
sinners . It is the only Sonne of God , begotten
from all eternity, in the presence of whome the
Angells prostrate themselues , and doe him homage , God infinitly wise, infinitly powverfull.
It is he alone, who doth this contemptible office,
who strippeth himselfe of this garments , who
powvreth vvater into the bason , who setteth it
before his Apostles feet . It is he, vvho makes
　　　　　　　　　　　　　　　　　　those

those sacred handes, (Creatours of thousands of vvonderfull beautyes)this day a cleanser & vviper of foule feete taking himselfe a pleasure to do this exercise, that exceedeth for humility, not permitting any other to put to his hand to help him therein. For at this tyme in particular he tooke vpon him the office and forme of a seruant, to teach by example vvhat he had before time preached by vvord, saying: Learne of me, that I am meeke & humble of hart.

3. To consider vvho they be, vvhose feete our Sauiour vvasheth. They are poore men, descended of the race of the terrestriall Adam, held for persons base and contemptible, euen among the refuse of the vulgar sort. To consider vvith vvhat an admiration S. Peter vvas surprized, vvhen he savv his Lord and mayster to kneele dovvne before his feete to vvash them. Heereupon he tooke occasion to deny him to vvash his feete, and to say: Lord doest thou vvash my feete, vvho am a poore, and miserable vvorme? To consider the vvordes, that our Sauiour vsed to Saint Peter, seeing him way vvord, and stiffe in his opinion of refusall: If I vvash thee not, thou shalt not haue part vvith me. As if ne had sayd, Thou shalt be no more my disciple, I vvill not suffer thee any longer to be one of my schoole, but I vvill banish thee out of my company, & from the inheritance of my Kingdome. Where may be seene, how much rebellion, and disobedience in following ones own iudgement, is displeasing to the diuine maiesty, though it be shadowed with the specious pretext of humility.

We

We may further conceiue the necessity we haue to be washed from our sinnes by the Redeemer of our soules , and therefore we must oftentymes say : wash me, Lord from my great wickednes, and cleanse me from my sinnes, not only once, but oftentimes, that I may be cleane before thy holy face .

4 . To consider, what manner of motion this our Sauiours threat wrought in Saint Peters mind: for it toucht him at the quicke, and in the most sensible part of his hart, wherein there burned the tender affection and loue he did beare to his mayster, with whome he had a desire to abide and continue alwayes, and for that cause he offered all his body to the washing How our Sauiour answered him : He, that is washed, needeth not but wash his feet . His meaning is, that those that be in grace by the Sacraments of Baptisme & Pennance , haue besides further need to be purged and made cleane of their terrene affections , and their veniall sinnes , vvherevvith none can haue any part vvith God, that is, enter into heauen . Of this vve are to learne to fly from veniall sinnes, in as much as is in vs possible.

5 . To consider, hovv our Sauiour vvent on the vvash the rest of his Apostles feete , and came in fine to Iudas, whome he would not exclude from that his fauour, to see whether so cōpassionate an action of his might mollify his stony hart . Heere I may represent to my mind the svveet speech , our Sauiour might perhapps vse vnto Iudas in his hart, and consider the inexplicable humanity of the same our Lord in kneeling

ling

ling downe before that rauenous wolues feete, who was neuer a whit moued to behold that meeke Lambe prostrated before his sacrilegious feet: a most strange hardnes of hart occasioned by mortall sinne, that maketh the soule more hard, and more insensible, then any rocke.

6. To consider these our Sauiours words: you know what I haue done to you · And these other following: If I, who am your mayster, & Lord, haue washed your feete, you ought also to wash one anothers feete. As if he should say, know you what manner of mistery is contayned and hidden in that I now come to doe to you? You must also by worke exercise the same charity one to another, that I haue exercised towardes you: which hath been mine exercise also all my life long.

7. Of the Institution of the most B. Sacrament shalbe treated after the meditations of the life of our Sauiour, vvhere is to be seene, that which concerneth this diuine mistery.

Meditat. V I I I. *Of the Apostles debate touching the primacy and first place.*

TO consider, how our Saniour had no sooner sayd, that the houre was come, wherin his heauenly Father would clarify, and honour him, but that there arose a spirit of ambition among the disciples, which made a question among them touching the matter of preheminence. But our Sauiour forthwith tooke

D d   vpon

vpon him to decide the matter of contention, & out of his wisdome represented vnto them, that he, who desired to be the greatest in his schoole, was to endeauour and seeke to be the very least of all, and he who had a will to preeede, should make himselfe the seruant : exhorting them further, that seeing they had persisted vvith him in his tentations till that present houre, they should continue, & perseuere to follow him still to the end.

2. To consider, how our Sauiour sayd to his disciples, that all of them should suffer scandall that very night, by wauering in their faith, to the end they might know, & vnderstand their owne weaknes. To consider the great courage, whereof Saint Peter made a shew, in saying that, though all the rest should be scandalized, yet he would neuer : wherein he ouer rashly contradicted his good mayster, and in some sort preferred himselfe before the rest of his companions, in presuming more of himselfe, then of them, and of his owne forces, yea and in promising more, then was in him to performe, and in witnessing that he had courage without humility, which is a cause of many errours, as the fall both of Saint Peter, & of the rest of the Apostles giueth ample testimony. Out of this, I am to draw a document and instruction neuer to presume of my selfe, but to humble my selfe in alll thinges, and to confesse, and acknowledge mine owne fragility.

3. To consider, how our Sauiour reprehended Saint Peters arrogancy in these termes :

X

I say vnto thee, that before the Cocke croweth, thou shalt deny me thrice, As though he should haue sayd, Thou, who presumest, and braggest more then the rest, shalt deny me, & shalt be scandalized more then all, this very night. To consider, what he sayd vnto the other Apostles, in these wordes : That Sathan would cist them, as corne in a Ciue &c. Where we may see, that the Diuell cannot tempt any without the permission of God, & that if our Sauiour had not prayed for Saint Peter and for the rest, they had been all in a piteous case, and Sathan had easily ouercome them. To ponder these wordes, that our Sauiour after this sayd vnto Saint Peter : And thou, after that thou shalt be conuerted, confirme thy brethren. By vvhich vvordes he tempered, and qualified the rigour of his former prediction of his fall, by this second of his uersion, that he might not fall into despayre, & that in acknowledgement of such pardon graunted him, he might help, comfort, animate, & confirme his brethren.

Meditat. IX.   *Of the Sermon of our Sauiour made after his last supper.* Ioan. 14.

TO consider, how our Sauiour, exercising the office of a sinner, exhorted his disciples to heroicall acts of vertue, and in the first place to the loue of God, alleadging many notable reasons to that end, saying : As my Father hath loued me, I also haue loued you : abide you

Dd 2   in

in my loue. Which is manifested most of all in
keeping Gods commaundements. If you loue
me, sayth he, keep yee my precepts. For he,
that keepeth them loueth me, & he that loueth,
shall be loued of my Father. Wordes, that merit due consideration, because they goe accompanyed with much consolation, sith they teach
vs, that the most sacred Trinity abideth, & dwelleth in the soule, that keepeth Gods commaundments.

2. To consider, how he also very earnestly recommended vnto them the loue of our
neighbour, & that with most ponderous speech,
in calling it a new commaundement, for that he
renewed it, when the malice of men had banished it out of the world, and left it vnto his disciples for a true ensigne of his schoole. He also named it his owne, for that though other commaundements were his also, yet this was his after a most excellent manner. For his law is foū-
ded vpon this precept, and therefore it is giuen
for a liuely example of this charity, and of the
loue of our neighbour. And for this he added:
These thinges I commaund you, that you loue
one another. Giuing to vnderstand, that all the
other commaundements are comprized in this
only of loue. And this he would reiterate the
third tyme, for the better imprinting it in our
harts.

3. To consider, how he further taught them
the exercise of continuall prayer, togeather with
the circumstances, that must goe in company
with it, by putting their trust in his diuine promise,

mise, and assuring themselues, that whatsoeuer
they should aske in his name, should be graunted them, adding further, that they should aske
oft, to make them see, that it was so, as he sayd
vnto them. To consider, that he, who maketh
this promise, is Gods only Sonne, yea the truth,
and infinite wisdome it selfe. Those, to whome
such a promise is made, be the faythfull, for the
sauing of whose souls his diuine maiesty vouchsafed to become man. That the Eternall Father
also made it by the mouth of his Son, who worthily meriteth to haue the same with him, because he is most sollicitous, and most affected to
the good of his children. That his beloued Son,
is God as well as he, & hath loued vs so tenderly, as he hath dyed for vs, togeather with the holy Ghost, who is very loue it selfe, who inspireth
vnto vs to aske for the desire, he hath to giue vnto vs. The tytles, and motiues of our petitions
be in the name of Iesus Christ, his vertues, his
meritts, his trauaylls, and his seruices he hath
done to his heauenly Father, &c. We must therfore aske that, which is fitting for vs, vvith
a great fayth, and certayne assurance, neyther must vve be remisse or slovv in presenting our demaundes, sith his Maiesty is so
liberall in condescending, and yielding vnto
them.

4. To consider, how our Sauiour alleadg-
ed many reasons vnto the Apostles for the co-
forting of them in their afflictions present and to
come, saying, that they shold remember their
Lord and mayster, sith the disciple is not to haue

more priuiledge, then hath his mayfter, nor the
feruant more then hath his Lord: faying further,
that they, vvhome the vvorld perfecuteth, be
not of the vvorld, but of Iefus Chrift; that all
thefe trauaylesare one day to be conuerted into repofe, thefe teares into ioy, thefe torments
into pleafure, as it hapneth vnto women, vvho
are in payne during the tyme of their trauayle
with child, and haue eafe, and comfort when
they are once deliuered. Euen fo they muft remember, that after thefe tempoeall afflictions
there followeth eternall repofe, befides this, that
this good alfo accompanyeth them, that when
they expect leaft, our Sauiour cometh to vifit
them, & leaueth not them orphelines: that thofe,
vvho fuffer heere on earth, are beloued of the
Father of heauen, becaufe their fufferings be as
it were the pledges of loue to them: and that finally we fhall remayne victorious ouer all our
enemyes, that affayle vs. Be yee confident, faith
he, becaufe I haue ouercome the world. that is
to fay, in vertue of my victory you may be affured of yours alfo: for I haue ouercome, that you
may doe the like, and it is I vvho fight vvith
you.

*Meditat. X.   Of the Prayer that our Sauiour
made at the end of the fupper.*

TO confider, how our Sauiour Iefus, lifting
his eyes vp to heauen with great reuerence
both outward, and inward, and with a fin-
                                        gular

gular deuotion, and with voyce somewhat raysed, prayed vnto his heauenly Father in this
manner: Father, the houre is come, glorify
thy Sonne, that thy Sonne may glorify thee.
This prayer may serue as a forme for well making and addressing of ours: for we must craue
of our heauenly Father, that he would please to
glorify his Son all the world ouer, that is, that he
would please to make him knowne to the faithfull, and to the vnbelieuing alike: We must also craue of him, that he vouchsafe to glorify vs,
though miserable sinners, vnworthy to haue
the name of his children, by the gifts of grace,
not for the seeking of our owne honour, but
for the procuring of his glory, and preaching of
his wonderfull workes all the world ouer. To
consider, how our Sauiour in this prayer allead-
ged the seruices he had done to his Father, obeying him in all thinges, to teach vs, that we may
other whiles with humility represent that we
haue done, to his diuine maiesty, not for any
glory to our selues thereby, or to stay there, but
to moue the diuine goodnesse to graunt vs what
we craue of him.

2. To consider, how hauing prayed for himselfe he praied for his Apostls also, saying to his e-
ternall Father, that he besoght him to haue a care
of them, because they were his, & that he would
giue them a perfect vnion of charity with him,
and among themselues: and that he would deliuer them from all that, vvhich may haue any
contrariety, or repugnance with that vnion,
and graunt them also perfection in all vertues.

Where

Where we are to vnderstand, that he teacheth
vs to aske great things.

3. To consider, hovv after prayer made
for his Apostles, he also prayed for all the faythfull; as well those, who haue euer been till this
present, as for them, who are to be, and confequently he prayed for me, sith all men were to
him present in his thought, crauing for the faithfull not only charity, and perfection in this life,
but also glory, and euerlasting repose in the o-
ther, where he is as man, with the enioying of
the cleare vision of God. To consider these words:
Father, whome thou hast giuen me, I will that
where I am, they also may be with me: that
they may see my glory, which thou hast giuen
me.

*Meditat. XI. How our Sauiour went into the
garden, and of the great heauines, wherewith
he was seyzed. Matth. 26.*

TO consider the causes, for which our Sauiour went into the garden. The first is,
because it was his custome to retire himselfe into some solitary place to make his prayer,
after he had preached all the day before. The
second, because it was a place, well knowne to
the traytour Iudas. The third is, for that his e-
nemies might find him, and lay hand vpon him
the more commodiously. The fourth and last,
for that as the ruyne of man began first in a garden, so his reparation might take the beginning

also

alſo in a like place.

2. To conſider, how when he came neere to the garden of Getheſmani, he ſeleſted out of the nūber of his diſciples three, whom he loued beſt,& began to be ſorrowfull & troubled in their preſence, pleaſing to depriue himſelfe of all ſenſible ioy, and to take vpon him the contrary paſſions, as feare and heauvnes, permitting his appetites to produce thoſe affections of ſorrow in a moſt violent manner, thereby giuing vnto vs the more ample proofe of his loue, which cauſed him to refuſe, & not to admit the ordinary ſawce of afflictions, that is to ſay, ſpirituall ioy. To conſider the multitude, & greatnes of our Sauiours ſorrowes. For the Euangeliſtes for the diſcouering of them, do giue them the name of feare, trouble, agony, ſadnes, being affections moſt violent & ſorrowfull, which like vnto a company of cruell and raging beaſts came with an impetuoſity to gnaw vpon the amiable hart of our ſweet Sauiour, by the repreſentation of the torments, that he was to ſuffer the ſame night, & the day following.

3. To conſider, how the remembrance of the multitude of the innumerable ſinnes, the infinit grieuouſnes of the ſame againſt the diuine maieſty, and the exceeding great domage and hurt they bring to men, by precipitating thē into eternall flames, were preſented altogeather before the minde of his innocent ſoule, which we muſt imagine we ſee actually tormented both for, and by our ſinnes, and in particular myne there among the reſt, that cauſe vnto him that

violent

violent fadnes, feare, and agony, and therefore I will ftirre vp in myfelfe a true forrow and repentance for them. Moreouer the confideration of this, that very few foules were to make their profit of his Incarnation, death, and Paffion, of the Sacraments, and of other graces and fauours we haue by his meanes receiued, afflicted him exceedinglv, by reafon of the ingratitude, blindnes, and wilfull obftinacy of men, among whome I will acknowledge my felfe for one of the moft ingrate, and I will humbly craue pardon of him for the fame. The reprefentation alfo of the afflictions, punifhments, and torments, that his elect vvere to fuffer, vvhen he fhould be gone, the perdition of the Iewes, whome he had chofen for his children, their extreme ingratitude to bereaue him of his life, at whofe handes they had receiued fo many and fo fingular fauours; the damnation of Iudas, whome the diuell had already drawne out of his fchoole: S. Peters denying of him, the fcandalous flight of the other difciples of his forfaking him, the extreme affliction of his moft deere mother. And all thefe togeather did vpon the fodayne feize vpon the compaffionate hart of our Sauiour, and drowned it as it were in a bottomleffe gulfe of forrow, & caufed this his extraordinary heauynes.

4. To confider thefe our fweet Sauiours wordes: my foule is fad vnto death: ftay yee heere, and watch with me. This he fayd to the three difciples, whome he fauoured, his meaning being, that his foule was furprized with fo

preffing

preſſing and ſore an heauynes, as it was inough
to take from him his life, if he ſhould not pre-
ſerue and keep it, that he might looſe it by a
long and crueil, and more tormenting death.
This he ſayd for a teſtification of the greatnes
both of his loue and of his heauynes, that we
might yield him due and reſpectiue thanks therfore: and for a declaration alſo, that he was true
man, voluntarily ſubiecting himſelfe to the ſorrowes, and feares of death, and for this cauſe
he did in ſome ſort comfort himſelfe with his
diſciples, to whome he communicated his ſore
affliction, as he had done his Tranſfigura-
tion before, meaning thereby, that as they had
been eye witneſſes of his ſhort ioy on the mount
of Thabor, they ſhould alſo be like witneſſes of
his long ſorroyves in his bitter Paſſion.

Meditat. X I I.   *Of our Sauiours prayer in*
   the garden.   *Matth.* 26. *Luc.* 22.

T O conſider, how our Sauiour willed his
   Apoſtles to watch and pray with him, that
   they fell not into tentation, as he ſhewed
them an example, teaching vs, that the true remedy for the moderating and eaſing of our heauynes, & ſorrow, is not to deale & treate with
men, but with God by reſtles & cõtinuall prayer. For to him we are to recurre in our afflictiõs,
as to the ſole cõforter of diſtreſſed ſoules, & prayer being the only remedy, that we may not giue
place to tentations, but rid our ſelues of them.
                                        We

We muſt ponder theſe words : watch with me: that is to ſay, in my company, & as I doe watch: for I am he, whoſe example you are to follow : where he giueth to vnderſtand, that he watcheth with the watchfull, and prayeth in company of the deuout. Finally we are to conſider this act of mortification in our Sauiour, by ſeparating himſelfe from the company of his diſciples in tyme of ſo preſſing and violent an heauines of mind, when men naturally deſire & ſeeke company for the diuerting of it, and putting of it a-way. Saint Luke obſerueth this effect of morti-fication in theſe wordes : He was pulled away from them a ſtones caſt, as one, who by the force and power of ſpirit did ouercome the in-clination of the fleſh. And of this we muſt make our profit.

2. To conſider the feruent prayer, he made to his heauenly Father, vpon his knees, & proſtrated with face vpon the ground, ſaying : Father, if it be poſſible, let this chalice paſſe from me: neuertheleſſe not as I will, but as thou wilt. We are heere to conſider fowre thinges, moſt remarkable in this prayer. The ſolitary retyre & going aſide, for the auoyding of diſtraction: the moſt great reuerence, and humility both inward and outward, ariſing of the great eſteeme and reſpect he had of his heauenly Father : the firme hope, and perfect loue, in ſaying (my Father) and the ſingular obnegation of his owne will, & the reſignation of it into the hands of God, with perſeuering long in that which he craued of his Father. In this muſt we imitate him.

3. To

3. To confider, how rifing vp all fad and heauy from his prayer, he returned to his difciples, and found them a fleep, when mildly blaming them, he fayd : watch and pray . Wordes, giuing teftimony of the paternall loue, he did beare to his, fith in the middeft of his extreme affli&ion he vifited them, interrupting his owne feruent prayer, with a fweetnes and moderation to put them in minde, what they were to doe, feeing it to be a fault, that in them proceeded of infirmity and weaknes. By the way we are to marke, by this the Apoftles fleeping the little care, men haue in affayres fo importing, which concerne their eternall good, and our Sauiours fo affe&uous care for the working & procuring of it .

4. To confider, how he returned once, & twice to pray, as before, and repeated the fame word (Father) twice, to giue vs to vnderftand his refpe&, and loue, and the confidence he had in his Eternall Father, by occafion whereof he continued long in his prayer, befeeching him (as we may thinke and beliue) that all might be faned, that his Paffion might profital, and that the fruit of his fo many and fo fore torments might not be fruftrate, fith he was the Redeemer of all men in generall . To examine thefe wordes : If this chalice may not paffe, but that I muft drinke it, thy will be done : As if he had fayd, If I muft drinke the bitter chalice, that myne ele& may drinke the fweet of it, I am ready to doe & accómplifh thy holy will.

5. To confider, how rifing from his prayer,

er, he went agayne to visit his disciples, and finding them sleeping, he pityed their weakenes, and therefore he left them, and returned to his prayer a third tyme. Where we may see the extreme anguish our Sauiour suffered in the inferiour part of his soule, without finding comfort from any. For his Eternall Father stopped his eare at his cryes, his sweet and most compassionate mother was absent, and his disciples who were at hand to giue him cõfort, slept for griefe, in so much as our Sauiour might iustly then say: I sought him who might haue cõforted me, & I found him not. And this other verse of the psalmist: my God, my God, why hast thou forsaken me? I cry day and night, and thou hearest me not. We must heere consider, that notwithstanding he were not ouerheard, nor comforted, yet he persisted in his prayer, to teach vs to be perseuerant in our prayers.

Meditat. XIII. *Of the apparition of the Angell, and of our Sauiours sweat.*

TO consider, how our Sauiour being in prayer, pressed with a deadly heauynes, his Eternall Father sent vnto him an Angell, which was Saint Gabriel, as it is most likely, to manifest that he despised not his Sonns prayers, but would then send him an Angell to comfort him, as another tyme he sent him many to serue him, after he had ouercome the Diuell in the desert. To consider, with how great reuerence the Angell spake vnto our Sauiour, proposing

pofing many good reafons that might make to
the eafing & mitigation of his anguifhes; as that
it was the will of his Eternall Father, that he
fhould drinke this Chalice:that neceffary it was
he fhould doe it for the redeeming of finners, &
for the helping of the iuft, who attended his coming in Lymbus, for the reparation of the
ruynes in heauen, for the accomplifhing, & fulfilling of the prophefyes, &c. Whereunto our
fweet Iefus gaue attentiue and humble hearing,
fhewing that as he was man, he ftood in need of
the comfort of his creatures.

2.   To confider, how when his forrow
& anguifh preffed him foreft, he began to fweat
great drops of bloud, which fell and trickled
downe from him vpon the ground. Wherebv
is to be feene the extremity of his inward heauynes, his foule being moft violently preffed with
the naturall feare of death on the one fide, and
with the zeale of Gods glory, and of mens faluation on the other. By this I muft learne to reftrayne, and moderate myne appetites. To confider our Sauiours exceffiue loue, vouchfafing
to fpend his precious bloud in fo prodigall a maner: and to thinke, that by fo doing he refem-
bleth the tree, that beareth mirrhe, which firft
diftilleth its owne liquour by a voluntary fweat
through the pores of the body and ftocke of
the tree, and after it is cut in the rine and barke,
that the myrrh may come forth in more a-
bundance. So is it with this myrrhe, of which
we muft make to our felues a little bundle to fet
in the middeft of our foules. To confider, bovv

our Sauiour in this his wonderfull and ſtrange ſweat did manifeſt the dolefull apprehenſion & feeling he had of our ſinnes, and of the mortall wounds, that ſhold be giuen to his holy Church, for the curing wherof he vouchſafed himſelfe, as the head therof, to take the moſt bitter medicine, not contenting himſelfe with his ſhedding of teares, but alſo adding his bloud. Moreouer, he would declare, that he tooke pitty on his e-lect, that were afflicted and perſecuted, as being himſelfe their head, & they his members. Laſt-ly, were are to conſider, how our Sauiour be-came very feeble & weake, through this ſtrange ſweat, whiles none was at hand to giue him any help in that extremity, or to giue him any linnen cloath to wipe of his ſweat. For the Angell, who was a beholder of ſo pittifull a tragedy, ſtood by aſtoniſhed with admiration.

3.   To conſider, how our Sauiour roſe vp from his prayer comforted, and went to awake his diſciples, ſaying vnto them, that he, who was to lay hand vpon him, and to betray him, was neere. Where we muſt obſerue the meeknes of our Bleſſed Sauiour in not reprehending their ſluggiſh ſleeping, in a tyme that required ſo much watchfulnes, and withall the efficacy of prayer. For where he was before filled with feare, he then found himſelfe full of courage, & of a noble reſolution.

¶   This Meditation ended, we muſt make another by the application of our inward ſenſes, after the manner, that our B. Father Igna-tius teacheth, as vve haue ſayd in the begin-ning

ning of the fecond , and of this third Weeke .

Meditat. XIIII. *Of the comming of Iudas with the fouldiers to apprehend our Sauiour.* *Matth.* 26. *Luc.* 22 .

TO confider the deteftable craft and policy of the traytout Iudas, feeking to apprehend our Sauiour partly by force,& therfore he brought fouldiers in his company , partly by guyle and deceit, fhadowing his treafon by
a kiffe of peace, which he moft impudently gaue
him. To confider, how this moft vnhappy man
of an Apoftle made himfelfe a captayne & lea-
der of theeues and robbers , and how he ferued
himfelfe of the knowledge , he had of our Sauiour, and of the place he frequented, for the compaffing of his more then diabolicall perfidy. To
examine the fingular meeknes of the innocent
Lambe our Sauiour, in receuuing this trayte-
rous kiffe, without conceyuing of any horrour
at the facrilegious mouth , that touched his facred face, in calling him friend, and in correcting
him fo meekly in thefe tearmes : O Iudas , be-
trayeft thou the Sonne of man by a kiffe ? As if
he had fayd to him , doeft thou make me warre
with this figne of peace ? O my friend Iudas ,
what is thy defigne in comming hither thus vnto me ?

4. To confider , how our Sauiour came
forth to meete the fouldiers, faying vnto them ,
that himfelfe was the man, whome they fought:

and

and how at those very wordes, they fell downe
backewardes, our Sauiour meaning thereby to
giue them to vnderstand, that he permitted them
to lay hand vpon him, and to take his life from
him, of his owne voluntary will, and not of any
necessity: also that the fall of the wicked is dá-
gerous, for it is commonly sodayne, & that they
fall when they thinke least of it. We must diligently weigh these wordes: I am he. Which
for the good be full of consolation, as if he had
sayd, I am he who am your Father, your Sauiour, your maister &c. And contrary wise dreadfull to the bad: I am your Iudge to punish you,
the God of vengeance, &c.

3.   To consider, how after he had giuen
leaue to those souldiers to rise agayne, notwithstanding they had seene so euident a miracle, yet
they gaue not ouer to put their Diuellish intention in execution, for that both Iudas, and the
rest of his most vnhappy crew were obstinate in
their sinne. To consider the infinite charity of
our Sauiour, who notwithstanding he did put
himselfe into his enemyes handes, did yet forbid
them to touch any of his disciples, who were present: where we are to obserue, what a care God
hath of his.

4.   To consider, hovv S. Peter, hauing a
will to defend his mayster, and permitting himselfe to be caryed away with the the violence of
his feruour, layd hand on his sword, and strooke
one of the souldiers: but our meeke Sauiour
willed him to put vp his sword into the scabbard
agayne; For all that take the sword, shall perish
                                                    with

with the fword. That is, whofoeuer killeth by the fpirit of reuenge, is worthy to dye. Wherin our Sauiour manifeſteth, how much he defireth that we fhould be moſt far from fuch a malicious fpirit: and therewithall he difcouereth his ovvne furpaſſing mildnes. I muſt confider thefe wordes: Wilt thou not, that I drinke the chalice, which my Father hath giuen me? Wherby he manifeſtly infinuateth, that he confidered not his paſſion, as proceeding from his enemyes, but as ordained by the will of his heauenly Father, and this was the caufe, that made it contenting and fweet vnto him, though of it felfe it was moſt full of paynes, and bitternes of this his voluntarily refignation into the handes of his enemyes, being of power to haue deliuered himfelfe, if he had pleafed, and to haue had of his Father many legions of Angells for his defence. We muſt learne to refigne our wills into Gods hands.

5. To confider, how our Sauiour of his moſt fingular goodnes did heale Malchus his eare, which S. Peter had cut off, teaching vs by fuch his rare meeknes to loue our enemies; meaning alfo to take away the occafiõ that the Iewes might haue taken to treate the Apoſtles ill for hauing refifted Iuſtice. We muſt make humble petition to the diuine maieſty to heale vp the the eare of our foule, that we may be more prõpt & ready to obey his commaundements.

Medi-

Meditat. XV.   Of the apprehension of our Sa-
uiour .   Matth. 26 .

TO confider , how our Sauiour was apprehended, and treated by thofe infernall furies, as a theefe , and robber , though they
might haue layd hand on him euery day in the
Temple, where he ordinarily preached. To examine well thefe wordes: This is your houre
now , and the power of darkenes . By which he
gaue vnto his enemies power to lay hand on
him , and to torment his body at their pleafure ,
without any limitation . Heere I muft conceyue
& ftir vp great commotions of forrow, loue, and
compaffion &c .

     2 .   To confider, how this wicked crew
of infernall minifters had no fooner receyued
this leaue, then that they furioufly ran vpon our
Sauiour, handling him fo inhumanely , as neyther tongue is able to declare, nor thought to cõ-
cevue . For thefe brutifh monfters left not a
part of his body, which they did not torment in
a moft cruell manner. To confider our Sauiours
moft profound humility , while his enemyes
trodde vnder their feete, him , who fitteth v-
pon the winges of the Seraphims : his inuincible
patience among fo many iniuryes of blowes,
buffetts, and torments, which he receyued as an
innocent Lambe, without either cõplayning or
fpeaking a word : his extreme meeknes in giuing his handes, that had created fo many won-
                                        ders ,

ders, to be so cruelly bound. The consideration
of these paynes ought to moue vs to take great
compassion on our Sauiour, to a most bitter sorrow for our faults, for which he hath suffered so
much, to a most singular loue of him, & to the
imitation of his vertues.

3. To consider, that the Apostles, seeing
how badly our Sauiour was treated, insteed of
dying at his feete rather then to forsake him, in
acknowledgement of so great fauours receiued
of his goodnes, and in particular of the fauours
he had done them a few houres before in their
supper, where they had put on a resolutió neuer
to leaue him, in tyme of this necessity ran their
wayes, and left their Lord and mayster in all the
broyle ; This we must apply to our selues. To
consider the extreme griefe, that pressed our Sauiour to see his flocke and company dispersed,
togeather with the ingratitude of his disciples, in
so much as he might then with good reason say
these wordes of the psalme 87. Those of my acquaintance be become straungers vnto me: they
haue me in horrour & in abhomination.

*Meditat. XVI.   Of the torments that our Sa-
uiour endured in the garden, till he came to
the house of Annas.   Ioan.* 18.

TO consider the vexations our Sauiour endured in this troublesome way, whiles his
enemies all the way long handled him
most inhumanely, some drawing him forwards
by

by the cordes, wherewith they had bound him,
some striking him with the truncheons , and
staues they had in their handes , others beating
him , and pushing on, as if he had been a beast,&
forcing him to make hast, whiles sometymes he
was forced to runne , sometymes he stumbled ,
sometimes agayne he fell downe , in so much as
his tender and delicate body,that had a little before for extreme anguish and heauynesse sweat
bloud, being agayne turmoyled, vexed, & cruelly treated , did open the poores once more ,
though not to put forth a bloudy, yet at least to
euaporate a painefull sweate, which his payne ,
labour in going , and wearysomnes , violently
caused in him .

2. To consider the outrages, blasphemies,
and ignominies , that these barbarians exercised
towardes him, whiles some called him a theefe
and robber, others seditious , and a disturber of
the people,and all this with extreme pride & incredible despight towardes him. To consider the
singular meeknes , humility, patience, and charity, wherewith our Sauiour receyued all these
iniuryes,offering vnto God his Father this painfull way of his , in satisfaction of so many bad
steps, as we make to offend him : endeauouring
in what we may,to excite and stirre vp commotions of loue , and of acknowledgement of all
this.

3. To consider the wordes of contempt,
and of mockery , that were cast out and vsed a-
gaynst our Sauiour , as he was entring into Annas his house , whiles the Scribes and Pharisies
scorned

scorned him, and abused him many wayes. For those the Diuells mynisters were assembled in that place of pestilēce, for the examining of him, who was true wisdome it selfe, where they began most prowdly to demaund of him about his disciples, and his doctrine, whiles our Sauiour gaue them the hearing with profound humility, and virginall modesty, and he, who with his wisdome filleth both heauen and earth, submitted himselfe to the examen of those Doctors.

4. To consider the discretion of our Sauiour, who answered, that he had not published his doctrine in secret, but openly in the Temple, and in the Synagogues, wherof he challenged themselues for both Iudges and witnesses, notwithstāding they were his enemies. And thogh this answere stopped their mouths, and they had nothing to say agaynst it, yet their damnable wils were not satisfyed therewith. But our Sauiour would not say a word touching his disciples, because he would not discouer their great disloyalty towardes himselfe.

Meditat. XVII. *Of the buffet, that our Sauiour receyued of the souldiar.* Ioan. 18.

TO consider, how one of those ministers of Sathan gaue our Sauior a blow on the face with his hand, and that very sore and cruell, because it was giuen him by the hand of one in choller, a most ignominious and shamefull one, because it was giuen, and receyued in the
presence

presence of many persons of nobility, and quality, for the person who receyued it, and for the
vility and basenes of him, who gaue it : an vniust
one, because it proceeded from a reuenge vnder
pretence of a calumny: an imprudent one, yea &
most impudent withall, for a most prudent and
wise answere. To be short it was approoued &
liked by the applause of al, that were preset, who
thereby also opened the way to other bad com-
panyons, gaue them the like assurance, and en-
couraged them to lay their violent and sacrilegious hands vpon that venerable face, which the
Eternall Father, the Angells, and the Blessed Virgin mother take pleasure to behold.

2.   To consider our Sauiours most milde
answere in these wordes : If I haue spoken euill,
giue testimony of euill : but if well, wherefore
strikest thou me ? We must take exaple of these
gentle and mild wordes, that we may put vp the
iniuries, that be done vs, without desire of reuenge. To consider further, how notwithstanding this answere were so reasonable, yet was it
not admitted of the standers by for such, neither
by them regarded.

3.   To consider, how our Sauiour was
from thence sent and conducted to Cayphas the
high Priest, that he might haue the iudging of the
cause in company of other Scribes & Pharisies,
who were with him. Thus was our meeke Iesus
agayne lead, and bound peraduenture with new
cordes, for feare least going along the streets he
he might get loose, and escape, with lowd cryes
and showtings, as he passed, at the noyse wherof
all

all the people came running out of their houses to see, what the matter was, in so much as the ignominies and paines, that our Sauiour endured, increased more & more.

Meditat. XVIII. *Of Saint Peters three denyalls of our Sauiour.*

TO consider the degrees, by which S. Peter descended to deny our Sauiour. The first was a coldnes in his loue, proceeding of a vavne feare. The second was an obliuion & forgetfulnes of what our Sauiour had told him, that he did put himselfe in danger of offending, by thrusting himselfe into company with that accursed crew, vnder colour of loue to his mayster, in so much as hauing sought out an occasiō, that might prouoke him to his fall, he was ouercome more by his owne imprudent fact, then by any violence of the tentation, hauing deserued to fall in so grosse a māner, because he presumed ouer much of his own forces, without reflecting vpon that, which his mayster had foretould him touching his imbecility and weaknes. To consider these the Euangelists words: It was night & cold: which giue to vnderstand the coldnes, & darknes, that S. Peters soule was in.

2. To consider, how the diuell assayled Saint Peter by mediation of a woman, as he did the first Adam by meanes of Eue. For he knoweth full well, that they be instruments most apt and proper for the executing of his designes,

and

and the ablest armes and weapons for the ouer-
throwing of the most stoutest, as this shamefull
fall of S. Peter by experience manifesteth . For
after he had confessed our Sauiour to be the naturall Sonne of the liuing God, notwithstanding
he were designed the Churchs fundamétal stone,
yet at the voyce of a poore chamber-mayde he
denied him, swore that he knew him not, dete-
tested, and blasphemed horribly, that he was not
a disciple of his, and that he had not to doe with
him . Where we are to obserue the frailty of our
infirme nature, how much an inordinate feare of
loosing the honour, or the life, hurteth, and how
little cause we haue to trust vpon our many
yeares, that vve haue liued in religion , or to re-
ly vpon our pious exercises, and works, sith our
weakenes goeth alwayes in company with vs: &
therefore we must euer liue in feare of our falling . To consider the greatnes of the iniury, that
Saint Peter did to his good Lord and mayster in
denying him so fowly , and the great griefe that
it might cause him , to see himselfe condemned
by him , who should haue been a witnes of his
innocency .

3.   To consider, how Saint Peter, seeing
himselfe in so great danger, went out of that vnhappy company, and got himselfe towardes the
dore , at what tyme the cocke crowed the first
tyme, and he obserued it not : but entring into a
place, where other persons were, & being asked,
if he were any of that mans disciples, he denyed
it, in swearing that he was not, and being againe
within a while after demaunded the same question ,

on, he fell to cursing and swearing, that he knew him not. O poore Peter, how hast thou demeaned thy selfe in the company of the wicked? we must heere consider the malicious craft of the enemy, who is wont to multiply his tentations, to ouerthrow a man, especially if he be vertuous. We are further to obserue, how dangerous a thing it is to persist a long tyme in the occasion of sinning, and not to correct one selfe after the first fault, or not to consider that one sin draweth another after it, as this poore Apostle doth manifestly teach vs. For as he rashly presumed of his weake forces, and that three seuerall tims, so many tymes also denyed he his mayster in testimony of his frailty, in so much as pride was then humbled, as alwaies it is.

4. To consider how S. Peter had no sooner made an end of this third denyall of our Sauiour, but that the Cocke did crow the second tyme, and that very instant his diuine maiesty beheld him with a compassionate eye, by occasion wherof he came to remembrance of what he had done, and forthwith getting out of the house of pestilence, he wept bitterly. Where we are to wonder at our Sauiours infinite charity, who notwithstanding he were cōpassed in round by his enewies, and were in the very middest of his afflictions, ill handled and tormented on all bands, yet, as though he had been insensible in so many his owne miseries, he forgot himselfe, that he might bring this his strayed sheep home to his fold againe, and deliuer him from out of the infernall wolues throte: & notwithstanding

the iniury, that S. Peter had done him, he mercifully beheld him, & recalled him by his effectuall grace, that he might both vnderstand and acknowledge his sins, & both weep, & do pennance for them. We must also craue this grace, & beseeching the diuine maiesty to cast his mercifull eyes vpon vs, and effectually to call vs to the acknowledgement & repentance of our sins.

5. To consider the most bitter teares, that S. Peter did shed both then, & all his life after, still remembring the speciall fauours he had receuued of his mayster, our Sauiour, & his owne extreme ingratitude towardes him in a time, wherin he shold haue giuen a thousand liues for the confession of his name. Euery one of vs may heere represent vnto himselfe the disgusts, that S. Peter conceiued towards himselfe, & the dolefull commotions, that he felt in his hart, and imitate the same in behalfe of his owne sinns. To consider the sodayne alteration & change, that followed in S. Peter vpon the fauourable countenance, that our Sauiour cast vpon him. For he did put him in remembrance of his wordes, caused him to leaue the occasion of his sinne, & did put him in mind to retire himselfe to some secret place, there al alone to lament his errour & fault in bitternes of hart. Such be the effects, that the diuine maiesty worketh and produceth in the soule, that he effectually calleth, and regardeth with his diuine & mercifull eyes.

Meditat. X I X . *Of the false testimonyes, that were deuised, and bought against our Sauiour.*
Matth. 2 6.

TO consider, how the Scribes and Pharisies laboured in all they could to bring it about, that our Sauiour might be sentenced to dye, and therefore they raysed many false testimonies agaynst him, whereunto our Sauiour returned them no answere at all, and held his peace to that wherein they falsely accused him. Heere we are to consider, what manner of men those be, who be the Sonns of Gods Iudges, with what a Diuellish fury they are transported agaynst him, the insupportable haughtynes and pride, that possesseth them: what manner of men his accusers be, and principally to consider, who is the person accused, and to see, hovv they make him to stand in their presence, vvith his handes fast tyed vvith cordes : What be the vvitnesses agaynst him, the extreme fury wherewith they proceed agaynst his innocency . To consider on the other side the surpassing purity and sanctity of our Sauiours immaculate life, vvhen as his enemyes sought vvithall the diligence, they possibly could, and vvith all the malice, that could come from men, some matter, vvhereof to frame an accusation against him, and could neuer find any . Moreouer to vvonder at his deep silence, vvithout opening his mouth eyther to defend himselfe, or to confute the false testimonyes, that

Ff 3   vvere

were produced againſt him : carrying himſelfe
as a Lambe, that is mute before him who theareth him, being aſſured of the innocency of his
owne life.

2.   To conſider the anſwere he made
to Cayphas, when he adiured him by the liuing
God to tell him, if he were the Sonne of God.
Wherunto hauing anſwered yea, for the reſpect
he caryed to the holy name of God, and repreſenting vnto them, that he whome they ſaw ſo
much oppreſſed now, ſhould one day ſit on the
right hand of God his Father, and ſhould come
vpon the clowdes of heauen to iudge the whole
world, he ſeemed to ſay the ſame, to ſee whether the apprehenſion of the latter Iudgement
might put any feare into them for the appeaſing
and ſtaying of their ſury and madneſſe agaynſt
him.

3.   To conſider, how Cayphas, and the
others his aſſiſtants thought this our Sauiours
humble and true anſwere blaſphemous, Cayphas renting his garment contrary to the law, &
peruerting al order of iuſtice in this, that he, who
was the Iudge, became both a party & accuſer
togeather, and made thoſe, who ſtood by, the
Iudges, inducing them to ſentence the innocent
party for a blaſphemer. We muſt heere ſtirre vp
our ſelues to compaſſion, in ſeeing our Sauiour
ſo falſely caluniated, meruailing with our ſelues,
that he ſhould be come to ſuch an extremity,
a to be reputed a blaſphemer, who is Truth it
ſelfe. To conſider, how peruerſe the iudgements
of men be in taking light for darkenes, & with
                                   what

what manner of courage our Sauiour heard and accepted this most vniust sentence, when it was sayd, He is culpable and worthy of death; especially when he saw the generall consent, & common accord of those, who condemned him to dye, who were bound vnto him for so many benefitts, & fauours, bestowved vpon them.

Meditat. XX. *Of the iniuryes and torments, that our Sauiour suffered in the presence of Cayphas, and his Councell, during the rest of the night. Matth.* 26.

TO confider, how the fentence beeing haftily, and precipitantly pronounced againft the Redeemer of the world, those, who held him bound, through the inftigation of Sathan began to treate him most iniuriously & contumeliously both by vvord, and by fact. And firft of all they did spit on his face, difgorging vpon him the fowle filth, that they rayfed out of their loathfome ftomackes: a kind of ignominy of all other moft abominable, and the more barbarous, becaufe it was done vpon the perfon of the Eternall Fathers Sonne, whofe face was moft venerable. And yet he endured this moft ignominious and reproachfull intreatement with an vnfpeakable meeknes, without faying a word, or cōplayning. The fecond iniury was in blindfolding him, that they might the more freely ftrike him, and fcorne him at their pleafure thinking that he could not fee them. For the maie-

F f 4   fticall

sticall grauity of his face did in a more exeel-
lent manner shew it selfe, by the serenity of
his beautifull eyes, so as their diuine clearenes
did in some sort hinder the extreme impudency
of those villanous monsters of hell, who in that
brutish action followed the inclination of most
abhominable & execrable sinners, whose desire
is, that God should not haue eyes to behold their
abhominations, to the end they may giue themselues the more liberty to commit them, as
thogh his cleare seeing eye could be obscured by
darkenes, or hindred by the obscurity of secret
corners. The third iniury was in inhumanely
smiting him with their sacrilegious hands, some
with their fists, some with open hand, buffeting
that diuine face at their pleasure, and by turnes
striking him on the head, necke, breast, & other
parts of his body, as madnes, fury, and cruelty
moued them, in so much as that most beautifull
visage of our Sauiour became blacke and blew
with the buffetts, & disfigured with their fowle
spitting on his face. The fourth iniury was in
pulling the hayre of his head, and beard, in
most ignominious manner handling this great
high Priest, and most beautifull Nazarean. Finally they misused him a thousand wayes in
wordes, in breaking their biting and bitter iests
vpon him, saying by mockery: Prophesy vnto
vs, o Christ, who is he that strooke thee: adding
cruelty to their blasphemous scoffing, & shewing that they held him for an impostour, and for
a deceyuing and false Prophet. For we must
thinke, that they would not forget any villany,
nor

nor reproach, that they caused him not to suffer, calling him a Samaritan, possessed of the Diuell, a glutton, drunkard, &c. And as they were rash, and shameles blasphemers, and filled vvith fury, and Diuellish enuy, credible it is, that they vttered vvhatsoeuer they could deuise, or imagine to be worst of all for the disgorging of their rage against him. Of all this I must endeauour to stir vp commotions of compassion, and to imitate the wonderfull vertues of our meeke Iesus, exercised in this action, as his meeknes, humility, patience, &c.

2. To consider what our Sauiour was likely to suffer all the rest of that night, being in the hands of that damnable and accursed crew, and to thinke that one part molested and tormented him, whiles another tooke breath, sleeping by turnes, without suffering their poore prisoner to take any ease, and inuenting new sorts of torments to afflict him, in so excessiue and extraordinary a manner, as impossible it is for the vnderstanding of man to comprehend it. For they handled the Redeemer of the world as a poore worme of the earth, as one, that were the abomination of men, the reproach of the wicked, and the sport and recreation of the most vnworthy creatures of the earth. To consider, how in this meane while our Sauiour was in his deep collection of prayer for the enduring of these his tormentes with the more constancy, and true resolution, representing to the eyes of his mind all mankind, for which he suffered, and me in particular

cular among others, and off;ring his paines vnto his Eternall Father, in satisfaction for our
sinners.

3.   To consider, hovv the newes of our
Sauiours passion was carryed to his most heauy
and sorrowfull mother, and to thinke how exceeding great and extreme the griefe was, that
transpierced he most piteous and compassionate
hart. And this we are to reflect vpon, and to represent vnto our mindes in euery action of the
Passion.

*Meditat. XXI.   Of the presenting of our Sa-
uiour before Pilate, and of Iudas his vnhappy
death.   Matth. 26.   Luc. 22. & 23.*

TO consider, how the Scribes, and Pharisies thought the tyme long till morning
was come, to bring their detestable designe
to a wished conclusion about the bereauing him
of his life, who had before called vp their
Councell very earely in the morning: by which
is insinuated, that the wicked be very diligent
in executing their malice. How our Sauiour also for his owne part desired the same day, which
he had expected the space of 3₂. yeares for the
accomplishing of the Redemption of mankind.
We must heere imagine, that we see that diuine
face most fowly disfigured through the most
bad intreatments of the night past, couered all
ouer with the loathsome matter, that those inhumane caytiffes cast out of their breastes, and
                                did

did spit on his face, and the same blacke and
blew through the blovves of their fifts, and the
sore buffetts they gaue him. If I should aske of
him, vvho it is, that hath handled him so inhumanely, his anfvvere vvill be, That my sinnes be
they, that haue done it.

2. To confider, hovv he vvas againe presented before thofe vniuft Iudges, vvho demau-
ded of him a second tyme, if he vvere Chrift. To
vvhich demannd he anfvvered vvith great liberty and assurance, that he vvas indeed, and
added, that they should one day also see it, &c.
to put them in feare, and to giue them to vnderstand, that after his humiliation there should one
day follovv his exaltation. To confider, hovv
he vvas brought before Pilate, as remitted from
the Ecclesiasticall Court to secular iustice. This
vvas the third ftation, that our Sauiour made,
vvho vvas lead in triumph vvith hands tyed in
great haft through the streets of the Citty, with
the lowd cryes and howlings of those rauening
wolues, at the noyfe wherof all the world came
running out of their houfes to behold that piteous fpectacle, among whome there vvas not any
found, that had hart and courage inough to deliuer him.

3. To confider, hovv the moft accurfed
Iudas, opening his eyes, that vvere blind before,
to see the moft horrible cry me, that he had done,
but not to confider the greatnes of Gods mercy,
fell in defpaire, as Cain did, & hanged himfelfe,
& bruft in the middeft, as the holy Euargelift
affirmeth. Whereby vve fee, hovv little his ca-
nable

nable auarice profited him, vvhich vvrought
vnto him the death both of body, and of soule,
and vvas the cause, that the siluer that he so loued before, serued him for the instrument to
hang him. To consider, vvhat an obstinacy that
vvas of the Ievves, who seeing the repentance of
the disciple, who had betrayed his mayster, and
confessed his innocency, did neuertheles proceed
and goe forvvardes in their Diuellish designes,
saying: what haue we to doe with him for his
innocency? Looke thou to it. To represent vnto our minds the griefe, that pressed our
Sauiour, to see the perdition of his disciple that
had been, and how willingly he would haue receiued him to grace, if he would haue recurred
vnto his mercy, as he did to the malice of the
Priests of the law.

4. To consider, how our Sauiour would
manifest the care, and loue, he did carry towardes the poore, causing by his diuine prouidence, that the price of his bloud was applyed
to the buryall of them, for as much as of the siluer that Iudas rendred to the Temple, after he
had receyued it for the hire of his detestable
treason, was bought a field, & peece of ground
for the buryall of the poore pilgrymes.

Meditat. X X I I. *Of the accusing of our Sauiour before Pilate.* *Matth.* 27. *Mar.* 15. *Luc.* 18. *Ioan.* 25.

TO confider the bad intertainment, that Pilate gaue our Sauiour, when he was prefented before him with hands bound, on of folemne a day, when & where fo great a multitude of people were prefent, come thither from all parts of the world. How at the very firft he imagined, that he muft needes be fome wicked man and great malefactour, that they brought before him, efpecially when he vnderftood the turbulent and confufed accufation of the Iewes, faying: If this man had not been a malefactour, and criminall perfon, we had not brought him hither.

2. To confider the fuppofed crymes, that the Scribes and Pharifies impofed vpon our Sauiour, hovv he was feditious, how he ftirred vp the people to rebellion; how he taught that tribute was not to be giuen to Cæfar: that he made himfelfe a King, and the Sonne of God; that he was the Meffias promifed in the law: to al which calumnies our Sauiour anfwered not a word. To confider, how Pilate examined him, taking him afide, and afking of him, if he were a King. To whom our Sauiour anfwered, that his Kingdome was not of this world, but that he was the King of heauen, and that he had alfo fubiects & vaffalls celeftiall, and fpirituall, to wit, the Angells,

G g gells,

gells, and the iuſt : and that further he was come into the world, to giue teſtimony of the truth, teaching it with conſtancy, and confirming it by miraculous works : that he neuer ſayd any thing, that was not veritable and true, and that all thoſe, who ſtand for the truth, vnderſtand his voyce, loue him, and yield him obedience. In which anſwere appeareth the authority of a Sauiour, who amiddeſt ſo many contempts, & reproaches, doth the office of a mayſter & Doctour. To conſider Pilates wordes, in ſaying : What is the Truth? without expecting any anſwere vnto them : becauſe he deſerued not to vnderſtand, what it was. Heere we are to conſider, how little the truth is knowne to the world : and on the contrary, how deep a roote Lying hath taken in it.

3.　To conſider, how Pilate hauing gathered by our Sauiors words, that he was innocent, admiring withall at his deep ſilence, and ſeeing how he excuſed not himſelfe, nor propoſed any defence on his owne behalfe, nor yet impeached his accuſers againe, was reſolued to deliuer him. But the chiefe Prieſtes greatly diſpleaſed thereat, charged him agayne vvith nevv impoſtures, and both of moſt grieuous, and moſt falſe crymes, thereby to incite the Iudge to giue ſentence of death agaynſt his innocency, ſhewing therein their implacable malice, and hatred they had conceyued agaynſt our Sauiour, who on the other ſide manifeſted for his part his owne inuincible patience, his inexpugnable conſtancy, his moſt deep ſilence,

and

and moſt ſingular humility .

Meditat. X X I I I. *Of the Preſentation of our Sauiour before Herod . Luc.* 23.

TO conſider, how Pilate hauing vnderſtood by the contents of the accuſations, that our Sauiour was a Galilæan of Herods Iuriſdiction, returned him vnto him, that he might proceed in iudgement vpon him, and ſo he was lead through the middeſt of the Citty with much more ignominy, then before, by occaſion of the concourſe of the people, and the fury of the Iewes, who feared, that if there were any delay vſed in the proſecution of his death, the Iudges would deliuer him as innocent.

2. To conſider, how Herod much reioyced to ſee our Sauior, not that his ioy proceeded of any charity, but of curioſity, thinking that he might ſee him worke ſome miracle, or other, which yet he would not doe, neither ſo much as ſpeake, or anſwere Herod, holding him for a perſon excommunicate, as well for the death of Saint Iohn Baptiſt, as for his ſcandalous adultery, and for the puniſhing of his vayne curioſity, and by the ſame meanes to giue him to vnderſtand, how willing he was to ſuffer & dye for our ſaluation. We muſt heere admire, and conſider our Sauiours moſt ſtrict ſilence.

3. To conſider, how Herod, and all his Court mocked him, & ſent him backe to Pilate, after they had put him into a white garment,

Gg 2   whils

whiles Herod meant to giue to vnderstand, that
he held our Sauiour for a foole, for a contemptible person, and not to be regarded: as if he had
said, I returne vnto you this blocke-head, this
witlesse foole, this King of straw, with other ignominious titles of the like kind. We must
heere admire our Sauiours surpassing humility,
and thinke how great a confusion & shame that
was of his, to passe along the streets of the Citty,
where all the world with a lowd voyce called
him a foole, a man without wit, an imaginary
King, and with what manner of laughter, and
showtings he was receyued into Pilates pallace,
when he came before him, clad in that white
apparell, at sight wherof all began to hisse at him,
in so much as his sorrowes and afflictions still increased vpon him. Whereupon we may conceyue, what was our Sauiours loue towardes
vs, sith for our sakes he would make himselfe
the matter of so many outrages, and torments.
Further to consider, how Herod and Pilate, who
were enemyes before, came to be reconciled by
meanes of our Sauiour. Whereby is giuen to
vnderstand that, which his death, hath principally wrought to the world, namely the vnion
of two people, the Iewes & the Gentills, by an
holy band of charity, with the price of his owne
bloud, & life.

Medi-

Meditat. XXIIII. *Of the preferring of Ba-rabbas before our Sauiour, and of our Saui-ours condemnation by the Iewes.* *Matth.* 27. *Ioan.* 18.

TO consider, how it was a custome among the Iewes, at the feast of the Pasch, to choose out two criminall persons, & that he, whome the people would, should be deliue-red and set at liberty, and thereupon Pilate, wil-ling to serue himselfe with this occasion, matcht our Sauiour with one of the most notorious malefactours, that were then in prison, named Barabbas, a man wicked in a most high degree, seditious, a theefe and homicide, and one who therefore merited to be abhorred & detested of all: proposing vnto the people, whether of those two their desire was should be released. This af-front was one of the most sensible, that our Sa-uiour euer suffered, by occasion of the ignomi-ny of being put in comparison with a most wic-ked assassinate and murtherer. To consider fur-ther, with what an heate the Scribes, Pharisies, and false Priests of the law sollicited and subor-ned the people to aske the deliuery and release of Barabbas, and the condemnation of our Sa-uiour. What ill they sayd of him, and how ma-ny false impostures and calumniations they did put vpon him. To consider heere, how Barab-bas euen at this day findeth many to defend him, and how wickednes is fauoured, suppor-

ted

ted, and borne out in preiudice of innocency, which abideth abandoned and all alone, & none so hardy as to speake a word in fauour of it, notwithstanding the cause it maintayneth, be full of equity, and iustice: as is to be seene in this of our Sauiour, who in this his extreme necessity found neyther friend, nor man in the world, among so many thousands, who were bound vnto him for the most great benefitts, he had bestowed vpon them, who would speake but a word to the Magistrate in fauour of his cause.

2. To consider, how the people with a lowd voice demaunded to haue Barabbas released vnto thē, & that Iesus should be condēned to dye, reiecting the authour of life, and postposing him to a most wicked murtherer, in so much as our Sauiours humility could not descend to any lower degree. To consider, how much the iudgements of men be deceiued, whē as in so cleere and euident a cause they giue their voice in fauour of iniustice, and condemne the truth: how strong the passion of Enuy is, which in so great a light dimmeth the vnderstāding with so great obscurity: how mutable and inconstant men be, & how little assurance there is in their fauour. & how little cause also to feare their disfauour. Heereupon we may consider, that he, who falleth into mortall sinne, maketh the very like election, in contemning our Sauiour, whome he postposeth to his sensuall pleasure.

3. To consider, how Pilate was much astonished to see the bad election the people had made,

made, in preiudice of our Sauiour, and of his innocency, though he had not the courage to deliuer him, but asked agayne, and agayne of the
people that was mad with malice, what he shold
doe with our Sauiour, making them the Iudges
of him, whome they pursued as parties: and all
this redounded to the dishonour of our meeke
Iesus. To consider these wordes, so oft reiterated by the people (Crucify him, Crucify him)
in testimony of their incensed malice agaynst
him; and to thinke how deeply our Sauiours
soule was toucht with griefe, to see himselfe condemned to death, & that so ignominious, and
cruell an one, by them, whome he had bound
vnto him, by so many diuine fauours as he had
done them.

Meditat. X X V.   *Of our Sauiours flagella-*
tion, or whipping at the pillar. *Matth.* 27.
Ioan. 19.

TO consider, how Pilate commaunded our
Sauiour to be scourged, as well for the ap-
peasing of the Iewes fury and the contenting of their enraged Passion, as also for the satisfying of the law of the Romans, which was, that
if any were to be crucifyed, he should be whip-
ped before. This sentence was most vniust, most
cruell, and most ignominious, because it was the
punishment, that was to be inflicted vpõ theeues,
& robbers, and slaues; besides that, that it was
pronounced against a most innocent person. To
Gg 4   consi-

consider, with what a courage our Sauiour receiued the sentence without eyther appealing, or contradicting, presenting his most precious body to that cruell scourging in satisfaction of my sinns; and offering vnto God his Eternall Father those most bitter paynes, and torments, togeather with the bloud he was to shed for our saluation, saying: I am ready to receiue all the stripes, that shall be giuen me: sith it is the pleasure of my Father it should be so.

2. To consider, how the souldiers layd hands forthwith vpon our Sauiour after an vnsupportable manner of pride, and surlynes, and stripped him naked to his very skinne, and then bound him fast to a pillar. Heere we must represent to our mindes the extreme confusion, that this our most beautifull, most noble, and most chast Sauiour suffered, in seeing himselfe all naked before so many persons, in an infamous place, destined, and appointed for malefactours, the whole assembly of the standers by mocking him, reproaching, and confounding him in the highest degree. And all this our most meeke Sauiour suffered most patiently: and we must excite our selues to commiserate his most piteous case by this consideration, that he endured all this for our sinns.

3. To consider, how our Sauiour beeing fast bound both hands and feete to the pillar, his most inhumane tormentors began to discharge an exceeding great number of most cruell blows with their whippes vpon his most innocent naked body, some with long and smarting rods
of

of greene and pricking twigs ; others vvith
sinnewes , accommodated with spurs, and sharp
iron prickes at the end ; some others with small
iron chaynes, that penetrated to the very bones,
and rent away the flesh togeather. These barbarians were wearyed agayne & agayne in laying vpõ him, whiles some succeeded still in place
of others : but our most meeke Sauiour was not
wearyed in suffering , though the stripes were
vnto him most sensible, and most cruell withall,
and fell vpon euery part of his body, no one part
of it remaining free from woundes frõ the head
to the feete , the very bones being discouered to
the eyes , & shewing their whitenes through his
purple and most precious bloud , and his most
delicate body being left like an anatomy , the
skinne flead off. For his tormentors did all this
vpon an emulation one of another for the contenting of the President, and the satisfying of the
Iewes fury, who vnder hand feed them with money , that they might whip him in the cruellest
manner they could , conformably to their fierce
and vnciuill nature , and to the Diuells malice ,
whereof they were the ministers, and executers
of his cruelty. Thus was the only Sonne of God
rent, & wounded with more then fiue thousand
blowes of his scourging , according to the more
common opinion, and this in all parts of his body . To consider our Sauiours inuincible patience in suffering so extraordinary torments
without giuing any signe of being troubled, or of
complayning, presenting vnto his heauenly Father those stripes of his scourging in satisfaction
of

of our finnes, with a defire & will to fuffer much forer torments then thofe, of it had bin neceffary for our, and for the fatisfying of the iuftice diuine. We muft heere conceyue an exceeding great horrour of our finnes, feeing they be the caufe of fo feuere a punifhment, executed vpon our Redeemers perfon, with a firme refolution to punifh them in our felues. We muft proftrate our felues at our fweet Sauiours feete, to bath our foules in the diuine fource, and fountaine of his precious bloud, and therin wafh, and cleanfe them of their fowle ftaynes. Finally, we muft confider, how when this moft inhumane and vn-iuft Iuftice was ended, the foldiers vnbound our Sauiour, whofe forces were fo fpent and decay-ed through his whipping, and the loffe of his bloud, as credible it is be fell downe: but feeing himfelfe naked in prefence of fo great a number of people, he got vp with exceeding payne, and vvent vp and dovvne to gather his gar-ments togeather, that lay difperfed heere and there, drawing the vpon the ground after him all bloudyed, & foyled with the duft. We muft heere put on an affection of compaffion towards our Sauiour, who found himfelfe fo abandoned, & fo deftitute of all humane compaffion, expo-fed to the cofufion both of heauen & earth, who doth himfelfe cloath the Angells with the beau-ty they haue. And therefore we muft loue him, who hath in fo affectuous a manner loued vs.

Medit.

Meditat. X X V I. *Of of crowne of thornes,
and of other iniuryes, done to our Sauiour
Iesus.* Matth. 27. Marc. 15. Ioan. 19.

TO Consider, how after the most cruell
flagellation of our Sauiour, there followed
another kind of torment more sore & more
painefull then it, namely, the crowning with
most sharpe thornes, and this in the sight of an
infinite number of people, who came running
thither, and were by the souldiers, (who did all
for the increasing of our Sauiours greater ignominy) inuited to the spectacle of his confusion.
Heere we must ponder the insatiable desire our
Sauiour had to suffer for loue of vs, permitting
his enemyes to inuent and find out new kinds
of reproaches, and punishments, to be exercised
vpon his person, therby to giue the greater testimony of his excesse of loue towardes vs, and
by the same meanes to cause vs to see, and take
notice of the grieuousnes of our sins, for which
he endured all this. To ponder the great malice
of these his tormentors towards him, in calling
the people togeather to the spectacle, to the end
their presence might cause the greater confusion
to our Sauiour, beeing exposed to be mocked
and scorned by them. We must heere endeauour to stirre vp our mindes to compassion by
consideration of these torments of his.

2. To consider, how these villaines stripped our Sauiour of his cloathing in a violent
manner,

manner and without any compaffion, or regard
of his perfon, which imbrewed with bloud, did
cleaue faft to the woundes of his rent body, a
kind of torment both new, and fhamefull, being done in the prefence of fo great a number of
lookers on, & thē clad a new with a poore purple
garment in derifion and fcorne of his Regality,
which thofe caytiffs efteemed counterfayte, they
did fet vpon his head a crowne of fharpe pricking thornes, that pierced to his very fcull, and
caufed the bloud to trickle downe in abundance
from his head, filling his body with extreme
paine, and his foule with confufion. Heere we
muft enter into the confideration of this new
tytle of Honour, which our Sauiour weareth
for the loue of our foules, reprefenting to our
felues, that our fynnes of pride, and our other
inordinate appetites, be as many thornes, that
pricke and payne him in a more cruell manner,
then did thofe, that the fouldiers put on his
head: and then by confidering him fo fore tormented, mocked, and wronged, we muft endeauour to ftirre vp in our felues the commotions, & affections of compaffion.

3.   To confider, howv after all thefe outrages they did put a reede into his had, infteed
of a fcepter, to giue the world to vnderftand, that
they held him for a counterfayte King, and reputed him for a foole, and mad man, in arroga-
ting Royalty to himfelfe. Heere we are to
to weigh the greatnes of the iniury, that was
done our Sauiour, in fo lightly regarding him,
and his Regality. To thinke, that the like is the
efteeme

ſeeme, that the world euen at this day maketh of his doctrine, and promiſes, which it deemeth as idle and vayne, though there be nothing more certayne, and more aſſured. To conſider, how our Sauiour admitted and receyued this affront with the ſame will, that he did all the reſt. To meditate, how much men are deceyued in their iudgements, when as to the terrene & periſhing Kingdomes, & Royaltyes they giue a ſcepter of maſſie gold, and to the euerlaſting Empire of our Sauiour they affoard but a poore, weake & crazed reede. To contemplate, how they mocked him, and with knee bowed in ſcorne ſayd vnto him : Hayle King of the Iewes. Wordes moſt highly diſpleaſant to his ſacred eares, that were worthy to heare the ſonges of prayſe, that the Angells ſing in exaltation of his glory.

4. To conſider, how to their words and ſpeeches of reproach, and of confuſion, they added worſe and more afflicting actions, whiles ſome ſtrooke him vpon the head with the ſame reede to cauſe the thornes to enter the deeper into the fleſh, ſome ſmote him with their hands, others did ſpit the fowle corruption of their loathſome ſtomackes on his face, others pulled the haires from his beard, and all in one word did their vttermoſt to torment him moſt. To wonder at his inuincible patience, his moſt profund humility, and his moſt incenſed charity: for his tormentors were wearyed in tormenting him, but he was not wearyed himſlfe in ſuffering, though his ſacred body were in a manner cleane ſpent with the torments, that had been

H b exerci-

exercifed vpõ nim, & with the loffe of his bloud, and forces decayed thereby &c. We muſt take pitty on our Sauiour for theſe his paynes, ſeeing there was not any there, who was toucht with any compaſſion towardes him.

Meditat. XXVII.   Vpon theſe words: BE-HOVLD THE MAN.

TO conſider, how Pilate ſeeing our Sauiour quite diſfigured, and thinking that the very ſight of him alone might mooue a compaſſion in the ſtanders by, cauſed him to be preſented & brought forth to the aſſembly in that poore and piteous caſe, ſaying: Behold the man: We muſt meditate & conſider theſe wordes, firſt as being Pilates words in the ſenſe he meant them. Behold this man, who ſayth, he is a King, & the Sonne of God. Behold him ſo ſeuerely puniſhed, as he hath in a ſort loſt the very figure of a man, and yet he is ſtill a man, as you are, and therefore you ſhould take pitty on him, as like vnto you. They may alſo be conſidered, as inſpired of the holy Ghoſt, ſpeaking by the mouth of Pilate thus: Behold this man, who is true God, though in outward appearance he be like vnto other men: this is the Meſſias, promiſed in the law: this is the head of all men, and the Bleſſed of all ſpirits: this is he, whom his infinite charity hath broght to this piteous ſtate: whome the loue of men hath charged with the paines, that is due to their

ſinnes:

ſinnes. Heere we muſt ſtir vp the commotions
of loue, and of admiration, in ſeeing what the
diuine maieſty hath done for the loue of vs. We
may alſo conſider theſe wordes, as proceeding
from the Eternall Father to all men in generall,
thus: Contemplate yee this man, whome I haue
ſent into the world, to be your mayſter, the mirrour of all perfection, and ſanctity. Conſider his
his vertues, his charity, humility, patience, pouerty, obedience, meeknes, &c. Weigh alſo
what he endureth both outwardly, and inwardly for your ſaluation. To offer vnto God the Father the meritts of this diuine perſon, crauing by meanes of him vertues neceſſary, & the
remedying of our neceſſityes, ſaying vnto him:
Looke, O Lord, vpon the face of thy Chriſt:
for impoſſible it is, that thou ſhouldeſt abandon
thoſe, whome he vouchſafeth to protect, & for
whome he hath endured ſo much.

2.   To conſider the little effect, that theſe
wordes of Pilate wrought in the hard harts of
that vngratefull people, who with a brutiſh fury fell a crying: Crucify him, Crucify him. To
conſider what a bitter apprehenſion our Sauiour
felt and had, touching the ingratitude of them,
who were bound vnto him by ſo many good
turnes, ſeeing the ingratefull and wicked recompence, that was made him therefore. To conſider the new accuſation, the Iewes brought a-
gayng our Sauiour, preſſing the Iudge to pronounce the ſentence of death vpon him without
any more delay, for this, ſayd they, that according to their law he was to dye, becauſe he made

him-

himselfe the Son of God. Where is to be seene
this peoples blindnes, who held the truth it selfe
for blasphemy, charging themselues with the
same cryme, that they would impute to our Sauiour.

3.   To consider, how Pilate hauing heard,
that our Sauiour was the Sonne of God, was
seized with a feare, & yet was on the other side
discontented, because our Sauiour answered not
a word to the accusations of the Iewes, nor to
his authority. To consider, that as our Sauiour
held his peace, when & where he thought it expedient, so did he also speake, when it was to
purpose, saying to Pilate: Thou shouldest not
haue any power against me, vnles it were giuen
thee from aboue: blaming by these wordes the
vniust Iudges insolency, and giuing to vnderstand, that all, that was done heere on earth a-
gainst him, was by the permission of his heauenly Father.

4.   To consider, how the Iewes, perceyuing that Pilate was inclined to deliuer, and release our Sauiour, said vnto him, that if he did
let him goe, & escape so, he should not be Cæ-
sars friend, with whose name they serued themselues to put the false Iudge in feare, who causing our Sauiour to be brought agayne forth,
sayd vnto them: Behold your King. As if he
should say, See heere this miserable person, this
poore and counterfayte King: see his scepter,
his crowne, and robbe of purple. A man may
meditate the same wordes, as by the holy Ghost,
spoken to the whole world. See, & behold the
                                                    King,

King, whome you haue so long expected for your deliuerance. Consider this King, the Son of Dauid, the annointed of God, to be your Prince and soueraigne Lord. See & consider, that he is wise & humble in the highest degree of perfection.

5. To consider the lowd cry of the Iewes, saying: Away with him, & Crucify him: for vve haue no other King, but Cæsar. Avvay vvith him, that vve may see him no more: for vve shall not be at quiet, as long as he shall liue: vve vvill not haue so much as one only hayre of his head remayning, but our desire is not only that he dye, but also that the very memory of him be quite abolished. To consider, vvhat vvas the blindnes of this people to reiect their lawfull Prince, vvhome God had giuen them to enrich and honour them, and to accept for King a Tyrant, vvhome they abhorred a little vvhile before, for spoyling them of their goods, and liberty, vvhich vvas vnto them so deere. I must apply this to my selfe, by considering, hovy often I haue abandoned and reiected my God & Lord, for the contemptible thinges of the earth.

Medit.

Meditat. X X V I I I.   *Of the Condemnati-*
on of our Sauiour, to the death of the Croſſe.
Matth. 27.

TO Conſider, how Pilates wife was in her
ſleep troubled with ſome perplexed dream,
whereof ſhe did the next day giue notice
to her husband to proceed no further in that affayre, much leſſe to condemne the innocent party. This dreame might come from the common
enemy, who ſeing the ſanctity of our Sauior, be-
gā to doubt that he might be the Meſſias, & the
Sonne of God, and ſo he ſought to hinder the
worke of the worlds Redemption by the means
of a woman, as he had before procured the de-
ſtruction of it by the meanes of an other woman. It may be alſo ſayd, that this dreame
was peraduenture occaſioned by a good Angell, by way of a threat to Pilates wife, and ſaying vnto her, that in caſe her husband ſhould
condemne our Sauiour to death, he ſhould be
damned himſelfe, & all the people of the Iewes
ſhould come to ruine.

2.   To conſider, how Pilate waſhed his
handes before the whole aſſembly, in teſtimony
of our Sauiours innocency, which the holy E-
uangeliſts haue alwaies pretended to manifeſt,
& make knowne in their Goſpells. To conſider
the malice, and fury of this wicked people, that
ſticked not to offer their owne liues, and thoſe
of their owne children, and to charge them with
that

that so execrable a cryme, rather then not to procure that our Sauiour should dye vniustly, so they might come to the conclussion of their malicious and Diuellish designe. Whereby we are to learne, how dangerous a festered and rooted passion is to the soule, whiles there is nothing that may stay it.

2. To consider, how Pilate sentenced our Sauiour to dye vpon the Crosse, and deliuered him into the handes of his enemies to doe with him as they pleased, contrary to the lawes, and to iustice, condemning him whome he knew to be innocent, for feare of men, to whose peruerse will he accommodated himselfe againft his own senscience. To consider the lowd cryes & show-tings, which that accursed assembly made for ioy, when they heard the sentence pronounced, & saw their wicked desire effected, whiles all this still redounded to the dishonor, & the greater reproach & ignominy of our meeke I E s vs: who on the other side heard his sentence of condemnation with most great deuotion, & receiued it, not as though it came from the mouth of an vniust Iudge, but as comming from the decree of his heauenly Father. So he accepted it most willingly, without appeale, replication, or complaint of any wrong done him, permitting himselfe with a right good will to the cruelty of his enemyes. To consider, how some of the disciples ranne forthwith to carry the newes of this heauy euent to his sorrowfull mother, whose soule was seized with an inexplicable griefe, though otherwise she absolutly resigned her selfe to Gods will. Hh 4 *Medi-*

Meditat. XXIX.   *Of our Sauiours carrying of his Croſſe.*   *Matth.* 27.

TO Conſider, how the ſouldiers ſtripped our Sauiour of the cloathing, that they had put on him in deriſion in the palace of Pilate, and of Herod, & did put him into his own agayne, that he might be the better knowne, and mocked the more, leauing withall the crowne of thornes ſtill vpon his head, to confound him the more, and to put him to more and greater payne. To conſider how the ſentence of death was no ſooner giuen, but that the ſame ſouldiers brought the tree of the Croſſe, that was both very great, vnhandſome, and heauy. Where we muſt repreſent vnto our ſelues the fearefull apprehenſion, our Sauiour might haue at ſight of his Croſſe, and the dolefull wordes he might haue within himſelfe, calling it one while the bed whereon he was to ſleep the ſleep of death, another while the tree of his life, vpon which he was to pay for the preuariation that was comitted on the other tree of death. Euery one may conceyue, what amorous and affectionate ſpeeches his diuine maieſty made to the Croſſe. To conſider, how our Sauiours companions, who went with him to the mount of Caluary, were two notorious theeues condemned to dye for their villanyes, which was diſhonorable vnto him alſo, becauſe it was as much, as to make him the chiefe Captayne of theeues, & robbers.

                                    2. To

2. To confider the fecond going of our Sauiour out of Pilates Pallace, at what tyme he carryed his Croffe in the middeft betweene two theeues, the trumpet founding before him, & all the people crying alowd after him. Thus went forth the true Ifaac, loaden with the wood for his facrifice, the eternall Father carrying the fire, and the knife for the immolating of the victime, for the fatisfaction of my finnes. To confider the fore payne our Sauiours body was put vnto, that had formerly been weakned throgh the torturings, and fore brufed with the blowes, and whipping: how he fell downe euery fteep he made, of very weaknes, vpon his knees vnder the heauy weight of the Croffe, be fprinling the ftreets and the wayes, where he paffed, with his moft precious bloud. My foule muft accompany him in this his laft ftation, pittying his pains, and fore trauayles, and reprefenting vnto it felfe, that it is not fo much the materiall wood of the Croffe, that furchargeth him, as the finnes of men, paffed, prefent, and to come, and efpecially mine among the reft, whereof I muft repent my felfe, and for them craue pardon of him.

3. To confider, how whiles he went on with his Croffe vpon his fhoulders, much weakned by the delicacy of his body, almoft deftitute of bloud, the Souldiers who guarded him on the way, did him a thoufand iniuryes both by word, and fact: which proceeding of theirs increafed his paynes exceedingly. But whiles they were afrayd, leaft he might peraduenture dye,

before

before his comming to the place of execution, they gaue his Croſſe to another to carry it after him, his diuine maieſty permitting it, to giue to vnderſtand, that his Croſſe ſhould be communicated to his faythfull, which were to cary it alſo, for as much as without a Croſſe it is impoſſible to lyue heere on earth, or to come after to heauen. To conſider, how during this painfull ſhort iourny, our Sauior found not any one to helpe him, or to comfort him in his affliction, becauſe it pleaſed him to drinke vp the bitternes of his Chalice without any companion all alone.

4. To conſider, how he, who carryed our Sauiours Croſſe after him, was called Simon, that is to ſay, obedient: how he was a ſtraunger, and was come vp about buſines to Hieruſalem: how the paynes he tooke, was of ſhort contynuance, & yet the memory of him, and of his Sonnes continueth ſtill in Gods Church. Out of this a man muſt draw profit and inſtruction for himſelfe, by conſidering, that the true obedient, & he who holdeth himſelfe for a pilgryme in this vvorld, vvhere the life is ſo ſhort, is he, that carryeth the Croſſe after our Sauiour.

5. To conſider, how amongſt them, who accompanied our Sauiour, ſome tormented him, others wronged him diuers vvayes, and ſome deuout Women pittyed him, and wept to ſee him ſo badly handled. But our Sauiour ſhevved them the ſubiect, and cauſe, for vvhich they vvere to ſhed their teares, ſaying vnto them, that it vvas their ovvne ſinnes, & thoſe of their children: for that vvas indeed the true cauſe of

his

his Paſſion. Wherein our Sauiour giueth vs to
ſee his diuine authority, vvhich he conſerued &
maintayned amiddeſt all his torments, & diſcouered his moſt burning charity. For as though
he had put all his ovvne paynes in obliuion, he
vvould teach vs to lament and vveepe for our
ovvne faults, and particularly for the punition
of them, vvho make not their profit of his moſt
bitter death & Paſſion, tovvards the obtayning
of the remiſſion of their ſinnes. To conſider
theſe ponderous vvordes: If in the greene vvood
they doe theſe thinges, vvhat ſhall be done in
the dry?

6. To conſider piouſly, hovv the B.
Virgin, vvho loued her Sonne ſo tenderly, vvent
from her houſe, accompanied with Mary Magdalen, & ſome other deuout Women, ſeeking her
beſt beloued, and follovving the trace of the
bloud, exceedingly afflicted vvith ſorrovv and
griefe. Hovv our Sauiour turning himſelfe tovvardes the Women of Hieruſalem, among
vvhome he beheld his ſorrovvfull Mother, vnſpeakable it is, hovv ſore a griefe ſeized vpon
the hart of the other, both of them being preſſed,
& afflicted vvith a nevv kind of torment in ſo
exceſſiue a manner, as impoſſible it is to declare
it by vvordes, vvhiles the deſolate Mother beheld her moſt deare child, vvho vvas the only
Sonne of God, and conſidered him all disfigured, mangled, and deſpiſed of men, for loue of
vvhome he ſuffered all thoſe torments. To admire the manner of Gods proceeding, vvho
afflicteth thoſe, vvhome he loueth beſt. To conſider

fider the affliction & griefe , that our Sauiour
felt in his foule , at his going out of Hierufalem
vvith thofe markes of a finner , calling to his
mind, that that vnhappy Cittv, which did in that
manner thruft him out after fo many & fo great
fauours receyued at his handes by his holy prefence,& miraculous vvorks, vvas one day to be
deftroyed for punifhment of its ovvne ingratitude .

*Meditat. X X X .   Touching that which fol-
lowed vpon the Mount of Caluary.*

TO confider , how our Sauiour pleafed to
be Crucified on the mount of Caluary,that
his torments might be the more vifible o
the world , and confequentlv the more ignominious : he vvould dye in a place deftined for the
punifhment of malefactours, where men were
executed for enormous & moft grieuous crims ,
to make it knowne, that he dyed for the fatisfying of the diuine iuftice , vvho punifhed vpon
his innocent perfon the crims of men, who were
malefactours indeed . He vouchfafed to be put
to death in that ftincking place , that he might
haue fo much the more payne : & that at noone
day , that all might the more cleerly behold his
ignominy & nakednes , and acknowledge the
excefs of his loue . For the fame reafon he pleafed further to dye on a folemne day , on which
an infinite multitude of people referued to Hierufalem , that the whole world might learne of
                                        this

this diuine mayster the wonderfull lessons , that
he taught in the holy chayre of his Croſſe . He
would be borne in the darke night, but he wold
dye openly and in publike , expoſed to the deriſion & reproach of men.

2. To conſider , how being come to
mount Caluary, they preſented him wine, mixt
with myrrhe, & gall to drinke, wherin thoſe inhumane wretches diſcouered their more then
beaſtiall cruelty; for inſteed of giuing him wine,
as is wont to be giuen to others, that are to dye,
they offered him a drinke , compoſed of moſt
bitter ingredients and drugges, that as his body
had been tormented outwardly by the crowning & whipping , ſo he might haue his inward
torment in like manner by the gall , and ſo that
not any part of him ſhould be exempted from
the particular paine . To conſider , how the bad
Chriſtians doe the very ſame, in giuing vnto our
Sauiour to drinke of the gall of their ſinnes, and
in increaſing the torments of his Paſſion , which
they contemne, & make no reckoning of.

3. To conſider , how the ſouldiers ſtripped
our Sauiour of his cloathing , & expoſed him all
naked to the ſcorne of the world , which was a
proceeding moſt iniurious , and moſt afflictiue
vnto him , & yet he did beare it with moſt great
patience, & humility, preſenting that his confuſion to his heauenly Father And ſo he would go
naked out of this world , as he came naked into
it , to teach vs to rid our ſelues , and ſeuer our
ſoules from the things of this world by imbracing pouery & contemning the vanities of it.

Medit.

*Meditat . X X X I.   Of our Sauiours Cruci-
fixion .*

TO confider, how the Croffe beeing layd v-
pon the ground , the executioners bid
our Sauiour to ftretch himfelfe a long v-
pon it , whereunto he humbly obeyed, & layed
himfelfe downe vpon that hard bed, lifting vp his
eyes to heauen to his Eternall Father, giuing him
thankes for hauing brought him to that point ,
whereunto he was now come neere, to fee himfelfe to be facrificed vpon that Altar , and offering vnto his diuine maiefty that bloudy facrifice for an expiation of our finnes .

2.   To confider , how his facred handes &
feete were pierced through with nayles , driuen
in by fore of hand and hammer, a torment moft
cruell , and moft painefull withall , by occafion
of thofe more fenfible parts , & that moft full of
finnowes of all the reft of the body , and therefore more apt to feele payne , befides that his
body was moft tender , and delicate . To confider , hovv one of the handes beeing nayled to
the Croffe , all the other members drew themfelues in by contraction of the fynnowes , that
were hurt ; in fo much as when the other hand
was to be nayled, it could not reach to the hole,
that was made in that arme of the Croffe , and
therefore they ftretched it out to reach the hole,
by force of cordes , in fo rude and inhumane a
fort, as they disioynted all the bones , conformably

mably to the prophecy, that sayth: They pierced my handes and feete, and counted my
bones. Thus was his precious body drawne, &
stretched vpon the Crosse, as is a stringe vpon
an instrument of musicke. We must heere procure to haue an affection of compassion, in seing
a yong man, so beautifull, so holy, so innocent,
who is the ioy both of heauen, and of earth, &
the splendour of the Eternall Father, so tormented for our sinnes, agaynst which we must conceyue an irreconciliable hatred, because they be
those, that haue brought our Sauiour into so lamentable, and dolefull a state. To thinke, what
inward & sensible feeling of sorrow the Blessed
Virgin was likely to haue, when she heard the
blowes of the hammer giuen vpon the handes
& feet of her most beloued Sonne, and by her
receyued into the most feeling part of her hart.

3.   To consider, how our Sauiour was
lifted vp on the Crosse, with the great showtings,
& outcryes of his enemies, who still added now
increase to his torments, and confusion, whiles
himselfe was oppressed with extreme paynes,
neyther had any part of his body from head to
foot free from wounds, but most of all the foure
holes of his handes, and his feet did powre forth
fowre streames of bloud, as though they had
been fowre riuers, comming out of the terrest: i-
Paradise. To consider, how dolefull a spectacle
this was to the Blessed Virgin to see her deere
Sonne in that state: whose sorrow was such, as
if God had not miraculously conserued her in
life, the very griefe must needes haue bereaued

Ii 3   her

her therof. For if the friends of Iob, when they
saw him sitting vpon a dunghill, all couered o-
uer with a leprosy, continued mute, and had not
a word to say for many dayes togeather, and
when they began to speake, it was but to make
passage for the sorrow, they had conceyued at
such a spectacle: how much more feeling in that
kind had the most sacred Virgin, in seeing her
Sonne, whome she loued incomparably more
then any tongue may deliuer, so cruelly & inhumanely handled by his? There were some other
womē of Hierusalem in company with her, who
contributed their teares also to her extreme heauynes, & wept in company with her.

Meditat. XXXII.   *Of the mysteries of Iesus
    Crucified*.

VVE must prostrate our selues at the
    foote of the Crosse, & consider, who
    it is, that is Crucifyed, his infinite
greatnes, his goodnes, his mercy, his wisdome,
& omnipotency, comparing all his perfections
with this extreme misery, and abiection of his
diuine person, nayled to the Crosse, by considering how different the throne of his glory, wheron he sitteth as God in heauen, is from the tree
of the Crosse, where he suffereth as man for loue
of vs. Heere we must cry out with an affection
of loue, and of gratitude, & yield him thankes
for so singular a benefit, stirring vp in our harts
cōmotions befitting the matter we meditate.

2.   To

2. To confider, how this our Lord is the great Priest according to the order of Melchifedech, the Churches fupreme Bifhop, the Paftor of our foules, whofe apparell is painefull & ignominvous vnto him, his Pontificall Miter being a crowne of thornes: his paftorall ftaffe and croyfier, an heauy Croffe; his rings be the nayls, that pierce his hands. Thus entred our Sauiour Prieft into the Holyes of Holyes, offering himfelfe for a facrifice and holocauft, burnt, and confumed with the fire of loue, & of payne for the remiffion of finnes.

3. To confider Iefus Chrift, as our Redeemer, & only mayfter, who about the end of his mortall life mounting vp into the chayre of the Croffe, made a briefe conclufion, and recapitulation as it were of all that, which he had formerly taught in the world, efpecially the eight Beatitudes, wherof he had preached vpon another mount. Confider, hovv the Eternall Father fayth the fame to vs now, that he fayd once to Moyfes: Doe according to the paterne, that was fhewed thee vpon the mount. Thus muft we endeauour to repeat and learne the leffon well, that this diuine Doctour hath giuen vs vpon the Croffe.

4. To confider, how this Lord, who hangeth on the Croffe, is the God of hofts, who like a valiant & generous Captaine hath fought, & ouercome in open field the infernall powers, hath deftroyed their forces, and ouerthrowne the Kingdome of finne. His armes be the Croffe, the nayles, the thornes, the blowes of the whip,

Ii 3   the

the iniuries and ignominies, he receyued, teaching vs if we haue a will to ouercome our enemyes, that we muſt help our ſelues with the like
armes, by mayſtring, and mortifying our body
by pennance.

Meditat. XXXIII.   *Of the tytle of our Sa-uiours Croſſe.*

TO conſider, how the tytle of the Croſſe
contained theſe wordes: Ieſus Nazarean
King of the Iewes, in which, as ſayth Saint
Marke, is comprized the cauſe, wherefore they
Crucifyed him. The firſt word is Ieſus, which
is as much as Sauiour, a name, that was giuen
him in his Circumciſion, when he tooke poſſeſſion of the office of Redeemer, and was againe
confirmed vnto him at his death, ſet ouer his
head vpon the Croſſe, for that in dying he accompliſhed all, that concerned the ſame charge
& office. The ſecond word is Nazarean, which
ſignifyeth floriſhing, for that our Sauiour by his
mounting vp vpon the Croſſe, produced and
brough forth the flowres of moſt excellent vertues, which he thereon taught by his owne example. This word alſo ſignifyeth Holy, to de-
monſtrate, that our Sauiour, who did hang, and
dye vpon the Croſſe, was the Holy of Holyes,
who dyed for the ſinnes of another, and not for
any tranſgreſſions of his ownn. The third word
is King, heauenly and diuine, whoſe Kingdome
tooke the beginning on the tree of the Croſſe, as
                                              that

that of sinne began in the forbidden tree. Wherof we are to learne this, that if we desire to raigne with Iesus Christ, we must begin to Crucify our old man now, and to destroy the body of sinne. The last word is, of the Iewes, though out of their wickednes & malice they would not then confesse him to be their King, as he was, & of all the world besides, and therefore this royall tytle was written in three tongues, that all nations of the world might vnderstand it.

2. To consider, how many, that read the contents of this tytle, were much scandalized, among whome were the high Priestes, and the Pharisies: others read it of curiosity without vnderstanding it what it meant: some agayne, as our B. Lady and S. Iohn, read it of deuotion, & conceyued the mystery it contayned, and them must we imitate in the reading of holy Scriptures.

3. To consider, how Pilate would not in any wise alter the Crosses tytle, though the Iewes importuned him to doe it. And this he did by inspiration diuine, to giue to vnderstand that what the tytle imported, was most true. Wherfore we must learne to be stable and firme in the good, we are onee resolued to do for the seruice of God, notwithstanding whatsoeuer obstacle, and impediment occurs from the common enemy, or from our bad inclinations.

Meditat. XXXIIII.   Of the diuision of our Sauiours garments.

TO confider, hovv the fouldiers, who cru-cifyed our Sauiour, taking his cloathes, deuided the fame amongft them, & caft lotts, who fhould carry away the beft. And this redounded to the difhonour of our Sauiour, which was as much as to fay, that fhe fhold need no more from thence forth to weare any cloa-thing. To confider, how it was our Sauiours will, that they fhould take them from him, to giue vs an example of perfect pouerty, depri-uing himfelfe of that, wherein confifted all his meanes and fubftance in this world, in fo much as he had neyther the vfe, nor the propriety of any thing left him, and thereby alfo giuing a te-ftimony of his moft burning charity, becaufe he gaue all that he had to men, his body, his bloud, & all he had befides.

2.   To confider, how they did caft lotts for his coate without feame, as the pfalmift had prophecyed long before : which the facred Vir-gin had, according to the common opinion, wouen with her owne handes : and how fory the fame B. Virgin was, when fhe faw it in the bandes of thofe inhumane and cruell executio-ners, all imbrewed with the precious, bloud of of her Son, that innocent & immaculate Lambe, whome the cruelty of enuy had fpoyled of life, & nayled faft to the wood of the Croffe.

3.   To

2. To confider, how the fouldiers fat them downe to deuide our Sauiours garmente, & to gard his dead corps alfo, at the intreaty of the Iewes, who were afrayd, leaft he might be deliuered aliue from the Croffe, or fome thinges might be giuen him to comfort him, as it was ordinarily to the Crucifyed. To confider, how our Sauiour though thus cruelly and ignominioufly tormented, his enemyes ceafed not to put him to more torments, by iniuryes, by blafphemies, and a thoufand outrages befides: all which he fuffered with an inuincible conftancy, in defpight of that, which Sathan did or could worke agaynft him, who fought, by meanes of his minifters, to caufe him to forget patience. And credible it is, that thofe accurfed monfters of the Diuell did a thoufand vnfeemely things by action, word, countenance and gefture, & all in derifion, and mockery, faying : If thou be the Sonne of God, come downe from the Croffe : if thou be the King of Ifrael, vnloofe thy felfe from the Croffe, and we will belieue in thee. He hath faued others, & he cannot faue himfelfe. He trufted in God, let him now deliuer himfelf, if he will. All thefe bitter fcoffes of mockery, and blafphemies our Sauiour heard with exceeding patience and meeknes : neyther were the two theeues, who were Crucified with him, behind in mocking, and blafpheming him alfo, as Saint marke obferueth. To confider the fingular great griefe, that the Bleffed Virgin had, when fhe heard the ininrious & reproachful fpeeches, that her Sonnes enemyes had of him, whofe brutifh

ferocity

ferocity alſo, as is very likely, was turned vpon her, in accurſing her for bearing of ſuch a Son: though ſhe ſuffered thoſe reproaches with patience, humility, & modeſty.

Meditat. X X X V .   Of our Sauiours firſt word vpon the Croſſe , praying for his enemyes.

T O Conſider , how the firſt leſſon , this diuine Doctour made in the Chayre of the Croſſe , was, when lifting his eyes vp to heauen, he prayed to his eternall Father for thē, who actually tormented , & blaſphemed him , ſaying : Father forgiue them, for they know not what they doe . He aſked not , that fire ſhould come downe from heauen to conſume them to duſt , but that the fire of loue might burne in their harts, & conuert them effectually to repentance . Wherein we are to wonder at the moſt ſingular charity of our Sauiour.

2.   To conſider euery word of this prayer: for though it be in our Sauiours power to pardon them abſolutely as God, as on his owne part he forgaue them alſo, yet he prayed his Father to forgiue them , by allegation of their ignorance , though it were affected in many of his enemyes, for the manifeſting of his infinite charity . For who is it , that will accuſe him who excuſeth him? Of this we muſt learne to excuſe the imperfections of our neighbour, yea though he ſhould be our enemy .

3.   To

3. To confider the effect of this holy prayer, accompanyed with teares. For if the diuine maiefty ouerheareth the prayers of the humble, how much more fhould he ouerheare his only Sonne, who was moft humble indeed, and moft humbled withall? Therefore Saint Paul fayth, that he was ouerheard for his reuerence, that is, for the refpect due to the infinite dignity of his perfon, and many of the Iewes, vvho ftood by, obtayned pardon through the efficacy of this prayer, & vvere aftervvardes conuerted by the preaching of S. Peter. To confider, vvhat an admiration this charitable prayer of his wrought in the minds of the ftanders by efpecially in our Bleffed Lady, Saint Iohn, & other deuout perfons, vvho hearing fo nevv and ftrange a prayer vvere aftonifhed, and vvere fory to fee him to dye, vvho prayed fo affectuoufly and hartily for his enemies.

Meditat. X X X V I. *Of the theeues Cruci-fied with our Sauiour : and of the fecond word he fayd to one of them, promifing him Paradife.*

TO Confider the profound humility of our Redeemer, that vvould dye betvveene tvvo theeues, vvho vvere likely to be tvvo moft notorious and moft criminall perfons. Confider, hovv our Sauiour, who the day of his Tranfiguration appeared betvveene Moyfes and Elias, being the only
Sonne

Sonne of the Eternall Father, and the figure of his substance, is novv on the mount of Caluary to be seene in the middest betvveene tvvo theeues, eyther as chiefe, or a companion of their cryme. Of this vve must learne willingly to humble our selues, and patiently to beare the iniuryes, & contemning of the vvorld.

2. To consider, how one of the theeues, vvho vvas on the left hand of our Sauiour, mocked him, vvhiles the other on his right hand, blamed the other theefe, saying, that themselues vvere punished according to their demerits, & that our Sauiour vvas innocent. Heere vve must consider, that the mockery, that came from the mouth of this infamous fellovv, and notorious cheefe, vvas most iniurious to our Sauiour. For the Scribes & Pharisies did not only blaspheme his innocency, but this vile & notorious theefe, who hung vpon the Crosse for his villanyes and great crymes, intermedled himselfe in wronging him as well, as did the others. To consider, how our Sauiour held his peace thereat, and the good theefe tooke vpon him to defend his innocency, inspired by God so to doe, and in that action exercised many heroicall vertues, as first to correct, & blame a publike blasphemer in sharp termes, saying vnto him, How was it, that he feared not God, who saw himselfe in extreme daunger of death? Secondly in the publike confession of his offences, for which he professed, that he merited that iust punishment. Thirdly, in maintayning our Sauiours innocency, when he sayd, that he was not any way culpable, an act most heroycall,

roycall, exercised in the face of the world, at a
tyme, that Pilate togeather with the Scribes, and
Pharisies, had iudged him worthy of death,
when the disciples were fled for feare, and his
secret friends were not so hardy as to open their
mouths to speake in his fauour.

3.   To consider, hovv this good theefe,
turning himselfe towards our Sauiour, sayd vnto him: Remember me, Lord, when thou co-
mest to thv Kingdome. By which wordes he in
the first place confesseth him Lord, then a King,
and lastly, he asketh of him, not that he would
deliuer him from the Crosse, nor that he should
giue him a seate in his Kingdome (for it is not
for a theefe, & malefactour to demaund so great
matters) but only that he would be mindfull of
him, in so much as his petition was full of faith,
of humilitv and hope, thereby crauing the remission of his sinnes. To consider, that, that
which moued this theefe to so sodayne a change
of life, was not our Sauiours preaching, or the
miracles, that were wrought by him but his heroycall patience alone, and singular meeknes a-
middest so many iniuryes, torments, and reproaches, and the prayer, he made for his persecutors. Of all which we are to learne, of what
efficacy good example is, and how we ought to
pray in imitation of this good theefe.

4.   To consider our Sauiours answere in
these wordes: Amen I say vnto thee, this day
thou shalt be with me in Paradise. In which is
to be seene the efficacy of the prayer, that he had
before made for sinners, for as much as he rea-

ped inftantly fruit of it by the conuerfion of this notorious finner. There is alfo heere to be feene the vertue of our Sauiours precious bloud, fhed vpon the Croffe, the very firft fruite whereof was this good theefe, in pardoning him his offences, in abfoluing and releafing him from both fault and payne, in promifing him Paradife, and in affuring him it without delay : his diuine maiefty graunting him more, then he craued, and telling him, that the very day he fhould be with him in his Kingdome, & fhould exchange the miferable condition of his Croffe and torments with the pleafures of the paradife of the Bleffed.

5. To confider the two different ftates of the good, and the bad, reprefented by the two theeues, the one of whome was chofen, and the other reprooued. For though the precious bloud of our Sauiour was moft fufficient to iuftify the one and the other, yet the vertue of it wrought but in the one of them, to keepe and contayne vs in feare far from vayne prefumption, and to giue vs withall a confidence agaynft pufillanimity, and fo to intertayne vs betweene feare and hope, and to teach vs, that none muft prefume, or continue long in thefe pleafures, by differring the amendment of his life vntill the houre of death. Finally to confider, what a motion this conuerfion, and anfwere of our Sauiour wroght in the foule of the moft glorious Virgin, who wondred, that among fo many affronts & torments of her Sonne, there was yet found one to to defend his honour, by the merits of whofe

death

death and Paſſion the gates of heauen, that had been ſhut vp for ſo many thouſands of yeares, were then opened to the greateſt ſinners. To cóſider how this moſt worthy Lady ſpake amiably vnto the good theefe, comforting him with good words, & increaſing the hope, he had in her Sonne, & incouraging him to dye well, and Chriſtian like.

Meditat. XXXVII. Of our Sauiours third Word to his Bleſſed mother, and to Saint Iohn. Iohn. 19.

TO Conſider, how among all the deuout ſoules, who out of their loue to our Sauiour ſtood at the Croſſes foote without fearing their enemyes, the moſt ſacred Virgin his B. Mother ſhewed more conſtancy then did the reſt, whiles the other were only there to accompany her. She approched to the Croſſe in body, but ſhe was much more neere to it in ſpirit; according whereunto ſhe was Crucifyed in company with her Sonne by a liuely apprehenſion of his torments, and by the exceſſe of the loue ſhe did beare him, as alſo by a compaſſion to ſee ſo holy, and ſo amiable a perſon, as he was, to ſuffer for the ſinnes of others. All theſe conſiderations cauſed ſo vehement a loue and ſorrow in her ſoule, as her paynes far paſſed, and went beyong the ſeuereſt and ſoreſt martyrdomes, that euer haue been.

2. To conſider the wordes, that our Sauior

vfed to his m ther : Woman, behold thy fonne,
Wherein he teftifyed his charity , in exercifing
the workes of piety amiddeft fo fore torments ,
and moft ignominious handling in praying for
his enemies, in promifing to the theefe paradife,
and in prouiding his mother another Sonne . He
called her woman , and not mother , to infinuate how far his foule was eftranged from all
carnall loue, being only attent to thofe workes ,
that concerned his heauenly Father . To confider, how fenfibly thofe vvordes toucht our Ladyes tender hart , in confidering the Adieu and
farewell her Sonne bad vnto her, and the fo vn-
equall chaunge , that he made by giuing her the
Sonne of a poore fiherman , for the foueraigne
and fupreme Doctour of heauen . To confider ,
how by thefe wordes our Sauiour did not only
giue S. Iohn to be the Bleffed Virgins Sonne a-
lone, but all the Chriftians his difciples alfo, who
then were, & euer fhould be to the vvorlds end,
his diuine maiefty obliging vs by this a new , in
making vs , through the exceffe of his liberality,
the children of his owne mother, who from that
tyme forwards thought her felfe bound to haue
a care of vs, as of her owne children, becaufe her
moft deere Sonne had fo recommended vs vnto
her in that very laft inftant , when he vvas to
dye.

3. To confider the other wordes , fayd vnto S. Iohn : Behold thy mother . By which he
imprinted in his difciples hart the affection of a
Sonne tovvards the holy Virgin, & reciprocally
in her will and affection of a mother towardes
him,

him, and towasdes all Christians : for Gods
wordes are alwayes accompanied with that vertue, effect and power, that they are able to work
that, which they signify . To consider , how S.
Iohn was priuiledged with this particular fauor
by occasion of his Virginty , and of the singular
loue, he did beare to his maister, in accompanying him alwayes euen to his Crosse, notwithstanding the difficulty and danger, that was presented : his constancy and charity, which we must i-
mitate in following our Sauiour in purity of
of mind, and of body .

4.   To consider , how S. Iohn did from
thence forth take the most glorious Virgin for
his Mother , and had a care to render and yield
vnto her the offices and duties of a true Sonne ,
in honoring , respecting, and seruing her with
great care and affection of loue, as well in regard
that his Mayster recommended it vnto him , as
also for that he esteemed himselfe happy to serue
so perfect and holy a mother, as she was .

Meditat. XXXVIII.   *Of the darkenes ,*
that couered all the earth : and of the fourth
word our Sauiour spake vpon the Crosse.

TO consider , how the diuine prouidence
permitted this miraculous darkenes, occasioned by the extraordinary Eclypse of
the Sonne , thereby to giue that ingratefull people to vnderstand , that they had highly procured his indignation and ire, in shutting their eyes
     K k 5   against

agaynft the charity of the Sonne of Iuftice,
whô their malice had brought to the darknes of
death. Moreouer the earth and all the world was
conuerted into obfcurity and darkenes, to the
end that all creatures by mourning for the death
of their Creatour, might giue a teftimony of the
innocency of his life, by thofe fignes of their forrow : the light withdrew it felfe, to take away
from our Sauiours perfecutors the occafion and
commodity of mocking and fcorning him finally this fodayne obfcurity hapned, to the end,
that whiles the filence of that night caufed a cef-
fation to the tumult, and ftir of the world, our
Sauiour might haue the opportunity to fpend
thofe few houres, that remayned vnto him of his
life in praying for vs with teares and feruour, as
his manner was, when he preached, to retyre
himfelfe by night into fome folitary place, or o-
ther, to pray. To confider, that our Bleffed
Lady did the fame fo long as that darkenes
continued, lifting vp her mind to contemplate
thofe high myfteries, that were there in accomplifhing in that very place.

2.   To confider the fourth word, that our
Sauiour fpake on the Croffe, in faying : my God,
my God, wherefore haft thou forfaken me? and
how he favd this, to giue to vnderftand, that he
found himfelfe inwardly abandoned, for that
his heauenly Father permitted him to fuffer all
thofe his tormêts without comfort, or affiftance
from him, whiles all the parts of his body had
their both generall, and particular paines : for
this alfo, that the diuinity abandoned the humanity

nity as touching sensible consolations , which it was wont to communicate vnto it , in permitting that the paynes it endured , were extreme, as may appeare by the agonyes , and mortall heauines he was pressed with , in the garden. He was also forsaken in another sort , when his disciples left him , and ranne their wayes for feare : and when the people of the Iewes denied him . Add heereunto the perdition of so many thousand soules , which he forsaw would at one tyme or other make wracke of their fayth , tread the diuine Sacraments vnder foote, and make no reckoning of so many trauayles and paines of his , endured for them .

3 . To consider , how though our Sauiour vsed these only wordes of the psalme, and spake them lowd : yet credible it is, that to himselfe and in silence he sayd the rest of the psalme, that comprehendeth the prophecy of his passion. To consider , how sharpe a knife of sorrow this was to the hart of our Blessed Lady : and how earnestly , and affectuously she craued of the Eternall Father not to abandon so his Sonne , so sore afflicted for the accomplishing and effecting of his diuine , & holy will .

Kk 4

Medit.

Meditat. X X X I X.   Of our Sauiours thirst: and of the fifth Word, he spake vpon the Crosse.

TO confider, how our Sauiour was fore altered, & thirfty, becaufe he had not drunke fince the euening of the night before, and had much trauailed, & in great haft alfo, & had withall loft much bloud: and though he had been a long tyme thirfty, before he complayned, yet would he difcouer that his fecret payne, being then within a while to giue vp his foule, to manifeft how much he fuffered for our finnes.

2.   To confider, how this corporall thirft reprefented three infatiable defires fpirituall in our Sauior. One, in all things to do what was for the fatisfying of the will of his heauenly Father without omitting the fulfilling of it in the very leaft thing. The fecond to fuffer yet more, then he had done, for the loue of vs, if it had been neceffary. The third, to faue all, wifhing that the fhedding of his bloud might profit all in generall, for as much as that incenfed defire of his did burne exceedingly within him. Heere I am to confider, that our moft compaffionate Sauiour did in particular thirft my foules good, and defired, that he might ferue him in a perfect māner. To thinke, how fimply his diuine maiefty propofed his own neceffities, to teach vs to propofe ours to our Superiours without importunity, or ouer great inftance, and moft of all in our

prayer

prayers, in which we muſt repreſent to the diuine maieſty our petitiõs, by reſigning our ſelues abſolutly into his hands.

3. To conſider, hovv that accurſed crew preſented vnto our Sauiour vinegar with a ſpong: Wherein was to be ſeene the extreme cruelty, and inhumanity of man in the higheſt degree towardes God, and contrary wiſe Gods infinite liberality towardes man: whiles his diuine maieſty gaue himſelfe vnto him to the very laſt drop of his bloud, & the ingratefull man anſwereth his goodnes agayne with ſo ſtrange a requitall. To contemplate our meeke Ieſus, abandoned of all ſuccour, whiles he found not any in that his extreme burning thirſt, to giue him the leaſt drop of water to quench it. For the ſacred Virgin, who would with a very good will haue giuen him not only water, but alſo the beſt bloud of her body, could not yield him that laſt ſeruice, the number of enemyes that were about the Croſſe, being ſo great, as ſhe could not come neere. To conſider, hovv great a payne and griefe it was to this holy Lady to ſee, how inſteed of a cup of water, they preſented vnto her moſt deare Sonne vinegar to drinke, mixed with the iuyce of bitter hyſoppe, as ſome Authors affirme.

Medit.

*Meditat . X L .   Of fixt Word , our Sauiour
ſpake vpon the Croſſe.*

TO conſider theſe wordes : All is conſummate : that is to ſay, he had ſuffered all that
the prophets had prophecyed of him frō
the firſt inſtant of his Incarnation , till the very
laſt moment of his life, his moſt Bleſſed ſoule re-
iovcing in it ſelfe for hauing glorifyed the eternall Father.

2 .   To conſider , how our Sauiour in
vttering this word, cōſidered the end, for which
he was come into the world , and the office his
Eternall Father had giuen him, which was to ſa-
tisfy for mans ſinne , to cruſh the infernall ſer-
pents head , to deſtroy death , to teach the doctrine of perfection , and to make himſelfe the
perfect paterne , & example of all vertue . And
therefore he ſaid : It is conſummate : for he had
then brought all thinges to a perfect concluſion .

3 .   To conſider, how he had alſo an eye to
the figures , that had repreſented him from the
beginning of the world . And eſpecially to the
ſacrifices & ceremonies of the old law : & therfore he ſayd, that all was accompliſhed . Wherin appeareth his moſt holy obedience , ſith he
would not giue vp his laſt breath , vntill he had
moſt exactly accompliſhed & put in execution
all , that his Eternall Father had commaunded
him to doe .

Medi-

Meditat. X L I.   *Of the seauenth Word, and of his giuing vp the Ghost.*

TO Confider, how beeing now at the point to yield vp his laſt breath, he cryed out with a lowd voyce, ſaying, Father: to ſhew that he had yet forces and ſtrength inough to extend and prolong his life, and to ſtay the violence of death, if he ſo had pleaſed, and that he would by conſent of his Father, & by obedience, dye willingly without any conſtraint. It was alſo to diſcouer the natural difficulty the ſoule had in leauing the body by occaſion of the good cōpany it had had with it, for the ſpace of thirty three yeares, as hauing been an aſſiſtant vnto it in the moſt noble worke of the Redeemer. Moreouer he yielded this lowd & miraculous voyce, in ſigne of the victory he had obtayned ouer the Diuell, hell, & ſinne, by meanes of his Croſſe, on which he permitted his body to be broken by torments, that as another Gedeon, breaking the earthen pot of his humanity, he might ouercome and defeate the infernall Madianites.

3. To cōſider euery one of the foreſaid words, that be moſt proper for the houre of death, for as much as our ſoule cannot be well aſſured in the handes of any other, but of our Father, who formed it. To conſider, how our Sauiour by recommending his ſoule to his Father, did alſo recommend the ſpirit of all his elect. For he,

                                                    ſayth

sayth the Apostle, that approacheth to God, becometh one and the same spirit with him; in so much as he did then also commend vnto his heauenly Father my spirit, & the spirituall life I ought to leade, praying him to please to take it wholy into his protection.

3.   To consider, how after he had vttered these words, he gaue vp his most holy soule into the hands of his Father, bowing downe his head in testimony of his obedience and humility, to giue vs to see the sore waight of our sinns, which is so great, as they caused it to bowe downe euen vnto death: as also to consider the place of Lymbus, whither his happy soule was to goe. Of all this I must seeke to make my profit, and to dravv out of it affectes of gratitude. To consider, how though our Sauiour gaue vp his soule of his owne voluntary will, yet vve must not affirme, that he dyed not through the the violence of his torments, & through the losse of his precious bloud, that issued forth of the infinite number of vvoundes of his body. For whē his bloud decaved and favled, his body became as dry, & destitute of forces, whereupon there followed an alteration and change of colour in contenance, which towardes his death vvaxed pale & wan, as is ordinarily to be seene in them, who be in their last agonyes. Thus did our most sweet Iesus giue vp his ghost on the tree of the Crosse, after he had gloriously ended his race, and accomplished all, that concerned the office of a most vigilant Pastour, soueraygne Bishop, most wise Doctour, most liberall Redeemer, and

true

true Sonne of Iustice, who with the light of his
doctrine and holy life illumineth the vniuerse,
and setteth it on fire. To consider, how piteously our Blessed Lady was affl.cted, when she saw
the body of her most deere Sonne destitute of
life, and how she became in his death a liuely paterne of sorrowes, what teares she shed,
with what manner of sighes and groanes, and
with what lamentable speaches she discouered
her griefe to the Eternall Father. To be short,
we must consider, hovv many Doctors doe affirme, that the Diuell was then in presence by the
Crosse, thinking to find & obserue some things
in our Sauiour, which he might make knowne
afterwandes, but he found himselfe deceyued
by his owne malice, & ouercome by the goodnes of Iesus Christ. It is also credible, that the
Eternall Father sent some of his Hierarchies to
be present there at the death of his Sonne, not
to help him in that his last passage, but to
honour him after.

Meditat. X L I I.   *Of the miracles, that
hapned at our Sauiours death.*

TO Consider, that these miracles vvere
wroght, to discouer the glory of him, who
dyed, and to controll the naughtynes of
the people, that had bereaued him of his life, as
also to giue to see, euen to the eye, the wonderfull effects, that were to proceed from such death.
The veile of the temple was rent in two, in signe

L l   of

of the blasphemy, and execrable sacriledge, the Iewes had committed in crucifying the only Sonne of God: and to insinuate also, that by his death were discouered & layd open the hidden mysteryes, that had layen hid for so long tyme, partly vnder the figures and shaddowes of the old law, and partly hidden from our eyes by the darkenes of our sinnes, that made a seperation betweene God, & men. The earth trembled, the rockes did cleaue, and the graues were opened, the insensible creatures witnessing in their manner the feeling they had of the death of their Creatour.

2.   To consider, hovv the Centurion, who had the charge of keeping our Sauiours body, seeing the wonderfull thinges, that had hapned, and hearing the extraordinary great and strong voyce, that our Sauiour gaue, when he was to dye, confessed, how that man was iust, and the Sonne of God indeed. As much said the souldiers of his company, & the people, that were present at all these wonders, knocking their breasts, and returning so to Hierusalem. To admire at the efficacy of our Sauiors precious bloud, which in so short a tyme changed & mollifyed those harts, that a while before were more hard, then the very rockes. Heere we must aske of God, that he would please to touch our harts, & make them soft, & pliable by his grace.

Medit.

Meditat. XLIII. *Of the opening of our Sa-*
uiours side, & of his fiue woundes.

TO consider, hovv the chiefe Priests prayed Pilate to commaund the legges of the
Crucifyed to be broken, that they might
be the sooner taken down from the Crosse. This
they did vnder a pretext of piety, and religion
for two ends, eyther to put our Sauiour to the
more payne, if he were still aliue, or to giue an
increase to his ignominyes, of he were dead.
And more then this, because they saw, that all
began euen then to be compunct and sory, and
to conceiue a remorse of conscience, they would
remoue and take out of sight the obiect of their
repentance, thereby to obscure the glory, that
might thereof rise to our Sauiour. To consider,
how the law commaunded, that the Crucifyed
should be taken downe the same day from their
Crosse, for as much as accursed was he, who dyed on it. And by this law our Sauiour pleased to
passe, in making himselfe accursed for our deliuery from the malediction of sinne. To consider, how the executioners comming to breake
the legges of the crucifyed, being arriued to the
mount of Caluary, and seeing our Sauiour then
dead, did forbeare to breake his legs: which
was done rather by prouidence diuine, then by
any humane will, God so disposing, to the end
the wicked intentions of men might be frustra-
ted of their effect. So the law decreed, that not

Ll 2   a

a bone of the Paschall Lambe, which was a figure of our Redeemer, should be broken.

2. To consider, how one of the souldiers, to assure himselfe of our Sauiours death, bent a speare against his precious body, & made an hole in his side, doing him this new iniury, because he might not breake his bones, as the Ievves desired. This wound of the speare was giuen more at the hart of the sacred Virgin, who stood at the foote of the Crosse, then at the body of him who did hang thereon, that was then deuoid both of sense, and life. And our Sauiour would receiue this woud for two reasons, the one, that there might not remayne any part of him from being hurt, in satisfaction of our sinnes: the other was, to discouer vnto vs his most affectionate hart, and that opening the gate we may goe in, and see, how it burneth within with the liuely flames of loue. In this sacred wound we must make our habitation, in it we must dwell & repose, as also in the rest his most precious body, therein placing our refuge, when our common enemy, and tentations come to assayle vs.

3. To consider, how out of the pierced sayd there issued bloud, and water, his maiesty vnwilling to retaine that little bloud, that remained in his hart, but giuing it to the very last drop for the loue of man. There issued forth bloud & water, to shew the efficacy of his death & Passion to wash vs from our sinnes, & to cleanse vs from them with the water of his grace, in quenching by its owne vertue the burning of our con-

cupiscence :

cupifcence : to fignify alfo, that from the fide of
our Sauiour Iefus, hanged vpon the Croffe, and
dead vpon it, by force of his loue, are to iffue the
Sacraments of the new Lavv, which haue vertue & effect to wafh, & fanctify our foules. Moreouer he pleafed to haue his fide opened, to giue
to vnderftand, that as Eue was formed of the
ribbe of Adams fide, fo the Church was to be
made & founded of his, as another Eue, the true
mother of the liuing. We muft proftrate our
felues at the foote of the Croffe, in company of
the moft facred Virgin, & of other the deuout
women, where we muft contemplate our Sauiours body, in euery part wounded, & then afke
of our foule, who it is we fee on this Croffe, &
for what caufe he hangeth on it : & thereof we
muft feeke to rayfe the commotions, & affections, we mentioned before, in the beginning of
this third Weeke.

Meditat. X L I I I I. *Of the taking of our
Sauiours body downe from the Croffe.*

TO confider the particular prouidence of
God towardes his, both liuing & dead.
For where our Sauiours body was nayled
to the Croffe in fo ignominious a manner, as
none of his acquaintance was fo hardy, for feare
of the Iewes, as to come neere him, & leaft his
enemyes fhould take him downe, & exercife
new outrages vpon him, he infpired vnto a certayne noble & rich perfon, named Iofeph, a iuft

man,

man, & one desirous to haue part in Gods Kingdome, & a secret disciple of our Sauiour, in that occasion to discouer himselfe, & boldly to aske of Pilate his maisters body. Wherein the singular vertue of the Passion sheweth it selfe, and driueth away feare & cowardize out of the harts of the faythfull. To consider our Sauiours humility & obedience in this, that he vouchsafed to passe by the lawes of malefactours, whose bodyes could not be taken downe from the Crosse without permission of the Iudge, he would be asked & obtayned, to declare that as he was by obedience nayled to the Crosse, so would he by the same obedience be taken downe from it agayne.

2. To consider, how the same diuine prouidence gaue to good Ioseph another companion, by name Nicodemus a man both noble & iust also, to assist him, who was a disciple of our Sauior also: for it importeth much, that the good be in comfort & company togeather about the doing of good workes. Ioseph brought a white & new sheete to wind the corps in, & Nicodemus brought a quantity of precious oyntment to annoint it. We must imitate these two holy persons in the like offices of piety.

3. To consider the deuotion & reuerence, the compassion & teares of theirs, wherewith they vnnayled and took down our Sauiours body, whiles they kissed his handes and feete, and with much sensible deuotion tooke the crowne of thornes frō his head, & held his body in their armes, vntill they came downe, & gaue him to
his

his sorrowfull mother, who tooke him into her lap. To thinke what teares our B Lady did the shed, what sighes and deep groanes she fetcht & raysed from her breast, what dolefull speeches she vsed: how Saint Iohn, Saint Mary Magdalen, & the other deuout womē that were present at this sad & piteous action. lamented, wept, and groaned.

Meditat. X L V. *Of the putting of our Sauiours body into the Sepulcher.*

TO consider, how after that the sacred Virgin had for a tyme held in her lap the precious dead corps of her most deare Sonne, those two holy persōs annointed it with myrrhe, aloës, and other oyntments, which they powred vpon the body in adundance, as there had been exercised ignominyes, reproaches, and torments vpon it in as great abundance a little before. For myrrhe, which is a bitter and funerall liquour, represented mortification, and the trauayles and trauerses our Sauiour suffered frō the first instant of his life till the last moment of his death. That done they folded the corps in a sheete, and bound his head vvith a napkin, according to the manner & custome of the country. To consider, how in all these thinges our Sauiour still practised pouerty: for the myrrhe, winding sheete, & napkin were bestowed vpon him of almes, & the sepulcher also was lent vnto him by another.

2. To

2. To confider, hovv it may be pioufly thought, that the corps was layd vpon a Beere, and carryed to the fepulcher by certayne denout perfons, who yielded him this their feruice, the B. Virgin follovving after weeping, and fighing with mournefull voyce for the death of her only Sonne, depriued of life in the flowre of his age. A man may in like manner meditate, hovv the Quires of Angells vve affiftant at thefe funeralls, to honour the body, that vvas vnited vvith the diuinity, and hovv, as the Prophet Efay fayth, The Angells of peace vvept bitterly: that is to fay, The fubiect and occafion of vveeping vvas fuch, and fo great, as if it had beene poffible for bleffed fpirits to weep, they vvould haue povvred their teares out abundantly in this heauy and dolefull proceffion.

3. To confider, the propertyes & circumftances of the Sepulcher, that vvas in a garden. For as the firft Adam by finning in a garden, incurred the payne cf death of body and of foule: fo the fecond Adam vvept for that finne, and all others in a garden, and vvould alfo be intombed in a garden, to deliuer vs from finne, and from death. The fepulcher vvas nevv, for that o[...]Lord, vvho became a new man, would choofe all thinges vvith the circumftance of nevvnes, a nevv mother, nevv difciples, a nevv fepulcher, &c. It vvas cut vvith iron out of a rocke, to infinuate, that it vvas to receyue vvithin it the folide and liuing ftone IESVS CHRIST, vvho vvas hevved, and cut

as is a ftone, by the torments of his paffion. In
this Sepulcher vvas put our Sauiours body,
his humility beeing in caufe, that he, vvho hath
his habitation in heauen, vvas buryed among
the dead, hidden vvithin the bowells of the
earth, for the releafing of vs from out of the
lovver lake. Thus may vve fee, that this fepulcher is for all refpects gloricus, and our foules
muft haue the forefayd conditions of it, that
they may be vvorthy places for our Sauiour to
abide in, vvhen he fhall come vnto them fha-
dovved vnder the Bleffed Sacrament of the
Altar.

Meditat. X L V I. *Of our Bleffed La-*
dyes folitude, and retyre.

TO Confider, how after this funerall office vvas ended, the Bleffed Virgin adoring firft the Croffe of her Sonne, returned home full of forrovv and griefe in a moft
high degree, taking heede vpon her vvay not
to treade vpon the bloud, our Sauiour had fp-lt,
as he vvent to his paffion, as certainely belieuing that it vvas the bloud of God. Beeing
come to her poore habitation, fhe thanked thofe
tvvo good perfons for the charitable office and
feruice, they had done to her Sonnes body, promifing them recompence for their deuotion &
piety.

2.   To confider, how fhe tooke her
leaue of them, and retyred herfelfe to her ordinary

nary poore chamber, vvhere she gaue scope
to her teares, and to her sorrovv of minde,
and intermingling sighes vvith colloquyes and
speeches addreffed one vvhile to the Eternall
Father, another vvhile to the soule of her
Sonne, vvho vvas in the Lymbus of the Fathers, and sometymes to the body she had left
in the sepulcher, she spake in so pittyfull a manner, as she would haue broken the very rocks of
pitty. Then turning her selfe to the deuout women, vvho vvept vvith her for company she
laboured novv and then to confirme and encourage them in their fayth and hope. To confider, hovv, though our Sauiours soule vvere
beneath in Lymbus, vvhere he deliuered the
foules of his friendes, and comforted them with
his holy presence, yet it forgot not in the meane
tyme those, vvhome it had left aboue on the
earth, vvho vvere, as strayed sheepe, difperfed, and feperated from their Paftour, infpiring
them vvith a defire to put themfelues in company vvith his holy mother, as Saint Peter, and
the other Apoftles did, vvho, as it is credible,
confeff:d vvith many teares their former feare
and pufillanimity: and the holy Virgin comforted them, refufcitating their hope in the Refurrection of her Sonne. To confider the griefe
of the fame Virgin, and of the Apoftles, finding the trayrour Iudas to haue hanged him-
f:lfe, vvhome queftionles she vvould haue receyued as she did the others, if he had retyred
himfelfe to her, as they did.

    3.   To confider, hovv the deuout vvo-
men,

men, thinking on that, which had passed at
the sepulcher, prepared themselues to seeke
nevv oyntments, to annoynt our Sauiours precious body, so soone as the feast of the Pasche
should be once past.

Meditat. X L V I I. *Of the Souldiers, who watched the Sepulcher.*

TO consider, hovv the Ievves did not
yet giue ouer to persecute our Sauiour,
euen after his death, and buryall, calling him a seducer, and praying Pilate to put
and set a guarde at the sepulcher, for feare least
his disciples should come in secret, and steale
avvay his body, and soe to make men belieue aftervvardes, that he vvas resuscitated
and risen agayne; so great povver an inordinate passion hath ouer the bad, and carryeth
them on to adde nevv faultes to their old ini-
quityes. But their malice blinded them, and the
diuine prouidence of our Sauiour serued himselfe of it, to make his ovvne resurrection the
the more authenticall, and the more celebrated.

2. To consider, hovv they vvere not
contented to haue a guard to vvatch the Sepulcher, but they further required, that the
stone might be sealed, shevving that they feared, vvhere no cause vvas. We must seale our
soules, after vve shall haue receyued I E S V S
C H R I S T, that our enemyes may not steale
him from vs.

3. To

3.   To confider, hovv the facred body, vnited to the diuinity, contynued three vvhole dayes free from corruption, according to the prophecy of the 15. Pſalme.

The end of the third VVeeke.

MEDITATIONS

OF THE FOVRTH

WEEKE.

HE Second Addition muſt be heere varied becauſe of the ioy of the Reſurrection, whereof we muſt be glad with Ieſus Chriſt. The ſixt muſt be chaunged alſo : for when we awake in the morning, we muſt ſeeke to call to mind ſome motiues of ſpirituall ioy. Touching the ſeauenth, that inſteed of darknes we muſt ſerue our ſelues with light, & vſe the open ayre. For the tenth beſides the moderating of our pēnance, we may vſe a moderation alſo in our meate, and drinke.

2. The meditations of the fourth weeke, in which be handled the myſteryes our Sauiour wrought in his glorious Reſurrection, & during all the tyme he conuerſed wirh his diſciples till his Aſcenſion, appertaine to the Vnitiue life, as we call it, which is the higheſt degree of ſpiritu-

all

all life, wherein the perfect soules are exercised by a most straite vnion with God, which comprehendeth three acts. The first is the vnion of the Vnderstanding, the office whereof is to cary God in it selfe, & to haue him in mind by thinking on him, and by knowing him by a true, proper, entiere & perfect knowledge, that may be as a liuely Image of God, wherunto the soule is transformed, according to that which the Apostle sayth: we behold with reuealed face, as in a looking glasse, we contemplate the glory of our Lord God, and are transformed into his Image diuine, passing from one clarity into another, carryed of the spirit of God. 2. Cor. 3.

3.   The second is the vnion of the Will, which going out of it selfe, is after a violent manner rayſed vp to an vnion with the goodnes, it hath vnderstood and conceyued, by louing it, & delighting in it, with a desire to enioy it in the best manner it possibly can. And this is that, which the commaundment of God, to loue him withall our hart, withall our soule, withall our forces &c. teacheth vs. Of this vnion arise the motions & affectiōs we must practiſe in the meditations of this fourth weeke, and be these that follow. To admire the maiesty diuine, his perfections, & his workes: to reioyce and be glad, that God is so great, and so perfect: to giue him thankes for the benefitts, that come from his liberall hand: to haue an earnest desire to see him, to possesse and enioy him, and to dwell with him for euer, to honour him, serue him, & pleaſe him in all thinges: To wish, that all the world may
know

know him, loue him, and serue him : to haue a most burning desire & zeale of his glory, & of the saluation of soules, & to be sory for the sins, that are committed agaynst his maiesty.

4. The third act resulteth and proceeceedeth of the second, which is an vnion of likekenes, and of imitation in the life, founded vpon a perfect conformity of our will with that of God in all thinges : and from this hath the fountayne and source the continuall exercise of all vertues. These three manners of vnion be linked & conioyned one with another, & they help the one the other very much to the producing of their effects. For the knowledge of God aydeth greatly to the loue of him, and againe serueth & helpeth to the imitation of vertues &c.

5. Saint Dionyse writeth, that there be two wayes to know God, the one by speculation, which is done by the naturall light of our vnderstanding, illumined by the cleere beames of fayth. For by consideration of the perfections of the creatures, and by meditation of the verityes, reuealed by the Scriptures, it is raysed vp to contemplate the glory of the Creatour. The other by practise, exercise, and experience, which proceedeth of the singular gift of the holy Ghost, which we call Wisdom, which is a certaine knowledge of God sweet, delightsome, and contenting, founded vpon the strange & wonderfull experiments we find in our soules, by meanes of the illustrations diuine, and the most comfortable affections, and commotions of the

charity,

charity, and loue of God. And in regard of this
sweetnes, and consolation the Prophet Dauid
sayd : Taft and see, hovv sweet our Lord God
is .

6. The Points, that we are to obserue in e-
uery one of the ensuying meditations, be like
vnto those whereof we made mention in the second weeke pag. 71. To see and behold the persons, to heare what they say, to consider their
workes and actions : to ponder, how the diuinity of our Sauiour, that seemed to haue beene
cleane hidden in his passion, appeared & shewed it selfe with so great glory in his miraculous
Resurrection : to consider the good office, our
Sauiour did to his friends in comforting them in
their griefe & sorrow, and weaknes of fayth.
Who desireth to find more and more abundant
matter for meditation, may recurre to the 5. §.
of the third Weeke.

*Meditat. I.   Of our Sauiours glorious descent
into Lymbus, and of the glory he communicated vnto the holy Fathers there.*

TO consider, how Lymbus is a place vnder
ground, whither the soules of them went,
who dyed in grace. For they could not
enter into heauen, how great Saints so euer they
had been, because of Adams sinne, vntiil our Sauiour suffered death for all mankind. In this
place were the holy Fathers, still sighing after
their deliuery, & beseeching the diuine maiesty

to come to release them, & to make them blessed with the cleare vision of his face : & besides this most affectuous desire they exercised many acts of deuotion, with commotions & affections that mans tongue is not able to vtter We must imitate them, in praying God to deliuer vs from this prison of body, that we may eternally enioy him in his glory of heauen .

2.   To consider, how the very instant, that he gaue vp his last breath on the Crosse, his body remayning still fast nayled vnto it , his most holy soule vnited togeather with the person of the eternall Word, went downe into Lymbus, to deliuer the iust ones, who there attended him. He manifested his infinite charity going downe in persom into that obscure & darke place, when it was in his power to haue remoued thē thence by his Word alone, or by an Angell : but he would let them see , how tenderly he loued thē, & what an esteeme he made of their good seruices , by applying vnto them the merits of his passion. Moreouer his humility exceedingly appeared in this his descent by entring into the prison of sinners, thogh true it be, that he was therin quality of a deliuerer, & of a Sauiour , & not as a prisoner .

3.   To consider, how he went downe in great maiesty , accompanyed with many thousands of Angells, who went singing these wordes of the psalme : Open your gates yee, Princes , & be yee opened you eternall gates , & the King of glory shall enter in &c. So the Princes of hell yielded themselues vnto him without any resi-

stance, the vertue of his most precious bloud breaking opē the gates, & the locks of that darke dungeon   We must reioyce at this omnipotency of our Sauiour, & at the efficacy of his death & Passion, beseeching his diuine maiesty to apply the same to our soules.

4.   To consider, how at his entire into Lvmbus, with his light he dispersed the darkenes of it, & communicated his glory to all the holy soules, who expected his coming, by meanes whereof they were glorifyed, & their prison vnder ground was sodainly chaunged into a celestiall Paradise. To consider, hovv great a ioy that was of those holy soules in that sodayne chaunge of their misery, & how thev thought all their passed payne now happy, in seeing themselues for the present in the glory of their felicity. To consider how these holy Soules came in their ranckes to yield our Sauiours most blessed soule thankes for the trauayles and paines, it had endured for their saluation & deliuerance, extolling it for the victory it had obtayned after so many assaults, & most cruell encounters. It is also credible, that Adam & Eue, our first parents, began this thankesgiuing, & that after them followed the Patriarkes, Prophets, &c. To consider, how the soule of our Sauior did at that time receyue an vnspeakable ioy & contentment, reioycing for hauing come into the world, & ransomed so great multitude of soules with the price of his bloud, holding his trauayles & paines well imployed.

5.   To consider, how whiles our Sauiour

wa

was still in Lymbus, the soule of the good theefe arriued thither, and was forthwith glorifyed, as were the other, according to the promise our Sauiour had made him some few howres before. He then and there honoured him in presence of all his friends, in lieu of the honour he had done him in the face of his enemies, all the other souls recommending the generous, & constant confession of fayth, he had made on the Crosse. We may also presently meditate, how during the same tyme, that our Sauiour was vnder ground, he spoyled Purgatory, giuing a plenary Indulgence & pardon to all the soules he found there, in vertue of his precious bloud, newly shed, cōmaunding his Angells to bring them vnto him into Limbus. Heere we must imagine, how glad they were, & how amiable a welcome our Sauiour, & all the other iust ones gaue them. In the last place to consider the fury, & despayre of the damned, who misdoubting of our Sauiours coming to Lymbus, were mad for despight, seeing themselues contemned, & forgotten, & especially Iudas & the bad theefe; as also Lucifer and his Angells, who found themselues ouercome & bound by his omnipotency; seeing on the other side, that the prisoners, whome they had held in durance for so many thousand years, were set at liberty. We must reioyce for this our Sauiours glorious tryumph.

Medit.

Meditat. II.   *Of the glorious Resurrection of our Sauiour.*

TO consider, hovv our Sauiour Iesus, alwayes the same, in his infinite charity pleased to accelerate & hasten his Resurrection, without omitting the very least thing, that had been prophecyed of him, to goe the sooner to comfort his most afflicted mother, & the rest of his friendes, to awake his disciples still sleeping in the night & darkenes of their infidelity, to illumine the world with the light of his glorious bodv, as he had already enlightened Lymbus with the clarity of his soule. To consider with what contentment our Sauiour departed from Lymbus, attended by that glorious company, tryumphing ouer death, & hell, which he had spovled. The songs of prayses, that the most blessed soule of our Sauior & the other iust ones did sing in that their going out, with much more cause, then had Moyses, and the people of Israel, when they passed ouer the red sea.

2.   To consider, how our Sauiours soule comming to the sepulcher, shewed vnto all the company the dolefull figure of the body, lying there disfigured with wounds, and rent with the scourging, that they might see at how deere a rate he had purchased their deliuerance, and for the same those iust souls gaue him thanks anew. To consider, hovv by his omnipotency, & perhaps by the seruice of his holy Angells, his

bloud,

bloud , that had been in diuerſe places ſpilt, was
all gathered togeather , & put into the vaynes of
the body againe : Some going to the garden
of Gethſemani, ſome to Pilates pallace , ſome to
the ſtreet of bitterners , & others to the mount
of Caluary,& in great reuerence gathered vp the
precious bloud vnited with his diuinity , as alſo
the hayres of his head & beard , which his tormentors had in moſt inhumane & cruell manner pulled away . To côſider, how this moſt bleſſed ſoule, entring againe into the body , & vniting it ſelfe a new with it , transfigured it with
much more glory,& in a far more perfect manner , then it did vpon the mount of Thabor , in
ſuch ſort, as it became without compariſon far
more beautifull, & more bright then the Sunne,
euery ſcar, wound, & part therof caſting forth a
moſt admirable ſplendour , and bright ſhining
light.It communicated vnto the body the foure
priuiledges of glory,to wit,clarity,impaſſibility,
agility , & ſubtility , by meanes whereof he roſe
out of the ſepulcher , penetrating and paſſing
through the hard & thicke ſtone, that ſtopped
the entrance, & going out . To conſider , how
our Sauiour lifted then his eyes,& handes vp to
heauen , as his manner was , whiles he liued a-
mong men, & gaue thankes to his Eternall Father for the Reſurrection, & glory of his body ,
ſaying that, which is writtê in the pſalme, Thou
haſt chaunged my mourning into ioy vnto me :
thou haſt cut my ſackcloth , & haſt compaſſed
me with gladnes, To imagine , that the celeſti-
all Hierarchies came downe from heauen, commaunded

maunded by the eternall Father to honour the glorious triumph of his Sonne. For if on the day of his Natiuity the Angells came downe from heauen, when he came to end his life vpon the earth; how much more credible is it, that they descended vpon the day of his triumphant Resurrection, when he was borne & became aliue againe, like as another Phenix of her aihes, to liue in heauen for euer? They doubtles renewed & song once agayne their heauenly song: Glory be on the highest to God, & peace on earth to men of good will. They also repeated this sonet: This is the day, that our Lord made: let vs exult, & be glad in it.

3.   To consider, hovv our Sauiour would not enioy this corporall glory alone, but he communicated it vnto many other of his friends, resuscitating & glorifying thē in body & in soule. And this he did to manifest his omnipotency, charity, & liberality, to the end they might be witnesses of his Resurrection, & that by their example we might be assured in our hopes, to rise agayne one day with glorifyed bodyes. To giue vs also to vnderstand, that his will is, we should rise againe spiritually, & begin a new life, as the Apostle seemeth to teach vs, when writing to the Romans he saith; Let vs walke in newnes of life. Let vs for the tyme to come lead a new life, abandoning & casting of the funerall, and deadly winding-sheets of our old customes, getting out of our old & inueterated sinnes, as out of so many sepulchers, & this with a firme purpose neuer to enter into the same any more.

Heere

Heere I muſt reioyce at the glory of our Sauiors body, & for that he would honour it ſo Royally for hauing faithfully ſerued his ſoule.

Meditat. I I I. *Of our Sauiours appari-*
rition to his mother : and how the Angells told
the deuout women, that he was riſen. Matth.
18. *Mar.* 16. *Luc.* 24. *Ioan.* 20.

TO Conſider, how our Sauiour would manifeſt his Reſurrection by thoſe Saints,
that were reſuſcitated with him, and appeared vnto many in the Citty of Hieruſalem,
by meanes of the Angels, who appeared to thoſe
deuout women, as they were on the way to annoint his body in the ſepulcher : and finally by
himſelfe, the more to teſtify his infinite charity
in continuing the ſpace of 43. dayes in the world
after his Reſurrection, doing the office of a perfect comforter, & like a good Paſtour gathering
his ſtrayed ſheep togeather. In theſe three manners God is wont to teach men, namely, by other
men, by Angells, & by himſelfe.

2. To conſider, hovv the firſt perſon,
to whome our Sauiour appeared, was his moſt
deere & moſt holy mother, who was moſt ſore
afflicted for the death of her moſt beloued Son,
though ſhe had a moſt liuely fayth, & a moſt aſſured hope of his future Reſurrection. And
therfore in the beginning of the third day being
in moſt high contemplation, ſhe made petition
to her Sonne to haſten his Reſurrection, accom-
payning

payning her prayers with teares, & sweet & deuout sighes and groanes. Arise, sayd she, my glory, awake thou out of the sleepe of death. To consider, hovv our Sauiour, soone heard the sighes of his mother, and presented himselfe vnto her most beautifull, and light as the Sunne, accompanyed with an infinite trayne of Angels, and with the soules, which he had deliuered out out of Lymbus, who, as it is credible, reioyced togeather with the Blessed Virgin for the glory of her Sonne, and gaue him thankes for all the paines, she had endured, & trauayles in cooperating to the worke of Redemption, acknowledging her for the tyme to come for their mother, sith she was the mother of their God, & Redeedeemer. We must heere represent vnto our mindes the sweet discourses, that past betweene the sacred Virgin, & her Sonne, the ioy of our Sauiour, the consolation of the Virgin, the most sweet imbracings, that passed betweene them. To consider, how after that our Sauiour had cōcontinued some good space with his mother, & that he had manifested vnto her many diuine & hidden mysteries, he tooke his leaue with promise to returne vnto her oftē so long, as he shold continue in the world, & so he left her replenished with ioy, & consolation. In the meane time she kept this visitation in silence to her selfe, as she had before time concealed the mistery of the Incarnation. We must heere be glad of the B. Virgins ioy, togeather with the glory of our Sauiour.

3. To consider, how Saint Magdalen, &
the

the other deuout women, went to the sepulcher with their oyntment , to annoynt our Sauiours body after the feast of the Sabbaoth was past , manifesting thereby their deuotion , & obedience they yielded to the law , in their religious keeping of the Sabboath day, for reuerêce wherof they did forbeare the doing of an office, which yet seemed vnto them very much pressing , and necessary . They discouered also their great diligence in rising before day to goe to exercise a worke of deuotion & piety, & therewithall they gaue a testimony of their firme hope & confidence, they had in God, togeather with perseuerâce in good, without leauing to prosecute what they had well begun , neyther for feare of them who guarded and kept the sepulcher, nor for the difficulty of remoouing the stone , hauing an hope, that God would prouide for all.

4. To consider, how when they were come to the Sepulcher , they saw , that the stone was remooued, & they beheld an Angell all resplendant, who tould them the newes of the Resurrection, saying vnto them, that they should not be afraid . We must heere consider the maiesty, and power of this Angell, who by this coming caused so great a trembling of the earth , therby terrifying them, who watcht the Sepulcher, & remoouing so great, & heauy a stone with so great facility . He named our Sauiour, Iesus of Nazareth Crucifyed : as knowing well the will of our sweet Iesus , who causeth glory of his contumelies, & holdeth it an honour to himselfe to haue been Crucified for loue of vs . To consider, how

Nn　　　　　　　　　　the

the Angell difpofed the women by degrees, that they might be worthy fee Iefus Chrift, by his fpeeches increafing their faith and charity, and willing them to goe withall diligence to aduer-tife the Apoftles of the Refurrection of their maifter, & S. Peter in particular, that he might not thinke himfelfe to be reiected for hauing de-nyed his Lord. In the laft place we muft medi-tate how thefe women purfuying their bufines, & entring into the Sepulcher, faw two other Angells, who affured them of the fame thing, that the other had done before: for perfeuerance in a good worke meriteth greater confolation.

Meditat. I I I I.   *Of our Sauiours appearing to S. Mary Magdalen. Mar.* 16. Ioan. 20.

TO confider, how after thefe deuout wo-men had deliuered their meffage, they re-turned backe to the Sepulcher where our Sauior made himfelfe known to Mary Magda-len, out of whome, as Saint Marke fayth, he had caft feauen Diuells. Wherin his diuine maiefty manifefted the exceffe of his loue & charity, in honouring the conuerted finner, & choofing her for the firft eye-witnes of his refurrection, in whome the Diuells had formerly made their ha-bitation. Of this we may learne, that thofe, who ferue our Sauiour with hartyeft good will and affection, fhall be priuiledged with the greater fauours.

2.   To confider, how fore Mary Magda-
len

len was afflicted & troubled, when she found
not the body of him, whome she loued best, in
the sepulcher: how she inclined herselfe againe,
looking in, and weeping bitterly, in so much as
with her brinish teares she bedewed the stones
of the Sepulcher: she sought, & found not him,
in whome were the desires of her soule: loue &
follicitude still made her to seeke, being ready to
dye, and spend her life, if she had thought she
might thereby haue learned & vnderstood any
thing of her mayster. Her feruour would not
permit her to goe from the sepulcher, though all
her companions were departed, though Saint
Peter and Saint Iohn were returned in as much
hast, as they came running thither. Neyther the
sight of the holy Angells, nor their consolatory
wordes could possibly stay the course of her
teares, because her hart, & affection, which
sought for none but her Creatour alone, could
not content it selfe with his creatures. Let vs
learne with this vertuous woman to seeke God
which care, teares, perseuerance & feruour, whē
eyther for our sinnes, or for other reason he ab-
senteth himselfe from our soules.

3.   To consider, how our Sauiour pleased
to comfort her, and therefore he did stand behind her, who turning herselfe saw in him the
likenes of a gardiner, & knew him not, because
her fayth was as yet somewhat feeble & weake.
How our Sauiour asked of her the cause of her
weeping, & of her diligent seeking, shewing that
her teares were occasioned of ignorance, and of
want of faith, because she wept for him, as dead,

whome she saw liuing : his diuine maiesty meaning to teach vs by this , carefully to examine ,
wherof our teares proceed . For they are for the
more part shed, not so much for the loue of God
or for hatred of our sinns , as for the losse of our
temporall goods .

4 . To consider, how Mary Magdalen,
thinking him to be some gardiner , said vnto
him : Sir, if thou hast carryed him away, tell me,
Where thou hast layed him, and I will take him .
In which few wordes she manifested the excesse of her loue, that transported her, & put her
besides her selfe . For it is proper to passionate
loue to take possession on the hart, and tongue
of him who loueth , causing him both to thinke
& speake continually of his beloued, perswaded
in himselfe , that all the world both thinketh, &
speaketh of him. By this manner of signe we shall
know whether we loue God . This is also an effect of violent loue , to cause one to forget himselfe , and to thinke of him , whome he loueth ,
& to cause him to humble himselfe in all things,
so he may attayne the end of his desires , carrying him to the doing and saying of those things,
that in humane iudgement seeme follyes , & yet
the same be the excesses of loue . Moreouer this
passion causeth them, who be indeed weake , to
promise themselues much strength, and maketh
them to vndertake more , then they are able to
performe , when there is question to serue the
obiect of their affection. All these properties will
giue vs to vnderstand , if there be any grayne of
the loue of God in vs .

5 . To

5. To confider, how our Sauiour, feeing the feruour and teares of Mary Magdalen, difcouered himfelfe vnto her, and called her by her name, Mary, and fhe prefently knew him, and therfore anfwered, mayfter: wherin we may fee, how eafy a thing it is vnto God to chaunge the harts by one word alone, and to driue away the darkenes, and heauynes of it, and to fill it with fupernaturall light, and exceeding ioy To confider the anfwere, that Mary Magdalen gaue him in faying, mayfter: a name of reuerence, & of loue. For fhe had made an experiment in her felfe of the effects of his affection to her by the plenitude & fulnes of the celeftiall light, that fhe felt in her hart. To confider, how fhe fodainly caft herfelfe downe at his feet to kiffe them: but he permitted her not, but gaue her to vnder-ftand, that fhe was from thence forth to vfe more refpect & reuerence towardes him, as beeing then glorious in the other life, for as much as in treating with him fhe fhould ioyne refpect with loue. Neyther did he fuffer her to kiffe his feete, to teach her to vnderftand the weaknes & want of fayth fhe had, in that fhe fought among the deac for him, who was liuing & glorious. And therefore we muft meditate his milde wordes in fending her to fay vnto his Apoftles: Goe and fay to my brethren; I afcend to my Father & to your Father, my God, & your God. And this he faid, that they might vnderftand & know, that the glory of his Refurrection had not chan-ged his affections towardes men, but that on the contrary ne did giue them greater fignes and

demonftra-

demonstrations of loue , in honouring his
vnworthy seruants with the honourable tytle of
brethren .

Meditat. V . Of the Apparition of our Saui-
our to the other women, togeather with Saint
Mary Magdalen. Matth. 28.

TO Consider , how Mary Magdalen , exceedingly glad , she had seene her Lord ,
ran in all hast , & ouertooke the other
women her companions , vnto whome she recounted her good fortune , in hauing seene our
Sauiour resuscitated, which newes gaue them as
great a desire to see him also: who,to satisfy their
deuotion , manifested himselfe visibly to their
eyes , & gaue them to vnderstand it by their
eares also , when he saluted them in these words
Peace be vnto you . Wherein he recompensed
the paynes of their watching & trauayle in coming to see his person . And where this comfort
was not yielded vnto them at the first , we must
thinke,that it is Gods custome to delay the communicating of his fauours, to giue them in their
due time & season when they shall be both greater, & content more.

2 .   To consider , how these holy women
glad in a most high degree to see our Sauiour, a-
dored him , & with his leaue kissed his feete , as
did Saint Mary Magdalen also, to whom he had
denyed that fauour a while before . To consider
what their comfort & affection of mind was
in

in this happy fight of him, and how happily they
thought their paines & the former nights watching imployed. We must also imploy the three
powers of our foule in the bufines of annointing
of our Sauiour, to the end that by addreffing
them to his feruice, we may deferue, that
our Sauiour may communicate himfelfe alfo to
vs.

3. To confider the meffage, he fent to
his Apoftles, willing the fame women to deliuer it them in thefe wordes: Tell vnto my brethren, that they go into Galily, & that there they
fhall fee me. We muft ponder well thefe fvveet
and comforting vvordes (my brethren) for he
fpeaketh not fo vnto his Angells, but by this he
meant to notify the exceffe of his infinite loue
towardes men. To meditate hovv his vvill
vvas, that his difciples fhould goe into Galily,
to the end they might there enioy their contenting fight of him, and his prefence, vvith affurance and quiet, and without feare, which
they could not doe in Hierufalem, vvhere in
the meane tyme he vifited the the fame day. In
this he meant not to teach vs, that to enioy God
we muft fhunne, & auoid the troubles, & ftirs
of the vvorld.

Medit.

Meditat. VI.   *Of our Sauiours appearing to Saint Peter.   Marc.* 16.

TO confider, how when the women deliuered this meſſage , the Apoſtles held it for fabulous, & idle : & by this is to be ſeene, how heroicall the acts of faith be, that cauſeth vs to belieue what we ſee not, & what mans ingratitude is towardes God , in perſiſting ſtiffe , and wilfull in his owne iudgement , though it be otherwiſe true, that he muſt not belieue all things lightly .

2.   To confider , how Saint Peter , and Saint Iohn , vpon the womens report, reſolued to goe to the ſepulcher , to ſee if it were true , as they had told thē: therby ſhewing that they were not of ſo hard belieſe & ſo incredulous , as were the other diſciples. We are heere taught to ſeeke Ieſus Chriſt by faith and charity, and by the actiue and contemplatiue life, which are repreſented by theſe two Apoſtles , who , as they loued our Sauiour more, thē did all the others, ſo were they alſo more diligent in ſeeking him, thē were the reſt, in his abſence.

3.   To confider , how Saint Peter beeing retyred into ſome place all alone, to thinke vpon that which he had ſeene in the monument, & vnderſtanding what was ſaid to the women , our Sauiour appeared vnto him, comforted him, & tooke from him the feare and confuſion, that his denying of him had cauſed in him. To confider,
how

how confounded, likely it was, that Saint Peter
appeared before our Sauiour: how vnworthy he
reputed himfelfe of fo great a fauour, and comfort, how he caft himfelfe downe at his feete,
wept bitterly, & craued pardon for his ingratitude: how our fweet Sauiour cofort ed him, gaue
him affurance of pardon with good & wholfome
inftructions, and fpake moft louingly vnto him,
as one who had no more remembrance of his
finne. To confider, how after this vifitation S.
Peter ranne in haft to his company to confirme
them in the faith of their maifters Refurrection:
& how his teftimony and report was of fo great
credit, and authority with them, as they abfolutely belieued his wordes: which they would
not doe vpon the womens report, and fayd all
with one and the fame voyce: Our Lord is truly rifen, & hath appeared to Simon.

Meditat. V I I.   *Of the Apparition to the*
  two difciples, that went vnto Emmaus.

TO Confider, how thefe two difciples went
    from Hierufalem, peraduenture for feare
    of the Iewes: how they went talking v-
pon the way about the thinges, that had hapned
the dayes before. To confider, how our Sauiour fell into company with them in forme of a
pilgrime, that he might draw them out of their
errour, as being the true Paftour of foules, and
to comfort them in their affl&ions, as beeing
proper vnto him to help and eafe fuch perfons:
                                                    he

he approached vnto thè, becaufe their talke was of good and pious matters, therein performing his promife, whereby he had giuen an affurance, that he would be in the middeft & company of them vvho were met togeather in his name, thefe two poore difciples knew not their May-fter, becaufe of their little faith, whiles our Sauiour difpofed them by little & little to the perfecting of it, for that the inward forrow of mind hindred outwardly the fenfes, & fufpended their knowing of him.

2. To confider, how our Sauiour afked of them newes, as though he had not knowne any thing of that, which had hapned the daves paft, with intent to draw them to lay open the the wound of their infidelity wherewith their foule was hurt, for the curing of it, and for the defire he had to heare them to report of the torments and pavnes he had fuffered for the loue of men. To confider the great and excellent opinion, thefe difciples had of their maifter, though otherwife it were def-ctiue in regard of his diuinitv, that he was a man powerfull in workes & in wordes before God, and all the people. We muft heere reiovce, that his diuine maieftv may be potent in all thinges, in which we muft imitate him. To medicate, hovv the difciples difcouered the weakenes of their favth, by thefe wordes: We hoped, that it was he, who fhould redeeme Ifrael. Where is liuely reprefented the imperfection of many foules, which for but one acccident contrary to their imperfect & weake apprehenfion, doe forthwith loofe the efteeme, opinion,

opinion, and hope, they should haue in God.

3.   To consider the sharpe rebrehension, our Sauiour gaue them, in calling them fooles, and slow of hart to belieue, and yet no wordes of choller, but rather of a côpassion of their fault, & of zeale of exciting their fayth, & of setting it on fire, being almost extinguished, & of drawing thê out of the ignorance, wherin they then were. For though they had heard him many tymes before speake of this mistery, yet they did not yet comprehend the secrets of it. To consider the efficacy our Sauiour had in declaring, & interpreting the Scripturs, enlightning their minds for the vnderstanding of them, and enkindling their affections towardes them, & towardes him who interpreted them, as they confessed afterwardes, when they said: did not our hart burne within vs, whiles he spake vnto vs on the way, & opened vnto vs the Scriptures?

4.   To consider, how being arriued to the village, our Sauiour made as though he meant to passe on further, though he had a desire to stay with his disciples, that they might inuite him, and hold him with them, to the end that by exercising that exteriour worke of charity, and hospitality, they might be the more vvorthy to intertayne his diuine maiesty within their soules. To consider, hovv the disciples forced him to stay with them, saying: Stay vvith vs, Sir, because it is tovvardes night, and the day is novv far spent. Our Sauiour indeed taketh a pleasure to be enforced by our teares, prayers, and pennances, and is content

that

that vve importune him , by reprefenting vnto him, how vvhiles our life dravveth tovvardes an end , & hovv vvhiles our dayes runne on vvithout ceafe tovvardes the occident of our death, we haue the more need of his help.

5.   To confider , how vvhen our Sauiour vvas fet dovvne at the table with them, he tooke bread , bleffed it , brake it , and gaue it them to eare , at vvhich inftant their eyes vvere fodainly opened , and he vanifhed forthvvith out of fight , to infinuate that his vifitations in this vvorld be not of any long continuance, but paffe quickly, as being but to excite and ftir vs vp, & particularly to teach vs the exercifing of the vvorkes of charity tovvardes our neighbours , For he pleafed to ftay vvith them , and to make himfelfe knovvne, to caufe them to fee, hovv he loueth hofpitality , and hovv he reputeth the vvorkes of mercy as done vnto himfelfe . In taking the bread vvith grauity, & modefty, in bleffing it vvith deuotion , & diftributing it vvith charity , vvas to teach them the exercife of thofe three vertues : as thofe , that opened the eyes of their foules for the knovving of him . In vvhich alfo is to be feene the efficacy & vertue of the moft B. Sacrament , that openeth the invvard eyes, & filleth the vnderftanding with diuine & celeftiall light, as thefe two difciples experienced, who prefently returned to Hierufalé to aduertife the Apoftles of that , vvhich had hapned vnto them .

                                        Medit.

Meditat . V I I I .   *Of the Apparition made to the Apostles, as they were togeather the day of Resurection.*   *Luc.* 23. *Ioan.* 20.

TO consider , how the night comming on , and the disciples beeing assembled in a certaine house, the doores wherof were shut, for the feare they had of the Iewes , our Sauiour Iesus appeared in the middest of them. He pleased to differ this visitation , till it was late , by little and little so to dispose the more incredulous among them , to trye the patience of the more constant , and to increase the desire of thē all by his long delay : For God is wont to comfort the afflicted , when they thinke least of it . To consider, how our Sauiour entred, the doors being shut, to manifest the gift of subtility, proceeding from the glory of his body , who by that meanes did penetrate where he pleased , thereby to declare his omnipotency, & to teach , that he entreth into the soules of his elect , when the ports of the senses be most of al shut vp to things terrene . He did put himselfe in the middest of his disciples , as the Sunne in the middest of the pianets to enlighten them , that he might accōplish what he had before sayd , That he would be in the middest of them, who should be gathered togeather in his name .

2 .   To consider the wordes, where with he saluted them. The first : Peace be with you I giue you the same peace now , that I left you,

when I went to my death, and I giue you it, for that I haue gayned it by my Paſſion. The ſecond: It is I: That is to ſay, I am the ſame, I was before both touching my returne, & touching my nature, and touching myne office: for I am your ſoueraygne Lord, and mayſter, &c. The third: Feare yee not: as if he had ſayd, There is no cauſe of feare at all, when I am with you. To conſider the ſweetnes, and ſupreme bounty of our Sauiour in this that for the confirmation of the truth of his Reſurrection, he would not only ſhew himſelfe vnto his diſciples, and talke with them, but would alſo that they ſhould touch his hands, feete, and ſide; in which parts of his body were his ſacred wouds, which were able, being but toucht, to heale vp thoſe wouds, that infidelity had made in their ſoules: as they were in effect cured, by being illumined & confirmed in the fayth.

3.   To conſider, how our Sauiour, not thinking this experiment inough, vouchſafed to aske of them with moſt ſingular affability to eate, as he alſo did with them, though it were a thing, that had nothing to doe with the ſtate of his glorifyed body, and this for the more confirmation of his Reſurrection. To conſider hovv, our Sauiour did eate of a roaſted fiſh, and of an hony combe, the one repreſenting his diuinity, the other his humanity, roaſted vpon the Croſſe in the fire of his torments. How, all this done, he expounded vnto them the Scriptures, ſhewing vnto them, that all, that had paſſed in his perſon, had been foretold by the Prophets,

and

and by the bookes of the Law. This meditation
ended, a man may vſe the application of the
ſenſes, as hath been ſayd in the beginning of the
firſt, ſecond, & third Weeke.

Meditat. IX.   *Of our Sauiour gaue the holy
holy Ghoſt to his Apoſtles, and the power of
pardoning ſinnes.* IOAN. 20.

TO Conſider, how our Sauiour, after he
had ſhewed himſelfe vnto his Apoſtles, en-
couraged, and comforted them, ſayd vnto them a ſecond tyme, Peace be with you: for
that a quiet and peaceable mind is diſpoſed and
apt for the receiuing of diuine illuſtrations. To
thinke, that the repeating of the ſame wordes
twice, was to diſpoſe the with the greater reuerence to receyue the office, he would haue them
take vpon them, in giuing them commiſſion to
goe all the world ouer to conuert men to God,
and therefore it was his will, that his peace
ſhould raigne amongſt them, and all others. To
ponder theſe words: As my Father hath ſent me,
ſo I ſend you: by which he made and cõſtituted
them his Apoſtles, that is to ſay, Sent. Which is
as much to ſay, As my heauenly Father ſent me
into the world to teach men the way of truth, &
of vertue: ſo doe I ſend you to proſecute & cõ-
tinue what I haue begun.
    2.   To conſider, that our Sauiour breathed
vpon them, ſaying: Receiue yee the holy Ghoſt.
A ceremony, that he pleaſed to obſerue, to giue

to vnderstand, that the holy Ghoſt, which he gaue them, was he, who proceeded from him, as the breathing cometh frõ him who draweth his breath. It was alſo to ſhew, that it was he, who formed Adam of a little maſſe of clay, and breathed into his face the ſpirit of life, that did quicken him, and put life into him, and that our ſoules ought to receyue of his liberality the ſpirituall vigour and life. To thinke, that that gift which he then gaue to his diſciples, was as a pledge of him, who was to be ſent them vpon the day of Pentecoſt.

3.   To conſider, how by the ſame meanes he gaue them power to pardon ſins, a thing that appertayneth vnto God alone, & which he gaue not to the Angells, nor to the Prieſts of the old law : & therfore it may ſeeme, that he communicated vnto them in ſome ſort the infinite dignity of Sauiour, becauſe he gaue them the power by his merits to ſaue, cure, and deliuer ſoules from their ſins. To conſider, that this was an act of infinite liberality, for as much as this authority of pardoning extendeth it ſelfe to all men, be their ſins neuer ſo great, exhorbitant, many, & grieuous, none excepted, as long as they be in this life, & this both all, & as oft, as need ſhall require. We muſt yield his diuine maieſty thanks for his ſo great mercy, by means wherof he hath pleaſed to ayde our frailty, graunting vs with ſo great a facility to enioy that, which himſelfe had with ſo great paynes, & torments gained.

Meditat . X. Of the Apparition made to his Apostles , when Saint Thomas was present. Ioan. 20 .

TO Confider, hovv Saint Thomas was a-way, when our Sauiour appeared to his difciples the very day of his Refurrection, & therefore would not giue credit to that, which his brethren reported , who aſſured him of that verity : and it came of this, that he had abfented ted himfelfe from the company of the Apoſtles, as alfo of the hardnes of his hart , and obſtinacy in maintayning his own opinion , without ſub-mitting of his iudgement to the relation , that his fellow diſciples made . And of this cometh that vayne preſumption to preſcribe vnto God the meanes to perſwade vnto him an article of fayth , ſaying , that he would not be ſatisfyed with the ſeeing of his mayſter , vnles he ſhould alfo touch him with his owne handes , and put his fingars into the woundes of his facred body. Of this alſo proceeded his pertinacy , which contynued for eight dayes , without yielding to that, which ſo many both ſayd, and auerred with ſo great aſſurance, and aſſeueration . Wherein a man may ſee, how bad a thing it is for a man to adhere ſtifely to his owne proper iudgement . For God permitted Saint Thomas to fall into this fault for the humbling of him , for the ac-knowledging of his owne weakenes, and to the end ne might rife againe with the more feruour,

and

and more solidity of fayth, by conuerting himselfe vnto his diuine maiesty.

2   To confider, hovv eight dayes after
the Refurrection, our Sauiour defirous to gather his difperfed fheepe togeather agayne, appeared to Saint Thomas in company of the o-
ther apoftles, to make him know, that he receyued that fauour in regard of thofe good perfons,
in whofe company he was; and to the end alfo
the reft might admire his infinite charity, who
for the doing of good to one among them, comforted, animated, and fauoured all the reft, and
would make them witneffes of his fayth, as they
had been his companions in his infidelity. To
confider, what meeknes and facility our Sauiour vfed in fpeaking vnto Saint Thomas, pittying his weaknes, & faying vnto him : But thy
finger into the hoales of my handes, & thy hand
into the wound of my fide. Wordes, that giue
teftimony of an incomprehenfible charity.

3.   To confider, how at this touching of our
Sauiour Saint Thomas opened the eyes of his
foule, & with the mouth of body cryed alowd,
faying : my Lord, & my God. Which was a
moft noble confeffion, proceeding from an hart
full of affection, in confeffing both the diuinity,
& humanity of Iefus Chrift. Vpon which we
muft meditate, in how fhort a tyme S. Thomas
his mind was chaunged. To confider, hovv our
Sauiour would not commend Saint Thomas for
that his confeffion, as he had done Saint Peter
for his, though he approoued the one & the o-
ther, becaufe he was ouer flow to belieue. Yet
                                                                    our

our Sauiour for the consolation of the faythfull
added: Blessed are they, that haue not seene,
and haue beliued.

Meditat. X I.   *Of the causes, wherefore*
  our Sauiour would rise agayne, with the woūds
  in his hands, feete, and side.

T O Consider how it was to confirme his
  disciples in the fayth of his Resurrection,
    and that by the same meanes we might be
confirmed in the same beliefe, and receyue an assurance to rise one day agayne with our ovvne
body, that vve may become like vnto our head:
for this also, that his vvounds might serue him
for a testimony of his victory, & be a perpetuall
memory of the esteeme, he maketh of his trauailes, and paynes endured for the loue of God,
meaning to honour them, by carrying them for
euer engrauen in his glorious body, set forth
with most excellent beauty, & diuine light. In
consideration vvhereof vve must take courage,
& suffer constantly of our Sauiour, yea and honour our selues for our sufferings, esteeming thē
much for our glory, and for a great fauour tovvardes vs.

   2.   To consider, that our Sauiour would
reserue his sacred vvoundes, to the end he might
be admired at, for that, vvhich for vs cost him
so deare, & that for the same reason be might be
moued to loue and pardon vs, sith the price of
our Redemptiō is vvritten in his piteously pier-
           O o 4   ced

ced hands, that he may replenish vs with his heauenly graces : & further that he may shew them vnto his Eternall Father, & therby appeaſe his Anger agavnſt men, by doing the office of a perpetuall Aduocate, & meditatour betweene them, & God, as the raynbow was bent between heauen & the earth, in ſigne of peace, & coue-nant : to prouoke and incite vs alſo to his loue, and ſeruice, in acknnowledgement of the loue, he hath borne vs, & for that he hath ſuffered to deliuer vs from euerlaſting paines. To theſe wounds of our Sauiour Ieſus, to theſe cliffes of the liuing rocke, we muſt make our recourſe, therein our ſoules muſt build their neaſts, and make their aboad, when they ſhal ſee themſelues purſued as doues by the infernall crue of raue-nous foules, or when the multitude of worldly affayres doth trouble, & diſquiet vs. For therin we muſt conſtitute and place our chiefe refuge, aſſurance, & repoſe, by conſidering the wounds, as ſo many diuine fountains, from whence there are deriued in abundance the waters of graces, & of ſpiritual conſolation for al the, who approach vnto them with feruor & deuotion.

3.　　To conſider, that he pleaſed to keepe theſe woundes for the confounding of the bad at the day of Iudgement, by manifeſting vnto the what he hath ſuffered for them, & the great de-ſire he had to ſaue them, & to comfort & reioice the good not only in that day, but alſo for all e-ternity. For that will be vnto them as many in-ducements & motiues to loue him, who hath re-ceyued them for loue of them.

Medit.

Meditat. X I I.   *Of the Apparition to the seauen disciples, who were fishing in the sea of Tiberias. Ioan. 21.*

TO consider, how the Apostles went to fish, both because their pouerty was great, and also for the auoyding of idlenes, vntill the tyme were come, that they should fish for men, all the others following S. Peter, who said, that he went to fish. Wherein is to be seene the conformity, and good manner of proceeding, that was among them• To consider, how all the night long they could not get any thing, insinuating by it, that humane industry can do no good for the gayning of soules, and the drawing them out of the gulfe of sinne, if God concurre not with his grace. By night is giuen to vnderstand, that it is a miserable thing with the sinner, before the Sonne of iustice be risen in his hart, for as much as the taking of soules dependeth vpon Gods fauour. We must also thinke, that the Apostles found themselues heauy, and sighed for his absence, being notwithstanding pleased and content with the paine & dolour they suffered in wanting his presence,

3.   To consider, how our Sauiour appeared vnto them about the breake of day vpon the shore, & willed them to cast in their netts, and to draw them on the right hand of their ship, and by so doing they caught a great number of fish. Wherin appeareth the Apostles obedience, who

submit-

submitted their iudgement vnto him, whome they did not then know to be their mayfter: and the happy euent of this obedience manifesteth, that the fpirituall fifhing of foules is done in the vertue of our Sauiour Iefus Chrift.

3.   To confider, hovv S. Iohn knew our Sauiour, and told it to S. Peter, who forthwith leapt into the fea: for his feruour of loue to his mayfter was fuch, as he would not expect the rowing to land. Saint Iohn alfo was illumined by the effect & force of the fame loue. To confider, how this fifhing infinuateth the catching that is euery day made of the predeftined, as alfo that which S. Iohn did in the beginning of his conuerfion, fignifying the fifhing for the both good & bad, & bringing of them within the cõpaffe of the Churches netts. To confider how, when the difciples were come to the fhoare, they faw a fifh put vpon coales, & bread miraculoufly prepared by the hands of our Sauiour, who pleafed to intertaine them with that refection & good cheere, becaufe they had trauayled & takẽ paines, as he commaunded them & for his loue, the holy heate whereof they carryed in their foules. By this is further fhewed, that if in the meane tyme, the iuft take paynes in this world for the loue of God, the diuine maiefty prepareth for them an eternall repaft & refection in the other.

Medit.

Meditat. X I I I. *How our Sauiour in this Apparition made* S. Peter *the chiefe Paſtour of his Church.* Ioan. 21.

TO conſider, how our Sauiour, meaning to put into Saint Peters handes the keyes of his Churche, which he had promiſed a while before, examined him by three demaunds about the affection of his loue towards him, that by thoſe three anſweres of his, that were accompanyed with much feare, and great humility, he might make amendes for his three negations, that had before proceeded from him throgh his pride, & preſumption. He examined him thrice touching his loue to him, to inſinuate, that ſuch as deſire to be Paſtours of Ieſus Chriſt his flock, muſt haue the vertue of charity deeply rooted in their ſoules, to the end they may purge, illumine, and perfect the ſoules of other men before God, in ſhewing them the way of ſaluation by the purity, and ſanctity of their life. He commaunded him to feede his ſheepe, that he might vnderſtand, that he was not the owner & Lord of the flocke, but only the Vicar of it, & that it appertained vnto him to haue a care of the faithfull, as of the flocke of our Sauiour Ieſus Chriſt, who is the ſupreme Prince of Paſtours, to whome he was to yield an accompt of his office & charge. In this appeareth the infinite charity of our Redeemer. To conſider, how the Paſtour is bound to giue three ſorts of paſturing to his
ſheep,

sheep; of spirit, in trauayling with them: of tongue, teaching them to worke & doe well: and shevving them the example of perfection.

2.   To consider, hovv our Sauiour said to Saint Peter, in testimony of the true loue he did beare him, that he should one day dye vpon the Crosse for loue of him, saying vnto him: whe thou wert yong, thou didest gird thy selfe, and didst walk where thou wouldst: but when thou shaltbe old, thou shalt stretch forth thy hands, & another shal gird thee, & lead thee, whither thou wilt not. In which words be meant two sorts of paynes, and mortification. The one, that a man taketh voluntarily of his owne election, in mortifying and maystring his flesh by pennance, & this is to make one subiect to himselfe. The other is that, which is inflicted and imposed by another, when men persecute a man, or the Diuells tempt him, or when God sendeth him afflictions, as maladies, sicknesses, paynes, disgraces, &c. And all this eyther for a tryall, or for a punishment. And he stretcheth forth his hands to his aduersityes, in imbracing and receyuing them with a good will, seeing it is the will of God: but it is for another alwayes to gird him, to Crucify him &c. in drawing & carrying him to that, which his carnall will inclineth not, and to which he hath not a will to goe. To weigh those words, that S. Peter should glorify God by that kind of death, in thinking that God is glorifyed, when we suffer any thing with a good will, for the loue of him.

3. To

3. To confider, how thefe wordes fayd to Saint Peter, that he fhould follow him, confirming by that figne, that he fhould follow him in the office of Paftour, and in the death of the Croffe. To confider, how Saint Iohn, carryed away with the vehemécy of his loue, that might not endure to be feparated from his company, followed after our Sauiour, though our Sauiour willed him not, whereunto he was alfo moued out of an holy and generous emulation to Saint Peter. And in this is to be feene, how great power good example hath to incite mens mindes to the imbracing of vertue. To confider, how Saint Peter out of his feruour and zeale of charity afked of our Sauiour, what fhould become of Saint Iohn: but our Sauiour reprehended him, becaufe that demaund of his fauoured of ouermuch curiofity, whiles he had a defire to know that which did nothing touch him, whé as he fhould leaue the care of that, and of other thinges to the diuine prouidence, and not intermeddle himfelfe in anothers affayres. Wherin we haue an inftruction and leffon giuen vs no leffe healthfull, then little practifed.

P p   *Medit.*

Meditat. XIIII.   *Of the Apparition to all the disciples on the Mount of Galily.* Matth. 28. Marc. 16.

TO Confider, how with how great a ioy the Apoſtles went into Galily, where they had an hope to enioy the preſence of their mayſter at leyſure: how they ſhould aduertiſe all the other diſciples, who were in diuers places diſperſed to the number of 400. perſons and vpwardes, all which went vp to the top of the mount Thabor, where our Sauiour comforted them with his diuine preſence: how a while before he had priuiledged three of his Apoſtles with the ſight of his glorious Transfiguration in the ſame place: and now credible it was, that he diſcouered vnto them ſome thing of the ſplendour of his glory, by occaſion whereof all of the adored him with moſt profound humility, and reuerence, whiles they receyued contentment in that, which they had ſeene, though ſome of the more imperfect, who were in company, made ſome doubt in their harts.

2.   To conſider, how he declared vnto them the power he had in heauen and in earth, which he had purchaſed, as man, by the meritts of his Paſſion, commaunding them to goe ouer all the world to teach all nations, & to publiſh the myſteries of our faith, as well touching thoſe things, that appertayned to the diuinity, as thoſe, that concerned the humanity of his perſon.

2.   To

2.   To confider, how he fayd vnto them, That they fhould baptize men in the name of the Father, and of the Sonne, and of the holy Ghoft: by changing the feueritv of Circumcifion into the facility of that wafhing, which is the gate of the new law of grace, and of loue, by which the Eternall Father admitteth and receyueth him for his child, the Sonne for his brother, and the holy Ghoft his foule for his Spoufe, by beftowing vpon it fupernaturall giftes, and vertues. We muft yield God thankes for this fingular benefit, by which the fruit of the dolorous Paffion of our Sauiour is applyed vnto vs.

3.   To confider, how he willed them to teach thofe, that fhould be baptized, to keep the commaundements, to giue thereby to vnderftand, that a Chriftian man muft lead a life, worthy the faith he profeffeth, and the baptifme, wherewith he hath been honoured, by meanes whereof we haue been fet free from the moft heauy and fore yoke of the auncient law, to receyue another both light and fweet one of the law of grace. To confider, hovv our Sauiour promifeth Eternall goods to them, that fhall belieue in him, & keep his holy commaundments, and contrarywife manaceth them, who infring the fame commaundements, and fhall not belieue, the euerlafting punifhment of hell.

4.   To confider, how our Sauior gaue vnto his difciples power to work miracles, as they did alfo in the primitiue Church, & fhall ftill do as oft as it fhalbe needfull for Gods greater glory. The preachers do euery day worke fuch miracles fpi-

ritually

ritually by their exhortations and sermons, and the Ghostly Fathers by absoluing from sinnes, which is, as if they should driue the Diuells out of the soules, and make men to speake a new language of heauen, in conuersing ordinarily with serpents, that is to say, with sinners, and not retayning any venine of their sinnes within them. Euery one exerciseth this power vpon himselfe, when by meanes of confession, and by a perfect sorrow & contrition for his sinnes, he thrusteth them out of his soule, and when he forgetteth the language of the old & terrestriall Adam, & speaketh that of the new and celestiall, by spending his tyme in continuall prayer, and holy conuersation, without receyuing any hurt from the venemous suggestions of the Diuell, or the dishonest & vncleane tentations of the flesh.

Meditat. X V.   Of the promise, that our Sauiour made of abiding with them vntill the worlds consummation.   Matth. 28.

TO Consider, that he, who made this promise, is our Sauiour Iesus Christ, true God, and man. The causes thereof were for the comforting of the Apostles, during their maysters long absence, who went vp to heauen, and for the solacing, and easing of the griefe, which the want of their good Father, and Lord caused them, by occasion whereof he promiseth not to leaue them as orphans : & further for the animating of them to goe on boldly & manfully

to

to the execution of that they had in hand, touching the worldes conqueſt, by the meanes of their preaching, ſending them forth to promulgate his holy word, to baptize, and to take pains as ſimple and innocent ſheepe among rauening wolues. For the conſideration of the preſence of our Sauiour, who was to be an eye witnes of their workes, was a moſt vehement motiue, and ſharp ſpurre to put them forwardes to doe their beſt. A man muſt accommodate, & apply all vnto himſelfe.

2.   To conſider all thoſe words in particular, but theſe moſt of all: I am with you. For it cannot be ſayd, that he is with thē after an ordinary and common manner, as he is in al his creatures, but as he is with the iuſt, & his elect, with whom he is by a particular prouidence, in hauing a care of them, as of his beſt beloued children. He is alſo in the moſt Bleſſed Sacramēt of the Altar, our ſpirituall refection and meate, gouerning vs, as our King.

3.   To conſider, that this promiſe is not to be vnderſtood for a day, nor for a yeare, but for the whole life, and euery houre, & moment of it. And this ought to mooue vs to a moſt diligent acknowledgement of our ſelues, hauing alwayes in mind, conformably to that, which S. Auguſtin ſaith: As there is not a moment, wherin a man receiueth not fauours at the diuine maieſtyes hands: ſo ſhould there not be a moment, wherein he ſhould not haue him ſtill preſent to his remembrance.

*Meditat. XVI. Of diuers Apparitions of our
Sauiour to his disciples, during the 40. dayes
of his aboad with them. Act. 2.*

TO Consider, how our Sauiour pleased to
reiovce his disciples with his presence, in
shewing himselfe vnto them in a visible
forme, & suffering himself to be touched of thē,
for a proofe of his Resurrection. He euery day
communicateth the very same fauour to the iust
soules, whome, besides their ordinary consolations, he visiteth and comforteth after a singular
manner, by giuing them the signes of his vndoubted presence.

2. To consider, howv in these Apparitions our Sauiour alwaies spake vnto his disciples
of the Kingdome of heauen, & intertained them
with pious discourses, repeating now and then
what he had sayd during his mortall life, & adding other thinges, that belonged to the founding of the Church, and to their particular good.
And this was a course, held by our Sauiour in
dealing with pure soules.

3. To consider, how in these our Sauiours visitations of his Apostles, some circumstances are to be obserued and marked, wherewith he was accustomed to honour his friendes.
The first, that these Apparitions were not continuall, but made at diuers tymes, and more frequent to some, then to others. The second, that
they were sodayne, and had but a short continuance,

ance, leauing them, who were viſited, with hony
as it were in their mouth. The third, that they
were not alwayes made in the ſame tyme, nor in
the ſame place. The fourth, that the Angells
ſome tymes came before the viſitations themſelues. The fifth, that the Apparition ſhewed it
ſelfe ſometimes ſhadowed according to the diſ-
poſition of the perſons, to vvhome it vvas
preſented. And all this paſſeth in the ſoules
of the iuſt inuiſibly, as they find by experience
euery day, ſome more, ſome leſſe according to
the diſpoſition it findeth in them, & conformably to the ordinance of the Eternall wiſdome.

Meditat. XVII.   Of the Apparition of our Sa-
uiour to his Apoſtles, vpon the day of the Aſ-
ſenſion.   Marc. 16. *Act.* 1.

TO conſider, how the Apoſtles being aſſem-
bled, and eating togeather in a roome
our Sauiour appeared vnto them, and did
eate with them, telling them that he was the ſame
day to aſcend into heauen to his Father, and to
goe to prepare for them a place there: how he
would be mindfull of them, when tyme ſhould
be: how, if they loued him, they ſhould haue
part with him of his glory, as they had ſorrow-
ed with him in his torments, and finally how his
aſcending vp to heauen imported them exceedingly, for that if he ſhould not goe, the holy
Ghoſt the Comforter ſhould not come, becauſe
they were ſtill through a certaine carnall amity

too much affected to his corporall presence: and
and therfore for the enioying of that soueraigne
Comforter, that was for him to come downe
into the earth, necessary it was, that himselfe
should ascend vp to heauen first. These and o-
ther the like reasons most probable it is, our
Sauiour vsed vnto them for the easing of their
sorrow.

2. To consider these wordes: Depart
yee not from Hierusalem, vntill you shall haue
receiued vertue from aboue. And this our Sauiour sayd to his Apostles, to teach vs, that the
quiet and tranquility of spirit, and repose of body is necessary for the receuuing of gifts and fauours from heauen: that patience and longanimity is very much required in them, who expect to be visited, and comforted of God. He
willed them to stay in the Citty, not in the desert,
to giue them to vnderstand, that the holy Ghost,
whome he meant to send them, was not for théselues alone, but to be communicated to men,
to whome he gaue them commission to preach,
he told thé, that they should receiue vertue from
aboue, by the efficacy of the holy Ghost for the
knowing and vnderstanding of their owne nakednes, imbecility, and pusillanimity of nature,
wishing them thereupon to haue most lowly e-
steeme of themselues before God, and not to
haue any thing to doe with vayne presumption,
by considering that nothing of difficulty, and
no great matter was to be vndertaken without
great prouision of help, ministred from the holy Ghost, and of gifts from heauen, which be
the

the apparell and cloathing, that God affordeth from aboue, & wherewith we must be clad.

3.   To consider, how after he had sayd these and the like thinges vnto them, he willed them to goe out of the citty to the mount of O-liuet, meaning from thence to ascend into heauen. His diuine maiesty pleased to choose this mount for his glorious Ascension, for this, that at the foote of it he had made his prayer with an agony, and bloudy sweat, was there abandoned and forsaken of his disciples, and deliuered into the hands of his enemyes, to giue to vnderstand, that he had gayned heauen there, whither he went to make his entry into it, & this by means of his passed trauayles. He specifyed and made particular mention of Bethania, which signifieth the house of obedience, & the mount of Oliuet, by which is meant Gods soueraigne mercy, to teach vs that the way to heauen is by obedience, charity, and compassion towardes our neighbour.

Meditat. XVIII.   *Of our Sauiour Ascension.* Act. 1.

TO consider, how when the most Blessed Virgin togeather with all the disciples were come to the mount of Oliuet, our Sauiour appeared vnto them in far more beautyfull and resplendent manner, then at other tymes, whiles also his sacred wounds dispensed a most fragrant smell, that comforted all, that

were

were present, all who (especially his B. Mother) fell downe at his feete, kissed them with all reuerence and deuotion, and humbly craued his benediction, which he gaue them with most diuine wordes, that made their harts to melt, and transported them with admiration. whiles he sometimes made his speach to his eternall Father, sometymes to his sweet mother, to whome he recommended his poore and little flocke togeather with the whole Church: one while he turned himselfe to his Apostles, another while to his other disciples, saying that he left vnto them his peace, that they might be assured he would neuer abandone them, and that they should fight manfully vnder his standard, & safe protection.

2. To consider, how our Sauiour began to raise himselfe by his owne proper vertue & power, by little & little from the earth, carryed vpwardes by the soules of the iust, and accompanyed by many thousands of Angells, who were come downe from heauen to honour his tryumph. To meditate, how the disciples had their eyes both of body, and of mind, still fixed vpon their mayster wondring at the sight of so strange a matter, that a man should mount so vp in the ayre with such a facility, maiesty and magnificence, reioycing at the glory of their Lord and mayster, and of the diuinity, that shined outwardly in his person, following him with eye, & and mounting vp with him in mind and affection, whither the force of their loue drew them togeather with him.

3. To

3. To consider, how a most bright cloud, cōming betweene our Sauiour and his disciples, tooke from them the sight of him, which serued him for a tryumphant chayre to carry him into the possession of his glory. And by this circumstance he gaue new matter of ioy vnto his Apostles, in seeing that all creatures did seruice to their Lord.

4. To consider, how whiles the disciples were transported with an admiration, & looked vp towardes heauen, two Angells, clad in white, appeared vnto them, and sayd: Yee men of Galily, what stand you looking vp towards heauen? This Iesus, that is assumpted from you into heauen, shall so come, as you haue seene him going into heauen. Which was as much as to say vnto them, that the comforts of contemplation ought not to be measured in this life, sith our end cōsisteth not in thē, because they be but the meanes to do the will of God with more facility, and to satisfy the obligations of euery ones profession: that ioyning the remembrance of our Sauiours ascension togeather with a firme beliefe of his future coming dòwne to iudge the whole world, they should preach the one & the other to the world, to the end that men may be induced & moued to doe what belonged vnto them, by the apprehension of that latter, & dreadfull day of doome. To consider, hovv the whole company had no sooner heard, what the Angells sayd, but that they looked down to the ground, kissed the places, where our Sauiours feete had stood, adored him with a liuely fayth, sitting in the

throne

throne of his glory, and then returned to Hierusalem in great ioy, that proceeded from the stability of their fayth, & of the hope they had, that
according to promise he would send them the
Holy Ghost. To consider the surpassing loue,
they did beare their mayster for his glory, wherof they were as glad, as if it had been their own,
being more in mind in heauen, then liuing in
body on earth. We must imitate all this, stirring
vp in our soules fayth, hope, & charity.

Meditat. X I X.   *Of our Sauiours Tryum-*
phant entry into heauen: and how he sitteth
on the right hand of his eternall Father.
Marc. 16.

T O consider the attendance, and company
our Sauiour had, namely the soules he had
deliuered out of Lymbus, and of some iust
ones, togeather with their glorifyed bodyes, and
all exceedingly reioycing. And all this ioy of
theirs was then redoubled, when they compared
their owne littlenes, and the misery of the place,
from which they came, with the beauty, greatnes, and felicity of heauen, whereinto they were
to goe: whiles also they heard the musicke of
of that celestiall Chappell, composed of an innumerable company of Angells, which went on
singing the glorious victoryes of our Redeemer, exhorting one another in extolling his
praise to their vttermost, sith all that they could
possibly doe, or say, came far short of the matter
of

of his prayſes. And this cauſed them an incomparable ioy. We muſt in like manner be glad of our Sauiours glory, and ioyne our feeble and vveake prayſes with thoſe of the Bleſſed ſpirits.

2. To conſider, how when our Sauiour had penetrated and paſſed all the heauens, & was come before the throne of his Father, he preſented him with this bleſſed captiuity, giuing him an accompt of that, which he had done heere on earth, for the glorifying of his name, ſaying: Father, I haue manifeſted thy name to men, and haue glorifyed thee on earth, in accompliſhing the worke, which thou gaueſt me to doe: and now, holy Father, clarify thy Sonne with that clarity, which I had with thee, before thou createdſt the world.

3. To conſider, with what contentment the eternall Father welcomed his beſt beloued Sonne, and receyued the gift, he preſented him, of thoſe ſoules, willing him to take his place on his right hand, that is to ſay giuing him the moſt excellent goods of his glory, exalting him aboue all the Angells, and making him the chiefe and head, as he was, of men. To conſider, hovv liberally the eternall Father recompenſed the ſeruices, his Sonne had done him, rayſing him aboue all, who had been abaſed beneth all, giuing him his owne throne for that of the Croſſe, that was full of torments and ignominy, and a crowne of infinite glory for that of thornes. Out of this we muſt draw a firme reſolution to trauayle, take paynes, and to humble our ſelues for

Q q   the

the loue of God, seeing after such trauayles, and mortifications there followeth so glorious a cōpensation.

4.   To consider, how our Sauiour, being set on the right hand of his Father, beganne forthwith to exercise his office in distributing the seates of glory to the soules, he had conducted with him out of Lymbus. Some he placed among the Angels, some among the Archangells, others among the Cherubims, and Sera phims. To thinke, what might be the ioy of these holy soules to see themselues raysed vp to so great honour in the middest of so holy a cōpany, and what was the contentment of the holy Angells to behold their Country peopled a new, and their seates filled vp that had continued empty from the time of the malignant spirits, that fell. To consider, our Sauiour, being set on the right hand of his Father, began to execute his office of Aduocate, by interceding for the men, that then were, and are yet this day vpon the earth, shewing & representing vnto him the wounds he receiued for the redeeming of them, and for the fulfilling of his commaundements. We must seeke heere to stir vp vehement affections of loue, and of confidence, by calling to our remembrance, that we haue an high Priest, who hath penetrated through all the heauens, that is, our Sauiour Iesus Christ, the Sonne of the liuing God, by whose meritts the gates of heauē be opened vnto vs, & our cause by his intercession defended on high in the Court of his eternall Father.

¶. *After*

¶ *After the precedent Meditations of the glorious Resurrection, and Ascension of our Sauiour Iesus Christ, who is now in heauen, where he raygneth for euer, and beatifyeth the iust soules: I haue thoght it to good purpose in this place to put downe meditations touching the matter of the glory of heauen, that the deuout soule, which shall by contemplation mount vp to heauen with her Spouse, may be the more affectioned to seeke, pursue, and find out the way of this eternall habitation, by beginning euen from this very tyme, to take the pleasure in the same by holy connersation.*

Meditat. XX. *Of glory, in as much as concerneth the condition, state, and company of the Blessed in heauen &c.*

TO Côsider, that Glory, Paradise, & Felicity signify a perfect state, that comprehendeth within it selfe the masse of all good, & the priuation of all euill, in so much as in glory is to be found the eternity of good, an immutability without euer changing, an enioying & fruition without being wearied or loathed, together with a continuall renouation of pleasure, as it was the very day it first began. We must compare these propertyes of the goods of the celestiall glory with the imperfect goods of the earth, and we

Q q 3   shall

shall find that there is not the very least comparison to be made betweene them: and of this
there will follow a contemning of the world, &
a desire of heauen.

    2   To consider, the excellency, beauty,
& splendour of heauen, that is, of an holy place,
where God sheweth his glorious face to the holy soules, the pallace of our supreme Emperour,
where is to be found whatsoeuer may be wished
good, and delectable in this world, the imperfections taken away, that we see therein, as sayth
S. Iohn Apocal. 21. and 22. and S. Paul 1. Cor.
2. To consider, how these beautyes and excellencyes doe incomparably exceed those of ours
heere. For the heauenly Empyre is most cleare,
most lightsome, beautifyed with a most pleasant
and diuine light, proceeding from the diuinity,
and from the splendour of the most sacred humanity of the Word, which giueth a perfection
to the ioy of the blessed. It is a place most temperate, not obnoxious to the variety of wether,
and seasons, that trouble vs heere beneath, one
while by excesse of heates, another while by an
extremity of cold: a place quiet, calme, & fayre,
because no corrupted ayre entreth in there; a
place replenished with all manner of benediction, and properly the land, and country of God:
a place durable, eternall, and most secure from
daunger; a place most beautyfull, & most pleasant: finally a place, that hath in it all that, which
can be sayd to be desired, and most perfect, and
therefore we must say with the Prophet: How
much to be loued be thy habitations, O God of
                    vertues.

vertues ? My soule hath so longed after them, as I am not able to desire more.

3.   To consider the dignity, worthynes, & maiesty of the inhabitants of this holy Citty, who be so many as they cannot be numbred, & yet they know one another most inwardly, and conuerse togeather most familiarly. They be most noble, most wise, most excellent and most intelligent in all arts and sciences, that may possibly be desired, most singular for their curtesy, discretion, affability, sweetnes &c. These be the lillies, & roses without thornes, and corne without chaffe, placed in wonderful order and variety, as be the starrs in the element, that be different in greatnes, and clarity, disposed with order and compasse. So be the blessed, liuing euery one in his rancke according to the degree, God hath assigned them: most contented with their felicity without desiring more, and reioycing at all the glory, that others haue, as if it were their owne. For there is a most inward, and most straight band of charity among them, and a most admirable conformity of one with another, though they be not otherwise in equall degree of happynes. We must meditate of all this, pondering euery one of these points by it selfe, the more to set our desire on fire with the thinges of heauen, & to liue so, as we may one day merit to become possessed of the same.

Q q 3   *Medi-*

Meditat. X X I .   *Of the essentiall Glory of the Soule, Body, and the Senses.*

TO Consider the greatnes of the glory, that the soules are rewarded with in heauen, which is such, as God cannot giue them greater, because they comprehend the diuinity it selfe, the most blessed obiect of the eternall delights and pleasures, the cleare vision whereof communicateth vnto the soules a perfect & consummate happynes, filleth them with the essence diuine, & desueth them by a certayne ineffable participation of it, his maiesty vniting himselfe with them, as doth the fire with iron, whereunto it communicateth the proper qualities, in penetrating therwith throughly, & into all parts. I shall be satiated, sayth the Prophet, when thou shalt discouer vnto me thy glory. Then shall the Memory enter into the powers of our Lord, alwayes hauing him in presence to it selfe, & shall ingulfe it selfe in the bottomles depth of his diuinity, continually thinking vpon his wonderfull workes: then shall the Vnderstanding haue the fill of God, by the cleare vision of the vndeuided Trinity, and vnity of it. There it shall vnderstand without shadow or figure, how the Father hath from all eternity begotten the Sonne, & how both of them togeather produce the holy Ghost: it shall see the perfections diuine, and all the mysteries, which it knoweth now but by fayth it shall see the deep secrets of the paternall
proui-

prouidence of God, whereby he shall haue conducted it into the way of saluation. Finally the insatiable desire of Knowledge shall then haue the fill in our soules, when we shall contemplate Gods essence, in whome all thinges be most perfectly comprehended. The Will shall also be filled with God, by louing him with a stable and durable loue, whereof shall proceed a perpetually flowing, and most abundant torrent of ineffable pleasures and contentments, whereof it shalbe inebriated to the fill, and shall thereby be ingulfed into the infinity of our Lords ioy, where it shall exercise all acts of vertue with delectation in the highest degree. For in saying that God himselfe is the happynes and glory of the soules, is to say all that, which may be imagined, and much more, for that in him be comprehended all good thinges without any imperfection. Of this we must learne to loue the exercise of mentall prayer, in which be exercised the acts of the three powers of the soule, by reason whereof we may well call meditation the representation & Image of the glory of heauen.

2. To consider the glory of the body with the foure gifts and priuiledges of it. The first whereof shalbe clarity, accompanyéd with an admirable beauty: For euery blessed body shalbe lightsome, and bright shining as the Sonne, conformably to the body of Iesus Christ And if it shal haue receiued any wound or mayme for the loue of God, it shalbe vnto it as an ornament of precious stones. They shalbe both without and within most contenting to see, their harmony

and

and composition shewing it selfe, and representing it selfe with the reuerberation of a diuine light, which shall fill them with a most gratefull lustre, and beauty. The second shalbe impassibility, and immortality, by meanes whereof neyther hunger, nor thirst, nor other payne can hurt them, but they shall liue eternally in one & the same good state, full of vigour, and immutable health. The third shalbe agility, which shall cause the soule to haue an absolute power ouer the body, in so much as it may transferre it and moue it from one place to another with most exceeding and sodayne swiftnes, without beeing wearyed at all. The fourth shalbe subtility, or, if I may say it, a spiritualization of the body, in so much as it shall not be subiect to eating or drinking, and shall be able to penetrate the heauens, and all other solid bodyes without obstacle, as did our Sauiour, when he entred into the chamber, where the disciples were met togeather, when the doores were fast shut. By this we must take courage, and resolue to suffer something for the loue of God, who rewardeth our trauails with so liberall an hand.

3. To consider the glory and pleasure of the fiue senses of the body. For the sight shall be glad in a most high degree to behold so many beauties togeather, especially in the sacred humanity of our Sauiour. The hearing shalbe delighted with the sweet wordes, and speeches the Blessed vse one to another, and with the harmonious concent of those immortall spirits musicke. The smell shalbe recreated vvith

the

the fragrancy of the moſt ſweet ſent of the
gloriſyed bodyes. The taſt ſhalbe ſatiated
with an vnſpeakable ſweetnes, that God ſhall
communicate vnto it, in a far more perfect manner, then a man can here find on earth. The touching ſhall haue the fill of holy, & pure delights
and pleaſures, in ſo much as euery bleſſed perſon ſhalbe as it were ingulſed with an infinite
Ocean of diuine pleaſures. The conſideration
of all this ought to excite vs to the mortifying of
our ſenſes in this life, that we may come to poſſeſſe theſe pleaſures, and infinite more in the
other.

Meditat. XXII. *Of glory, as it comprehen-*
deth the reward of Beatitude.

TO Conſider, that the glory, and Kingdome
of heauen, which our Sauiour hath promiſed to the poore of ſpirit, is the cleare viſion
of God, and the poſſeſſion of his infinite riches,
as we haue declared in the precedent meditations. This Kingdome is in euery one of the
Bleſſed entiere and whole in ſuch ſort, as if there
ſhould be but one alone in paradiſe, he ſhould
poſſeſſe the Kingdome of God whole to himſelf,
and the reaſon is, for that all the Bleſſed be in holy writ called Kings.

    2. To conſider, that the price of the ſe-
cond Beatitude conſiſteth in the fruition of the
heauenly countrey, which was promiſed to the
meeke, the land of benediction, and of diuine
                                            conſo-

confolations , where there is neyther weeping ,
nor paynes , nor griefe.

3.   To confider, that the contentments promifed to them that weepe , be infinite , & therewith pure , without any mixture of any difcon-
tent . For all this bleffed countrey hath a moft
abfolute felicity by the cleare vifion of the diuine effence, by the facred humanity of the eternall word , and by the prefence of his moft B.
Mother : the company of the Hierarchves of the
holy Angells, the Angells, Martyrs, Confeffors,
and all the Saints : the affurance of beatitude, the
eternity of it, & finally all that, which in this glorious place may be expected by the inhabitãts is
a foueraigne ioy & gladnes. Moreouer the fatia-
ting that is promifed to thofe, who haue hunger
and thirft of iuftice in this world , is in another
abundance of all good things, that may poffibly
be defired, and ftore and prouifion, that cannot
be found on the earth , for that all is there intermixt , and defectiue , but in heauen all thinges
be accomplifhed folid, and perfect: for that is the
place, where are filled all the defires of the foule,
and from whence is banifhed all, that may giue
occafion of payne, or griefe .

4.   To confider , that the recompenfe ,
promifed to the mercyfull , confifteth in the fulnes of mercy, which is no other thing , then the
glory it felfe , the diuine maiefty rewarding on
high , though his infinite goodnes , the workes
that be heere done in grace , and this compenfa-
tion hath the name of the Crown of Iuftice, and
of mercy , whereof we muft make our profit .

                                                    To

To confider that the reward of thofe, that fhall be cleane of hart, is the glorious vifion of the face of God, (which we call the effentiall beatitude and glory). For he glorifyeth the foule the very day it entreth into heauen, and enricheth it with the gifts of glory, adorning and beautifying it, as his deere and beloued Spoufe. Faith is recompenfed with the light of glory, by means whereof the foule beholdeth cleerly the effence diuine, togeather withall the myfteries, that it beleeueth heere in this life. The Hope is changed into comprehenfion, that is, that the foule fhall enioy, and poffeffe, as the owne, all that, which it hoped for in this life, as being then and there for euer vnited with God, and its owne Spoufe. Charity fhall be rewarded with the fruition, and enioying of God, and louing in a fupreme degree the good, that it fhall fee with an ineffable contentment, delight, and pleafure. And therfore it is written in the Canticles: my beft beloued is all for me, and I all for him.

5. To confider, that the reward of the peace-makers, whome through a fpeciall priuiledge our Sauiour hath honored with the title of Gods adopted children, is the fame glory. For the iuft be, by the Sacraments, and the graces that God communicateth vnto them, adopted in this life, and yet this adoption is ftill imperfect, and attendeth another perfect indeed, whereof the foule fhall haue the full poffeffiō when it fhal enter into the glory of God the Father, when it fhall receyue the right of vniting it felfe with its

owne

owne body agayne in the end of the world, and then make it glorious & immortall. And all this for that adoption, whereunto holy men haue euer sighed and longed for in this life, and wherof our Sauiour pleased to giue as a certayne passing representation in the day of his Transfiguration, on which he was declared the Sonne of God by his heauenly Father, the first adoption beeing made in his baptisme, where also he had the tytle and name giuen him of the Sonne of God.

Meditat. XXIII. Of glory, in as much as it comprehendeth the seauen kindes of rewardes, that our Sauiour promiseth to them, who shall become victorious. Apoc. 2. 3.

TO consider the great compensations our Lord promiseth to them, who shall ouercome their passions, become victorious ouer themselues, and tryumph ouer the world, flesh, and Diuell. The first reward is promised to them, who shall perseuere in their first feruour, or by the meanes of repentance shall returne vnto it. I will giue to him, that shall ouercome, to eate of the tree of life, which is in the Paradise of my God. This tree is God himselfe, togeather with all his perfections, the Paradise is the Empyrean heauen, the meate is the cleare vision of the diuinity, and of the humanity of our Sauiour, a meate of so soueraygne vertue, as it conuerteth all those, who eate it, into trees of life,

and

and maketh them to beare fruit continually in
abundance, that is, new and delectable commotions, and most sweet affections of heauenly
things. The second is promised to them, who
perseuere alwayes faythfull till death amiddest
tentations, and persecutions, saying, That he
will giue them a Crowne of life; & that he, who
shall ouercome Sathan, shall not be hurt by the
second death, as be those, who willingly put
themselues within the enemyes power. For
though those, who withstand and fight agaynst
the enemy, be toucht by the former death of body, yet the second death of the soule hath nothing to doe with them, and God will deliuer
them from them both. From the first, by the finall Resurrection of bodies, which shalbe glorifyed, & from the second by a crowne of life, that
shalbe giuen the soule.

2. To consider, that the third recompence
is promised to them, who make resistance to
Gods enemyes, and fly from their bad company. I will giue, sayth he, to the ouercomer the
hidden Manna, and a white Meddall, wheron
shalbe written a new name, which none knoweth but he who receiueth it. This mánna is sweetnes of the diuinity, which cóprehendeth in it all
sorts of delicacies. The white Meddal is the most
noble testimony, that God giueth to the Blessed,
who by that meanes knoweth, and is assured,
that he is approoued, & elected to enioy the diuine esséce for eternity, without feare to be euer
separated from it. And if in this world the testimony of a good conscience causeth so great a
R r   comfort,

comfort, how much greater will this most happy testimony of the diuinity cause, that is signified by the white Meddall, being a signe of approbation, as is the blacke one of reprobation? The name, that is written on this Meddall, is, Sonne of God, and inheritour of his Kingdome. And this name is sayd to be new, by occasion of the new and perfect adoption, which they shall receiue to enioy for euer. The fourth recompence is promised to them, who shall ouercome, and keep his commaundements till the end. I will giue him, sayth he, power ouer people, and he shall rule them with a rod of iron, and he shal breake them, as a pot of earth, euen as I haue receyued the same power of my Father: and I will giue him the morning-starre. Wherein is to be seene, that the conditions of the good and of the bad shall be wholy changed, for as much as the wicked & sinners shall then find themselues vnder the feet of the good, contemned, and placed among the refuse and most contemptible of this world, though they were before Kings, and Monarkes of the whole world. The morning-star is Iesus Christ, God and man, giuen by his Eternall Father in recompense vnto those, who haue heere imitated his vertues, that they may there be raysed aloft, as bright shining starres in the firmament of eternity.

3. To consider, that the fifth recompence is promised to them, who haue not defiled their garments, & do full & perfect works in the presence of God. He, that shall ouercome, shall be vested in white, & I will not put his name out of the book
of

of life, & I will cōfesse him before my Father, &
before his Angells. That is to say, I will beautify their soules with glory, with the rich cloa-
things of grace, and of most excellent gifts, I will
reuest their bodyes with the precious ornament
of immortality, & they shall haue their continuall habitation in the tryumphant Church, without feare of being excluded, where their holy
workes, and good seruices, done to the diuine
maiesty, shall be published, and this, that all the
world may honour them. All which shall be effected at the day of Iudgement, when our Sauí-
our shall celebrate their prayses in the presence
of all both men and Angells. The sixt reward,
that our Sauiour promiseth to those, who conserue & keep the good they haue receiued
from his liberall hand, is recorded in these
wordes: He, that shall ouercome I will make
him a pillar in the temple of my God, and he
shall goe out no more: And I will write vpon
him the name of my God, and the name of his
Citty the new Hierusalem, which descendeth
downe from heauen, and my new name: meaning, that those, who shall be stable and constant
in their good workes during this mortall life,
shall in the other of immortality be as most artificiall pillers placed in the Temple of that heauenly Hierusalem, there to stand and abide for
eternity, promising to write vpon those holy pillers, the most sacred name of God, that of the
new Citty of Hierusalem, togeather with his
owne, as they are indeed the workes of his own
omnipotent hands. In the last place we must

confider the recompence, that God promifeth to
them, that fhall ouercome the flouthfull & fluggifh
luke-warmnes of life, that prouoketh vomiting,
in thefe wordes : He, that fhall ouercome,
I will giue him to fit with me in my throne ; as I
alfo haue ouercome, and haue fitten with my Father
in his throne. Wherein is infinuated the
greatnes, and maiefty, the Saints fhall haue in
glory, where they fhall be in company of our Sauiour
Iefus Chrift, conuerfing familiarly with
him, made partners in his goods, and in his owne
throne, in fo much as they fhall be made Gods,
in fuch fort, as they fhall be capable fo to be : a recompenfe,
that he promifeth to them, who fhall
fuffer, and ouercome, euen as he fuffered and ouercame
himfelfe. And as after his fufferings, &
his victory he was exalted by his heauenly Father;
fo fhall they be exalted, who fhall humble
themfelues in this world for the loue & honour
of God.

¶ *We will fpeake of the loue of God in the Meditations
of the Perfections diuine, following
therin the proceeding of our Bleffed Father,
S. Ignatius, who treateth of it in the fourth
weeke of his Exercife.*

Medit.

Meditat. X X I I I I. *Of the Apostles retyre,
and prayer after the Ascension of our Sauiour , vntill the comming of the holy Ghost.
Act . 1 .*

TO consider, how our Sauiour being ascended into heauen , the Apostles returned to a chamber, where being separated from the noyse and trouble of the world, they attended to prayer , the better to dispose théselues to the receyuing of the holy Ghost, at what time to their prayer they added the Exercise of many other vertues, as of Charity being in cõpany togeather euery one collected in himselfe , of perseuerance in prayer with out relenting in their first feruor , making prayer in company of the most Blessed Virgin, whome they vsed from their Aduocate , whiles she animated them to pray as wel by her own example, as by her holy, sweet, and encouraging speeches . We must vse this manner of proceeding , that the holy Ghost may vouchsafe to descend into our soules .

2 . To consider the motiues of this the Apostles retyre, among which one of the principall was their maysters commaund, who willed them to stay in Hierusalem, which they did , & there they withdrew themselues into a certayne roome , which since that was conuerted into a place of prayer , by occasion of the great mysteries, that were therein accomplished . Moreouer the knowledge of their owne weakenes , &

pusil-

pusillanimity, was another inducement vnto thē
so to doe, and made them feare in themselues the
like faults vnto those , wherinto they fell vpon
the day of their maysters Passion. Being thus retyred to this place, and shunning all occasions of
their owne mistaking , they in most affectuous
manner besought the diuine maiesty to satisfy
his promise, and to send them the holy Ghost, &
comforter , addressing themselues in their prayers one while to the Eternall Father , another
while to their good maister, the word Incarnate,
and then to the holy Ghost, whose consolation
they them attended. God also in this manner disposed them by little and little by feruent desires,
which they felt in themselues , to set their harts
on fire more and more , the neerer the tyme of
his coming was at hand . We must dispose our
selues in like sort , euer and anon repeating the
the Hymne , that the Church vseth in the sacrifice of Masse in honour of the holy Ghost.

3 .   To consider that , our Sauiour pleased
to differ the coming of the holy Ghost the space
of ten dayes, to teach vs longanimity & perseuerance, if we desire to obtaine any fauour at Gods
handes, without being wearyed , or giuing ouer
the prosecuting of our petitions, though he may
seeme not to ouerheare them of a long tyme to
teach vs also to be diligent on our owne part ,
without omitting any thing, that ought to be required of vs : for the number of ten is a signifi-
cation of perfection . Moreouer, what are we not
to doe for the obtayning of so excellent a gift, as
is the holy Ghost ? Heere we must imagine, that
for

for nyne dayes after our Sauiours Afcension in heauen, the nyne Quyers of Angells celebrated the feaft of his Afcéfion, euery one for one day, and that the tenth day the expected holy Ghoft came down vpon the Apoftles.

Meditat. XXV. *Of the election of Saint Matthias to the Apoftleship. Act.* 1.

TO confider, how in this meane while, that the Apoftles were in their retrayte, Saint Peter as the chiefe of all, and of the whole Church, propofed the election of an Apoftle in place of the travtour Iudas, and for that end feleĉted Mátthias and Barfabas out of their whole number. By this is Gods fingular prouidence to be feene, vvho caufeth that there be alwayes in his militant Church perfons fit to be elected and chofen to the dignityes therof: & that if any one favle in fayth, or in Religion, there be found thofe, that may enter into his place. To confider, in hovv high an efteeme God hath his Church, and the orders of religious, that adorne and beautify it, & protecteth them: & heerhence Religious ought to draw an argument & motiue to humble themfelues, and to feare the forgoing & loofing of their degree, and leaft another enter into poffeffion of their place.

2. To confider the care, Saint Peter had to difcharge his office. For it is not to be doubted, but that for the better fatisfying of it, he côfulted with our B. Lady as with the maiftreffe,

and

and supreme Woman of the whole Church. To consider the great obedience, and subiection of the other Apostles in submitting their iudgement to Saint Peter: the singular vnion & concord of those two, who were selected among the rest, without ambition on their part for that Apostolike charge, whereof none of the hundred and twenty persons, who were there in company, deemed himselfe worthy. All of them fell to their prayers, crauing of God, that he would please to manifest, whether of those two should be chosen to the Apostleship, confessing thereby, that men may easily be deceyued in their elections, if they be not assisted with light from heauen.

3. To consider, how God choose Saint Matthias to the Apostleship, to honour him: for Barsabas was most highly esteemed of men in regard of his holynes, and by that occasion had merited the surname of Iust, and S. Matthias excelling for his humility, discreetly concealed his sanctity vnder the shadow of simplicity, and therefore he was not so much regarded before men. But God the searcher of secrets meant to exalt him, raysing him vp from the dust of the earth, to make his vertue apparant to men: therby teaching vs to subiect our iudgement to that of Gods, which is far different from that of men, as is to be seene in this election. To consider, that Barsabas was nothing discontented, or troubled, that his companion was preferred before him, but conformed himselfe, as a iust man, to the diuine will, and was glad of the honour, that was

cast

caſt vpon Saint Matthias, who on the other ſide
was not a whit prowd of his dignity, but deemed himſelfe vnworthy of it, and the leaſt a-
mong the reſt, aſcribing all to the grace of God,
who had conferred it vpon him. We muſt
learne to doe the ſame, and to reioyce at our
neighbours good.

Meditat. XXVI. *Of Gods ſupreme benefi-*
cence towardes Men, *in ſending them his*
Holy Spirit.

TO Conſider, that the Eternall Father did
out of his only goodnes and mercy, ſend
this moſt ſingular gift: the very ſame
goodnes and mercy, that had moued him before
to giue vs his moſt deere Sonne, without meri-
ting on our part any ſuch fauour at his hands,
whereas on the contrary we had infinitely de-
merited for the bad intertaynment the eternall
word had receued at the worlds handes. To
conſider, that the death and paſſion of our Sauiour merited vs this gift, and moued the Eternall Father to ſend vs it, through the compaſſion he had of our miſeryes, in ſo much as in this
diuine gift there concurreth iuſtice on the part
of the meritts of our Sauiour, and mercy on the
part of our Eternall Father. To conſider, that
our Sauiour alſo did, togeather with his Father
ſend vs the ſame holy Ghoſt, to the end he might
in moſt effectuall manner perfect the Redemption of the world, bring to a côcluſion the work,
he

he had heere begon on earth. In like manner the
fame holy Spirit giueth himfelfe vnto vs for the
great loue he beareth vs, himfelfe being both
the gift and the giuer togeather, as one & fole
God, togeather with the Father, and the Sonne.

2.   To confider, that the holy Ghoft came
into the world to fucceed our Sauiour in the Office of Protectour, Aduocate, and comforter,
working thefe effects inuifibly in the Church: as
alfo to exercife the function of mayfter and doctour in perfecting, and confirming the fame
heauenly doctrine, that our Sauiour preached
himfelfe during his mortall life. He came alfo to
giue teftimony of the diuinity of our Sauiour,
by inciting the Apoftles to publifh this verity all
the world ouer, & to mayntaine it with the perill of their liues. The fame teftimony is by the
holy Ghoft giuen vs, by meanes of the abundant light, that is infufed into the foules of the
faythfull. Moreouer he came to blame and correct the vices of the world, to condemne men of
finne, to ratify the victory that our Sauiour got
ouer the Diuell, by euident fignes & teftimonies
confirming the integrity & holynes of his life, &
fhewing that by meanes of him the Kingdome
of finne was deftroyed, and Sathan togeather
with all his infernall troupes ouercome.

3.   To confider the infinite greatnes of this
gift, which is by an excellency called Almighty
Gods gift. For his diuine maiefty contented not
himfelfe with giuing vnto vs Charity, and other
the fupernatural vertues, togeather with the feauen gifts of the holy Ghoft alone, but he further
pleafed

pleafed to giue vs the very fource, and fountaine of all thefe goods. And therefore we are bound to yield him thankes, being affured that he, who hath giuen vs the greater thing, will not fayfe to giue vs what is leffe.

4. To confider, that the greatnes of this gift doth yet appeare the more, by reafon of the bafe condition, and quality of them, to whome it is cōmunicated, being men fimple, idiots, fear-full, fifhers by profeffion, and perfons of fuch like rancke: yea the liberality of God was fo great to impart himfelfe to all, without excepti-on eyther of nation, people, or of any one per-fon at all of any condition whatfoeuer. Heru-pon I haue moft iuft caufe to wonder at Gods infinite charity towardes men, fo vnworthy of it.

Meditat. XXVII. *Of the manner in which the holy Ghoft came downe vpon the Apoftles, on the day of Penticoft. Act.* 2.

TO Confider, how the moft B. Virgin be-ing in the chamber in company of an hun-dred and twenty perfons vpon the day of Pentecoft, which was a feftiuity of the Iewes in-ftituted in memory of the Law, that God gaue them on the mount of Sina, fifty dayes after the refurrection of Sauiour, the holy Ghoft defcen-ded vpon all, that were there affembled, & were vnited in charity, and had their foules prepared by feruent defires, that be the meffengers, and

fore-

forerunners of this most Blessed Spirit.

2. To consider, that sodainely there was made a sound from heauen, as of a vehement wynd cōming, to giue to vnderstand, that the cōming of the holy Ghost, or of holy inspiration, is not vpō a determined day or houre, but all dependeth vpon his wil, who produceth his operations in the time, and manner, that best pleaseth him & good inspirations come not from the earth but downe from heauen, whence all, that is good, cometh. The sound of the ayre insinuateth the effects of diuine inspirations, that put spirituall life into the soules, and mortify the heates of concupiscence, by separating that, which is precious, from what is vile, & the graynes frō the chaffe, mouing the harts, and putting them forwards to all that, which is good. We must earnestly desire the impulsions, and mouings of this most holy wind. This wind was vehement and very strong, to signify the impetuosity, & feruour, wherwith the holy Ghost moueth the soules to vertue with a certayne both sweet and amiable impulsion, without any constraint of the will, & expelling out of it all drowsynes and luke-warmenes withall. The same wind causeth a cleere sound, as a thunder-clap, that was heard ouer all the Citty of Hierusalem, to shew that the comming of the holy Ghost, produceth by the iust who be the instruments therof, the effects that sound, and are heard in the eares of all the world, by causing great alteration in the liues of men by the holy example of good persons, as was to be seene in the time of the Apostles, & is ofté also to be seene at this day.   3. To

3. To confider, how this vehement, ftrong & loud wind filled al the houfe, where the difcipls were; to infinuate, that the holy Ghoft is giuen in abuldance in the law of grace, where in the law of Moyfes it was comunicated in a very fparing manner: & this is effected by the merits of our Sauiours Paffion. There was not a place in the houfe, which was not filled with this admirable wind, as there is not a corner in the world, where the holy Ghoft hath not a will to enter, & prefenteth not it feife to all, that defire to haue any dependance on it. To confider, how when the holy Ghoft entreth into a foule, it filleth all the powers of it with what is good, as the memory with good thoughts, the vnderstanding with holy difcourfes and reflections vpon God, and things appertayning vnto him; the will with feruent and pious defires: finally all the foule is filled with God, and whatfoeuer it hath, and is in it, apprehendeth, confidereth, and breatheth nothing, but the diuinity it felfe. To confider, that the holy Ghoft came downe vpon the Apoftles, when they were fitting, to giue vs to vnderstand, that it hath no commerce or conuerfation with the vagrant, whofe will is inconftant, wandring, and difperfed about thefe exteriour thinges of the world, but abideth with them who are prefent to themfelues, collected, and bufying their mindes in good thoughts, & pious works.

4. To confider, that the holy Ghoft appeared in fiery tongues deulded, which came & fat vpon euery one of them, to fignify, that in manner of a diuine fire it purifyeth the foules,

illumi-

illumineth them, enkindleth an heate and feruour in them, rayseth them vp to heauen, vniteth them, and transformeth them into it selfe in a much more perfect manner, then doth the naturall fire materiall thinges. We must learne of this to stir vp in our selues an earnest desire, that we may haue our part in this most blessed spirit, that it may produce all these, and other effects in our soules It cometh not in forme of harts, but of tongues, because it was not communicated vnto the Apostles, that they should only loue it, and be themselues alone conuerted into that diuine fire, but that their tongues guided, directed and moued by the holy Ghost, might illumine the whole world, and set it on fire with the loue of God by their preaching of the Ghospell. To consider, that they were deuided tongues, to insinuate the diuersity of gifts and graces, that the holy Ghost communicateth, by producing many different effects, though the cause be alwayes one and the same We must heer stir vp in our soules deuout affections, in giuing thankes to the diuine goodnes for communicating so great priuiledges and high fauours to men. To consider what is sayd, that it sat vpon euery one of them, giuing thereby to vnderstand, that as touching it selfe, it cometh into our soules, therin to repose, & make a stay, desirous not to leaue them, vnles they abandone & forsake it first.

5. To consider, how all were replenished with the holy Ghost. Wherein appeareth Gods liberality, in replenishing with the holy Ghost all those, who were then in the chamber, and in the

the houfe , by communicating vnto them a perfect light to vnderftand the Scriptures , and
by putting into them a moft harty and affectioned loue to their neighbour . Finally wonderfull was the chaunge , they found in themfelues, and far other, then that they were before.
To confider , that though all were replenifhed
with the holy Ghoft , yet fome receyued more,
and greater giftes and grsces, then did others, according to the more or leffe difpofition, that was
in euery one , and conformably to that , they
were capable of . A man muft difpofe himfelfe
to the receyuing of the holy Ghoft by feruent &
pious defires, purity of hart, a good confcience,
great humility, and truft in God , long continued , and feruent prayers : For the more we fhall
haue of thefe vertues, the more and better fhall
we be difpofed to receyue the graces of the holy
Ghoft .

6 .   To confider, hovv they began to fpeake
with diuers tongues , accordingly as the holy
Ghoft gaue them to fpeake, giuing them to vnderftand, that this great fauour, he had beftowed
vpon them, was not intended fo much for themfelues, as for the whole world , whereunto they
were to preach the Gofpell , and the true fayth
of Chrift, & fo they began forthwith to fpeake,
not as beft liked them, but as it pleafed the holy Ghoft , who inftructed them in the way ,
did put into them feruour , and gaue them the
wordes into their mouth , that they were to
preach and fay vnto men . For preaching, and all
other found doctrine profiteth no further , then

in what it proceedeth from the holy Ghosts inspiration. To consider what strange & wonderfull thinges the holy Virgin, the Apostles, and the disciples were likely to vtter, and preach that day, and all their life after. We must imitate them herein, in speaking with diuers tongues, that is, in stirring vp in our harts diuers & sundry commotions and affections of deuotion, and in exercising pious works both pleasing to God, & profitable to our neighbour.

Meditat. XXVIII.   Of the wonderfull workes, that the holy Ghost wrought the day of Penticost by the Apostles. Act. 2.

TO Consider, how the Apostles, who had till the day of Penticost contynued shut vp and silent, expecting the comming of the holy Ghost, could not contayne themselues, after they had receyued it, but went abroad, & made themselues knowne to the world, & began to preach the wonders of God without feare. For Gods pleasure is, that the talents he giueth, be not hidden, nor idle. Thus being come forth, and seeing the great number of people, that came running vnto them at the lowd and great noyse of that vehement wind, they preached the Ghospell vnto them.

2.   To consider, hovv some of the standers by mocked the Apostles, thinking that what they sayd, proceeded of drunkenes, and that they had taken ouer much wyne. For there

are

are neuer wanting peruerſe and bad perſons,
who report ill of vertue, & interprete all things
ſiniſterly, and in the worſt manner: and God
permittetb it, that his ſeruants may haue matter
for the exerciſing of humility. To conſider, how
S. Peter taking an occaſion therof to inſtruct the
people, that neyther himſelfe, nor any of his cōpany were drunke with materiall wine, but with
the ſpirituall, which is no other thing, then the
diuinity it ſelfe, according to the promiſe it had
formerly made by the prophet Ioel cap. 1. ex-
plicated vnto them the Prophecy, and told thē
that the eternall loue of God moued them, both
to ſay, and to doe ſo prodigious and wonderfull
thinges.

3.   To conſider the effects, that the holy
Ghoſt produced in Saint Peter; how cleerly and
expreſly he diſcourſed in that his ſpeech, wherby he gaue a demonſtration of his profound wiſdome, of his great dexterity in propoſing the
truth, and in explaning the myſteryes of our Sauiour, his moſt confident liberty of ſpirit, his cō-
ſtancy, and moſt generous reſolution, without
the leaſt feare of the whole people, who a while
before had been terrified by the voice of a poore
ſimple mayde: his feruent and incenſed zeale,
that ſhewed it ſelfe in his wordes, by which he
entred into the very bottome of mens harts, and
conuerted them to God. For preſently after he
had ended his ſpeech, three thouſand perſons
deſired to be inſtructed in that which they were
to doe for the ſauing of their ſoules.

4.   To conſider what ioy the B. Virgin,

& the other disciples conceiued, when they saw, that the bloud of our Sauiour began to fructify so happily , and our Sauiour to be acknowledged in that place , where a little before the people had hā dled him so ignominiously, contemptibly , and cruelly.

Meditat. X X I X.   *Of the most perfect life which the Holy Ghost inspired into the first Christians.* Act. 2.

TO Consider , how it is proper to the holy Ghost to incite men to the doing of good workes , and principally to the hearing of Gods word , the reading of good and spirituall bookes, the frequenting of the holy Sacraments, and perseuerant and continuall prayer For the faythfull of the primitiue Church spent their tyme in these three manners of spirituall exercises, because they be the three most soueraigne, and most effectuall meanes for the conseruing of Gods grace in our soules.

2.   To consider , that it is another property of the holy Ghost to vnite the faithfull in a most straite manner among themselues, & one with another. For though they were of diuers Coūtreyes, and of different humors and conditions, yet they were but one hart , and one soule , according to that saying of the Prophet Isay : The wolfe, & the lambe , the lyon, & the sheep shall keep togeather. And this is the worke of Gods omnipotency, to shew vs, that the holy Ghost is

the

the God of vnion , and of charity . He further
inspired them to put all their goods and possessi-
ons in common for the conseruing of charity a-
mongst them , whiles they so lyued in Euangelicall pouerty, for as much as Myne and Thine be
the causes of diuision. Agayne in the distributing
of goods they followed not euery one his owne
iudgement , and will , but that of the Apostles ,
at whose feet they layd what was theirs: that is,
they did in such sort renounce all that they had,
as they would not so much as say, This is myne.
And of this it followed , that though all were
poore, yet none endured necessity, for as much
as all things were common, as houses, cloathing,
money , &c. Of this the Religious must learne
the affection , that they held , and kept in bringing them to their most happy state.

3.   To consider, that the holy Ghost inspired thē also to go to the Temple, & there to perseuere in prayer, & yet none forgot to doe what
was his office, and that done , they went to the
houses one of another, and this with most great
conformity, to take their corporall refection, one
exhorting another to the praysing & seruing of
God, & to the exercising of good workes , & liuing in a most perfect vnion of minds, & affections .

S f 4   Medi

*Meditat. X X X.   Of perfection, which the holy
Ghost communicateth by inspirations.*

TO consider, how the holy Ghost maketh
them like vnto it selfe, whome it regene-
rateth by grace in the holy Sacrament of
Baptisme, and perseuereth still going on to rayse
them vp to such a degree of perfection by the
meanes of holy inspirations, as they may be named spirits togeather with it selfe, according to
that, which S. Iohn sayth : That which is borne
of the flesh, is flesh, and that, which is borne of
the spirit is spirit : that is to say, a spirituall man,
for as much as euery one engendreth his like.

2.   To consider these wordes : The holy
Spirit breatheth where it pleaseth : that is. It
communicateth the inspirations, when, and to
whome it seemeth good. And this is sayd, to
giue to vnderstand the liberality of it, according to the proceeding of the eternall Prouidence, in communicating sometymes great and
effectuall inspirations to the soules, that are
in no sort disposed, and to sinners, that be the
most obstinate in the world. We must pray the
holy Ghost to please to touch our harts with his
efficacious inspirations, that his infinite goodnes may appeare & be seene in vs.

3.   To consider, these words : His voyce
you heare. For the inspiration is sayd to be a
voyce : That is, when it pleaseth the holy Ghost
to inspire, there is not a gate so fast locked vp,
nor

nor any disturbance so great in our soules, as may hinder it for comming in. For it is the mayster of all, and is of power immediatly at the very first to penetrate our hart, and to cary it in a most sweet manner thither, whither it will, without constrayning or forcing it. To consider, that as euery man is known by his voyce, that distinguisheth him from others: so the holy Ghost hath particularities, by which it is knowne, and they be these, to mollify the harts, and awake them out of their dead sleep of sinne, to put an heate & fire into the frozen cold, to giue strength to the weake: to cause them to contemne the earth and earthly thinges, & to desire heauen, & the things appertayning vnto it: to mortify the disordred appetites, to cause & worke many such effects sometimes with a sweetnes, sometymes with a feare. So we say, that the man whom we see modest in his actions, discreet in his words, pure in his intention, prompt to obedyence, diligent in that which concerneth the seruice of God &c. is inspired of the holy Ghost.

4. To consider, that the holy Ghost hath yet another propriety, which is this, that we know not whence it cometh, nor whither it goeth: hiding from our sight the comming of the inspirations of it by a wonderfull secret and skill of prouidence, as touching the tymes, places, & exercises. Sometymes it cometh vpon some day of festiuity, sometymes vpon a working day: one one while by day, another while by night, &c. Of this we must learne to be alwayes attentiue to the motions of our hart, with gratitude, and thankes-

thankef-giuing to receyue the inspirations of the
holy Ghoſt, & to execute thē with promptitude.

Meditat. X X X I.   *Of the ſeauen giftes of the holy Ghoſt.*

TO conſider, how, beſides the three Theologicall vertues, which be fayth, hope,
and charity, the holy Ghoſt communicateth vnto the iuſt ſoules ſeauen giftes, well
knowne, by meanes wherof they follow the holy Ghoſts impulſions and inſtinᶜts ſo ſoone, as
they feele the very touch of them, euen as the
maryner or pilot, who ſtanding at the ſterne,
by meanes of it, wyndeth and turneth the
ſhip what way he liſteth. And by this it is moſt
apparant to the eyes, how earneſt a deſire the holy Ghoſt hath, that we obey his inſpirations, for
ſo much as for that end he communicateth the
ſeauen giftes of his grace, that giue teſtimony of
the great deſire he hath of our ſaluation.

2.   To conſider, how the ſame holy Ghoſt
draweth vs from euill by meanes of theſe gifts,
and furniſheth vs with armes both offenſiue and
defenſiue againſt the principall roots of tentations, which maintayne a reſtles warre againſt the
ſpirituall life. For by the gift of wiſdome is diſſolued the ſoules frozen coldnes, and the diſtaſt
of it driuen away, & the eternall good, thereby
become ſweet and taſtefull vnto it. By the gift
of vnderſtanding be infuſed into vs the lighſome
illuſtrations, which diſperſe all darknes, doubts,
and

and perplexities, that troubled vs before. By the gift of Counsayle we are taught, how to ouercome indiscretions, precipitant, & headstrong motions, of things that happen vnto vs sodainly, and which we cannot morally preuent, or foresee By the gift of knowledge be discouered vnto vs the fallacies and treacheries of the D uell, the deceits of the world, & the guylefull & deceyuing pleasures of the flesh. By the gift of strength our soule is fortifyed, receyueth new forces, and is made to beare all temporall losses with iov for the gayning of the goods, that continue for euer. By the gifts of piety be our harts mollifyed, & we moued to vse mercy, when occasion is giuen vs to reuenge our selues. Finally by the gift of feare we are armed against the tentations of pride, presumption, & vanity, by repressing & keeping downe our pride, to teach vs to apprehend the terrible & secret iudgments of God. We are to render the holy Ghost immortall thanks for his paternall prouidence towards vs, in affoarding vs so singular and soueraigne helps for the remedying, & redressing of our miseryes & necessityes.

2. To consider, that there be three most important & effectuall wayes to obtaine the inspirations of the holy Ghost. The first is to be most confident in the holy Ghosts bounty & liberality, & withall cōceiue, that he will do vs the same fauour now, that he hath at other times done to many, though we be otherwise most vnworthy of it. The second is to vse all our possible diligence in frequenting of spirituall exercises,

cifes, in which the holy Ghoft is accuftomed to impart his infpirations: fuch be prayer, to intertayne the minde with good & holy thoughts, & actions, to be continually exercifed in pious & profitable works. The third, to giue the holy Ghoft all poffible & moft affectuous thanks for the fauours, he doth intend to do vs, holding our felues vnworthy of them, & in a moft exact manner executing his infpirations & inftincts, though the fame be otherwhiles repugning and contrary to our defires.

¶ *The meditations of Gods Effence, and of his di-*
uine attributs appertayne to the fourth Week,
which correspond to the Vnitiue Way. We
will make a Treatife of them apart by them-
felues, that thofe, who haue deuotion to me-
ditate them, may find matter for the rayfing of
their minds to the loue of God, & of moft
ftraitly vniting thefelues vnto the diuine ma-
iefty by the band of Charity.

The end of the fourth VVeeke.

DIVERS

DIVERS OTHER
MEDITATIONS
CONFORMABLY

To that which hath been ſaid in the firſt
Paragraph of the Preface. And firſt of
the moſt Bleſſed Sacrament.

*Meditat . I.   Vpon that which our Sauiour did
and ſayd before the inſtituting of the moſt holy Sacrament of the Altar .*

TO Conſider, how our Sauiour wold
waſh his diſciples feete before the inſtituting of the B. Sacrament of the
Euchariſt, to teach, the great purity
they ſhould haue, who would participate of this
heauenly banquet. For they muſt not contayne
themſelues from mortall ſins only, but alſo from
veniall, and from the diſordered paſſions both
of body and of ſoule, for that this diuine and ſoueraigne Lord, who is receyued in the Sacra-

Tt   ment,

ment, is purity it selfe. He would also wash their feet for another reason, which was to accommodate himselfe to the custome, which was, that he who inuited any, washed his feet in signe of humily, and fraternall charity, and this our Sauiour meat to teach vs, that those who were to be present at this banquet, should in the first place exercise themselues in the works of humility & of charity, which is the best disposition a man can possibly haue to communicate vvorthily.

2. To consider, how the legall supper of the Paschall Lambe went before the other mysticall supper of the holy Sacrament. For as that Lambe was sacrificed in acknowledgment of the fauour God did to the people of Israel, in deliuering them from out of the seruitude of Pharao: euen so in the sacrifice of Masse is offered the true Lambe Iesus Christ our Redeemer, in acknowledgement of the good, he did vs in deliuering vs from the captiuity of the Diuell, and of sinne, by the meritts of his Passion, nourishing and intertayning vs with with his precious flesh heere on earth, vpon hope that he will one day nourish vs with his diuinity aboue in heauen. He would further teach vs, with what dispositions we ought to come to this diuine Sacrament. For such as wil receiue it worthily must be very chast, & pure: a vertue, that they must also purchase by mortification of the flesh: they must also haue a diligent and continuall guard ouer their hart, and keep their affections pure & vndefiled from the fowle and vnsauory pleasurs of the earth: a great confidence in the Crosse of

our

our Sauiour : a great desire , and an hunger of
this diuine meate : a singular purity of mind , &
mortification of the body : and finally a burning
loue towards him, whome our fayth teacheth vs
to be present in the holy Sacrament of the Altar.

3.　To consider and ponder these words:
I haue with great desire longed to eate this Pas-
chal with you , before I dye . Where we are
taught to come to this holy Sacrament with a
great and harty desire, proceeding from the consideration of the singular benefit, God hath done
vs therein , being perswaded that as often as we
shall communicate , it may be perhaps the last
tyme, that we may dispose our selues thereunto
with the better deuotion .

Meditat. II. *Of the tyme , place , and com-*
pany , our Sauiour chose for the instituting of
this diuine Sacrament .

T O Consider , that our Sauiour instituted
this Sacramēt the euening before his most
bitter Passion, in testimony of his singular
great loue to men . For at what time they practised to bereaue him of his life , he prepared for
them an heauenly and diuine banquet , for the
preseruing of them from death; in so much as the
impetuous and violent waters of his torments
were not inough to quench the heate of his charity , and therefore there must not be any affection in vs , that may separate vs from his loue .
Moreouer he instituted it, to shew the exceeding
　　　　　　　　　　　　　　　　　　　　great

great desire he had to abide with men, and to beare them company in this miserable exile : for what tyme enuy wrought to get him out of the world, his piety and ineffable goodnes thought vpon staying in it. He also inftituted it, that he might leaue to his Church a memoriall of his Church, a memoriall of his Paffion, and a facrifice for the appeafing of the wrath of God : and to oblige vs to haue a remembrance of him, and of his moft dolorous and paynefull Paffion with the more tendernes of loue, he would inftitute it about the very tyme, he was to prefent himfelfe to death, for that the charges and precepts of Fathers, when they are neere the tyme of yielding vp their foules, abide the more imprinted in their childrens minds.

2.   To confider, that the place, that he choofe, was a great & large chamber wel accommodated, which one had offered him of good will. Wherein is giuen to vnderftand, that the foule, that hath a will to receyue our Sauiour, muft haue a will prompt and affectioned towards him. For fuch a difpofition is much pleafing vnto him, and the foule, that hath it, is receyued and accepted of the diuine goodnes, as a thing proper and peculiar vnto it, after a fingular manner of propriety, by working therein great myfteries, as was done in the chamber there, both before and after our Sauiours Refurrection.

3.   To confider, how our Sauiour choofe the company of his Apoftles, and the traytour Iudas among thereft, but yet with a difpofition
much

much different from the others, who attended
with deuotion to that, which their mayster did
and faud, and difposed themfelues to the receyuing of that celeftiall meate, whiles Iudas his
thoughts were carryed away about the putting
of his Diuellifh defignes in practife, and therfore
that diuine refection was vnto him conuerted
into poyfon, and into an occafion of his eternall death.

Meditat. III. Of the miraculous Tranfub-
ftantiation of bread, into the body of Iefus
Chrift. Matth. 26. Luc. 22.

TO fuppofe that, which holy fayth teacheth
vs, that is, that our Sauiour taking bread
into his facred hands, and vttering the
wardes of confecration, changed the fubftance
of the bread into that of his precious body, couered and fhadowed with the exteriour Accidents. And we muft confider the infinite wifdome of God, for hauing found out fo wonderfull a way to communicate himfelfe to man, that
he might giue him a nurture of life, as that alfo
was another meruayle to become incarnate by
ioyning in an hypoftaticall vnion for the fame
effect, two thinges of fo great difference and di-
ftance, as is God and man. He manifefted his
omnipotency, by one word working fo many
and great miracles in an inftant, in changing the
fubftance of bread into the fubftance of his body, being all in all the hoft, and all in euery part

Tt 3   of

of it without being deuided in himselfe, He witnesseth his infinite charity in giuing vs all that,
which was in his power to giue vs, that is to say,
himselfe, in making himselfe our meate and
drinke. The Eternall Father discouered also his
goodnes & loue to vs in giuing vs his most deare
Sonne in such a manner. The most incensed
zeale, our Sauiour had of our saluation, appeared in a most high degree in this, that he vsed so
extraordinary a meanes for the applying of the
merits of his most bitter Passion vnto vs.

2. To consider the woders, that are coprehen-
ded in these wordes of the Consecration, This is
my body, reall, & true body, not a figure, & representation of it For he would himselfe in person be the sustenace of our soules, as the mother,
who tederly loueth her own child, giueth it not
vnto another to bring vp, but giueth it suck with
the milk of her own breasts Euen so God giueth
vs his owne body whole & perfect, to giue vs to
vnderstand, that his meaning is to sacrifice al our
members by his owne most holy members, to
cleanse our harts by his, our eyes by his eyes &c.
And therefore when we are to receyue the holy
Communion, we must craue of him, that he
would please to sanctify all the parts both of our
body and soule. To consider, that our Sauiour
sayd; This is my body, that shall be deliuered
for you : that we may vnderstand, that the same
body, that was deliuered vp to be nayled to the
Crosse, was giuen vs for our meate and food, the
one and the other proceeding from the same
source of loue, & of charity.

3 .   To confider , that the Apoftles receyued this moft facred bread with great reuerence, and belieued with a moft fteedfaft and vndoubfaith , that vnder thofe appearing likenes they receyued the very body of their mayfter , & felt within their foules moft fweet and moft contenting affections of deuotion in that their firft communion . The traytour Iudas alone found no taft at all in that moft teftfull meate , and this in regard of the moft bad difpofition , that was in him . To confider , how our Sauiour tooke a peece of this moft holy bread , and communicated himfelfe , thereby to excite and moue his Apoftles to doe the fame , and gaue them an example of modefty and deuotion , wherewith they fhould recevue it , and reioyced in his hart, that he had inftituted fo wonderful a Sacrament. We muft feeke to ftir vp in our foules the commotions of admiration , of ioy , and of prayfing fo good a God, and fo liberall a Lord, who vfeth fo many holy artificiall inuentions, and wayes for our greater profit .

Meditat. I I I I .   *Of the conuerfation of wyne into the bloud of our Saviour : and of the great treafures which be contayned in this precious Bloud .*

T O Confider, how after the confecration & receyuing of the bread , our Sauiour confecrated a cup of wine , which by vertue of his wordes was by his omnipotency changed

T t 4   **into**

into his bloud, in testimony of his supreme chɑ-
rity towards vs. For he then gaue vs no lesse
thing, then the precious bloud of his owne
vaynes, contrary to the humour, disposition,
and custome of the Kinges of this world, who
drinke the bloud of their subiects, enriching
themselues by their goods, and intertaining thē-
selues by their substance.

2.   To consider, that he called the Chalice
of bloud, his new Testament, to shew the difference, that is betweene the new Testament and
the old. For he promiseth vs in this, that was
made the night before his Passion, the remission
of our sinnes, the grace and adoption of Gods
children, charity, vertues, the gifts of the holy
Ghost, & the inheritance of heauen. Such was
the banquet our Sauiour gaue vs in his last
testament, sealed, signed, and confirmed by the
effusion of his owne bloud: and therefore we
must heere humbly craue of the eternall Father,
that he please to graunt vs that, which his most
deare Sonne hath left vs.

3.   To consider what our Sauiour sayd,
That he did shed his bloud for his Apostles, and
for many in remission of sinnes: to moue them
by those his wordes to compassionate him, to
acknowledge him as they ought, and therefore
he added these expresse wordes (for you) speaking vnto them. We must apply this to our
selues. He sayd also: which shall be shed for many. For all the men of the world, as touching
the sufficiency of it; and for many, as touching
the efficacy: and this (in remission of sinnes)
witnout

without excepting any , be it neuer so grieuous.
He declared his infinite loue in vsing this word
(to shed) that insinuateth the excesse of his
charity .

Meditat . *V* .   *Of the Sacramentall kindes of*
Bread and Wyne, and what they represent.

TO consider, how our Sauour would institute this feast and banquet of bread and
wyne, to insinuate the perfection of it, and
that where principall meates of a terestriall banquet consist of these two , so the same haue the
chiefest place in this heauenly feast , whiles our
Sauiour is also serued at this diuine table vnder the kindes of the one & of the other : to signify also that all his precious bloud was wholy
seuered from his Body , when it was in the passion shed for our sinnes , and so must we represent them vnto our selues in the holy Sacrifice of
Masse .

2 . To consider , that he would remayne
hidden vnder the veyle of accidents for the humbling of himselfe , and for giuing vnto vs an example of patience. For as, when he became man,
he concealed his diuinity vnder the robe of his
humanity; and therfore was knowne but to few,
and despised of many : euen so hidden vnder the
Sacramentall kindes , he is not acknowledged ,
but contemned , and more then that otherwise
ill handled by many vntoward and bad soules .
To consider , howv he did this , to giue vnto vs

a

a new and continuall occasion of exercising our fayth by renouncing our senses, and ascending higher, then our ordinary discourse and reason can reach vnto, by subiecting and captiuating our vnderstanding vnder the obedience of faith: and therefore this Sacrament is named a mysterie of fayth, in so much as when we heare Masse, or enter into the Church, we must excite and reuiue our faith, that our merit may be greater. He would hide himselfe vnder the appearance of bread and wine, for the imboldening of vs to come freely vnto him, to touch, take, and eate him. For if he were not disguised in this sort, who is so hardy, as he would approach or come neare vnto him without horrour, and extreme feare?

　3.　To consider, that he would be shadowed vnder these kinds, to incorporate himselfe with man by the most inward vnion, that can possibly be. For there is nothing, that vniteth it selfe more perfectly to man, then meate and drinke, that penetrateth him in all parts, and is conuerted into mans owne substance. It was also to signify, that it worketh spiritually in our soules, that which the meate doth materially in our bodyes. For it sustayneth vs, it conserueth vs, it augmenteth in vs a spirituall life, it comforteth and reioiceth our harts, it quencheth the intemperate and excessiue heat of proper loue, it repayreth the domages and hurts it doth vs, and to say in one word, it maketh vs to resemble our Sauiour himselfe, by making vs participant of his diuine vertues. To signify also, that

that as bread is made of many gra ynes of corne,
put into a masse togeather , and Wyne of many
grapes , pressed , and put togeather : euen
so this diuine meate, and celestiall drinke require
harts and mindes vnited by true charity, and that
it tendeth only to this wōderfull vnion, of which
this most noble Sacrament hath taken the name
of Communion.

Meditat. VI.   *Of six thinges full of mystery,*
which our Sauiour did , and sayd , when he
consecrated the Bread, & Wyne.

TO consider, how for the making of this
wonderfull conuersion of bread into the
substance of his most precious Body , our
Sauiour tooke it into his handes , giuing to vnderstand that they were the omnipotēt workers
of the vniuerse , into which the Eternall Father
had put all things,& by shewing also his great liberality. For as the Psalmist sayth : He openeth
his hand , and he filieth all creatures with his benediction . And what greater benediction can
there be, then for him to giue himselfe vnto vs ,
to accompany vs in our exile , and to solace and
ease vs therein, as long as we lyue in this vale of
teares? He tooke bread into his hands , to insinuate that by the labour of them, and the sweare
of his browes he had gayned vs that bread of
heauen , that was not the meate of the idle and
slouthfull, but of those that trauaile, take payns,
and

and spend their tyme in purifying their soules by the exercise of vertue.

2. To consider, that he lifted his eyes vp to heauen, to teach vs that this bread was from heauen, and not from earth, the bread of Angells, and which maketh men become like vnto Angells; that we may lift vp our eyes to heauen by hope, prayer, and purity, by disposing our selues in such sort, as we may receyue him worthily. He gaue thanks to his Eternall Father for the benefit he did to the world by his meanes, in giuing it so diuine bread for the refection thereof, teaching vs with what manner of thankesgiuing we ought to receyue it. He blessed the bread with a most efficacious and powerfull benediction, that made such a miraculous conuersion & change of the substance of bread into that of his owne Body. He brake the bread, and gaue it to his disciples, to giue to vnderstand, that all should eate of one & the same bread, that must vnite them one with another : that the bread might be deuided without deuiding him who was contayned vnder the same, and that this celestiall bread was to be eaten in little peeces, that is to say, that is was to be chewed agayne & agayne with the teeth of consideration, and the mysteryes therein contayned, were by particular reflection to be ruminated.

3. To consider, how he gaue it to his disciples, communicating them with his own hands, and giuing himselfe vnto them: the noblest, and most excellent gift, that he could bestow vpon them, which they also receyued with such reuerence

rence, as they would neuer haue been so hardy
as to touch it, if his diuine maiesty had not commaunded them.

Meditat. V I I. *Of the power our Sauiour gaue to his Apostles, to doe that which he had done: and of the power that Priests haue to consecrate, and offer the sacrifice of his precious Body, and Blood.*

TO consider how our Sauiour, hauing instituted the holy Sacrament of the Altar,
sayd to his Apostles : doe this in memory
of me. By which wordes he gaue them power
to doe the same, that he had done, testifying his
infinite charity more and more by this, that he
gaue power vpon his true Body, and Bloud, not
to the Angells of heauen, but to men on earth,
that in his name they should doe what he had
done, by the representation of his owne person.
He discouered also by this his endles liberality,
in that he would not limit or abridge this power
eyther to a certayne number of persons, or to a
determined tyme, or to any one particular place,
but gaue power to all Priestes to consecrate his
Body and bloud in all tymes and places, whiles
they obserued the circumstances required therin. He manifesteth also his profund humility, in
binding himselfe from that very instant till the
end of the world, to come at the voyce of the
Priest that did consecrate, though he were ne-

V u   uer

uer so bad, or had neuer so ill an intention, eyther to abuse it, or to commit whatsoeuer villany towards it, & all this for the vtility and good of his elect.

2.   To consider, how our Sauiour would haue the Apostles, and Priests to doe it in remëbrance of his Passion, shewing thereby the desire he had, that we should neuer forget this infinite band, but should alwayes acknowledge the benefit, by extolling and praysing the benefactour, with desire to doe him our best seruice. But our Sauiour knew well inough, that it was not in our power to render him any seruice, that might in the least correspond to the infinity of the price of our Redemption, and therefore he vouchsafed to prouide vs of a sacrifice, as infinite as it, that by making a frequent oblation thereof to his diuine maiesty, we might in some meane sort giue a testimony of the apprehension and conceite we haue of it. He would also haue vs celebrate this mystery in memory of the heroycall vertues, he practised himselfe both in his life, and in his death, whereof this most excellent Sacrament is a most liuely representation. We may also imagine, that his maiesty sayth vnto vs: Learne of me, that am meeke, & humble of hart.

3.   To consider, that our Sauiour commaunded, that this sacrifice should be offered in place of those sacrifices of the old law. Where we are to meditate; that Sacrifice is a certayn oblation, that man maketh vnto God, of something that is pleasing to him, and maketh to his honour,

honour, by recognizing his excellency. And this
oblation is made eyther for the expiation of
sinnes, or for the rendring of thankes, or for the
obtayning at Gods hands that, which we desire
and craue, eyther temporall or eternall : Wherin is to be seene the obligation, we haue to our
Sauiour for hauing giuen vs this sacrifice, that
infinitely surpasseth those of the law of Moyses,
by the merit wherof we may obtayne, of the E-
ternall Father, all that we craue of him.

*Meditat. V I I I. Of Gods singular proui-
dence, which appeareth in the institution of the
holy Sacrament, for the spirituall intertayning
of our soules.*

TO Consider, that if for the nouriture and
intertainment of the first man, God created in Paradise so great a diuersity of trees,
and in particular that of Life, which out of his
singular prouidence he planted in the middest
of paradise; we must needs say, that he hath much
more excellently prouided for the disposition of
his Church, in putting in the middest of it this
diuine tree of life, the most B. Sacrament of the
Eucharist, the only liuing and viuifycall food for
the nouriture of the faythfull, infinitly in price,
worth, and perfection, exceeding that terrestriall
tree, and producing most wonderfull effects in
the soules, that eate of this vitall fruit.

2.   As touching the excellency of this diuine nouriture, we must consider the properties

of the manna, which was that wonderfull food, wherewith God in tymes past fed his people in the desert. This Manna was the heauenly and Angells bread, which God made with his owne hands: but this diuine bread came downe from the highest heauen, not as then the Manna, by the ministry of the Angells, but by the operation and working of the holy Ghost, comming downe as an heauenly dew, to make the earth of our soules fertile. The Manna was a medicinall food, that preserued the bodyes from malady, infirmity, and sicknes: but this bread cureth the maladyes of the soule, and preserueth it from sinne, & eternall death, whither sin leadeth vs. The manna had but one naturall gust, but for the good it had an infinity of tasts, in so much as euery one of them had the tast, that he most desired: euen so this diuine meate hath but one naturall sauour of the Sacramentall kindes which hide it, but yet for the iust ones it hath all manner of spirituall sweetnes, they can possibly desire. The obedient tast obedience, the humble humility, the chast purity, &c. Euery one gathered of the Manna a certayne prefixed measure, that was inough for the refection both of the great ones, and of the little: but the very least particle of this diuine meate, sufficeth to satiate, and spiritually to sustaine the soule, that taketh it with deuotion. For as much receyueth he, who taketh but the least part of a consecrated Host, as doth he who taketh the whole Host, & the Chalice togeather.

5. To consider, that euen as God commaū-
ded

ded, that they should rise in the morning to gather the Manna : so must we haue an exceeding great feruor of spirit for the receiuing of this diuine Sacrament, & rayse our harts to the meditating of the wonderfull thinges it comprehendeth, and gather the most sweet Manna of prayer, by praysing and glorifying God for so singular a benefit, which we ought to haue alwayes in remembrance, but most of all the day vve communicate.

Meditat. I X. *Of the Blessed Sacrament, as it is a memoriall of the wonderfull thinges which God hath done for men.*

TO Consider the wordes of the Psalmist, when he sayth : Our mercyfull Lord hath made a Memoriall of his Wonders, in giuing himselfe to them to eate, that feare him. These meruayles be, that in this diuine Sacrament the Person of the Eternall word is vnited with the sacred Humanity, & the whole Trinity, with all the diuine attributes and perfections, whereof that which appeareth in this Sacrament most, is goodnes accompayned with wisdome, for that it pleased in such sort to vnite it selfe with man, as that it might be the more conioined with him, and so become mans very meate and drinke.

2. Our Sauiours omnipotency had a great part also therein. For the accidents being separated from the subistance of the bread and wyne,

they remayne still in their ordinary apparence, and the substance is after an extraordinary manner chaunged into the Body and Bloud of the Sonne of God , besides that , a little substance is conuerted into a great and perfect body , togeather with the glory he hath aboue in heauen , and all this in an instant . This is also one effect of his omnipotency , that the Body of Iesus Christ is in the Host indiuisibly, as a spirit, in so much as he is whole in the whole of it, and whole in euery part : and of this it cometh, that though the host be deuided,yet the Body of our Lord is not deuided , and so the life of our Sauiour in the Sacrament is but a life of flesh , but yet seemeth alsogeather spirituall Another miracle of this mystery is, that our Sauiour being in heauen aboue , there occupying the place of his supreme greatnes,cometh neuertheles downe to the earth in the Sacrament , without leauing his place in heauen, and is that very tyme & instant in many places in the world . Heere we must admire his power, and extoll his infinite goodnes , sith for the honoring and sauing of men he hath pleased at all times and seasons to worke so great wonders.

3. To consider , that this holy mystery is a memoriall of the offices, that our Sauiour hath exercised heere below,in euery one whereof we are to consider three thinges , namely , how he hath exercised them on earth : how he still exerciseth them in this Sacrament : & the great need we haue,that he should exercise them in behalfe of vs . How our Sauiour did the office of a Phisitian

sitian in curing maladyes, and resuscitating the
dead : how he doth it in this Blessed Sacrament,
where being toucht by the meanes of the Sacramentall kindes, he cureth the spirituall infirmityes of those who receyue him. We must consider the extreme necessity we haue of such a
Phisitian, seeing our maladies be great & grieuous, the perfect cure whereof dependeth on his
liberality. We may in like manner meditate v-
pon his other offices of mayster, Pastour, &c.

4. To consider, that it is also a memoriall
of the hero, call vertues, that our Sauiour exercised, when he lyued on earth, & still doth practise in this Sacrament, as humility in concealing his owne greatnes vnder such a littlenes : his
exact obedience in obeying at the voyce of a
Priest: his meeknes and patience in enduring the
iniuryes done him by heretikes, infidells, & bad
Christians, who receyue him in mortall sinne :
his burning charity & most singular mercy, that
he exerciseth towardes soules, in coming to visit
them. We must consider these points with hma-
turity, attention, and leysure, and endeauour
therof to make our best profit. Our Sauiour also
exerciseth perseuerance in abiding continually
present in the Host, and chalice, vntill the consummation of the kindes. To consider also, that
the holy Sacrament is a signe of the three greatest benefitts, that God euer did, or will bestow
vpon men, that is to say, of Redemption sanctification, & Glorification. And this ought to be
vnto vs a vehement motiue to desire it affectuously, & to receyue it deuoutly.

*Meditat . X .   Of the Sacrament, as it repre-
senteth our Sauiours Passion .*

TO Consider, that where our Sauiours pleasure was , that the memory of his Passion
should abide alwayes infixed in our soules,
for that by it he consummated our Redemption, he instituted this diuine Sacrament , that he
might represent by it not by ignominious and
dolorous signes, as it was in it selfe , but by proposing a most magnificall and most contenting
banquet, in testimony of his great charity, which
appeareth vvonderfully in this , that where
he reserued , and tooke vnto himselfe all that ,
which was bitter and paynefull , he would giue
vs the sweet ; and delightsome that remained ,
by applying by that ocasion vnto vs the fruit of
his paynes, and teaching vs, that he suffered for
the sauing of our soules with so great charity, as
the vehemency and excesse of it , made all things
in that respect both easy and pleasing vnto him .
He pleased to ordaine a pledge & signe of remembring him in a thing , that was most full of
sweetnes , as is this diuine banquet , to the end
we might haue a memory of him, & of his Passion with pleasure, and thankes-giuing : and further, that we might see, that his law is sweet (for
his burden is light, and his yoke sweet)& withal
that he might bind vs therby to imitate his patience in bitter & painfull things. For both gratitude & ciuility require , that the more cōtenting

a

a feast he meant to make vs of that , which was to himselfe so dolefull, and paynefull in his most bitter Passion , the more ought we by an holy contention to endeauour to punish our selues in testimony of the acknowledging of it , by mortifying our selues, by fasting, pennance, & other the like austerities , that by so doing we may in some sort conforme our selues to our sweet I E-S V S , who was crucifyed for our sinns.

2. To consider, that he would not, that this Sacrament should be an idle signe, but a reall, & effectuall one, truly contayning his Body & precious bloud , that we might see in how high an esteeme he had his Passion, and what an esteeme we also should make of it : and further that he might the more notify vnto vs his superabundant charity . For as he offereth himselfe in the holy sacrifice of Masse to be ofte sacrificed without effusion of his bloud: so would he willingly offer himselfe agayne to be immolated on the Crosse with the shedding of his bloud, if it were necessary for the saluation of men. We must also make an oblation our selues, euery day to suffer some thing or other for the loue of God . Moreouer he vouchsafed to be present in person in this Sacrament, by his owne presence to supply the default of mens gratitude towardes God , as well for his benefit , as for all others that we receiue dayly from his munificent hand , which, because they are without number, cannot be acknowledged inough by any pure creature , and therefore this Sacrament is called Eucharist , which is as much as thankes-giuing . And this

ought

ought to moue vs to yield God thanks from our hart for the care he had to supply our defaults.

3.   To consider, that this diuine mystery is a memoriall of our Sauiours passion, for that as bread is made of many graynes of corne groune and brused in the mill, and wine of many graps pressed : euen so was his holy body ground, and tormented by the blowes of whippes, nayles, and thornes, &c. and ignominyously and opprobriously intreated by them, who iniured him : So must we breake and bruise our owne harts with the hammer of contrition, pennance mortification, by the example of our Sauiour, who loued vs so tenderly.

Meditat. XI.   *Of the holy Sacrament, as it causeth Grace, Sanctification, and vnion with our Sauiour Iesus Christ in this life.*

TO consider, that the Sacraments were instituted for the instruments of grace, thogh this Sacrament doth also contayne the authour himself of it, who vouchsafed to put himself therin, to shew, how much he esteemed our sactification, not doing as doth the Phisitia, who doth ordayne a portion to his patient, & giueth charge to another to giue it him; nor as did the rich ma, who sent to redeeme the captiue by means of his seruant; nor as the mother, who being deliuered of her yong infant, giueth it vnto another woman to nourse and bring vp, but our most good and most charitable Sauiour Iesus would in our

behalfe

behalfe doe all these offices and good turnes in his owne person, being himselfe present in this most diuine Sacrament.

2. To consider, that the soule in this Sacrament filleth it selfe with grace, with the gifts of the holy Ghost, and with all vertues more abundantly, then it doth in the other. For as when a King giueth almes with his owne hand, there is a far more reckoning made of it, then when it is giuen by his Almoner: euen so when the King of Kings communicateth himselfe to the soule in this spirituall refection, he much more effectually exciteth vertues in it, and in particular setteth loue and charity on fire, with desires and wishes to vnite it selfe with its owne soueraigne good. And thus he proceedeth to stir vp euery vertue in particular; as Religion, which he putteth forwards to actions of reuerence, of prayse, of gratitude, of deuotion, &c.

3. To consider, that our Sauior hath instituted this Sacrament for the vniting of himselfe particularly with our soules by vnion & charity during the race of this our mortall life, and this is that, which he sayth by S. Iohn cap. 6. He that shall eate my flesh, and drinke my bloud, shall abide in me, and I in him. For his diuine maiesty abideth with the soule, not only so long as the kindes abide without being consumed, but also after their corruption being present by his diuinity, and vnited with it by a reciprocall amity, as sayth the same Apostle: God is charity, & he that abideth in charity, abideth in God, and God in him. To consider, that it is God him-

selfe,

felf, that inuiteth vs to his table: that the meate he fetteth before vs, is himfelfe: that the end, which is by this feaft intended, is the vnion of his charity, God taking a pleafure to abide in vs, as in a place of recreation.

4.   To confider the excellencyes of this foueraygne vnion, briefly touched by our Sauiour in S. Iohn cap 6. in thefe wordes: As I liue by my Father, fo he, that fhall eate me, fhall liue by me. That is, as the Sonne of God doth by his Eternall Father receyue being and diuine life, as alfo all the perfections of his incomprehenfible effence, being the fame with him by the meanes of eternall generation. Euen fo he, who doth in this holy Sacramen receyue Iefus Chrift, doth participate of his being, life, perfections, vertues, and all, in fuch fort, as he may fay with the Apoftle: I liue, not now I, but Iefus Chrift in me. And for this he is called the bread of life, for that we liue by him.

5.   To confider the wonderfull effects of this diuine food. For as it is moft delicate, fo alfo it engendreth fweet, healthfull, and holy humours, which be vertues. And therefore they, that eate of it, may be called celeftiall, borne of the fecond Adam, as the fame Apoftle fayth 1. Cor. 13. We muft further confider this Sacrament, as a lincke or chayne in our foule, to vnite them vnto it, togeather with all their powers, in regard of the influences it communicateth vnto them, and therefore we muft make petition to his maiefty to be pleafed to cleafe our harts, & to cut away all the fuperfluityes of vices, that haue

any

any interest in them . We may also consider this
Sacrament as a good graffe of a fruitfull tree ,
graffed vpon a barrayne and wilde stocke , as it
was done in the mystery of the Incarnation, and
is dayly done in this Sacrament , and we must
beseech God , that he would vouchsafe to graffe
it in our soules, that they may beare fruite, worthy euerlasting life .

s.   To consider, that our Sauiour would
institute this Sacrament with bread and wyne,
that be common and ordinary foode , for the
great desire he had to frequent this banquet with
vs , his goodnes being such , as he holdeth it an
honour to him if we come ofte to his table, from
which he excludeth none, but communicateth it
alike to poore and rich , to great and little &c.
for the comforting of their soules . For, as Dauid
sayth : Bread strengthneth mans hart , and wine
maketh it glad & merry .

Meditat . XII .   *Of the Blessed Sacrament,*
as it is a pledge of life euerlasting .

TO consider , that the pledges that men ordinarily giue for assurance of some debt ,
be eyther of equall , or greater value, then
is the debt it selfe : but our God , though he be
most faythfull and sure in his promises , that are
no wayes subiect to chaunging , pleased to giue
vs a pledge , that was to him the dearest , and
most precious of all his treasures , and that was
his only **Sonne** , God , as himselfe , vnder these
    X x   kindes

kindes of the holy Sacrament for the affuring of the glory vnto vs, that he hath promifed. Vpon this we muft meditate how deeply we are indebted, and bound to fo good, and liberall a God.

2. To confider, that this Sacrament is a pledge of the glory, that we expect, as it serueth vs for a meanes to come therunto. For by it we obtayne pardon for our paffed faults, preseruation from thofe that are to follow, conseruation in the grace we haue receyued, and perseuerance till death. And therefore our Sauiour faith in S. Iohn cap. 6. This is the bread, that defcendeth from heauen, that if any man eate of it, he dyeth not. For the vertue of it deliuereth frō all, that is contrary to euerlafting life. To confider, that this diuine pledge proceedeth yet further: for it caufeth in the foule fome thing, that is a part of eternall life, and as the very roote, and fourfe of it, and that is, an vnion with Iefus Chrift by his grace, and by the charity of the holy Ghoft: and fo we may fay, that it is not only the gage, but alfo the earneft-penny of glory, which will neuer fayle, till the principall be payed. For the gages may be recouered and redeemed, but the earneft-penny remayneth aiwaies vnto him, who taketh it: euen alfo as charity, which is an earneft-penny of glory, is not fruftrated, or euer decayeth.

3. To confider, that this Sacrament is a pledge of glory, becaufe it contayneth the King of glory, who being in heauē on high caufeth nis to fit downe at his table, where be intertayneth

tayneth and welcometh them with his diuinity,
and most sacred humanity, & is the same Lord,
who feasteth his faythfull ones on earth, in the
holy Sacrament of the Altar. There is this difference only in the one and the other, that on high
this meate is seene face to face, & heere beneath
it is to be seene shadowed to the eyes of the body, and open and discouered to the eyes of faith:
and yet the soule is satiated with it both heere &
there, according to the proportion of the different capacities, and the measure correspondent
to both states. We must heere resolue vpon a
pure and celestiall life, that we may deserue to
be called to this bacquet. To consider that it is
giuen vs for our viaticum, as being the pledge of
glory, when we are at the point to exchange
our countrey, that the faythfull soule may haue
strength and force inough, as another Elias, to
bring it to the mount of God, if euery tyme
vve communicate, vve goe vvith this apprehension, that it may be perhaps the last, and
this will help vs much for the stirring vp of
deuotion.

¶ *We may heere meditate all that concerneth the*
Blessed Sacrament, by vsing that manner of
Meditation, which we call the Application of
the senses, as is before set downe in the place
of this Booke. For it importeth very much to
comprehend well the wonders of this diuine
mystery, by shutting vp the eyes of our body,
and opening those of our soule.

Medit.

Meditat. XIII. Appropriated to the feaſt of the Bleſſed Sacrament, that we may be preſent at the Proceſſions with deuotion, as well on the feaſt day it ſelfe, as during the Octaue.

TO Conſider, how it ſeemeth our Sauiour meant to renew in this Sacrament all that he did during his mortall life, when he cured the ſicke, preached vp and downe, rayſed the dead, draue the Diuells from out the bodyes vvhich they poſſeſſed, and did good to all, in ſo much as what way ſoeuer he went, euery where left he ſignes of his diuinity and omnipotency. We muſt heere repreſent to our mindes, how we ſee our Lord & Sauiour marching in company with men, and excite in our ſoules the ſame deuotion, that we would doe, if he were ſtill preſent with vs in his mortall life.

2. To conſider, that the Proceſſions that are wont to be made in the ſtreets, do ſpiritually renew and repreſent to our mindes the entry that our Sauiour made into Hieruſalem vpon the day of Palmes. For as he then entred in much meekenes, ſitting vpon a poore beaſt, and the people came forth to meete him, with ſinging, & acclamations of prayſes, & he manifeſted the great contentment and pleaſure he had to be in company with the people, though many of thē were at that tyme practiſing about his death: ſo we may apply the ſame circumſtances to the ſolemnity of this day, with deſire that it may be celebrated

lebrated with feruour & deuotion .

3. To confider that the eternall Father mea-
neth by these solemne processions to recompense
the ignominious, and paynefull goings & com-
mings too and fro, of his most beloued Sonne
the night and day of his Passion , whiles he was
led through the streets of Hierusalem from
one Tribunall to another . We must conceyue a ioy
on our part for this recompence, and how faithfull a rewarder God is of his seruants in this life,
exalting them by the very same , whereby they
be humbled .

4. To confider that our Sauiours will is,
that we on earth celebrate a solemnity after our
manner , in imitation of that , which is done in
heauen , that the diuine benedictions may def-
cend and come downe to vs from aboue . Thus
must we by the example of the Cittizens of heauen, who keep a continuall festiuity of this holy
mystery, celebrate, and obserue it by humble &
deuout affections , and by a liuely fayth and apprehension of his infinite greatnes , presenting
vnto him the vessell of our hart , filled with the
incense of feruent prayers , accompanyed with
the mortification of our inordinate passions, setting our soules on fire with the fire of his loue ,
that the odour of this our sacrifice may be pleasing vnto him : finally celebrating this feast in
the best manner we possibly can , and admiring
withall , that he vouchsafeth to make an esteeme
of so meane, and vnworthy a seruice, who is honoured with such solemnity on high, in the glory of his Father .

X x 3   *Medi-*

Meditat. XIIII.   For the better preparing of our selues, to the receyuing of the Blessed Sacrament.

TO consider this Lords greatnes, who ioineth to our soule, his diuinity, that is, the person of the eternall word, which is, hath been, & euer shalbe in the bosome of his Father: his omnipotency, his infinite maiesty with the rest of his diuine Attributes. His sacred humanity, that was conceyued in the pure and immaculate wombe of the B. Virgin, the very same that preached to the world, that wrought so many miracles, that dyed for vs on the crosse, that rose againe glorious and tryumphant, that mounted vp to heauē the day of his Ascension, that is, our Redemer, our Phisitian, maister, pastour, &c. We must here awake and stir vp our fayth in all things, and the acts of loue, of praise, of admiration, and gratitude.

2.   To consider the amiable manner, our Sauiour vseth, when he commeth to visit sinners so miserable, as we be, why les he contenteth not himselfe with this, that for the curing of our spirituall woūds, we looke vpon him, as did the Israelites on the brazen serpent for the healing of the bitting of naturall serpents; or that we touch him with our hand, as did the woman, that had the bloudy fluxe: but his pleasure is to enter into vs, who be nothing but vilenesse, filth & rottennes it selfe. We may here make a
reflecti-

reflection vpon our selues, by considering who we are , for the more exaggerating of Gods goodnes towards vs.

3. To consider, that our Lord cometh vnto vs , as a Sauiour to pardon our offences ; as a Phisitian, to cure vs of our infirmityes; as a maister , to instruct our ignorance:as an high Priest, to apply vnto vs the fruit of his bloudy sacrifice; as a Pastour, Redeemer, heauenly food, & spirituall drinke, for the intertayning, sustayning, & nourishing of our soules. To ponder our great necessities, and to compare them with the excellent offices of our Sauiour, by exciting our selues to affectionate & earnest desires to receiue him. For this is that , which he desireth, that we prepare a place for him to abide with vs , by a certaine extreme hunger, caused by the esteeme we haue, and make of so singular a benefit : And so we must seeke to receyue him with all the purity, that we possibly may.

Meditat . XV . Of spirituall receyuing, which serueth for a disposition to receaue the Blessed Sacrament .

TO Consider, that spirituall Communion is an exercising of most excellent inward acts, by meanes whereof without the receiuing of the Sacrament a man participateth of the fruit and merit of it, which consisteth in an vnion with Iesus Christ our soueraigne God, by exercising the acts of fayth, opening the eyes of the

soule

foule, and mortifying the fenfes of the body, by a ftedfaft beliefe, that vnder thofe kindes of bread and wine is contayned Iefus Chrift, true God & true man, who inuiteth to his feaft all the men of the world to beftow his benedictions vpon them. We muft heere help our felues with the meditations of Gods excellencies. We muft alfo ftir vp in our felues the acts of hope, & repofe our felues vpon the omnipotency of God, & his inuiolable fidelity in his promifes, fith he both knoweth, hath a will, and is able to performe them, and therefore we muft reuiue our hope in him, with affurance, that he can graunt vnto vs the good that we defire, for the defire alone we haue to receyue it, though we take it not in the Sacramentall kinds. We muft alfo ftir vp the acts of charity, by meanes whereof our foule is fpiritually vnited with Iefus Chrift, by taking our contentment & pleafure in his goodnes, charity, omnipotency and liberality, which be the vertues, that are particularly to be feen in this banquet, and giuing him thankes for his exceffiue loue in giuing himfelfe vnto vs in meate and drinke.

Meditat. XVI.   *Contayning a thankef giuing, after the Receyuing of the holy Communion.*

TO confider, that we haue God within our foule, and that it is the beft tyme then to treate our affayres with him. Therfore we muft must reuiue the fayth of the presence of this our Lord, as certainly, & more then if we should see him with our corporall eyes, attended vpon by milions of Angels, that prostrate theselues before his holy face . We must moue our selues to many acts of humility , and of confusion in regard of our selues, and of reuerence in respect of him, saying : Whence is it , that our Lord and God cometh vnto vs? or other the like wordes , by making exclamations now and then in prayse and acknowledgement of this supreme benefit, and inuiting all creaturs both of heauen & earth to prayse so good , and liberall a Lord &c.

2. To consider the offices , that our Sauiour exerciseth in this Sacrament, and the principall end, for which he vouchsafeth to come to visit vs , and to reioyce that we haue with vs our Redeemer, our Father, Pastour , Mayster , &c. To represent vnto him all our necessities one after another : For though he knoweth them right well , yet he taketh a pleasure, that we lay them open before him, that we humble our selues before his diuine Maiesty , and acknowledge our own nothing .

3. To make some holy oblations, that be pleasing vnto him , in recompence of the wonderfull fauours he hath done vs , in offering him our soule with all the powers, our body, and the senses of it, and all that we are, or can be, to imploy our selues wholy to his seruice, to renew our vowes, and desires, and good purposes and intentions , & to offer him something in particular, as the mortifying of some Passion : and so
to

to conclude the meditation with some sweet &
affectuous Colloquy to his diuine maiesty.

¶ *After these Meditations it seemeth to good pur-*
pose, to add some others in this place concerning
the Sacrament of Pennance, because the same
ordinarily accompayneth the Blessed Sacra-
ment of the Altar.

Meditat. *XVII.   Of the Excellencyes of the*
Sacrament of Confession.

TO cósider the singular benefit God hath
bestowed vpon his Church, & cósequent-
ly vpon euery one of vs as members of it,
in instituting the Sacrament of Pennance. For
whereas it is proper to God to pardon the sinns
of men, he pleased to communicate that power
of his to Priests, who be men, subiect to sinne, as
be the rest, and need the same Sacrament they
administer to others, by giuing them power to
absolue from all sinnes without reseruation or
lymitation, with promise to approoue aboue in
heauen what the Priest shall do heere on earth,
and mercifully putting vs in mind of the most
strict iudgement of our life, which is to be exercised at our death, and at the consummation
of the world, in so sweet, facill, and secret a
manner, as that of the Sacrament of Confession
For God neuer chasteneth the same thing twise,
and,

and therefore if man punisheth his sinnes by this Sacrament, God will not punish them any more for euer. To thinke that the holy Confessiõ is a sourse of liuing water, which God hath placed in his Church for the washing away of all our filth and fowlenes, and for the repayring of the beauty of our soule. We are heere to reioyce for this, that God hath giuen vs so inestimable a good so cheape, though it cost him as much as his life.

2. To consider the excellency of the act of Confession, for as much as the faythfull by occasion of their sinnes, doe in it exercise great acts of Fayth, Hope, Charity, Obedience, Humility, Iustice in punishing themselues, as criminall persons, and of singular magnanimity & courage in ouercoming themselues, and inforcing themselues to discouer their sinnes to another man. And these & other the like acts make Confession very meritorious.

3. To consider the graces and fauours, that God communicateth to them, who come worthily to this Sacrament; as Iustification by making them friends of enemyes, which they were before: by adopting them for his children with promise of the inheritance of heauen; by giuing them spirituall peace for the victory they haue gayned ouer themselues, in destroying their sins, in dryuing away the Diuells, and subiecting their carnall and sensuall passions to the superiority of reason: the ioy of the holy Ghost, who expelleth feare and sorrow out of a badd conscience, disburdening the soule of the insupportable

table weight of sinnes, that depresse it to the ground. For all this, and much more we must make an high esteeme of this Sacrament, and make our profit therof.

Meditat. XVIII.   *Of the preparation, which is to be made for receyuing of the Sacrament of Pennance.*

TO Consider, that in this Iudgement vve must our selues doe the office of an Accuser, Witnes, Iudge, and Executioner, all togeather. And therefore Saint Gregory sayth: The conscience accuseth, reason iudgeth, feare bindeth, and sorrow tormenteth. That we are highly bound to yield God thankes, who is cōtented, that our acts of contrition, confession, & satisfaction, should be the instruments of his grace, whiles by them we are disposed to receaue it: therfore we must practise them in as perfect a manner as we possibly may, as being the three essentiall parts of this Sacrament. Contrition, which is a sorrow for our sinnes, must be as great, as we can possibly procure, in being grieued for our faults, for that they be offensiue to the diuine goodnes. And this disgust, and sorrow must proceed of the loue of God, who is to be loued aboue all thinges: neyther must we cōtent our selues with Attrition alone, because it is an imperfect sorrow. We must lament and be wayle our soule, as did the mother, mentioned in the Gospell, weepe for the death of her only
                                                        Sonne

Sonne, in vvhome vvas her only hope and comfort: or as the Bride wept for her Bride-grome, when she had lost him, on whome depended all her good, when she saw her selfe desolate, and comfortles. This consideration also, that we haue by our sinnes, as much as hath layen in vs, crucifyed the only Sonne of God, ought to be a great motiue also vnto vs to be-wayle them with bitternes. And if these consi-derations worke no effects of true sorrow, we must serue our selues with the meditations of the foure last things.

2. To consider, that we must plainely & di-stinctly confesse all our sins without concealing any from our Ghostly Father, who holdeth the place of God, for feare least the confession, that should turne vs to good, be conuerted into our hurt, & dānation. And therfore we must come to Confession with very great humility & diligent preparation, and with a good will admit the re-hensions of the ghostly Father, and purpose to obserue & keep his good counsayles.

3. To consider, that the third act is satis-faction, which is an effectuall and firme purpose to performe all, that our Confessarius shall command vs for our soules good. For reason it is, that the sicke person obey his Phistian, and receyue at his hands the potion he prescribeth him, be it neuer so bitter, so it be good & health-full, and the debtour pay what he oweth to his creditour. We must therefore giue testimony to our ghostly Father, that we haue a will prepa-red and desire to doe what he shall inioyne vs, &

Y y   this

this is a signe of true sorrow . And to induce vs
the more easily to take the pennance, and exactly to performe it , we must call to remembrance
the painefull pennance our Sauiour did in his
Passion ; for the expiation and purging of our
sinnes : and thereunto also adde the reflection
vpon the paynes of Purgatory . We must labour to make a good purpose of amending our
life , with a resolution neuer to returne to the
committing of our passed and former sinns .For
if this good purpose be wanting, the contrition is
defectiue , also the confession sacrilegious , the
satisfaction little profitable , and the absolution
of no effect.

Meditat. XIX.   Of thankes-giuing after
    Confession .

TO Consider , how much this gratitude is
    due to the diuine goodnes for so singular a
    benefit, that in it selfe comprehendeth ma-
ny others, as for hauing pardoned all our sinnes,
confessed, and forgotten without malice : for hauing cured vs of our spirituall maladies : deliuered from eternall death , whereunto we were
obnoxious by reason of our sinns : crowning vs
with mercy , in healing vs from innumerable
euills : filling our desires with good thoughts ,
by infusing into vs his grace , and giuing vs his
charity , and other vertues with a new increase
of them all. He reneweth my yong yeares, as he
doth that of the Eagle, saith Dauid, in deuesting
                                                vs

vs of our old Adam, and of our depraued & bad customes. We must doe, as did that Leaper of the Ghospell, who finding himselfe cleansed, returned to giue our Sauiour thankes, who tooke as much pleasure in his gratitude, as he was displeased for the ingratitude of his companions.

2. To breake forth into exclamations of the prayses of God, with a most vehement affection, in acknowledging the miserable state, out of which his mercy hath drawne vs, for as much as of the slaues of Sathan, & condemned to euerlasting paynes, he hath made vs his children, & inheritours of his heauenly Kingdome. To consider, that this fauour that we haue receyued, cost the Sonne of God deerly, who did with the price of his precious bloud ransome the pardon of our sinns, which we obtayne with such a facility.

3. To resolue in earnest vpon a good purpose of amendement, neuer any more to commit the sins then confessed, & concealed, thinking those wordes, that were sayd to the infirme persō at the Pond side in the Gospell, to be spokē vnto vs: Behold, thou art now healed, go thy way and sinne no more, least some worse thing happen vnto thee.

Y y 2   MEDI-

MEDITATIONS

VPON THE LIFE,

VERTVES, EXCELLENCIES,

and Feasts of the BLESSED VIRGIN MARY, the Mother of GOD.

---

*The I. Meditation of the B. VIRGINS ele-
ction to be the Mother of G O D. ¶ Of this
see, what is sayd in the 4. Meditation of the
second Weeke.*

*Meditat. I I. Of her most pure, and imma-
culate Conception.*

HE Prayer preparatory is euer the
same. The composition of the place
shall be to represent to the mind the
most Blessed Trinity, sitting in a glorious throne, compassed round with the Angels,
which seeing that the time was now come, wherin

in it was determined vpon the redemption of mankind, and vouchsafing to lay the first stone of the most sacred edifice and building of the Redemption, created the soule of the B. Virgin Mary. The petition must be to craue diuine light for the clearing of our vnderstanding, that we may be able to comprehend the greatnes & excellency of this most noble worke.

To consider, how God, hauing from all Eternity elected the B. Virgin to be the mother of his only Sonne, bestowed most singular perfections vpon her, for as much as God is wont to giue gifts, graces, and priuiledges, and meanes conformable to the offices, and dignities he conferreth. And because the office, and dignity to be the mother of God, is in some sort infinite, certayne it is, that the prerogatiues of the sacred Virgin did incomparably surpasse all the graces, that God euer gaue to the rest of his creatures.

2. To consider, that all her prerogatiues may be reduced to foure principall heades. The first is, to haue been preserued from originall sin, whereunto she was by nature subiect, as being a child of Adam. For as God created the Sunne, and the light, in one and the same instant: euen so did he create the soule of the Virgin, and sanctified her, making her chovse as the Sunne, not permitting the darkenes of originall sinne to come neere vnto her, and redeeming her in the noblest manner, that it was possible for the supreme Redeemer to doe. And thus she continued beautifyed with his diuine grace, that the

Y y 3   mother

mother might resemble the Son in purity, who
had that by priuiledge, which he had by right of
nature, because she was in some sort to cooperate
to the worke of our Redemption. We must be
glad of this singular prerogatiue, wherewith God
honoured the Virgin, and in her person all mankind besides. The second prerogatiue is, to haue
exempted her from that, which Deuines call
Fomes peccati, that is to say, the roote, seede, and
nutryment of sinne, that consisteth in the rebellion of the flesh agaynst the spirit, by causing an
vniuersall, and vniforme concord in the soule of
the Virgin, and in all her powers, in so much as
sensuality in her was euer at the commaund of
reason, euen as there neuer was to be trouble in
the house of the Prince of peace. The third is to
haue been confirmed in grace, and that in a
particular manner, in assisting her by a singular
prouidence in all her workes, and wordes, and
thoughts, in such sort, as she neuer sinned actually, but euer chose what was the best in all
thinges, and that with the greatest purity of intention, that could possibly be. The fourth is
for hauing at that very instant replenished her
with grace, charity, and other vertues and giftes
of the holy Ghost, in so plenteous a measure, as
she therein surpassed the very Cherubims, and
Seraphims. For as her dignity of being the Mother of God exceeded theirs, so was she to go beyond them in graces, according to that of the
Psalmist: Her foundations are on the holy hills:
our Lord loueth the gates of Syon aboue all the
tabernacles of Iacob. And these high, and holy
                                                moun-

mountayns be the Saints in highest dignity . To imagine, what might be the ioy of the Blessed Trinity, to behold this yong Virgin, that was to be the worthy Mother of the second Person in Trinity. Heere we must reiouce with the Virgin for so great excellency , and holynes conferred vpon her.

3. To consider, that it was most conuenient for the glory and honour of the diuine maiesty , that the Virgin should be conceyued without o-riginal sin. For it might haue seemed to derogate from his honour , if she , of whome the eternall Word was to take the immaculate flesh , had been at any time in bondage to the Diuell by the meanes of sinne. For what conneniency is there betweene light,& darkenes?

4. To consider, that if it be true, that the perfections, that are seuerally found in the crea-tures, be all togeather in the Creatour, and that the beast, named Ermine, had rather dye , then enter into a place, where the very least filth is,& therefore these wordes are appropriated vnto it: *malo mori , quàm fœdari* , I choose rather to dye , then to be defiled : we must needes affirme, that God, who is purity it selfe, hath not permitted , that the house, which he had chosen to make his aboade in , should euer be distayned & soyled with the filth of sinne , sith it is written of him , That he is white and ruddy, choise among ma-ny thousands : and that he taketh his pleasure , and is fed among the white lylies.

5. God in tymes past required great purity in them who entred into his Temple , & much

Xy 4   greater

grater in the high Priest who approached neere to him, then did the reft : how much greater thē will he require of that creature, that toucheth him so neere ? If Saint Iohn Baptift, and Ieremy were sanctifyed in their mothers wombes ; & if the lips of the Prophet Isay were purifyed for nothing but for the exerciſing the office of a preacher, what are we to thinke of her, who was to be the mother of the God of purity ?

6.   For the better weighing of this verity, we muſt ſtill caſt our eyes vpon this honourable tytle of mother of God, for it comprehendeth all, that may be ſayd in commendation of the moſt holy Virgin : yea moſt certayne it is, that the greateſt & higheſt prayſes of all would come infinitly ſhort of that, which this ſoueraigne & moſt excellent dignity contayneth.

*Meditat . I I I .   Of the Natiuity of the Bleſ-
ſed Virgin .*

TO Conſider how the Bleſſed Virgin had the vſe of reaſon from the firſt inſtant of her immaculated Conception, or within a very ſhort tyme after, and ſo the conſecrated & deuoted herſelfe to the diuine maieſty by a particular vow, offering vnto him her both body & ſoule. For if we know, that S Iohn Baptiſt had the vſe of reaſon put into him but ſix monethes after his conception, we muſt not meruayle, if the Virgin receiued the ſame, and a greater priſiledge. We muſt reioyce togeather with this most holy Lady, for this, that she was the very first in the world, that wholy consecrated herselfe to God.

2.   To consider the ioy, that is probable her parents had, especially her Mother S. Anne, that she caryed in her wombe, her who was the Temple of the holy Ghost. And if S. Elizabeth were priuiledged with the gift of prophecy, and receyued many other graces, because she was with child with the precursour of the Messias, what graces and benedictions did not S. Anne receiue, who carried in her wombe her who was to be the Precursors mistresse, and the Messias his mother? To consider the ioy of the Angels of heauen, of the Patriarkes in Lymbus, and of mē on earth, who vnderstood that the Redemption of the world had the beginning in this Blessed yong child, which S. Anne carryed in her wōbe, and of whome was to be borne the Lambe of God, that taketh away the sinnes of the world. To consider, that if the natiuity of S Iohn caused so much ioy, how much greater did the natiuity of the most Blessed Virgin cause? For she was as the dawning of the day between the light and darkenes, that is, betweene God and men, doing after a manner the office of Mediatresse. And so the deuout vvomen vvere astonished to see the excellency of her beauty, and sayd with the spouse in the Canticles cap. 4. Who is this, that appeareth as the bright morning, fayre as the Moone, chovse as the Sunne, terrible as an army set in battayle ray? To thinke, that as the natiuity of the Virgin gaue great ioy to the world,

world, becaufe it was an affured argument and figne of the Sauiours comming neere at hand for the redeeming of men: euen fo the deuotion of pious foules towards this Bleffed Lady, muft needes caufe their fpirituall ioy and comfort, becaufe it is a certayne pledge, that the fame Sauiour will come to faue them. For as S. Anfelme faith: To be deuout to the B Virgin is a figne of predeftination.

3. To confider, that the Virgins progenitors were Patriarks, Captaines, and Prophets, all whome fhe far furpaffed in vertue and holynes, which is the only and true nobility, that God loueth, and the more noble fhe was by defcent, the more humble and lowly was fhe in fpirit.

4. To confider, that this diuine Child was named Mary by a particular infpiration of God, as it hapned alfo to Saint Iohn Baptift, who had his name giuen him of God. Mary is as much as a ftarre of the fea, the bitter fea, a woman exalted, illumined, or illumining, a miftreffe of people, all which fignifications ought to excite vs to loue her the more affectuoufly, & to make petition vnto her, that fhe would pleafe to exercife in our behalfe the offices, that are meant by her name, and that fhe would be contented to be the ftar of our nauigation, the myftreffe and inftructreffe for the reforming, informing, & conducting of our ignorance, &c.

5. To confider, that the malediction, that fell vpon all the reft of men, was fufpended vpon the moft happy day of this Bleffed Virgins natiuity,

ty, vvho vvas exempt from sinnne, and therefore she cannot say this versicle of Iob: The day
of my Natiuity perisheth : but she might say on
the contrary : Blessed be the day, wherein I was
borne : for that day was happy both for me, and
for all the world besides.

6. The children of Israel reioyced much,
when being beset by the Philistians, they saw
the Arke of the Testament come into their cāpe:
and on the contrary the Philisthians were sory,
& sayd in lamenting manner : Vnhappy are we.
Euen so men were glad, when this noble little
child came first into the world, who is the true
Arke of couenant, wherin was shut vp the bread
of heauen, Iesus Christ : & the Diuells were sory, fearing that, which hapned vnto them a while
after.

7. The sicke man that liueth languishing in
misery in his bed, whiles the nights be darke &
long, longeth for the comming of the light of
the morning, that he may find some ease of his
payns. Euen so the world, sore decayed by sinne,
and languishing therein, pressed round with all
manner of infelicities, and come almost to the
extremity of misery, was glad of the rising of this
diuine morning, that was by its brightnes to
disperse the long darkenes of the afflictions, it
was in.

Medi-

Meditat . IIII.   Of the B. Virgins Presen-
tation in the Temple.

TO consider, how the holy Ghost, who had
selected the B. Virgin to so high a dignity,
did inspire into her a mind and desire to
retire herselfe into the Temple . Wherein God
manifested the care, and paternall prouidence he
had of this holy child , in drawing her from out
of the tumult, & noise of the world, into his own
house, where she disposed and prepared her selfe
to be the Temple of Gods eternall Sonne . To
imagine , that God vsed these wordes of the
Psalme 44. Heare daughter, & incline thine eare,
and forget thy people, and the house of thy Father , and the King will couet thy beauty. The
Virgin vnderstood this voyce and inspiration of
God , and became forthwith obedient to what
was commaunded her, vowing herselfe to God,
and consecrating herselfe in his holy Temple in
her so tender age (for she had not at that tyme
three yeares complete) forsaking her parents , &
the commodities, which she might hope to haue
by abiding with them , to goe to liue in another
place with vnknowne persons , and to deuote
the prime of her tender age to the diuine maiesty .

    2.   To consider, how the Priests receyued
this oblation with a certayne spirituall ioy , and
deuotion , because they had neuer seene the like
oblations , or receyuings before . To consider
with

with what a contentment the most Blessed Trinity accepted and receyued this noble gift . For the Father admitted her for his daughter; the Sonne for his mother; and the holy Ghost for his Spouse, and consequently the Angells acknowledged her for their soueraygne Lady, in seruing and attending her, during the tyme of that her retire .

3. To consider the deuotion of Saint Ioachim, and of Saint Anne, who neither diswaded, nor diuerted their yong daughter from her good purpose, but rather confirmed her therein, by particular inspiration, they receyued from heauen, and offered vnto God the fruit, that God had bestowed on them, with no lesse deuotion, then did the other Anne offer her yong Sonne Samuel .

4. To consider with what a spirituall ioy the holy Virgin, being come to the Temple, began to mount vp the fifteene steps therof, with a feruour, that exceeded the strength of her age, making a resolution in her hart to mount vp to all the degrees of vertue, and not to cease till she came to the perfection of them, being a manifest and certaine signe, that God did help her with his strong hand, as Dauid sayth.

Meditat. V. Of the vertuous Example the B. Virgin gaue, whiles she contynued in the Temple; and of the vow she made of Virginity.

TO consider that the B. Virgin, whē she had passed the steps, and was come into the Temple, adored the diuine maiesty humbly vpon her knees, and offered herselfe for euer to serue him. Behold, my Lord God, sayd she, I am come into thy house to yield my selfe to be thy perpetuall handmaid. Receyue me into thy seruice, in state as I am, for I aspire not to any higher degree, nor to greater glory, then it. And God might returne her answere in these wordes: Come, my beloued spouse, enter into my garden: for I meane to put my throne in thee.

2. To consider, that as this yong Virgin grew in age, so she increased and waxed in vertue before God and men, in so much as the increase & progresse of her meritts did correspond to the continuall augmentation, & growing of her body. For the holy Ghost did incessantly sollicite and put her forwardes by good inspirations, whereunto she cooperated to her vttermost, endeuouring to excell in all her workes, & alwaies seeking perfection. Thus she increased in charity and holines, togeather with wonderfull prudence & constancy, in all her actions proceeding with a most pure intētion. We must imitate all this.

3. To

3. To consider the B. Virgins exercises, & occupations, which were, reading, contemplation, meditation and prayer, in time of which exercises she was often visited of Angells: Also she spent some tyme in labouring and working with her handes, for the seruice and vse of the Temple, and for the vtility of the rest of her cōpanions, and these her externall imploymens were alwayes accompanyed with internall Meditation. Her life was a perfect paterne of humilitv, obedience, temperance, abstinence, silence, & of infinite other vertues: she was the first in all busines, her deuotion, & modesty made her amiable to all her companions: in few words, she was the true mirrour, and looking glasse of perfection.

4. To consider how at that tyme this yong holy Virgin made an oblatiō, which was to God most accepted, & was withall very strange and new, in vowing vnto him perpetuall Virginity, which she did by a particular inspiration of the holy Ghost with great deuotion. For the exceeding great loue, she did beare to God, moued her to consecrate her selfe wholy to him, and to make him her Spouse, to the end she might deuote vnto him her body & soule. Thus this most sacred Virgin continued, as it were, in guarde, shut vp, & kept for the only Sonne of God, who togeather with the Father, & the holy Ghost recreated himselfe with the most fragrant & sweet smeling odour of her incomparable vertues.

Meditat. VI. Of the Marriage of the Blessed Virgin. with Saint Ioseph her spouse.

TO consider how, when the tyme of the INCARNATION of the Eternall Word drew neere, it was Gods will, that the B. Virgin should mary with a certayne iust man, called Ioseph, with assurance, that her chastity should not in the least iote be preiudiced. And thereunto she obeyed with promptitude.

2. To consider the causes, wherefore God would haue his mother marryed, which were these, to conceale the mystery of the Incarnation for a time: to conserue the honour of this most chast Virgin: and to giue her an assistant, and comforter in her afflictions, and long iourneyes.

3. Another cause was to giue a foster-father to his Sonne, who might haue a care of him, and to honour holy Ioseph by making him the Virgins spouse, and the reputed Father of the eternall Word.

4. To consider the fayth and prompt obedience she exercised in this action, in accepting by commaundement that which she thought to be contrary to her vow, and in resigning herselfe absolutly to Gods will.

5. To consider how, though the B. Virgin far excelled her spouse in vertue & holynes, yet she obeyed him, honored, and respected him, as
her

her Superiour, by considering in him God himselfe, who had giuen him her: and though she
were so much affected and giuen to contemplation, as she was, yet she omitted not to haue a
care of her house, which gaue an occasion to Ioseph to wonder at.

*Meditat. VII. Of the feruent desire which
the Blessed Virgin had, of the Incarnation of
the Word.*

TO Consider, how the neerer the tyme of
the Incarnation approached, the more
feruent desires did the holy Ghost put
into her mind, to see the Word made Flesh,
that she might haue the better apprehension and
knowledge of his wonders, and conuerse the
more familiarly with him. Who will graunt vnto me, sayd she, o my brother, that I may see thee
in the bosome of my Mother? Cant. 8.

 2.   To consider, that so great was the Virgins zeale of Gods honour, as she was most hea-
uily afflicted to see the offences and sinnes, that
were committed agaynst him, and to consider
the perdition of men, and therfore with humble
petitions, and most deep and sorrowfull sighes
& groanes she prayed continually for the comming of the eternall Word, saying: shew me thy
mercy, o Lord God, and giue me thy saluation.
O that thou wouldst break throgh the heauens,
and come downe heere amongst vs! And many
other speeches of the like affection.

3.   To confider, that her prayers were fo effectuall with God, as, though the world deferued nothing leffe then his comming, yet they wrought fo much, as they ouerweighed the demerits therof, and accelerated the Incarnation of the Son of God. We muft difcouer our own exceeding ioy for this, that the facred Virgin hath fuch power, & fo great auctority with God.

Meditat. VIII. Of the Annunciation. ¶ See what is fayd of this myftery in the 5. 6. 7. 8. and 9. Meditation of the fecond VVeeke.

Meditat. IX. Of the Vifitation of S. Elizabeth. ¶ It is the 11. and 12. Meditation of the fecond VVeek.

Meditat. X. Of the affliction of the B. Virgin, occafioned by the perplexity of S. Iofeph ¶ It is the 14. Meditation of the fecond VVeeke.

Meditat. XI. Of the expectation and tyme of her deliuery, and of the iourney fhe tooke to Bethleem. ¶ It is the 15. & 16. meditation of the fecond week.

Meditat. XII. Of that which hapned to the Bleffed Virgin the very night of her deliuery in Childbirth. ¶ See the 17 meditation of the 2. weeke.

Meditat. XIII. VVhat befell her in the Circumcifion of the little Iefus; and Adoration of three Kings. ¶ See the 20. meditation of the 2. weeke.

Meditat. XIIII. Of the Purification of the B. Virgin, & of her flight into Ægypt. ¶ See the meditations 24. 25. and 26. of the fecond VVeeke

1. We may meditate also vpon this flight, how the Blessed Virgin, being come into Ægypt, she found not any prouision for intertayning of her life, nor any stable place to remayne in, or to retyre herselfe vnto, after so long, tedious and paynefull a iourney, and therefore credible it is, that for some dayes after her arryuall, both she, and B. Ioseph, with their little Iesus, found place in some hospitall, or other.

2. To consider, that though the Virgin wanted many thinges necessary for the maintayning of her little and poore family, yet she alwayes found time for her deuotions and spirituall exercises, neyther yet omitted any thing, that appertained to the care & busines of her house.

3. To consider, that being in this pouerty in a strange and barbarous countrey, she prouided with the labour of her owne handes for the necessityes of her most deere little one.

Meditat. X V . *Of the death of Saint Ioseph.*

TO consider, how this holy man, now grown in yeares, and loaden with merits, came to dye, our Sauiour Iesus and his most holy mother being present at his death, to help him to make an happy end, after which the Angells receyued his soule, and carryed it into the bosome of Abraham, where the holy Fathers welcomed it with great ioy for the woderfull things, that happy soule reported vnto them of Iesus, &

Z z 4   his

his holy mother, thereby conceyuing a certayne affurance of their owne deliuery neere at hand.

2. To confider how the B. Virgin conformed herfelf to Gods will, bearing patiently the griefe for the death of her deare and faythfull fpoufe, whofe company, good conuerfation and exemplar life gaue her much comfort, in helping her towardes the intertayning of her moft deere Sonne.

3. To confider, how notwithftanding fhe continued all alone, poore, and increafed in age, yet fhe complayned neyther of her poore ftate & condition, nor of the prouidence diuine. Her care was principally and only fo to difpofe of her felfe, as fhe might become more and more pleafing vnto God, and to labour to her vttermoft to the higheft degree of perfection as neere as her ftate would permit her. True it is, that from that time forth all the care of family lay wholy vpon her, and yet that was not any impediment to her exercifes of fpirit. For fhe fo tempred the active life with the contemplatiue, as the one did not let the other, and fhe vfed them both without trouble, or confufion in her life, and actions.

4. To confider, how her conuerfation was fo modeft, and her comportment fo fweet and gracious, as they gaue an occafion vnto all to loue her, and all, that faw her, did euidently cóceyue in her a fenfible affection of the loue of God, and of vertue, in fo much as none was fo hardy in her prefence, to doe any thing, that was

vnde-

vndecent : but on the contrary those, that were of themselues of a more free nature, did forbeare, moued with the sight of her modest grauity.

Meditat. X V I. *Of the seperation and parting of our Sauiour from his mother, when he went to offer himselfe to death.*

TO consider, how, when the B. Virgin vnderstood, that the houre, determined by the eternall Father for the most bitter Passion of his Sonne, was come, her compassionate hart was transpierced with the sharpe sword of sorrow, as she witnessed by the teares, that fell continually from her eyes.

2. To imagine the affectionate & pittifull speeches, that the B. Virgin was likely probably to vse to her Sonne, & what answere agayne he was likely to make her in that dolefull separation.

3. To consider, what she did, after he was departed, & how she withdrew herselfe to her prayers, presenting herselfe to death in company with her Son, & to suffer all sorts of torments, if it had been necessary for the glory of God, & for the saluation of men.

¶ *See of this matter more in the 6. meditation of the third Weeke, & the 2. point therof.*

Medi-

*Meditat. XVII. How the Blessed Virgin
went to the Mount of Caluary.*

TO consider, how the Virgin, hauing had
intelligence of the sore torments, that her
Sonne was put vnto, went from home in
company of some other deuout women to seeke
him, and she was not gone far, but she found the
traces and drops of his precious bloud spilt on
the way, which brought her to mount Caluary,
whither being come, sorrow and compassion
strooke her at the hart, when she heard the horrible blasphemies, and the execrable imprecations, vttered agaynst her most Beloued Sonne.
¶ *See the 29. Meditation of the third VVeeke.*

2. It was also a sore hart-breaking vnto her
to see, that all the disciples had forsaké their maister in that his extreme necessity: that Peter had
denyed him in the house of the high Priest: that
Iudas had betrayed him, & that not one of the
rest had the courage to defend the innocency of
him, who had for so many particular titles, boúd
them vnto him.

3. To consider the exceeding sorrow, that
afflicted her soule, when hauing a desire to approach neere vnto him, she saw him all disfigured, bloudy, battered, and bruized with blowes
& stripes, his skinne fleaed, and the flesh of his
body rast with the scourging, his face couered o-
uer with cold bloud, on his head a crowne of
thornes, his shouldets charged & loaden with an
                                    heauy

heauy Crosse, and lead to death betweene two theeues, as though he had been their Captayne. ¶ See the 29. *Meditation of the third VVeeke, and the 6. point thereof.*

4. To consider, what a deadly knife that was which pierced the most sensible part of her, whē she heard the cryers voyce, who published the sentence of death against her most innocent Son, & what a feeling she had in herselfe, when she heard the blowes of the hammers, & the tumult of the people, crying out, & blaspheming against him . ¶ *See the 11. Meditation, and the second and third points: the 37. 39. & 41. Meditations, of the third VVeeke.*

Meditat. XVIII. *How the Blessed Virgin receyued her Sonne dead into her armes.*

TO Consider what manner of affliction that of the B. Virgin was, when she saw her Son dead vpon the Crosse, and had not any to help her take him downe from it, that she might yet once imbrace him after his death, sith she could not doe it, when he was aliue. At least she gaue this poore comfort to her excessiue sorrow, which was increased, when insteed, of finding some one to do her that good office, she beheld a souldier to opē his side, & thrust it throgh vvith a speare. True it is, that that thrust wrought more in her hart, then it did vpon her Sonnes body.

2. To consider, how in the middest of all these

thefe her afflictions the diuine prouidence fent her certaine iuſt & good men, who tooke down the body from the Croſſe, & did lay it into the ſorrowfull mothers armes, who receyued it as the deereſt, & moſt precious treaſure, that could poſſibly be preſented her.

3. To conſider what teares diſtilled, & how abundant, from her eyes vpon the body, what deep ſighes were rayſed from the bottome of her hart, & what words ſhe vttered, in beholding the ſacred wounds, which ſhe kiſſed often. One while ſhe tooke the ſharp pricking crowne into her hands, another while ſhe did put it vpon her owne head, another while her eyes did for griefe powre forth great fluds of teares, wherewith ſhe bathed that precious corps. O how different was the bitternes of her ſoule, whiles ſhe held her Sonnes dead body in her armes, from thoſe ſweet contentments, that ſhe had felt, when ſhe held him a little child, hanging at her ſacred beaſts.

4. To conſider, how great a griefe it was vnto her, when perſwaded by thoſe deuout perſons, ſhe was much agaynſt her will induced to render vnto them the body, to be carryed to the ſepulcher. *See the meditations 44. & 45. of the 3. VVeeke.*

Meditat. XIX. Of the ſolitude and retyre of the Bleſſed Virgin. ¶ See the 46. meditation of the ſecond Weeke.

Medit.

Meditat. XX. How she saw her Sonne resuscitated.

¶ *See concerning this matter, the third Meditation of the 4. Weeke, and the second point, as before.*

VVE may add, how the B. Virgin seing her Son glorious, adored him first, as her God: then she imbraced him againe and agayne, as her most beloued Sonne, kissing his diuine wounds, that gaue most admirable & comfortable light. To thinke with what deuotion she reuerenced those precious markes and testimonyes of our saluation. For then her teares of sorrow were chaunged into teares of ioy, and of contentment. Moreouer a man may meditate, how after she had thanked her Sonne for his so visiting her, she besought him to goe to comfort his Apostles, who were most anxious and much afflicted, togeather with the deuout women, who had their part in the same sorrow, and in gathering togeather his poore & little flocke, that was dispersed by his death and Passion.

2. To consider, the great ioy, the Blessed Virgin had all those fourty dayes, that her Sonne conuersed on earth after his Resurrection. For credible it is, that he visited her oftentymes, and comforted her much with the vision of his diuinity. For God communicateth

his

his confolations according to the meafure of the forrowes, and therfore why fhould we not beliue, that the B. Virgin, who had been afflicted in the death & Paffion of her Sonne more then all Creatures befides, receyued more comfort then all, by, and after his Refurrection.

3. To confider, how fhe often tymes prayed her Sonne, that fhe might accompany him to heauen, fith fhe found not any thing, that might giue her contentment on earth, but to enioy his moft beloued prefence. But yet fhe manifefted her wonderful ready refignation into his hands, knowing that fhe was yet to ftay in the world for a tyme, for the greater glory of God, for the directing & inftructing of the Apoftles, and the comforting of all the faithfull.

4. To confider how the day of the Afcenfion being come, the B. Virgin was in company of the Apoftles, & difciples, to bid the laft farewell to her Sonne, & to receyue his holy benediction: For it is not to be thought, that he wold refufe to his mother that, which he yelded to his Apoftles. To confider the fweet & contenting talke, that was between the Son, & the Mother: how fhe befought him to remember his Church and the faithfull of it, to deliuer them from their neceffities, & to ouerheare the prayers it fhould oft prefent vnto him for al the afflicted therof. To reprefent to our mind the ioy, that the B. Virgin was moft likely to haue, when fhe faw her Son afcending by his owne power, accompanyed with legions of Angells, and with all the holy foules, that he had releafed out of Lymbus, lea-
ding

ding them with him, as a certayne conquest
made by his owne precious bloud, tryumphing
ouer the world, the flesh, & the Diuell, & opening the way to heauen, that had been so long
tyme shut vp and stopped : & for this the Blessed Virgin could neuer make an end of rendring
thankes to the diuine maiesty. We must in her
imitation, praise God with all affection of our
hart, and reioyce with her for her ioy, and consolation she had, as we haue been before sory
for her sorrowes, & in payne for her dolours
& paynes.

Meditat. XXI. *Of that which the Blessed*
Virgin did after the Ascension, vntill the com-
ming of the holy Ghost.

TO Consider, how after our Sauiours Ascension into heauen, the Blessed Virgin &
the Apostles retired themselues to the cha-
ber, that was in mount Syon, so commaunded
by our Sauiour, there to stay within the Citty of
Hierusalem, & not to depart thence, till they had
receyued the holy Ghost: & therfore the B. Virgin, as the mystresse of all, exhorted them to o-
bedience in that behalfe.

2. To consider, that her exercises in that
meane tyme of ten dayes, were in continuall &
deepe contemplation, for as much as her mind
& soule was more there where it loued, then
where it gaue life, by the same meanes being a
motiue to the disciples to doe the like, that she
might

might the better difpofe herfelfe to the receiuing of the holy Ghoft. She exhorted them alfo to charity, vnion, concord, & conformity one with another, encouraging them with a liuely hope to attend the holy Ghofts comming, which was vndoubted and moft certaine, though it might be differed longer then they defired, for that the promifes of her Sonne and Lord, were inuiolable.

3.   To confider, that the neerer the comming of the holy Ghoft was at hand, the greater was our B. Ladyes deuotion, & feruour of prayer, & by her owne example excited all the reft of the company to the like feruour. Moreuer the holy Ghoft replenifhed her with moft excellent gifts & graces beyond all the reft there prefent, as being his Spoufe, & mother of the eternall Word, who was Incarnate in her Blefled & fanctifyed wombe. For if in the Incarnation the holy Ghoft fhewed fo great liberality towardes her, as the Angell Gabriel promifed her, we haue iuft caufe to belieue, that the day of his comming brought her greater graces, & perfections without comparifon, then all the Apoftles had, becaufe God had made her capable thereof. We muft reioyce togeather with her for the moft excellent gifts, wherwith the holy Ghoft enriched her vpon the day of Penticoft.

Medit.

Meditat. XXII.   *Of the Blessed Virgins most glorious Death.*

TO consider the most longing desire, the Blessed Virgin had to go to heauen, to enioy the diuine essence, and the presence of her most beloued Sonne, and this desire proceeded not of any loathing of this terrestriall and mortall, nor of the trauayles & paynes, that it abundantly brought with it vnto them, who imbrace vertue, but it had the origene of her surpassing loue to God, in sighing and longing incessantly to haue the fruition of the obiect of her loue, which moued her frequently to vse these wordes: Alas, how long is the tyme of my pilgrimage prolonged? And these: As the hart desireth to the fountaines of waters; so my soule longeth vnto thee, my God? Sometymes she addressed her plaints to her deere Sonne: sometims to the sacred Trinity: sometymes to the Blessed Angells and soules &c. But the conclusion euer was, that she resigned her selfe, into the handes of the diuine prouidence, & therefore she added and sayd: Lord, if I be still necessary for thy people, I refuse not the taking of paynes for them.

2. To consider, how knowing that the time of her life was come neere to an end, she prepared herselfe to death with a new feruour, by exercising herselfe more and more in the works of vertue, in so much as she disposed herselfe to

Aaa 3

goe

goe out of this world accompavned with three things most of all, that is, by inflamed desires of seeing God face to face, by an absolute & perfect resignation of her owne will; and by more perfect & more feruent acts and workes, then before.

3. To consider, how Gods pleasure was, that the holy Virgin should passe the way of death, as other men do, that she might in that be also conformable to her Sonne, and that by the same she might giue the greater increase to her merit, in ouercoming by force of her mind the naturall repugnance the flesh hath of death. To consider, that as God had before sent vnto her the Angell Gabriel to declare the Incarnation of the word, so did he also send vnto her the same Angell to notify vnto her her glorious passage. And credible it is, he saluted her with that Haile, he had done before, in giuing her to vnderstand the great desire the most sacred Trinity, & al the Cittizens of heauen had to see her placed in her throne of glory. To represent to our mindes the B. Virgins spirituall iubilations at the message & deliuery of so ioyfull newes. My spirit, sayd she, reioyced for the things, that were said to me: for I shall goe into the house of my Lord God. And then turning herselfe to the Angel; Behold, quoth she, the handmaide of my Lord God, be it vnto me according to thy word. To consider, how the Apostles, and many other of the disciples were by miracle present at her glorious death, & lamenting with bitter teares her future absence, and her present departure, besought
her

her not to forget them, when she should come
to her glory. She then comforted them with
sweet & amiable words, & gaue them good and
healthfull admonitions, with promise to be their
Aduocatresse in heauen, & still to present their
petitions in fauour of them to the diuine maiesty, & in fine gaue them her benediction.

4. To consider, how our Sauiour Iesus
Christ came downe from heauen, attended with
an infinite company of Angells, to receyue the
soule of his most deere Mother, & droue all the
diuells of hell away before him. And when he
called vnto her with a sweet, & amiable voyce,
she answered him saying: My hart is ready,
Lord, my hart is ready. Into thy hands, my God,
& my Sonne, I commend my soule. And saying
so, she gaue vp her most pure soule. To consider, how she dyed not so much of infirmity of
body, as of spirituall loue, & she dyed without
any paine at all. For she had suffered at the foot
of the Crosse the strong panges, that might naturally haue caused her death: but their effectes
were suspended till this last houre of hers. Moreouer the exceeding ioy, she had of seeing her
Sonne, was the cause, that she felt no payne in
dying. To consider, how all her good workes
were then discouered to the world by the omnipotency of her Sonne, the representation
whereof increased her ioy and assurance much.
Of this we must learne to exercise our selues
in good workes, that when we come to dye,
they may be our guarde, as a squadron in bat-
tayle-array.

Aaa 4

4. To

4. To confider, how the foule being once-feperated from the body, the Apoftles confulted about the preparing of an honourable buriall for her facred Corps, and thereupon both they, and all the reft of the faythfull, that vvere then found there prefent, began to prepare her Funeralls vvith great reuerence, and the fhedding of many teares, and fo condu&ed her corps to the fepulcher, vvherein it vvas to be layed, finging of Hvmnes, and Canticles in honour of God, and of his holy mother. The Angells alfo honoured her Funeralls in follovving her facred corps, and contvnued the fpace of three dayes in her fepulcher, honouring their Queene vvith heauenly muficke. To confider, hovv both the Apoftles, and the reft of the faythfull, found themfelues much comforted, as vvell vvith the moft fragrant odour that proceeded from her precious Body, as for the affurance they had, that their mother vvas in heauen, and prayed for them, vvho remayned behind on earth. We muft reioyce togeather with the Bleffed Virgin for her moft happy paffage out of this vvorld, beeing fuch, as beft conforted vvith the dignity of the Mother of God.

Medi-

Meditat. X X I I I. *Of the Bleſſed Virgins Aſſumption, as touching her ſoule*

TO conſider how, after that her Bleſſed ſoule was deliuered from the bandes of the body, the Son & the Mother imbraced one the other ſpiritually, with an ineffable ioy on the part of the mother, who might then well and truely ſay: I haue found him, whome my ſoule deſireth, & I will not leaue him, vntill he ſhall bring me into the houſe of my mother: that is, into the heauenly Hieruſalem. To conſider, how the B Virgin was brought into her Sonnes armes, who then repayed her the reward of the ſeruices, & the Motherly intertaynments, he had receyued at her handes in his infancy & tender age, when ſhe carryed him at her breaſts, & dandled him in her lap. And this cauſed no little admiration to all the Hierarchies of heaue̅, who ſayd: Who is this, that commeth vp from the deſert abounding in delightes, leaning vpon her beloued? So did the Angells ſalute her, euery one with new ſalutations, that expreſſed her greatnes: & thus entred the B. Virgin in a triumphant chaire into the Empyreall Heauen, with the common and vniuerſall ioy & applauſe of all the Cittyzens therof. We muſt in imaginatio̅ accompany this diuine pompe & tryumph, and with the Bleſſed Angells celebrate this ſolemne entry of the Empreſſe of the Vniuerſe into heauen, in prayſing her to our vttermoſt, as did the

Hebrewes

Hebrewes of Bethulia in tymes past the victorious Iudith. To represent to our imagination the speeches, that were betweene the soule of the B Virgin, & the sacred Trinity, & with ech one of the diuine Persons seuerally, whiles she yielded them thankes for the fauours, she had receyued of their infinite goodnes.

2. To consider the greatnes of the essentiall glory, that was conferred vpon her soule: For as on earth the Virgin did not lymit the seruice she did to God, but alwaies did what was in her vttermost power, & desired to doe more, then she did: so the diuine maiesty did not in a māner lymit the remuneration of her deserts in heauen, in so much as her vnderstanding was filled with the cleare knowledge, & glorious vision of the essence of God, in so full & perfect a manner, as the very Cherubims, compared with her, came not almost by infinite degrees neere vnto her. Her will was filled with so great a loue of God, as the Seraphims, who are sayd to be all fiery, matcht with her, were as frozen cold. And to speake in one word, there is not any created vnderstanding, that can possibly comprehend the immensity of the glory, this diuine Lady possesseth aboue in heauen. We must be glad of her ioy, & of the abundant recompense, that God hath made her for her trauayles.

3. To consider, how the B. Virgin was crowned, as Lady, & Queene of heauen, & of Earth, raysed aboue all the Quyers of the Angells, placed on the right hand of her beloued Sonne in a throne of Maiesty, & of glory, that is,

that.

that she enioyeth on high the best of the infinite treasures of grace & of glory in the excellentest manner, that a pure creature can possibly enioy them, & as is most fitting for the dignity of Gods mother to enioy. The eternall Father crowned her with a crowne of power, giuing her full power & authority, next vnto her Sonne, ouer all the creatures of heauen, of the earth, & of hell. The Sonne crowned her with a crowne of Wisdome, by communicating vnto her the cleare knowledge not only of the diuine essence, but also of all thinges created, appertayning in any sort to the office of the Mother of God, & of the Aduocatresse of men. The holy Ghost crowned her with a crowne of charity, infusing into her not only the loue of God, but also that of the neighbour, togeather with a most burning zeale of their eternall saluation. She was also crowned with the prerogatiue of Virginity, of a Martyr, & Lady. She was further crowned with twelue Stars, whereof mention is made in the 11. cap. of the Apocalyps: that is, all the prerogatiues, excellencies, & eminencies of all the orders of heauen concurred in the glory of our B. Lady, & therefore she may truly say that, whch is mentioned in the Prouerbes: many yong damosells haue amassed riches togeather, but thou hast gone beyond them all. Finally we must consider the ioy, & admiration, that the comming of a pure creature to heauen, so highly beautifyed, & richly set forth with graces, as she infinitly in a sort surpassed all the Cittizens thereof, caused vnto them.

Medit.

Meditat. XXIIII.   *Of our Blessed Ladyes Assumption in body : and of the place, she hath in heauen.*

TO côsider, how her sacred body lay in corrupted in the sepulcher, hauing by a speciall priuiledge, the same integrity, that it had in life, and of the immaculate sanctity of her soule, wherinto no worme of mortall sinne euer entred, nor dust of veniall to soyle it, or destaine it in the very least. And therefore reason it was, that the worms, or putrifaction should not haue any power vpon her body, sith withall this singular priuiledge concerned the honour of the Sonne, who had taken incorruptible flesh of the Virgin, with whom we must also reioyce for this her greatnes.

2.   To consider, how God the Creatour caused the B. Virgins soule to returne to the earth to enter into the body againe, which was much to her contentment, by occasion of the naturall desire, common to all soules, to vnite themselues with the other part of their being, that the body & the soule of the B. Virgin might continue for all eternity in that coniunction, wherof they had a beginning in this world, in a restles pray sing of the diuine maiesty, & that thereby also we might haue an assurance of our future Resurrection, sith not only our Sauiour did rise againe, but his mother also, who was a pure creature, as we are. This consideration ought to a-
wake

wake & ſtir vp in our harts a deſire to goe to ſee
our common mother. Moreouer this reunion
of the ſoule and body was for this cauſe, for that
from that tyme forth the B. Virgin tooke vpon
her for euer the tytle of the Mother of God, and
did the office of Mother and Aduocatreſſe of
men, whiles ſhe layeth open vnto her deere Son
in heauen her Virginall breaſts, that gaue him
ſucke on earth, for the appeaſing of his iuſt Anger agaynſt vs, wretched ſinners.

3. To conſider, what a ioy that likely was
to be of hers, in ſeeing herſelfe reſuſcitated: and
how often ſhe repeated her ſweet melodious
ſong (Magnificat), We muſt giue the eternall
Word thankes for the ſingular fauour, wherewith he honoured his mother, with whome we
muſt ioyne our ioyes for the glory of her body,
that vvas indewed vvith the foure glorious qualityes.

3. To conſider, how many thouſands of
Angells guarded & kept her ſepulcher, & ſong
this verſe of the pſalme 139, Riſe vp, O Lord, in
thy repoſe, thou, and the Arke of thy ſanctifica-
tion. This arke diuine began to mount & rayſe
it ſelfe on high, accompanyed with the Cherubims, & Seraphims, paſſing through the ayre,
& the heauens, & filling all with the light, without making any ſtay till it came to the Holy of
Holyes, the higheſt place in the Temple of God,
that is to ſay, in the Empyreall Heauen, which by
the arriuall of ſo fayre, and new a Sunne, receyued an increaſe of light, and beauty. The Bleſſed Angells reioyced much at the preſence of

ſuch

such a mother, by meanes of whome next vnto
God they had hope of the repayring of their
ruynes, and the filling vp of their seates, from
which pride had cast down the Diuells. We must
reioyce with this most humble Virgin for her
exaltation to so eminent a greatnes, and learne
to be humble with her, sith God rayseth vp the
humble, and causeth them to sit and take place
among the Princes of his Kingdome.

*Meditat . X X V . Of the care, that the Bles-
sed Virgin hath in heauen to protect them, who
honour her on earth .*

TO Consider, that if in all Countreys and
prouinces of the Christian world there be
to be found some particular Images of the
B. Virgin, by meanes whereof this our most
worthy Lady worketh many miracles in fauour
of them, who recurre to her protection : hovv
much more reason haue we to belieue, that she
fauoureth them in heauen, where the greatnes
of her glory hindreth not, but that she may still
remember their necessities . But on the contrary
great likely-hood there is, that she there remem-
breth them better, then she did, when she was in
this world, because her charity is more perfect in
the other .

    2.   To consider, that the B. Virgin is so plea-
sing vnto Gods eyes, as she doth not only obtayne of him what she asketh, but God also taketh a pleasure to fauour them, who honour her
                                              heere,

heere, though they should not make petition vnto him in their behalfe.

3· To consider, that in heauen she vseth the
honour she hath of Mother, to the vtility of mē,
for as much as she holdeth herselfe bound to assist and help them, and to handle their assayres
before the tribunall of God. And therefore we
must take courage to runne vnto her vvith
confidence, to be shadowed vnder the winges
of her protection, by considering our miseryes,
& the perils, that cōpasse vs round in this exile of
ours. And so to do, will induce vs the infinite examples of miraculous things, which we read to
haue been wrought by this our B. Lady, in fauour of them, that be denout to her.

Bbb   MEDI-

MEDITATIONS

OF THE VERTVES

OF OVR

BLESSED LADY.

THE Life of the most Blessed Virgin is like vnto a most excellent garden, furnished with diuersity of flowres, both most beautyfull, & sweet smelling. For the rich variety of her heroycall works doe more gloriously adorne her round, and on euery side of her, thē doth the variety of a thousand sorts of beautyfull floures recommend and set forth the excellency of a garden on earth. And though the precedent meditations vpon our B. Ladyes holy Life, did lay open vnto vs many rare vertues of hers, some worthy our admiration, others fit for our imitation: yet to the end the deuout soule may with the more facility and ease help it selfe by the example of them, & imitate them with the more alacrity, I haue thought
it

it to purpose to make some meditations by thē-selues vpon her more remarkable vertues, to the end that in meditating them vve may enioy the sweetnes, & diuine fragrancy that they yield, & still hold on the way to higher degrees of perfection. For most vndoubted it is, that the holy Virgin is next vnto her most Blessed Sonne the most perfect patterne, that can be found of all sanctity and purity, possible vnto the deuout soule to follow, in so much as to imitate her life, is to imitate Iesus Christ, of whome she was a liuely & perfect Image, and representation.

Meditat. I.   *Of the Blessed Virgins Fayth.*

TO consider, that fayth is a rare treasure, & diuine light, that sheweth vnto vs the way to heauen. It is the Sentinell, that discouereth vnto vs the treacheryes, and treasons our enemy worketh agaynst vs: the roote of all vertues, the fountaine of graces, an heauenly Doctour that teacheth vs the way, how we may remedy our necessities. We must heere giue God thankes for vouchsafing to haue honoured vs with this precious gift.

2.   To consider, how necessary it was, that man should belieue the supernaturall things, & that vvhich concerneth the glory of God for the attaining of eternall beatitude. For the knowledge of this supreme perfection must be in a most high degree, correspondent in some sort to so great a maiesty. And because it was not in the

Bbb 3   power

power of man naturally to attaine to the knowledge thereof, becaufe it exceedeth all humane vnderstanding, it was neceffary that God fhould reueale, the Church propofe, and man belieue the truthes that Fayth teacheth vs.

3. To confider, that the Bleffed Virgin hath giuen vs an example of this noble vertue, in firmely belieuing the profound mysteries, that the world neuer cleerly vnderstood before, as the holy Trinity, the Incarnation of the eternall Word of her felfe, and al that, which the Angell faid in faluting her. That our B. Ladyes fayth fo excelled, as fhe particularly merited the commendation of S. Elizabeth, when fhe fayd, Luc. 1. Bleffed art thou, who haft belieued, becaufe thofe thinges fhall be accomplifhed, that were fpoken to thee on the part of God. Though it was a moft great happynes to the Bleffed Virgin to haue been elected for Gods Mother, yet I dare fay that a greater glory it was vnto her to haue giuen her confent thereunto, with fo a liuely a faith: for by fo doing fhe conceiued the Son of God more in her foule, then in her immaculate body.

4. To confider, how this wonderfull Faith of hers appeared exceedingly in her on the day of her Sonnes Paffion: for when all our Sauiors friends left and forfooke him, fhe alone perfifted moft ftable and conftant in confeffion of the faith, not mouing a foote from the Croffe, and confeffing her Sonne, her God, and Sauiour. She alfo neuer doubted of the Refurrection, nor of the accomplifhment of all that which our Sauior

had

had foretold during his life. Heere we are to reioyce for this, that our B. Lady was so perfect in
the vertue of Fayth: and we must imitate her in
her constancy therein. To consider, that it importeth vs much to aske vertue of God, and the
increase of it, and to endeauour to conserue and
keep it by holynes of life, & purity of hart. For
as the Apostle 1. Timoth. 5. sayth: Some by re-
pelling and loosing a good conscience, came to
make a wracke of their fayth.

Meditat. I I.   *Of the Hope, which our Blessed*
    Lady had.

TO consider, that Hope is a vertue diuine, by
God infused into the will, by meanes wherof a man hopeth, and is assured, that God
will not be wanting on his part infallibly to contribute his assistance, and to communicate his
mercy in all, that shall be vnto a man necessary
for the bringing & conducting of him to beatitude. This is that excellent vertue which vniteth
the soule vnto God, as he is the authour of the
good it aspireth vnto. It hath the source of the
knowledge, a man hath of the goodnes & mercy
of God, & of the consideration of this, that we
haue the Sonne of God for our Redeemer, who
hath by his precious bloud, shed for vs, opened
vnto vs the gates of beaue. To consider, that Hope
is conserued, intertained, & increased by the purity of conscience, when a man auoideth the doing of any thing that may offend the diuine ma-
    B b b 4   iesty,

iesty, as Saint Iohn teacheth vs 1. Epist. cap. 3. in these wordes : If our hart doe not reprehend vs , we haue confidence towardes God : and whatsoeuer we shall aske, he will giue it vs . This vertue also receyueth increase by the exercise of good workes.

2.   To consider, how the Blessed Virgin hath giuen vs many examples of this vertue. For first notwithstanding she made a vow of perpetuall Virginity , and was in a most high degree affected vnto it , yet she accepted of Ioseph for her spouse, and did put all her trust in Gods protection, without feare of loosing that which she so highly esteemed, as was her Virginall purity . Secondly , when she was with child , and saw that S. Ioseph was very much troubled at the matter, and had an intent to leaue her, she vvas nothing moued herselfe, but permitted all to the diuine prouidence, being assured , that her own innocency would at length come to be knowne. Thirdly, being at the Marriage in Cana of Galily, she prayed her Son, out of the hope she had, to supply the want of wine, that the mayster of the feast might not be confounded before the vvhole company . And this vertue appeared the more in her , when she willed them who serued, to do as her Sonne should bid them to doe, notwithstanding the answere she had receiued from him , which seemed in appearance somwhat harsh .

3.   To consider, that of what hath been said, we must learne this excellent vertue of the Blessed Virgin, with hope that God will graunt

vs what we shall aske, though the tyme of performance, and of the effecting of our petitions be other whiles differred. We must also resolue with our selues neuer to loose our hope, though we should see, that all thinges went contrary to our desires by the example of our Blessed Lady, who in the middest of so many ignomynies, crueltyes, and torments, exercised vpon her Sonne the day of his Passion, was not for all that out of Hope, but that the worlds Redemption should be accomplished by him thereby, imitating heerein the Patriarke Abraham, who, notwithstanding he had receyued a commaundment from God to sacrifice his Sonne Isaac, in whom he had made him all his promises, hoped agaynst hope, that God would performe his word, by such meanes as he knew best.

Meditat. III. *Of our Blessed Ladyes Charity, and Loue towardes God.*

TO consider, that though she had all the vertues in a most high degree of perfection, yet the charity and loue, that she did beare to God, surpassed all the rest. For this Vertue is giuen according to the measure of grace, wherewith because she was replenished from the very instant of her immaculate Conception, she also receyued charity in a most abundant and full measure. To consider, how she continually proceeded, & increased in grace and charity all her life long, from the tyme she began to haue the vse

of

of reason: whereby it may be conceyued, that the degree of perfection, that she had therein at the end of her life, was in a manner incomprehensible.

2. The more knowledge a soule hath of God, the more doth it loue him, and his supreme goodnes. And wheras the B. Virgin knew the greatnes & the goodnes of the Creatour, & vvas besides most faythfull & loyall vnto him: who seeth not, that the greatnes of her loue towardes him was inexplicable? Againe, according as the measure of the benefitts that haue beene receyued be greater or lesser, we are wont therefore to loue more or lesse the benefactour, and giuer thereof: If then the Blessed Virgin receyued so great and extraordinary benefitts at the liberall hand of God, as she professed herselfe in her Canticle, when she sayd: Because he that is mighty, hath done great thinges in me; manifest & most certayne it is, that her loue was in a most perfect degree towards God.

3. To consider, that the property of Charity is to vnite the soule with God: there is not any creature, hath been so inwardly & neerly vnited to God, as the sacred Virgin, and consequently none euer loued him so much. And of all this I must draw a desire of vniting and conioyning my selfe with God. To consider, that this loue of hers vvas so much the more pure, the further it was of from particular interest and respect, and the more in all thinges it sought the honour and glory of God, in conforming it selfe absolutely to the diuine vvill, as our Blessed
Lady

Lady did in taking a Spouse, in belieuing the mystery of the Incarnation, and all the rest of the life of our Sauiour, especially during the tyme of his most bitter Passion. Of this vve must learne to seeke God in all thinges, and not our own will.

4. The Blessed Virgins Loue vvas most feruent, and most constant vvithall, and therefore she could not endure to be idle. For that Loue moued and incited her continually to imploy her selfe for the seruice of God, and therefore she might say much better, then any other, that of the Canticles: My beloued is all for me, and I all for him. She also did all thinges vvith most great perfection, and most singular perseuerance, as vvell in aduersity, as in prosperity, as vve may perceyue by her constancy amiddest so many trauerses and Crosses, that befell her, especially in her Sonnes Passion. She further gaue testimony of her Loue to God by the continuall care, she had to fly from all thinges, that vvere bad, vvere the same neuer so little, eyther vvordes, or thoughts, this being an infallible signe of the Loue that a soule beareth to God alone.

Meditat. IIII. *Of the Blessed Virgins Charity towardes Men* .

TO cōsider how, that out of true charity towards God resulteth the true loue towards man. For in what measure a man loueth God

God, in the same he loueth his neighbour, for the loue of him who commaundeth it. And for this reason did holy men trauayle, and take so much paynes, as they did, for the sauing of their neighbors soules. And if the Loue of the neighbour be to be measured by the loue of God, we may well affirme, that the Blessed Virgin, who Loued God in a most high degree, did also loue men in an extraordinary manner: & this should giue vs courage to recurre to this Blessed Virgin in all our necessityes, when we know the Loue, wherwith she tendreth vs.

2.   To consider, how, whiles she liued in the world, she gaue frequent testimonyes of this Loue of the neighbor. For she prayed with most harty affection for the worlds saluation, & when she saw the beginning thereof within her owne wombe, she made a iourney to see S. Elizabeth, to make her glad, as well for the fauour, that God had done her therby, & all mankind besides, as also for that, which that good woman had receyued in her old age. The very same charity appeared also very much at the marriage in Cana of Galily, by the care she had, when there was want of wyne at the feast, that it might not redound to the confusion of him who made it.

3.   To consider, how the Blessed Virgin gaue yet more cleare signes of her loue towards man after her Sonnes Ascension into heauen, for as much as she instructed the ignorant, comforted the afflicted, animated the fearfull, wrote to the absent, and sometymes tooke the paynes to goe to see them, with S. Iohn in her company, in so

much

much as ſhe was the conſolation of all the faith-full of the primitiue Church.

4. To conſider, how ſhe further exten-ded her charity euen to them, who had ſpoyled her moſt deere Sonne of his life, and loued them with ſo tender an affection, as, if it had been ne-ceſſary, ſhe would moſt willingly haue ſpent her life for euery one of them in regard of the loue, that her Sonne did beare them, which was ſuch, as the very firſt word, that he ſpeake on the Croſſe, was in fauour of them. To conſider, that this her loue towardes both friendes and enemyes increaſed, when our Sauiour gaue her Saint Iohn in place of himſelfe. For in his per-ſon ſhe receyued and adopted all men in gene-rall for her children, and holdeth vs ſtill at this day for ſuch, and hath a care of vs from heauen. And this conſideration ſhould be a motiue and inducement to loue her agayne as our Mother, & humbly to reuerence & reſpect her, as our ſo-ueraigne Lady.

5. To conſider, how the ſame loue moued her to offer vnto the eternal Father the innocent life of her beloued Son, for the Redemption of Man. And this alſo, among other reaſons ſhould excite vs to loue her with moſt tender affection, & to offer vnto her our lyues for the ſpirituall profit of our neighbour.

Medi-

Meditat. V.   Of the Blessed Virgins zeale of Soules.

TO Confider, how the glorious B. Virgins loue towards God caused her earneſtly to deſire the ſaluation of Men, & how ſhe neuer intermitted, or gaue ouer to pray for their conuerſion. It is alſo credible, that many ſoules were by occaſion of her continuall prayers deliuered out of the bottomles gulfe of their infidelity, & rayſed vp to the heauen of the Chriſtian faith, & brought forth from the darkenes of ſin to the light of grace.

2. To conſider, how ſhe ſought to excite all to the exerciſe of vertue by her owne example, for exemplar life is a double preaching. Her holines gaue admiration to all, that conſidered it, & there ſeemed ſenſibly to appeare in her the bright ſhining beames of a certaine diuinity For her manner of cariage, comportment, & doing was all celeſtial & diuine, & her words & ſpeech were like vnto fiery darts, that tranſpierced the harts that heard her.

3. To conſider, how ſhe was ſore afflicted in ſoule, when ſhe ſaw any fall into ſinne: and tooke compaſſion of their weaknes, in ſo much as ſhe might ſay with the Apoſtle: who is ſcandalized, & I am not burnt? & with Dauid: The zeale of thy houſe hath eaten me. And this was was it, that preſſed her to pray moſt hartily for men, & to her vttermoſt, to procure their ſouls good,

good, wherein we muſt imitate her.

Meditat. VI. Of the Bleſſed Virgins Pray-er, and Contemplation.

TO Conſider, how the Bleſſed Virgin ex-celled in contemplation, wherein ſhe ſtill increaſed, as ſhe grew in age. And this is apparant by this, that in her moſt tender yeares ſhe retired herſelfe to the Temple, with the more commodity to attend to prayer. The holy E-uangeliſts giue teſtimony heerin, whē they ſay: Mary conſerued, & conferred in her hart all the myſteries of the life of her Sonne.

2. To conſider, that ſhe was free from all obſtacles & impediments that trouble prayer, namely from thoſe, which S. Bernard mentio-neth in his 23. Sermō vpon the Canticles, which be, ſinne that biteth, care that pricketh, ſenſe that troubleth, the multitude of vaine thoughts that diſtract the imagination. To conſider, how the Bleſſed Virgin had the eyes of her ſoule con-tinually fixed on God, without any the leaſt di-ſturbance to her ſight. For ſhe was eminent in thoſe vertues, that diſpoſe to prayer & contem-plation, as in liuely fayth, in profound humili-ty, in moſt burning charity, togeather with a di-uine wiſdome, & the reſt of the gifts of the holy Ghoſt. And as all this increaſed togeather with her years, ſo did her prayer and contemplation increaſe more then other, in ſo much as ſhe was continually conioyned with God.

Ccc 2

3. To

3. To confider, that the mysteryes (as hath been reuealed) of her Sonnes life & death, continued fo liuely imprinted in her foule, as the thought vpon them day & night, euer ftirring vp in herfelfe the tender, affectionate & deuout commotions of compaffion, forrow, gratitude, and charity, whereupon fhe oft vifited the holy places, wherin her moft beloued Sonne accomplifhed the mifteryes of our Redemption, as the manger, her houfe of Nazareth, the garden of Gethfemani, & the mount Caluary, vfing euery one of thefe places for the raifing of her mind to heauen.

4. To confider, how our Bleffed Lady, following the counfayle of her Sonne, when he faith Luc. 18. we muft alwaies pray, and neuer ceafe; prayed in all places, and at all times, côtinuing as much and as long, as it was poffible for any pure creature to do in fuch fort, as when fhe laboured with hand by day, or flept by night, her hart was ftill awake, and fhe treated fpiritually with God. To thinke how fhe was ofté vifited not only of the Angells, but alfo of the Lord of Angells & of all creatures, from whom fhe receyued moft high illuftrations, and knowledge in the moft profound mifteryes of all. For credible it is, that fhe was honoured with greater fauours, then euer any Saint had receyued at Gods hands. To confider, how the Bleffed Virgin receyued the Bleffed Sacrament euery day, and that with an admirable faith, reuerençing her Sonne with moft fingular deuotion, & voifing her felfe by charity with him, of whome fhe
receyued

receued euery day new degrees of graces, occaſioned by her moſt excellent diſpoſing of her mind. Thus conuerſed ſhe in the world with her Sonne, ſhadowed vnder the Sacramentall kinds, and ſometimes appearing in his owne likeneſſe vnto her, as it hath been graunted to many other Saints, vntill at length ſhe beheld him in heauen face to face reuealed, & in company of him for all eternity.

Medirat. V I I. Of the Bleſſed Virgins profound Humility.

TO conſider, hovv the Bleſſed Virgin excelled in profound humility, whereunto may in particular & eſpecially be attributed her exaltation, becauſe ſhe humbled her ſelfe more then all the creatures of the world, as ſhe teſtified by the ſilence wherewith ſhe concealed her fauours, & perfections, without euer giuing any demonſtration thereof eyther by ſignes, or words. And this is to be ſeene in the Annunciation of the Angell; which ſhe would not diſcouer or reueale ſo much as to Ioſeph her Spouſe, though the ſuſpition he had of her Chaſtity, ſeemed otherwiſe moſt ſtraitly to bind her thervnto. She alſo gaue a teſtimony of her humility, when ſhe was troubled at the recitall & commemoration of her prayſes, becauſe of the little opinion, and conceite ſhe had of her ſelfe. For the truly humble perſon referreth all glory vnto God, & deſireth that all the world ſhould doe

the

the same, when his graces and vertues come by Gods will to be knowne. And so did the Blessed Virgin, as her cáticle Magnificat maketh plaine, which she made, when S. Elizabeth deliuered her prayses.

2. To consider, how our Blessed Lady, being by Gods mercy eleuated to the most high dignity of the mother of God, abased herselfe by humility to the very lowest rancke, and beneath all creatures, naming herselfe the Handmaide of God. Of this most profound humility it came, that being in Bethleem, she tooke vp for her lodging the most cótemptible place, that was there to be found, namely a poore stable & further put her selfe vnder all the lawes & ceremonies, that did not any way bind her; as the Purification by name, by húbling herselfe not only to her betters but to her inferiors also, as she did to S. Elizabeth, who was her inferior in dignity. Moreouer she exercised her selfe in base & contemptible offices with much cótentment of spirit, as being the spouse of a poore tradesman, & did the busines that is required in the house, as if she had been some poore seruant in drudgery. Besides this, she shunned, as much as she could, offices of honor, as to worke miracles, to preach in publike, though she were an instructour of the Apostles, leauing to thē the office to preach to the world, and contenting only to teach the faithfull in secret. Yea it is credible, that when occasion fell out that she was in the assemblyes of the first Christians, she tooke vp her place in company of the other Women, that were there present

present, giuing eare to Gods word, and reuerencing the Priestes, who preached there in
place.

3. The Blessed Virgin also gaue a remon-
strance of her voluntary pouerty, and by her
patient suffering of iniuries. For all her life long
she carryed her selfe for a poore person: witnesse
the stable at Bethleem, and her Purification in
the Temple. She tooke a pleasure to conuerse, and keep company with the poore,
and did patiently beare the iniuryes, and contempts, which persons of such condition & quality are wont to receiue and beare at the handes
of the rich, besides those, which she endured frō
the enemyes of her Sonne, who did, as it is credible, oftentimes conuert their rage and fury v-
pon the mother. She declared also at other
tymes, how deep and fast roote this noble vertue had taken in her soule, when she did with a
sweet and quiet mind beare the refusalls, and
sharp words of her Son vpon diuers occasions;
as when she found him in the Temple, after she
had sought him for three whole dayes: & at the
marriage in Cana of Galily.

4. Finally, she made her surpassing humility knowne, when he would participate in the
reproaches and ignominyes of her Sonne, when
he was Crucified, when she presented herselfe at
the foot of the Crosse, & there stood of purpose,
that the whole world might take notice, that she
was Mother to him, who did there hang in the
middest betweene two theeues: & credible it is,
that whils she there stood in so infamous a place

in the opinion of Men, she was many wayes iniured, misused, and mocked by her Sonnes e-
nemies and persecutors. And in this the holy
Virgin seemed to follow the counsaile of the holy Ghost, (saying Eccl. 2. The greater thou art, the
more, humble thou thy selfe in all thinges, and
thou shalt find fauour before God. Moreouer
she was so perfect in this vertue, as she was crowned with a crowne of twelue starrs, in recompense of the twelue principall acts of humility,
which we haue heere touched before. Of all this
we must learne to stirre vp a feruent desire and
affection to humility, and endeauour to exercise
our selues therein, & to conserue it in all things,
and vpon all occasions, in imitation of the
Queene of heauen.

Meditat. **V I I I .**   *Of the Blessed Virgins*
    Obedience.

T O consider, how the Blessed Virgin, know-
    ing that this vertue was most pleasing to
    the diuine maiesty, did therein exercise her
selfe from the very time of her infancy, in a most
exact obedience to her parents in all thinges in
their house, to the high Priest in the Temple, &
to S. Ioseph in her owne little family.

    2.   To consider, that her obedience ap-
peared much more in this, that she obeyed bad
Superiours, as when she went that long iourney
from Nazareth to Bethleem to obey the Edict
of the Emperour, that was a Tyrant, & an In-
                                        fidell

fidell, though it were accõpanyed with many & great incommodities. as well for the difficulties of the way, as for the vnſeaſonable time of the winter, and notwithſtanding all this ſhe o-beyed without eyther murmuring or complayning.

2 Her obedience excelled alſo in this, that ſhe had a care to the obſeruation of the Law. We haue her Purification to witnes the matter, from which the ſame law in expreſſe wordes ex-cepted her, but ſhe willingly ſubieċted herſelfe vnto it, becauſe ſhe knew that by ſo doing ſhe ſhould the more pleaſe God. For to the obedient it is inough to knew the wil of his maiſter with-out expeċting what he will commaund him. Moreouer ſhe made a declaration of this excel-lent vertue, when for the loue of God ſhe depri-ued herſelfe of all, that might giue her content-ment, as of the preſence of her Sonne, who was more deare vnto her, then ſhe was vnto herſelf, in enduring his abſence patiently, and in reſig-ning herſelfe to the diuine will, not only thoſe three day, that he was loſt, & the 40. dayes of his aboad in the deſert of ſury, and thoſe three yeares, that he preached the Kingdome of hea-uen, but alſo in bearing with patience the death of the ſame her Lord, and onlv Sonne, and his corporall abſence after his Aſcenſion into hea-uen. And therefore we may probably belieue, that ſhe oftē repeated theſe words: Thy will be done.

4. She alſo exerciſed the ſame obedience after her Sonns Aſcenſion to heauen, in punċtu-ally

ally obſeruing all, that he had commaunded, whiles he liued on earth; & more then that, the very ordinations of S. Peter, & of the reſt of the Apoſtles, in whoſe perſons ſhe conſidered God himſelfe.

Meditat. IX. Of the Vow of Virginity, that our Bleſſed Lady made. ¶ See the fifth Meditation before.

TO côſider, that where the B. Virgin deſired with all her hart to doe the will of the diuine maieſty, her deſire was not to doe what was ſimply pleaſing vnto God, but ſhe ſought to doe what was beſt, and moſt perfect. And therefore knowing, that Virginity excelled Marriage & Wedlocke, and that with it ſhe might ſerue God more perfectly, & giue him a more abſolute poſſeſſion of her hart thereby, ſhe reſolued to keep it, binding herſelfe thereunto by a perpetuall, & irreuocable vow. To conſider, that this work was ſo much the more noble, the leſſe it was in practiſe in thoſe times, in ſo much as then a woman barraine was infamous, & diſhonoured before all the people, & ſterility was held for a malediction of God: & notwithſtanding this, the Bleſſed Virgin did put on a reſolution to ſuffer all for the loue of God, & of Virginity. To conſider, that ſhe made this vow without any precedét exáple, or law, or coûſaile, that might induce her ſo to do, but ſhe was moued only with a deſire of that which might be
moſt

most acceptable to God, and out of the loue &
affection, she did beare to this Angelicall, & celestiall vertue.

2. To consider the most high esteeme
the Blessed Virgin made of Virginity, seeing at
what tyme the Angell deliuered his message,
and offered vnto her on the part of God the dignity of being Gods mother, she seemed to make
a greater reckoning of Virginall purity, & stood
vpon the refusall of that most soueraigne condition, if her integrity might haue peraduenture
been preiudiced thereby. For her answere seemeth to insinuate no lesse, when she sayd: how
shall this be done? because I know not man.

3. To consider, that Virginity is so highly esteemed also in this most pure Virgin, as the
Church holdeth it not inough to giue her the tytle
of Virgin of Virgins, but giueth her also the nam
of Virginity it selfe, whē it saith in honor of her:
O holy and immaculate Virginity, I know not
with what manner of praises I may best extoll
thee. For this Blessed Virgin was in a most supreme degree, most pure both in Body, and in
Soule. To consider the exceeding great fruit,
the Church hath reaped by this first vow of the
B. Virgin by binding herselfe to perpetuall Virginity. For by her example an infinite number
of persons of both sexes haue liued in singular
purity, and many haue been found, who chose
rather to suffer whatsoeuer torments, then in the
very least to destaine their Virginall purity. To
consider the circumstances of the times, wherein the Blessed Virgin made an election of this

noble

noble vertue, with what manner of affection she made profession of it, & with how great a purity she kept it. Of this we must make our spirituall profit.

4. To consider, what manner of vertues the B. Virgin practised for the conseruing of her immaculate candour, & purity, to wit, a singular temperance in her meate and drinke, and manner of liuing, long watchings, little sleep, indefatigable prayers, diligence and circumspection in exteriour workes that concerned the honour of God, the seruice of her Sonne, the gouernement of her poore family, and the profit of her neighbour, a sollicitous guard ouer her hart, frō which proceedeth both death and life, a seuere mortification of her senses, knowing that they were the windowes, by which death entreth into the soule: a graue modesty in her actions, silence and a meruailous recollection of her mind in God. We must in imitation of her, endeauour to procure to our selues the same vertues for the conseruing of this precious iewel of chastity.

Meditat. X. *Of the Blessed Virgins Modesty, Silence, and solitary Retire.*

TO consider, how our Blessed Lady omitted not any meanes, which made, or were proper, for the conseruing of Virginal purity, and therefore her retyre was admirable, as is manifest by her aboad in the Temple: and when the Angell brought her the newes of the Incarnati-

Incarnation, she was found alone in her little oratory. Where we are to consider, how not being accustomed to see, or treate with any man apart or alone, she was troubled at the sight of the Angell. And the Gospell further teacheth vs, that when she went to see her Cosen Elizabeth, she made hast, & vsed diligence to come thither soone. Besides this, we read not, that she euer went from home, but vpon most pressing necessity, & in company of other women : and credible also it is, that she obserued the same course after her Sonnes Ascension into heauen, with as much care, as she had done before.

2. To consider, that this B. Virgin was graced with so singular modesty, & with so graue, modest, and remarkable a comportment in her countenance, wordes, actions, gestures, & outward carriage, as she was a perfect patterne and represētation of sanctity & deuotion, in so much as her exteriour apparence testifyed most euidently the beauty, that was hid within, and this by a certaine glittering of a certaine diuinity, that shined in her in so effectuall a manner, as if faith did not teach vs, that she could not be a Goddesse, she might haue been thought one, so many and so great were her perfections : for neuer was any creature on earth to be seene so excellent, as she.

3. To consider the meruaylous silence she kept all her life long. For we find, that she spake very sparingly, in few wordes, and with much circumspection. For as her conuersation was ordinarily with God, she would not haue to doe

D d d   with

with men, but when eyther necessity, or the neighbours soules good bound her thereunto, and then her words also were precisely necessary, holy, edifying, and full of the spirit of God, as is to be seene in her canticle (Magnificat). Whē any saluted her, we may piously belieue, that she answered them with saying, *Deo Gratias*, or some such like wordes, as being wholy absorpt in God.

Meditat. XI. *Of the Blessed Virgins voluntary Pouerty.*

TO cōsider how, that voluntary pouerty is willingly and hartily to forsake all temporall thinges for the loue of God, and not to possesse more then is precisely necessary, & yet to depriue our selfe sometimes also of that for the loue of God, to whome such abridging of what is necessary is most pleasing, for that the soule by abandoning and renouncing these perishing goods of the earth, may by that meanes with the more facility raise it selfe vp to those other eternall in heauen.

2. To consider the excellent examples, that our Blessed Lady hath left vs of this vertue, as that knowing that it was Gods will she should marry, she disdained not to take a poore craftesman for her spouse, though she were herselfe so nobly descended, as she was, and excelled in so many rare & singular vertues. That the very night of her happy deliuery of child, she found

not

not any other place, whither to goe , but to the corner of a poore ſtable , the ordinary place for beaſts: at what time alſo ſhe had none but a few poore, but yet cleane,cloathes to wrap the King of glory in , & a poore maunger to lay him , inſteed of a cradle.

3. To conſider, how in her Purification ſhe made her offering, as the offering of a poore perſon . For though the three Kings of the Eaſt, had a while before preſēted gold vnto her yong Sonne, credible it is,that the Bleſſed Virgin had diſtributed all to the poore , as being an Euangelicall poore perſon herſelfe : and that in Ægypt ſhe was in the like poore ſtate of pouerty , where ſhe liued vnknowne in a forraine Coūntrey.

4. To conſider , how after the Aſcenſion of her Sonne ſhe lead her life in extreme pouerty ; whereof we may piouſly meditate that ſhe made a vow, if ſhe had not made it before;in ſo much as ſhe liued of almes, that was by the Apoſtles diſtributed to the faithfull , whiles ſhe contented her ſelfe with very meane intertainment , that might ſerue the turne for maintayning of life, and poore and honeſt cloathing,alwaies retayning in memory the gall , vinegar, and nakednes of her moſt deere Sonne on the Croſſe . There wanted not in her a deſire to ſuffer far greater effects of Euangelicall pouerty, in accommodating her ſelfe to liue of almes , as other poore widdowes did , and in teaching by her owne example the practiſe of this vertue , and of all others , as being herſelfe alone a

great

great part of Euangelicall perfection.

Meditat. XII.   *Of the vertue of Patience,*
    wherein the Bleſſed Virgin excelled.

TO conſider, that the degrees of Patience
be theſe. The firſt, patiently to beare iniuries, & contempt that ariſe of ſinne. The
ſecond, and more perfect, is to ſuffer the ſame
iniuries without deſeruing them. The third, and
that the moſt perfect of the three, to ſuffer for
hauing done ſome good and holy worke, that
merited praiſe. The fourth to ſuffer the ſame
not only at the handes of enemies, and ſtran-
gers, but alſo of our owne friendes, and brethren.

2.   To conſider, that the Bleſſed Virgin
practiſed all theſe degrees of patience, & that in
a moſt perfect manner, except the firſt, which
ſuppoſeth a fault, from which this Bleſſed Virgin was moſt free, and had her part in moſt
heauy ſorrowes, and moſt ſore trauerſes, and
afflictions, as is to be ſeene in the courſe & pro-
greſſe of her whole life.

3.   To conſider, that Bleſſed Virgins ſorrowes and afflictions were ſore and grieuous in
a moſt high degree, becauſe ſhe ſuffered in the
perſon of her Sonne, whome ſhe loued more,
then ſhe did herſelfe, & therfore her ſorrowes
were proportioned to her exceſſiue loue. To cōſider, that the Bleſſed Virgin was more then a
Martyr, in ſeing her beſt beloued in his tormēts,
                                                    and

and dying so cruell & ignominious a death. And
notvvithstanding this she persisted stout and
constant amiddest the excessiue panges and
grypes of sorrowes, that in a most violent manner pressed her , without giuing any the least
signe of intemperate passion , as euen the most
discreet & best aduised women are wont in like
cases to breake forth into .

4.   To consider the patience, that she manifested after her Sonns Ascension into heauen,
when she saw with her eyes the persecutions &
afflictions, that fell vpon the Apostles , and
faythfull of the primitiue Church, by the cruelty of that barbarous people, that was so deeply
bound vnto her Sonne . It was also no little affliction vnto her to see so few to receyue the holy Gospell, and fewer to make their profit of our
Sauiours copious and abundant Redemption.
Moreouer her long stay & banishment in this
world much afflicted her , & the tyme seemed
vnto her long, till she might enioy the obiect of
her loue : & therfore she still longed to be deliuered and released from out of the bands of body , though otherwise she resigned herselfe alwaies to the diuine will . But yet this was not a
bar to the griefe, that that she tooke for the absence of her best beloued, the loue of whom was
vnto her a new & continuall Martirdome.

Meditat. XIII.   *Of the deuotion which we
owe vnto the Bleſſed Virgin, for the good, that
hath come vnto vs by her: and in what we -
ought to witnes it .*

TO Conſider, how reaſonable a thing it is,
that we loue and ſerue the Bleſſed Virgin,
ſith the holy Trinity loueth her more, thẽ
he doth all the Angells and Saints togeather.
Moreouer, wheras ſhe is the Mother of our Sauiour, a tytle and dignity that is honorable vnto her in a moſt high degree, aboue all thinges
next after God, his pleaſure is, that all ſhould
honour and loue her, as the diuine maieſty ho-
noureth and loueth her it ſelfe. Furthermore
ſhe is the cõmon mother of all men, who ought
to anſwere her with loue for loue, who ceaſeth
not doing good continually to men, by praying
and interſeding for them, and taking care for
their ſaluation, as a true and compaſſionate mother, in particular to thoſe, who be deuout vnto her. She is powerfull & in credit with the diuine maieſty, & euer and none becometh an in-
terceſſour in fauour of thoſe, that inuocate her,
as many haue, to their ſingular good, by experience found: Who haue been deliuered from
their neceſſities, rather inuocating the name of
the B. Virgin (ſavth S. Anſelme) then the moſt
ſweet name of Ieſus, whiles God vvould ſo haue
it for the honouring of his mother. We muſt
further be moued to this deuotion towards her
by

by the consideration of that, which the same holy Man saith in these wordes : It is a signe of eternall predestination to be hartily deuout to this holy and diuine Lady. For she solliciteth most carefully aboue in heauen the meanes of predestination for those her seruants, who honour her beneath on earth. These motiues, & the like ought to be incitements vnto vs to exercise deuotion towardes this most glorious Princesse.

2. To consider, how the holy Ghost hath inspired to the faithfull a deuotion towardes the Blessed Virgin, by teaching them certaine exercises for the stirring vp of their deuotiō towards her. For first he hath shewed, that she is to be adored with an adoration, inferior to that, which belongeth to God alone, but yet greater then that which is giuen to other Saints, and is called Hyperdulia : and that certaine tytles and names appertayning to the diuinity, are to be appropriated vnto her, as one, who in some sort participateth them. So we call her mother of mercy, of Life, Sweetnes, and by other names and tytles, that are contayned in the *Salue Regina.* Secondly, he hath taught vs in honour of her to dedicate sumptuous, magnificall, and costly Churches, Oratories, and Chappells, where by her intercession be wrought great miracles ; and to institute and found Religions, and Societyes vnder her protection. Thirdly, he hath inspired vnto the faythfull to celebrate the frequent memory of this Blessed Virgin, by annuall solemnities and feasts, wherein they ho-

nour

nour her , craue her interceffion , and ayde ,
and confecrate in honour of her the Saturday
with particular feruices , deuotions , offices , &
Maffes , vvherein are graunted many Indul-
gences and pardons, as when we fay the Angells
falutation vvith deuotion at thofe tymes and
houres , that the Aue-bell (as we call it) foun-
deth &c .

3.   To confider , that among all the deuotions , wherewith we honour the Bleffed Virgin , the moft remarkable , moft common , and
that by meanes whereof greateft benefits and
fauours haue been obtayned, is the Rofary , or
Beades , as we tearme it , which we are to fay
with fome precedent preparation of mind , and
to endeauour to be attentiue to what is fayd ,
togeather with a confideration of her, to whom
the prayer is addreffed . The Beades may be
faid in diuers manner , as in meditating of fome
particular vertue of hers after the faying of ten
Aues , and one Pater nofter : or in crauing help
of God for the ouercoming, or rooting of fome
vice out of our hart, or in pondering fome word
of tue Aue Maria , or of the Pater nofter , by
prefenting at the end of euery decade , or ten
Aues , one or other of the feauen Petitions of
the Pater nofter . Or, which is more ordinary ,
and more in vfe, by confidering after euery de-
cade|one of the fifteene myfteries , as we call
them , of the Rofary , and whereunto we attribute the names of ioyfull, dolorous,and glorious , in which is familiarly contayned the life
of our Sauiour , and of his holy Mother , making

king a short Colloquy after the Mediation of
euery mystery, and crauing of God that, which
we desire by intercession of the most sacred
Virgin, to whome be glory for euer and e-
uer. Amen.

MEDITATIONS

VPON THE MISTERIES
OF
GODS ESSENCE,
AND PERFECTIONS.

Togeather with the Naturall, and Supernaturall Benefits, that the diuine Maiesty hath bestowed vpon men.

The Preface.

THE end of Christiã perfectiõ is charity, & loue of God, by means wherof the soule is vnited with the diuine
maiesty. And to the attayning of this
end, the contemplation of the excellencyes and
perfe-

perfections of the Diuinity, is a moſt aſſured way, and a moſt effectuall meanes. For by them we learne, that it is worthy of ſupreme loue, prayſe, ſeruice, and ſubiection, togeather with an infinite affection, if it were for vs poſſible to giue it. And becauſe it is not in our power, all theſe perfections, and euery one of them, bind vs to conceiue in our ſoules a moſt vehement, inſatiable, conſtant, and perſeuerant deſire, as neere as we may, to loue this ſupreme goodnes with all our hart, and with all our forces to ſerue it. And for this end will ſerue vs the conſideration of the innumerable benefitts, we haue receiued of Gods liberall hand, for which we ſtand bound vnto him, with the greateſt correſpondence we can poſſibly yield him: and therfore the enſuing meditations ayme altogeather at this marke,

2. Vpon euery benefit we are to conſider fiue thinges, to wit, the infinite greatnes of the benefactour, and the loue wherewith he imparteth vnto vs theſe benefitts, the baſenes, and vnworthines of the perſon that receiueth them, that is man, miſerable, ingrate, and obliuious: the infinite liberality of God, in doing vs ſo much good, without any hope of recompence on our part, and withall ſo far from deſeruing them, as on the contrary we are moſt vnworthy of them, and we cauſe him to ſhut vp his hands, in as much as his liberality is withdrawne from vs, occaſioned by the multitude of our ſinnes.

3. We muſt anſwere theſe benefitts with gratitude, eſteeming them, as is meete, for the

reaſons

reasons heere declared, publishing & extolling
Gods liberality, exhorting and inducing all creatures to prayse him, and doing him seruice, with
hoping for new benefitts at his hands, sith the
foresayd be inough to induce vs to serue him
for the loue of him only, &c.

Meditat. I. Of the *Essence*, *and Being of*
God.

TO consider, that Fayth teacheth to belieue, that there is a God, that is to
say, that in this visible world is a soueraygne and inuisible Spirit, the beginning & ending of all thinges, that he hath created, & conserueth, and gouerneth them. All creatures
preach vnto vs this verity, as well in heauen, as
in earth, That they made not themselues, but
that God gaue them their Being, and dispersed
them, as they are. This verity ought to excite vs
to resound Gods prayses.

2. To consider, that the thinges, that be
within our selues, doe manifest vnto vs the cer-
titude of this verity, as the psalmist affirmeth in
these wordes: Thy knowledge is become meruaylous of me: it is made great, and I cannot
reach vnto it. And els where he saith: The light
of thy countenance is signed, o Lord, vpon vs.
This light is a certayne participation of the diuine essence, as also the beauty, and diuersity of
the powers both within and without vs, the
vaynes, the arteryes, the sinnewes, &c. The
wonder-

wonderfull order, and difpofition of all thefe; aboue all the foule, a moft noble thing, which is within our body, exercifing the vvonderfull operations bv it ovvne povvers, fuch as be fciences, arts, &c. All thefe thinges cry vvith a lowd voyce, that there is one God, who gouerneth, directeth, and difpofeth them.

2.   To confider all the miferyes, that man fuffers, as pouerty, ficknes, rebellion of the flelh agaynft the fpirit &c. All which teach the fame verity, for as much as vve fee, that being preffed vvith thefe euills, we eftfoones make our recourfe vnto God by the very inftinct of nature. To confider, that hauing this fayth and beliefe alwayes in our remembrance, we doe with facility reftrayne and keep in our vitious paffions, inclinations, and appetites, and bv the fame meanes excite vertue in our foules. For moft certayne it is, that there would not fo many finnes be committed in the world, if the memory of this verity vvere ftill prefent to mens mindes. We muft heere deplore the infelicity of finners : Who with their lips doe confeffe, that there is a God, and doe deny him by their vvorkes.

Meditat. I I.   *Of the Eternity of Gods Being.*

TO côfider, that this foueraygne being had neuer any beginning, and neuer fhall haue any ending. For he it is, who is, as he anfwered

wered Moyses; his meaning is, That he euer
was, and shall be without end, without tyme,
and without limitation. And for this we must
be glad, and prayse the diuine Maiesty to our vttermost.

2. To consider, that this diuine Being
appertayneth so to God, as it cannot be appropriated to any other, because he is and sub-
sisteth of himselfe, and euery other thing receyueth being from him, in so much as the creatures properly be not indeed, because their being, to say well, is nothing at all. From this we
must draw a true knowledge of our selues, and
a most great esteeme of the Diuinity.

2. To consider, that Gods Being is most
simple, without any composition, and yet
comprehendeth in himselfe the perfections of
all creatures in a more high and more perfect
degree, then can be imagined: in so much as
in comparison of him, all that which is created,
is nothing at all. Of this we must learne to make
a most high esteeme of God, and contemne our
selues, because we are very nothing it selfe, if
vve enter into a comparison with the diuine
Essence.

*Meditat. I I I.   Of God Infinity, and In-
comprehensibility.*

T O consider, that God is not any thing, that
may be perceyued by sense : for he neyther hath colour, nor smell, &c. And it
    E e e   is

is vnworthy his greatnes to compare him to visible creatures. We must reioyce and be glad, that he infinitly exceedeth all, that is created.

2. To confider, that God is nothing of all that, which the vnderstandings of men, and of Angells be able at all to comprehend. For they are finite, and limited, & God is not, in so much as God is neyther wise nor good in such sort, as men, or Angells are able to conceyue, but in an other manner infinitely more excellent. And this is that which the Scripture sayth, that Moyses entred into the mist, where God was, and that which S. Paul teacheth vs, saying: That God dwelleth in an inaccessible light, which no mortall man neyther hath, nor can see, much lesse comprehend his infinite greatnes. We must admire, & wonder at so soueraygne a Being.

3. To confider, that Gods being is in such sort infinite, as all his perfections, whereof the Scriptures make mention, be also infinite: neyther may any vnderstanding eyther conceyue, or imagine any end or bound of them, in so much as when we shall haue imagined whatsoeuer we can, our capacities come infinitly short of that, which they are in themselues, so ineffable and incomprehensible his Being is. For as the whole vniuerse cannot be comprised within the compasse of a pricke, euen so impossible it is for any created vnderstanding to enter into the diuine Essence, much lesse to penetrate it. And for this we must be glad, and withall admire it. To confider, hovv great a fauour God hath done vs, in

graun-

graunting vs to belieue these sacred mysteries, that exceede all vnderstanding. And this should be an inducement vnto vs to submit our owne vnderstanding, and to captiuate it to belieue that which exceedeth any capacity to comprehend, knowing that it is God himselfe, who hath reuealed it. And of this we must draw a firme hope, that we shall one day come to see these mysteries, which we now belieue, giuing the diuine Maiesty thankes for hauing discouered thē vnto vs by his Prophets, and in particular by his deere Sonne, our Lord Iesus Christ.

Meditat. IIII. *Of the Vnity, Essence, and Trinity of the diuine Persons.*

TO Consider, that God is an infinit & soueraigne good, wherein be contayned all sorts of goods and perfections, and is the supreme moderatour & gouernour of his creatures, to whome all thinges doe homage and yield obedience, and nothing can oppose against him to resist him: the only independent lawmaker, to whome it appertayneth to prescribe and appoint lawes to all creatures, and vpon this it followeth, that there can be but one sole God in one only Essence. For if there were more Gods then one, their lawes would contradict one another, &c. Out of this we must learne to referre all our affections to this only supreme and soueraigne Lord, without diuerting them towards the creatures. And this is the very firſt Article of our Fayth.

2.   To conſider, that though God be but one in Eſſence, yet he ſubſiſteth in three perſons. We muſt heere captiuate and enforce our vnderſtanding and iudgement to belieue this verity, though we cannot haue any other euidency of it. Theſe three Perſons be but one ſole Eſſece, and but one will, power, &c. And heerehence we muſt learne to admire and reuerence this ineffable myſtery, and reioyce at the moſt perfect vnity of theſe diuine perſons in one & the ſame eſſence, and endeauour to vnite our ſelues to God by a conformity of will, and with our Superiors, who hold the place of God on earth.

3.   To conſider, how the Father contemplating, and comprehending his owne Eſſence, formed within himſelfe a liuely repreſentation, & Image of himſelfe, which we call the Sonne of God, and ſo engendring his eternall Word, he loueth him, nature forcing him ſo to do, & he loueth him with an infinit loue, as doth the Sonne in like manner his Father. This loue common to both, is that, which we call the holy Ghoſt, who proceedeth from one & the other, & is one God with the Father, and the Sonne. And all this is in God frō all eternity : for all the three Perſons be coeternall one to the other, without precedence, or primacy of nature, of tvme, or dignity. Out of this we muſt draw affections & commotions of admiration, of prayſe, & of loue, for the wonderfull things of theſe three diuine Perſons.

Medi-

Meditat. V. *Of the infinite Perfection of God.*

TO Consider, that God is so perfect in him-selfe, as he comprehendeth within his Es-sence all the perfections, and excellencies of all creatures, by infinit degrees exceedeth them, and hath nothing of those imperfections, that be in them.

2. To consider, that all that which is in the world consisting of Bodyes, & without life, as the heauens, the Sunne, the Starrs, &c. be in a most eminent manner in God, and therefore he can do all that, which those his creatures can do, & infinitely more, for as much as all the good, that is in them, is but a shadow of that, which is most truly in him. We must be glad, that God doth by an eminëcy cöprehend all, that the crea-tures (which haue bodyes, & those which haue a vegetatiue life, such as haue grasse, hearbes, trees, plants, &c. or a sensitiue life, as haue the beasts, &c.) haue of perfection, or goodnes in thë. And though their diuersity & multitude be wonder-full, yet their goodnes & perfection is nothing in regard of that, which they are in God, and ther-fore by the consideration of them we must rayse our selues vp to contemplate the Creatour.

3. To consider, that in God be all the per-fections of all those creatures, that haue vnder-standing, as of Angells, & men, whome he hath created to his owne image & likenes, & therfore

when

when we caſt our eyes vpon the excellent inuē-
tions, arts, ſciences, & other the like things, we
muſt mount a degree higher to the infinite wiſdome of God, from whome all ſuch perfections
originally proceed. To conſider, how as the
goodnes of the tree is known by the goodnes of
the fruit, ſo the perfection of God is conceyued
by his workes, by which we may vnderſtand,
that his diuine maieſty is the infinit paterne of
all perfection, wherunto we ought to conforme
and faſhion our ſelues as neere as we can, and
recurre vnto him, that we may haue what we
want. Euen as the thinges, that be in any quality or kind imperfect, recurre to that, which is
perfect in the ſame kind, for the perfecting of
that which they want, as where heate is wanting, there is recourſe made to the fire to get it,
& this nature it ſelfe teacheth.

4.   To conſider, that all theſe perfections
diſtributed, and ſeuerally deuided in euery creature, though they be otherwiſe not to be numbred; and in a manner infinite, be, for all that,
but one, and moſt ſimple perfection in God, euen
as many hūdreds of pence are contayned in one
peece of gold. We muſt learne by this ſo to doe
all our works, as they may alwayes goe accompanyed with a pure & perfect intention to pleaſe
God alone: for in it be comprehended many o-
ther vertues beſides.

Medit.

Meditat . VI . Of Gods soueraygne Goodnes, and Holynes.

TO Consider, how God is infinitly good, and in the compasse of his Essence comprehendeth all the degrees of goodnes, that are to be found in creatures, hauing this goodnes of himselfe, and not by participation from any other, and infinitly exceeding that of all creatures, that now are, or may be . Of this we must learne humility towards God, so common to holy persons, who abase & contemne themselues in presence of him, by considering that their owne goodnes and holynes is no more, then accidentall, by participation, communicated, nothing alike to our nature, and subiect to change, and is indeed nothing at all, compared with that of God .

2. To consider, that the diuinity comprehendeth all the vertues of Angells, and of men, in such sort, as he is infinitely wise, prudent, iust, &c. That his vertues be the modell and paterne of those, that the Saints haue, or can haue, for that theirs be more or lesse perfect, accordingly as they come more or lesse neere vnto those of God . We must heere excite our selues to the prayses of the diuine maiesty, and desire, that all creatures may blesse him, because he is the God of vertues, and make a generous and noble resolution not to content our selues with the getting of common vertues, but still to rayse our

selues

selues vp to the more perfect, and to profit in them more & more in imitation of God, who is perfection it selfe.

3.   To consider Gods infinite purity, and holynes in all his workes, which be so pure, as they admit not the admixtion of any thing, that is not most perfect: He also cannot possibly sinne of his own nature, nor can properly be the cause of sinnes, because that is contrary to his soueraygne purity. Of this we must draw our instruction, and learne to make a greater reckoning of vertue in this world, then of honour, riches &c. For that is it, which God regardeth most, whē he sayth: Be vee holy, as I am holy: and therefore we must liue with the greatest purity, we possibly can.

Meditat. V I I.   *Of the great inclination God hath to communicate himselfe to men.*

T O cōsider, that God by his soueraygne goodnes is most inclined to communicate his being, as he is the soueraygne good, & that his naturall liberality maketh him to communicate himselfe, not for any need he hath of his creatures, but for the inclination & propension he hath, which cānot be idle; for as much as he communicateth himselfe in all manners possible.

v.   To consider, how in communicating himselfe to creatures, he hath giuen himselfe to some their corporal Being, with diuersity of properties,

pertyes, & perfections, as we see in the heauens, in the elements, in mixt creatures &c. to others a life vegetatiue, as to the plants, trees, &c. to some a life sensitiue, as to beasts &c. to others an intellectuall Being, as to the Angells. And all these foure differences of being doe concurre in man, who is composed of body and soule. And for this we must yield God thankes, and excite our loue towards him for hauing communicated such wonderfull thinges to creatures.

3. To consider, that God hath found an other more wonderfull way of communicating himselfe, which is by a certayne supernaturall quality, which we call grace, by which the Angells and men come to be his children & friends, by meanes of his charity, imparted vnto them, togeather with the other supernaturall vertues. How his goodnes hath yet found another more perfect manner then it, and that is the Being of glory, that maketh the iust like vnto God. Moreouer the personall, and hypostaticall Being of the eternall Word, vnited with the nature humane, is another inuention of his ineffable loue for the communicating of himselfe to men. And to this we may adde another miraculous vnion, which is made in the most Blessed Sacrament of the Altar, a most great testimony of his infinite liberality, and charity. To consider, how particularly liberall the goodnes of God hath shewed it selfe towardes men, in communicating vnto them only, and not to Angells, the two last and most excellent manners of vnion, giuing thereby to vnderstand, that it is his

singular

fingular pleafure to conuerfe and keep company with the children of men . To thinke , how
by communicating himfelfe fo to man , he hath
in him honoured all other creatures , for as much
as in him be comprifed all their perfection , and
that man is the compendium as it were , and abbridgement of all the world .

*Meditat . V I I I .   How amiable the Di-
uine Goodnes is .*

TO confider , that as the goodnes of God is
infinite , fo ought it alfo to be infinitly loued, and fo he can but only loue himfelfe ,
becaufe no creature , nor all of them togeather
can poffibly loue his goodnes , as it meriteth :
And therefore we muft take a pleafure and enforce our felues to loue God aboue all thinges ,
& that for himfelfe . For that muft be the chiefe
motiue of our loue , togeather with his confideration , how abhominable finne is , as the finner
alfo , who by his offenfes eftraungeth himfelfe
from the loue of God , who in regard of his infinite goodnes deferueth infinite loue . We muft
defire , that all the creatures may loue our Good
God , who is fo worthy both of all loue , and of
honour .

   2 .   To confider , that this fupreme goodnes
is infinitly amiable for the propenfion it hath to
doe vs good , as thofe endlefs fauours , and benefitts in behalfe of our Redemption beare re-
cord : And therfore we remayne bound to a fu-
                                        preme

preme gratitude and loue. For we are to thinke,
that God sayth to euery one in particular : Take
and render. And if we be so much bound vnto
him for the goods of nature , what shall we say
of those , that transcend it , and be supernaturall? To consider , how he is amiable also in a
supreme degree , because he comprehendeth in
his Essence , all sorts of good , that may profit ,
without admixtion of any imperfection , for as
much as in God consisteth the accomplishment
of all our desirs, & this ought to incite vs to loue
him the more.

3. To consider , that he is to be loued in a
supreme manner for this , that he contayneth in
himself all good, that is delectable, & that causeth
a tranquility , quiet , & peace of minde in him
who possesseth it , and therefore God is amiable
for the infinite ioy , and contentment , he hath
in himselfe, and in production of all his creaturs,
and because he is the cause , and beginning of all
delectable good, that is to be foud in this world,
and principally for the pleasure, he hath to haue
his conuersation with the children of men. To
consider, that seeing all things delectable are foud
in God in a supreme degree of perfection, we
must serue him with serious affection,& alacrity
of mind,& seeke no pleasure any where , but in
him alone.

**Meditat. IX.   *Of Gods infinite Chari-*
ty, *and Loue.***

TO consider, that God loueth himselfe infinitly, by occasion of the infinite goodnes,
that is found in his Essence, wherein he
pleaseth himselfe, as in his own, & proper good,
and this loue is in him most holy, and most perfect withall. For in the three diuine Persons
there is found an equality one with another, an
vnion of wills, a communication of all thinges,
and a most inward conuersation, accompanyed
with a supreme ioy and contentment. We must
be glad, that God so loueth himselfe, & as much
as he is able, and he deserueth to be loued; and
that this loue is cause of that, which he beareth to
his creatures.

2.   To consider Gods surpassing loue to
his creatures, in louing them, and doing them
good: for to doe good vnto them, is to loue
them. To consider, that God loueth without any comparison man, more then all other
creatures of the world, because he is created to
his Image and likenes, which naturally causeth
loue. Moreouer he hath created him for himself,
as being his last end, and the rest of the creaturs
for his help to attaine vnto it. And this ought
to be vnto vs a singular motiue to loue God, &
serue him, and to meruayle, that his maiesty hath
vouchsafed so highly to honour vs: & we must
say with the Prophet Dauid, psalme 8. What is
man

man, O Lord, that thou art mindfull of him, or the Sonne of man , that thou visitest him ?

3. To consider, that Gods loue is most noble , because it comprehendeth all creatures, and for this we should not hate any, but loue all for the loue of him , enuring our harts continually to this loue , and not hating any thing besides sinne alone, because God detesteth it aboue all things.

4. To consider the great charity , that God beareth to man , with whome he pleased to contract a true, and since amity, making him in a manner his equal, raising him vp to a most excellent being aboue his owne nature , and remunerating him with the most precious gifts of his grace, by which he is made his adoptiue child, & an inheriter of his glory. And this ought to giue vs iust cause of great admiration, by considering so surpassing a goodnes , that supplyeth the defect of man , to proportion him in some sort to this amity. And of this there ariseth a second property of true friendship , which is to wish to the friend the being, life , and all the good , that may be giuen him : and this God also doth by a singular liberality towards man, vnto whome he communicateth life, grace, and glory, togeather with innumerable goods, that proceed of them. True friendship also causeth vnion , and therefore a friend is sayd to be another selfe , & this condition hath been meruayously obserued of God towardes man , in making him one spirit with himselfe by the meanes of loue, and in cherishing him, as the ball of his eye, because his de-

light

light is to be with the children of men. And therfore we muſt heere ſtir vp in our ſoules affⱥⱦions and commotions of loue, and of admiration, and put our ſelues forwards to loue him, who hath ſo tenderly loued-vs.

Meditat. X. *Of foure, ſingular Excellencyes of Gods infinite Charity towards men.*

TO conſider, that the firſt excellecy of Gods charity towardes men, which is Eternity, is as ancient(if I may ſo ſay)as is God himſelfe. For God hath loued him from all eternity, and had a will euen then to beſtow thoſe goods vpon him, which he did afterwardes communicate vnto him, by which it appeareth, that the loue of God precedeth ours: and as this loue had not any beginning, ſo neyther ſhall it haue any end, & no creature ſhall euer be able to diſſolue or breake it. And though ſinne cauſeth a breach therof, yet our Lord God ſtill abideth the ſame, firme and ſtable in his loue, and deſireth continually, that man returne into amity with him, and giueth him without ceaſe the meanes for the effecting of it. Of this we are to learne, how hartly we ought to loue ſuch a Lord, who hath loued vs from eternity, and to endeauour, that no creature may euer diuert vs from this loue of God.

2.   The ſecond Excellency of Gods loue is, that it is vniuerſall, and comprehendeth all, in as much as is in it ſelfe, and excludeth none, of

what

what condition so euer they be, desirous for his part, that all be saued. For he is as the Sonne of Iustice, that riseth, and giueth light vpon the good and the bad, imparting his benedictions to all the word. And though God loueth all men in generall, yet we must not therefore say, that his loue is deuided into so many obiects, or that for it, it looseth the force: for it extendeth it selfe to euery one, and in particular to the elect, as if there were but one alone: in so much as the great number neyther diuerteth it, nor maketh it lesse, nor hindreth it in any sort. And this ought to be a vehement inducement, & motiue vnto vs, most affectuously to loue God.

3. The third Excellency of Gods charity towardes men is the greatnesse of the benefits which he communicateth: for so great they be, as they cannot be more, because they rayse vs vp to the supreme dignity of Gods children, & inheritours of his Kingdome. And this Excellency yet appeareth the more in the vnion hypostaticall of the diuinity, in which a man of our owne nature is raysed vp to the most high dignity of the Sonne of God, not adoptiue, as we be, but naturall. It manifesteth it selfe also exceedingly in the holy Eucharist, wherein God giueth himselfe vnto vs, the more cordially to vnite vs vnto himselfe, as it doth also in this, that he giueth vs the holy Ghost, the eternall fountaine of loue.

4. The fourth Excellency is the profoundnes & depth of this charity of God, which is discouered in the profound humiliations, that God

pleased to vndergoe for the loue of man, in annihilating himselfe for the raising of him vp, and in suffering and dying for sauing of him. It appeared further in this, that his diuine maiesty couerted all those his tribulations, and paynes to the good and profit of man.

Meditat. XI.   Of the desire, that God hath to be beloued of men.

TO Consider, that God, desirous to purchase the loue of man, gaue him a commaundement of loue, saying: That he shold loue him withall his hart, withall his soule, strength and vertue: that is, in as perfect a manner as possibly may be, without any limitation at all of our loue towards him, as he neither limiteth his owne towards vs. To consider, that this commaundement is the first, and foundation of all the rest, as also of spirituall life. It is the first in dignity, because it commaudeth the supreme and highest act of vertue, the first in merit, the first in sweetnes, in mildnes, in efficacy, for that it is cause of the obseruing of all the other commaundements. Of this we must learne to make a great esteeme of this precept, so much recommēded vnto vs by our Sauiour, so excellent in it selfe, & so profitable for vs.

2.   To consider, that God, who giueth this precept, giueth also ability & meanes to accomplish it, by infusing into our harts charity, wherwith we ought to loue him, & by sending vnto

vs

vs his holy inspirations, & which is more, the fountayne it selfe of charity, that is to say, the holy Ghost, the lyuing, & viuificating loue. We must acknowledge this benefit with all our hart.

3. To consider, that God deserueth to be loued for the loue of himselfe, thogh there shold not be any precept that bound vs so to doe: and that ouer and aboue all this, he promiseth vnto them who shall loue him, most great priuiledges both temporall and eternall, as glory that is giuen in heauen, answerable to the measure of the charity and loue a man had heere before on earth. That he bindeth vs euery day, and from tyme to tyme by celestiall gifts and fauours, and by innumerable benefitts, by meanes wherof he seeketh to draw vs vnto him with the ropes of Adam, incessantly by new graces and fauours en-kindling the fire of his loue in our harts. And to excite vs to loue him in earnest, he is not conten-ted to promise vs a recompense, but he further addeth most seuere threates, as to depriue vs of life euerlasting, & to send vs thither, where we shall be punished for euer, if we shall faile to loue him. Whereby he giueth to vnderstand, how much he desireth to be loued of vs, for our owne good alone, & not for any particular profit of his owne.

Meditat. XII.   *Of Gods infinite Mercy.*

TO consider, that this Perfection sheweth it
selfe wonderfully in God, as is to be seene
by the effects, and therefore Dauid sayth:
That the earth is ful of Gods mercy. For before
God punisheth, he vseth mercy, yea he inter-
medleth the one with the other. And this moued the same Prophet to say elswhere: The mer-
cyes of God be aboue all his works.

2.   To consider, that this mercy is infinit,
because it is founded vpon omnipotency, as is to
be seene, if we reflect our eye of consideration v-
pon all the creatures, wherin his Infinity exce-
dingly discouereth it selfe. The holy Scriptures
confirme as much, for that there is scarce a line
to be found therein, that maketh not mention of
this diuine attribute.

3.   To consider, how it appeareth also greatly in this, that it extendeth it selfe towardes all
sinners, be they neuer so abhominable and wicked, in giuing them helps to rise vp from out of
their iniquities, and in patiently expecting them
to pennance. For it is written: Thou takest pitty, o Lord, on all: and thou hatest none of those
thinges thou hast made.

4.   To consider, how when Dauid often
tymes craued pardon of God for his sinnes, he
represented vnto him nothing, but his great mercy, as is to be seene in the 50. Psalme, and is to
be gathered by the parable of the prodigal child,
& of other passages of holy writ. How this mer-

ey also appeared in the iust, in whose behalfe
there is no end of it. For it preuenteth them, it
rayseth them vp agayne, it accompanyeth them,
and euer followeth them, till their death, after
which it exalteth them to the most excellent
goods, that be in God, that is, to his glory, and
in this vvorld he fauoureth them with his particular grace, and protection. What hath beene
sayd, ought to mooue vs most cordially to loue
so compassionate, and mercyfull a Lord.

5. To consider the demonstrations, and
testimonyes, that God hath giuen vs of his infinite mercy, as to become man, that he might
sorrovv for our miseryes: to lament and be-
vvayle them, as if they had been his ovvne:
yea to take them vpon himselfe, and to suffer
for them euen vnto death, in so much as by that
experience he learned of himselfe to take compassion on vs, after a new and miraculous manner, and such as was neuer heard of before. The
same mercy yet passed on further in the Sacrament of the Altar, wherein he became meate &
drinke for the infirme, and sicke, &c. Wherehence vve are to learne to be mercyfull tovvardes the poore, and to hold it an honour
to condescend to the infirmityes of our neighbours.

Eff 4   *Medit.*

Meditat. XIII.   *Of Gods infinite Liberality towardes man.*

TO consider, that this liberality of God cósisteth in giuing and bestowing innumerable benefits vpon his creatures, without any obligation of his part so to doe, and without hope of any retribution, or requitall from them. And his infinite liberality discouereth it selfe towards men, particularly in this, that without any exception or obligation at all, he giueth them the gifts of nature, & of grace, & without expectation of any recompéce from them, whils he only followeth his owne naturall inclination to giue. That if he demaund any thing of vs, he doth it that he may thereby haue an occasion to giue vnto vs the more abundantly, & to reward our seruices. And therfore we must on our part be agayne liberall to God, and offer both body and soule to serue him, and our neighbour, in ayding him, & doing him good, sith God hath been so liberall towards vs.

2. To consider, how liberally God requiteth the Liberality that we vse in his seruice, whiles he at the very first ouerheareth his prayers who sheweth himselfe liberall for the loue of him: whiles he inspireth, and incessantly sollicireth him to aske of him, what he hath a desire to giue him, yea & giueth him oft tymes though he aske not, because he hath a regard of this necessity. He sendeth him spirituall consolations

in

im ftore, he beftoweth excellent gifts vpon him s
he imparteth vnto him great prouifion of his
graces, and receyueth him into his protection s
and particular prouidence. And this Religious
mé experiéce more then others, who haue fhewed themfelues liberall towards God, whiles they
renounced themfelues, & forfooke all that they
had, for the loue of God.

3. We muft heere confound our felues,
by confidering, how niggardly and fparing we
haue been towards God, whiles by that meanes
we hindred his liberality, and ftopped the iffue
of it, as much as lay in vs, for that we haue ferued him coldly, and haue not anfwered the very leaft part of our ability to ferue him, but haue
done all our affayres on his behalfe imperfectly,
and diftractedly, &c. And therefore if we defire to enioy, when tyme cometh, the recompéfe,
promifed to the liberall, we muft now for the
prefent begin to be liberall, and fo to continue.

Meditat. XIIII.   *Of Gods Immenfity, and
of his prefence in all places, and in all thinges.*

TO confider, that God is fo immenfe and
great, as he filleth all his creatures with his
his infinite Greatnes, and is more inwardly prefent in all thinges, then they be
in their owne Eßence. And notvvithftan-
ding all this, he is not imprifoned heere in the
world: and though there were many milions of
worlds more, yet fhould he be ftill infinitly greater

ter then they, in so much as it is impossible to fly from him, sith he is by his essence, presence, and power in all places, and all creatures be filled with his greatnes. This consideration should make vs more present to our selues in all our actions, both priuate, and publike, by representing to our selues, that Gods eyes be vpon vs; & making vnto our selues an Oratory in all places, sith he is euery where. We must excite in our selues affections of ioy, and of admiration, at so wonderfull a greatnes.

2. We must consider our selues, as liuing, and doing our actions in God, who enuironeth vs round, as doth the water of the Ocean compasse in the fish that swym and liue therin. And this consideration should keep vs from going & wandring out of our selues, seeing we haue God present within vs, as though we were his house, or by considering our selues enuironed without, and penetrated within by God, as though he were our owne, & belonging vnto vs.

3. To consider, how God sheweth himselfe in heauen to his Elect with reuealed and open face, working in them most glorious things, and he giueth in some places on earth particular signes of his presence, as Iacob saw him on that mysticall ladder whereof the Scriptures make mention. God also hath his aboad particularly in the Churches, and Oratories, and in a more excellent manner in the iust, with whome he abideth by his grace, and worketh strange and wonderfull thinges in them. But aboue all he is with some great friends of his in this life, producing

ducing spiritually within them miraculous effects, as illustrations, discourses of the soule, re-
uelations of diuine mysteries, which be all signes
and testimonyes of his particular presence. All
this ought to make vs the more attentiue, and
present to God, & our selues, & to coposed both
within, and without.

*Meditat. XV.   Of Gods infinite Wisdome,
and Knowledge.*

TO Consider, how God by his infinite Wisdome, & knowledge comprehendeth himselfe, and filleth the infinite capacity of his
vnderstanding with the contemplation of his
owne Essence, togeather with a supreme ioy and
contentment therein, in such sort, as he neyther
desireth, nor can desire to know any thing, that
he knoweth not most perfectly. He hath this
knowledge of himselfe without receyuing it frō
any other and therefore he is alone essentially
wise & intelligent, with an illimited knowledge:
who comprehendeth all, that hath been, is, and
shall be, and all that which is possible to be,
and which therefore shall neuer be. We must
admire so wonderfull a knowledge.

2.   To consider, how by this knowledge
God inuented whatsoeuer is in nature For from
it proceed all acts, sciences, & inuentions, the fa-
shion, and framing of heauen, and of earth, the
visible world, the creation of man, the communication of the being of Grace, and the manner
of

of ioyning the diuine and humane nature togeather in one person: finally if we should runne o-
uer all the works of nature and of grace, we shall
find, that the infinite wisdome of God doth euery where wonderfully discouer it selfe. To consider, how God disposed, and ordered all things
of the world, with order, weight, and measure,
with a wonderfull composition in all. He knoweth the number of all the starrs of heauen, of the
graynes of sand, & drops of water, that are, haue
been, or shall be in the sea: he knoweth the number of the leaues of the trees, and of the grasse of
the earth: the number of men, and of Angells:
he numbreth the hayres of our head: he mea-
sureth the earth, the elements, and all creatures
with three fingars: and to say in one word, he
penetrateth all, and graspeth both ends of the
world in his hand.

3. To consider, how the infinite Wisdome of God is eternall, immutable, most profound, and most cleare, seeing with the only
glympse of an eye, all that eternity comprehendeth, & all that, which may be seene and known
without forgetting any thing of that he knoweth, in so much as he hath alwayes a remembrance of euery one of vs, and hath vs still preset
in his diuine memory. He also knoweth all, that
he now createth or doth in the world: at one &
the same instant he penetrateth all the secrets of
the harts of euery man liuing, how secret soeuer
they be. He knoweth all, that is to happen for all
eternity, and all that, which dependeth of the
liberty of the created will, togeather with all
thinges

things possible, though peraduenture they shall neuer be. We must reioyce & be glad, that God is so infinite in his knowledge, and that he comprehendeth all thinges, and that nothing can be hidden from his sight, drawing heerhence a great motiue of loue and esteeme of Gods wisdome, & a great feare to see, that we cannot fly from him, & that nothing whatsoeuer we do, can be cōcealed from him.

Meditat. XVI. Of Gods Omnipotency.

TO consider, the Omnipotency of God, that it consisteth in this, that it is of power to doe whatsoeuer his infinit Wisdome seeth possible, where there is not any contradiction of being, in so much as it can make infinitly more thinges then it hath made, & can chaunge & alter those that are made, & doe, & vndoe them agayne at his pleasure. Finally God is able to do all that he pleaseth, els his Essence should be defectiue.

2. To consider, how this Omnipotency cannot be communicated with any creature, and so God alone is able to do by himself that, which all creatures are able to doe seuerally : but they cannot do any thing without his assistance, because their power & vertue hath the dependance of his operation of omnipotency, that communicateth vnto euery creature an ability conforme to their nature.

3. To consider, hovv the Omnipotency of God is alwaies busied and imployed in doing vs

good,

good, becaufe togeather with Wifdome, and goodnes it is the fountaine & fource, from which be deriued & iffue all the benefits, which we receyue dayly from Gods liberality.

Meditat. **XVII.** *Of the Omnipotency of God in the worlds Creation, and of the greatnes of this benefit.*

SVPPOSING what fayth teacheth vs touching the creation of heauen and earth, togeather withall the vifible creatures, we are to meditate, how all thinges haue had a beginning of their being, not hauing been before, but as it were ingulfed in their owne nothing. How God created thē out of his own liberality of nothing without any need of them, nor had any other modell or patterne for the making of them befides himfelfe, who is their firft caufe, & their laft end. And heerin God difcouereth his infinite wifdome, & incomprehenfible goodnes. We muft confider our felues fhut vp within this endles gulfe of nothing, for the abating, & confounding of our vanity.

2.   To confider, that when God made this wonderfull worke of the vniuerfe, he needed not any preexiftent, or precedent, or preiacent matter, as the Deuines call it, after the manner of Angells, and men, who cannot produce their actions without matter: how he had not any other help therin befides himfelfe, to the end man, for whome he created all thinges, might contynue
                                                        the

the more gratefull , as being therefore the
more bound vnto him . For in behalfe of him
he pleased to take this payne, as it were, in building him the world for his house , before he
had yet any being, with most abundant prouision of all thinges for his vse . This wonderfull
effect was produced by his word alone, wherunto all creatures were most prompt to obey. And
though he might & could haue made all immediatly of nothing , yet he pleased to draw one
from out of an other , as the fishes & fowles out
of the water, the beasts & plants out of the earth,
to shew that he hath full power ouer his creatures, & can doe with them, what himselfe best
pleaseth .

3. To consider , that though it was in his
omnipotent power to create the vniuerse in an
instant , yet it was his will to dispose & frame it
in six dayes, to giue vs the better to vnderstand
the proceedings of his wisdome, and the necessity of the things he created, in causing to be seene
the first day what was to be created the second ,
that we might côceyue by this worke the means
and wayes he obserueth in our sanctification, towards which he proceedeth by degres, disposing
& directing vs so in this life , that in the other
life we may haue and enioy the Saboth of the e-
ternall rest , Of what hath been before sayd we
may learne a motiue to prayse, in what we may ,
the infinite ompotency of God , and withall our
hart to loue his ineffable goodnes .

Meditat. X V I I I. *Of that , which God created in the firſt inſtant , or beginning of tyme .*

T O Conſider, that the firſt creature, that was made, was the heauen Empyreall , bright ſhining as the fire , that, as a Court of that euerlaſting Kingdome , it might comprehend vvithin it ſelfe all the machine and frame of this viſible world . God alſo created the Angells , almoſt infinite for number, and deuided them into three Hierarchyes , to whome he gaue in one and the ſame inſtant , all perfeƈtions of nature , and of grace , conuenient for euery one . To conſider the pleaſure & contentment, the Angells had to ſee themſelues then newly created, and how the good ones rendred humble thankes to their ſoueraigne Creatour & Lord .

2 . To conſider, how God created the earth in an inſtant , and placed it in the Center and middeſt of the concauity of heauen , where it continueth hanging without any ſtay to ſupport it, notwithſtanding the mayne greatnes, & without moouing one way or other . And this ſhould ſerue vs for a motiue of confidence for putting our whole truſt in ſuch a Lord , whoſe armes be ſo ſtrong, as they ſuſtayne without being wearyed, ſo heauy a weight as it is, whils we may be aſſured, that he is of power to deliuer vs from all aduerſity . To conſider , how the earth

was

was in that instant voyd, and empty, and without light, & most imperfect: wherein is represented vnto vs the state of man, conceiued in sin,
filled with obscurity, and darkenes. To consider, that if the earth had, had vnderstanding for
the knowing of what it wanted, and wherein it
was defectiue, it would no doubt in that instant
haue cryed out to the Creatour, and haue besought him to giue it light, & to set it forthwith
trees, grasse, and fruits. And this must we doe,
vpon whom God hath bestowed reason.

3.   To consider, how the holy Spirit vvas
carryed vpon the waters, and impressed in them
an effect and vertue for the producing of those
things, that might afterwards serue for the ornament and beautifying of the Vniuerse. And of
this we must learne to know, how proper it is to
the holy Ghost to succour & help the poore &
needy. Moreouer, the vertue that he afterwards
communicated to the water, to wash away mens
sinns, & to serue for an instrumēt of Gods grace,
was at that time, & afterwards represented in figure: The very same is wroght by the holy Ghost
in the soules of iust men, who causeth them by
his heate & protection to produce & bring forth
the fruits of vertue & holynes. To consider, that
the three Persons diuine concurred to the worke
of the creation, because it depended on the omnipotency, wisdome, & goodnes of God.

Meditat. X I X . *Of the thinges , that God made the first Day .*

TO Consider, how God first made the light, for he sayd : Let the light be made : And it was made, euen as when we light some torch in a darke house . To consider , how miserable the world should haue byn without corporall light, and what good this beautifull creature bringeth vs : for by it we behold the Creatours workes, we goe , and walke to and fro , we trauayle and take paynes, and we doe all thinges : besides that , it greatly comforteth vs, & reioyceth vs , and communicateth vnto vs healthfull influences . In acknowledgement of which benefit we must prayse God, and yield him thanks, & ascend from this corporall light to the contemplation of the spirituall, examining the euills, that the priuation & want of it causeth vnto vs , that we may in a most harty manner both desire & seeke it , if it be our hard hap to be depriued of it .

2 . To consider , how God made the light the first day , because there could not be day without light : Euen so the spirituall bright shining light is the first perfection, that God putteth in our souls : for without it, impossible it is to do any thing spiritually : & all this day God made nothing but the light, holding it inough to haue driuen away darkenes; manifesting thereby the esteeme he made of light, which seemed vnto him

him beautyfull and good ; teaching vs thereby , how great a reckoning we ought to make of the spirituall light , and how carefully we should keep it, when we haue it , & seeke for it agayne, when we shall haue lost it.

3 . To consider , how God deuided , and separated the light from darkenes, causing ther- by night & day, that the one might serue for rest, & the other for labour & trauaile : For this pre- sent life is intermixt with pleasure and payne, with tentations and consolations , and with a vi- cissitude , and interchange of one and the other. And this ought to comfort vs in our afflictions , being perswaded and assured, that peace will fol- low warre, as the day cometh after the night .

Meditat . X X.   Of the thinges , that God made the second Day .

TO consider , how on the second day God made the firmament , which comprehen- deth all the earth, and the water to the first heauen, that is to say , all the ayre , and the fire . Out of this we must draw a motiue to prayse God , and to yield him thankes. For we breath , liue , enioy light, & all pleasure by meanes of this element of the ayre , which is called the fir- mament, not for that it is most easily moued , as we see, but because it is firme, stable, permanent in doing the offices , for which God hath crea- ted it.

2 . To consider, how God separated the
waters ,

waters, that were aboue the firmament frō those, that were vnder it. For of the grosse and heauy waters, that couered the face of the earth, he chose the subtile and light, and put them in the middle region of the ayre, & turned them into clowdes, for the watering and fruƺifying of the drye earth, when need should be. And this worke of mercy is so great, as God would haue himselfe named, as witnesseth the Prophet Iob, the Father of Rayne, which being by a singular & diuine prouidence suspended, & stayed in the ayre aboue, falleth not downe all at once or together, but by little drops, for the movstning & fruƺifying of the earth. Moreouer the clouds serue for a pauilion, tent, & curtayne for the tempering of the Sunne: & in all this we must obserue the omnipotency, and paternall Prouidence of God, & apply all to our spirituall profit.

3. To consider, that God calleth the Aire Firmament, in regard of the resemblance it hath with the heauen, from which it receyueth its light, and the other impressions that it communicateth vnto it: a figure accommodated to the propertyes of the soule, wherof God is as it were the heauen, for as much as it receyueth of him the light, & other diuine qualities. The grosse & heauy waters are seuered from the subtile, and light, that is to say, there is a separation between the terrestriall affections, & the celestiall, which are wont to fatten the dry earth, & to conuert the terrene, & grosse body into a spirituall one.

Medit.

Meditat. X X I. *Of the thinges, that God made the third Day*.

TO Confider, how God commaunded the waters that were fpread ouer all the face of the earth, to gather togeather into a certavne piace, which they did in an inftant, though they were fo huge and great, as the mayne Ocean, & other feas be compofed thereof. And in this Gods omnipotency greatly appeareth, as alfo the waters precife obedience whiles it left the naturall place, and withdrew it felfe into that, which the Creatour appointed it for the common good of the vniuerfe, wherin in fuch fort it containeth it felfe, as it neuer paffeth the bounds within which it hath been limited by God. Out of this we muft draw affections & commotions of admiration, and of feare. For God would be feared for this his meruaylous worke, as he faith himfelfe exprefly by the mouth of his Prophet Ieremy in thefe wordes : Doe yee not feare me, who haue giuen the fands for a boûd to the fea, by a commaundment for euer?

2. To confider, that this day God made the earth, which was round, & made in the middeft of it great concauities & deep places for the receyuing of the waters, rayfing in circuite about it, high & great mountaynes, & hills, &c. And the fame tyme the earth became drye, watered, notwithftanding with many fweet fountaynes, out of which their iffue continuall running

ning streames of water in great quantity, which empty themselues into the salt sea, whence they haue their first beginning, though sweet and gustable in themselues; and this by the prouidence of the Creatour, who hath made all for man, the chiefest worke of the Vniuerse. To consider, that God disposed the earth in such sort, as one part of it was fit for the bearing of plants and trees, another for the yielding of gold, siluer & other mettalls, &c. And for this we must giue thankes to God for his paternall prouidence.

3. To consider, that the same day God beautifyed the earth, & garnished it with a rich and most beseeming variety of trees & plants, causing it in a moment to put forth grasse, herbes fruites, and flowers in their maturity, and conuenient greatnes and perfection, and this with great facility, deuiding the whole into many parts of the world, and giuing them vertue and effect to bring forth seede euery one according to its kind, to the end that his workes might by that meanes be perpetuated, and continue. To consider Gods paternall loue to man, in creating so great a diuersity of obiects for the recreating of his senses, and for the prouiding of him so great variety of medicinall herbes for the curing of his infirmities. All this should excite vs to loue, & prayse God.

4. To consider, how God the same day, out of his singular prouidence, planted the most excellent garden, which we call the terrestriali Paradise, for the habitation of man, the

most

most temperate place of all the world, as well for the sweetnes, salubrity, and healthfulnes of ayre, as for the fecundity and fertility of the ground. It was garnished, and set forth with fruit-trees, disposed and set in a wonderfull order, fayre to the sight, and delectable to the tast. In the middest was the tree of life, the wonderfull fruit whereof preserued from sicknes, old age, and corruption, and prolonged the life as long as it pleased God. There was therein a fountayne of sweet and soueraygne water, that deuided it selfe into foure riuers for the watering of the whole face of the earth. It extended it selfe so far and wide, as it was capable to contayne many thousands of men within it. Heere we are to admire the loue of God towards man, for whome he built so goodly an house, furnished with all both necessary, and delectable thinges, before he was made himselfe. And therfore euery one of vs in particular hath most iust cause to giue the diuine goodnes thankes for the goods, that he hath prepared for vs in the terrestriall Paradise, with so great an affection, as if we possessed them, seeing there was no fault in God, that we did not enioy them.

Meditat. XXII. *Of the thinges, that God made the fourth Day.*

TO consider, how God on the fourth day made the Sunne, the Moone, & the Stars. The Sunne as a second beginning of light, alwayes

alwayes continuing the same without any diminution at all, euer carrying the same light, giuing both heate, and fertility to the earth, then which it is an hundred tymes bigger. It giueth heate, life, and increase to plants, & to all liuing things in this world beneath, and by its owne ordered, and constant motion causeth the diuersity of seasons, dayes, & yeares. We must heere wonder at Gods infinite power, that hath produced so beautyfull a creature : a representation of his diuinity, that greatly appeareth in the vvonderfull properties of this fayre Planet, vvhich vve are to imitate, in yielding him immortall thanks for this so great a benefit, bestowed vpon vs.

2. To consider, how it vvas not a little fauour to giue vs the moone, that is a vvonderfull creature, & receyueth the light of the Sunne, that it might communicate the same vnto the earth in time of the nights darknes, & in its own composed motion, with a certaine harmonious course, follow that, as a glympse & small beame of the beauty whereof it receyueth, on the part that looketh towardes it, causing heere on earth wonderfull effects in all thinges that haue life, or receyue mouing by the cold influence it hath, and by the motions distinguishing and deuiding the moneths of the yeare. We must conuert all this to our spirituall profit, and imitate the effects of this noble Planet, that it may be sayd of our soule, That it is fayre, as the Moone.

3. To consider, how God hath created an infinite number of stars, which he alone is able to count, and reckon vp by their proper
names

names. He hath made them fixed and ſtable in
the firmament, and diſpoſed them in a wonderfull order, in which they giue light to the night
vpon earth, ſerue for guides, and directions on
the ſea, beautify the heauens with their preſence, and worke wonderfull influences heere
beneath. Of all this we muſt take matter, & occaſion of extolling Gods omnipotency, & imitate the properties mentioned, in what we are
able, and ſtir vp our ſelues to our hart, ſith for
loue of vs he hath created ſo many, ſo wonderfull creatures, that may by their conſideration
conduct and lead vs to the knowledge of him.

4. To conſider, how God created the element of fire, which by night ſupplyeth the abſence of Sunne, and the Moone, and giueth light,
and heate without diminution at all. It ſerueth
vs for an inſtrument vniuerſall for all vſes, for
the ſeething, roaſting, and ſeaſoning of our
meates, for the purifying, working, and accommodating of mettalles, for the melting, and ſoft-
ning of thinges that be hard. For this we muſt
render thankes vnto our Creatour, who hath
giuen vs creatures, ſo profitable for the life of
man.

Meditat. XXIII.   *Of the thinges, that God*
    did the fifth Day.

TO conſider, how the fifth day God created
in the element of water great ſtore of fiſhs
of diuers kindes, formes, and propertyes,
    H h h   ſome

some lesser, some greater thē those liuing things of the earth, and prouided all, of that which was necessary for the conseruation of euery one, giuing them vertue to engender their like, and that in most great abundance. And though their number be so great, as it is, yet they want nothing, that maketh for the conseruation of their life in the sea, and in the ryuers, that prouide them of nouriture sufficient to serue their turne. To consider, that this so abundant multiplication of fish receyueth the efficacy from Gods benediction, for vvhich vve must yield him thanks, who hath shewed himselfe so prouident towardes man, in creating such a quantity and variety of fishes for his intertaynment, & in giuing him the meanes, commodity, & industry to take them.

2.   To consider, how out of the same element of water, God hath produced great store and variety of fowles to liue in the ayre, & gaue them his benediction to multiply, and conserue their kindes. We must thinke vpon the greatnes of this benefit for hauing created them, some for our recreation & pleasure, some for our setting forth & brauery, some to delight vs with their melodious & sweet singing, some with their fayre & fyne feathers, good to intertayne & content vs by their diuers & different vses & properties, to teach vs many thinges, that we know not, & to giue vs our pleasure with their own payne & labour, as do the Bees, &c.

Meditat.

Meditat. **XXIIII**. *Of Gods workes of the sixt Day.*

TO consider the multitude and wonderfull diuersity of beastes, different in nature, forme, and properties, euery one with the owne naturall inclination, prouided of armes defensiue and offensiue, some for the nouriture of man, some for his sport & pleasure, but all so profitable many wayes for his vse, as impossible it is to number them : for by their meanes he is cloathed, he hath shoes for his feet, he hath helps for all his occasions, learneth and vnderstandeth many secrets, & findeth out many medicines & remedies for his sicknesses.

2. To consider, how God, when he had made and perfected his worke, found that it was good, and approoued it. For though among the beasts there be found some fierce, cruell, & venemous, yet all be profitable to man . For the vnprofitable and dangerous teach him to practise many vertues, and to shunne many vices, doe awake the feare of God in his soule, and an hope & confidence in his mercy, & finally serue for executioners, according to the degree of diuine iustice, for the chastning and punishing of sinners.

3. To consider, how God did not giue his benediction to the beasts of the earth, as he did to the fishes of the sea, and to the fowles of the ayre, because he ment to giue it afterwardes to

man,

man , for the feruice, for which they were made
and this benediction was to be extended to them,
to giue them to vnderſtand , that the benediction or malediction , the multiplication or diminution of the beaſts depended on the meritts ,
or demeritts of man.

Meditat. X X V.   *Of the Creation of Man.*

TO conſider , how the ſame day , that God
created the beaſtes of the earth , he created
man alſo , for that he is the ſame with the
in the part ſenſitiue of the body , to the end he
might found himſelfe in humility , acknowlege
his owne baſenes in that behalfe , and not rayſe
himſelfe vp vpon the wings of his pride, for the
great excellencyes & giftes, he was to beſtow v-
pon him . He created him after the beaſts, to inſtruct vs , that as his diuine maieſty began the
production of the beaſts by the leſſe perfect , ſo
muſt we proceed in imitation of him, and aſcend
by degrees from imperfection to perfection, endeauouring euery day to doe ſome new good
thing , as did God during thoſe ſixt firſt dayes .
To conſider, that man was the laſt creature, that
God made , that he might vnderſtand that he
was the end of all , and the compendium of the
world, wherunto all things were reduced, as to
a little booke .

  2 . To conſider the ioynt conſent of the three
perſons diuine about the creation of man , as is
recorded in theſe words : Let vs make man to
our Image, & liknes. Which ſeeme to inſinuate,
                                                    that

that there was some difficulty in creating this
chiefest work of nature, for that the most sacred
Trinity knew, that it would become extremely
ingrate to the Creatour, & that it would cost the
diuine maiesty most deerly to ransome it, to sanctify it, & finally to bring it to the last end. And
yet, notwithstanding all these difficultyes, it was
created, to teach vs to vndertake good & holy
things, be they neuer so hard to compasse.

3. To consider, how God created man to his
own image & liknes, giuing him a soule, wherin
this Image is principally grauen, a most great excellency of our soule, which is an immortall spirit, and inuisible to the eyes of the flesh, indiui-
sible, all, in all the body, & whole in euery part
of it, endewed with most noble powers, giuing
life to the suppositum (as we call it) communicating vnto it both life, and motion, endewed
with freewill, both to will and nyll, as it pleaseth, inuiolable, & able agayne to be forced in
the liberty of its own inclination, only subiect
to the Creatour, capable of knowledge, of Wisdome, of Vertue, of Grace, of Glory, & of all the
gifts of nature, & aboue nature, of capacity so
great, as God is able alone to fill it, & none but
he. And therfore man is superior to all creatures
visible & corporal, yea to the heauens theselues,
beyond which he goeth in dignity & perfection. Of what is heere sayd we must gather, and
consider the nobility of our soule, that it may
yield it selfe wholy vnto him, to whome it belongeth, by deuoting it selfe perpetually to his
seruice, not degenerating in the least from the

naturall excellency, he hath beſtowed vpon it.

4. To conſider, how God created man not only to his own Image according to nature, but to his owne likenes alſo according to grace. And ſo, whē he created Adams ſoule, he did not only rectify it, & conforme it to himſelfe, but further gaue it the gouernement, commaund, ſuperiority, & full power ouer its owne Paſſions, in ſo much as when it would, it could commaund its own appetites, & they to obey without contradiction: and of this redounded vpon the body the immortality that the ſoule communicated vnto it: and we had for euer enioyed this gift, if our firſt parent had not byn diſobedient vnto God. We muſt heere extoll Gods infinite liberality towards man, &c. And exaggerate on the other ſide mans ingratitude to God.

5. To conſider the excellency of man, who for hauing the honor to carry the Image of God imprinted in his ſoule, was made Lord & Soueraigne ouer all the corporall creaturs, who becauſe they wanted reaſon, had an head & gouernour, who had reaſon, ſet ouer them, that he might guide & direct thē to their end. And therfore all were brought vnto him, that he might giue them their names, & take poſſeſſion of his principality, & be known for their Soueraigne, in ſuch ſort as the beaſts & liuing things might acknowledge him for ſuch. This dominion hath yet in part been cōſerued euen in ſinne, in that man hath & doth tame, & ouercome the fierceſt beaſts of all, eyther by force, or ſkill. Out of this we muſt draw motiues of prayſing, & of louing God.

Medit.

Meditat. XXVI. *How God formed the body of man, and infused the Soule into it : and of the creation of Eue.*

TO Confider, how God would not create the body of Adā of nothing, but formed it of earth, mixed with water, that man might acknowledge whence he came, & ground himselfe in humility, for the attayning whereof necessary it is, that he thinke agayne & agayne of the dust, wherof he was made. Of this we must take an occasion of humbling our selues, and therewith of putting our trust in the diuine goodnes, & assure our selues, that sith we are the worke of his hands, he will not abandon vs, & cast vs off.

2) To confider Gods omnipotency in hauing made of so base a matter a thing so excellent, as is the body of man, the perfection wherof is to be seene in the wonderfull proportion & composition of the parts, disposed, and vnited so artificially one with another, hauing the figure straight, looking vp to heauen, being great, fayre, and semely to looke vpon, indewed with diuers powers, and senses, subordinate to the soule that informeth it, and by reason, and industry supplyeth that, which other liuing things want.

3. To confider, how God created the soule, which the scripture teacheth vs, when it sayth : He breathed vpon his face a spirit of

Hhh 4   life,

life, to giue him to vnderstand, that the spirit
and life, that he gaue him, came not from the
earth, but from him only, vvho out of his great
loue to him created him, breathing vpon his
face, as though he drevv him out from his owne
bovvells. This spirit & breath is called the life,
because it giueth life to the house, vvhere it
entreth, For the body liueth so long, as the soule
abideth vvith it, euen as the soule also liueth a
spirituall life as long as God continueth it by
meanes of his grace, and intertayneth the life of
it by the breathings of his holy inspirations. We
must yield God thanks for hauing composed vs
of tvvo such so excellent parts, as be the soule
& body.

4. To consider how God, after he had
created man, did place him in the terrestriall paradise, which he had made for his place of dwei-
ling. We must consider the two motiues, that
Adam might peraduenture haue in his soule, in
knowing by infused knowledge the obligations
wherby he was bound vnto his diuine maiesty,
who had made so many & diuers creatures for
his seruice, had made him Lord, and Soueraigne
of the whole Vniuerse, honored him with originall iustice, & other both naturall & supernaturall gifts, which be the ropes wherewith God
would haue Adam, & his posterity tyed, for the
acknowledging of him for their Creator, & benefactour.

Medi-

*Meditat . X X V I I.   Of the reflection that
God made vpon the workes , which he made
during the six Dayes .*

TO confider , that it is a condition proper,
& peculiar to God, that he fholud fay, that
his workes be good & perfect without a-
ny imperfection therein , no leffe then in thofe
of Iefus Chrift , God and man , and by a fpeciall priuiledge in thofe of the moft Bleffed Virgin alfo. For the reft of men, it is a law of courfe,
that in them be found faults , be they neuer
fo great Saints . For it is written Iac 3. In many
thinges we offend all . We muft learne by this
to make often reflection vpon our actions , and
examine them exactly , fith it is a matter fo ordinary with vs to offend, & fall .

    2.   To confider, how , after that God
had ended his worke of the Vniuerfe , he re-
fted , not that his omnipotency was wearyed ,
but for this , that what he had done , was inough for the perfecting of the world accordingly as his diuine vnderftanding had defigned
from all eternity . How he bleffed and fanctifyed the feauenth day , beginning from thence to
doe good to his creatures after another more excellent manner , which confifted in conferuing
them . How his pleafure was , that all thinges
fhould be in action , trauayle , and labour, and
man moft of all , for whofe vtility the reft were
deftinated and appointed . We muft alfo take

paynes

Paynes to get fanctity, and confider heere, that the celebration and obferuation of Feafts is taught vs, and this with foure circumftances, that is, by ceafing from feruile works; by attending to Gods feruice in prayer and contemplation; by prayfing him in finging of Hymnes and Pfalmes in thankef-giuing; and in offering vnto him facrifices, as to our Creatour, and fanctifyer. And thofe, that fhail obferue feafts in this manner, merit well to haue their part in Gods benediction.

Meditat. XXVIII.   Of the benefit of Conferuation of all creatures.

To côfider, that this côferuation is no other thing, but a certaine côtinual creatiô in fuch fort, as ifGod did but fufpend his help, all thinges would forthwith returne to nothing. And herehence we muft draw diuers motiues of confidence, of feare, and of hnmility, feeing we haue our dependance fo abfolutely of God, not only for our being, but for our conferuation alfo.

2. To confider the innumerable benefits, comprifed vnder this of Conferuation. For by it God ceafeth not to produce ftil new things for the conferuing of the order of the old, in fo much as when one is corrupted and decayed, another fucceedeth in place of it. The greatnes of this benefit appeareth much by côfidering that, whereof we ftand in need euery day. Fos ir feemeth

meth according to our weake vnderstanding,
that God trauayleth incessantly for vs, as fearing
our want in any thing. Many other benefits be
comprehended in this one, whiles God remoo-
ueth & taketh away an infinite number of impediments, that might greatly annoy & preiudice our conseruation, in deliuering vs from many perills, that would ouerthrow vs, which vve
can neyther foresee, nor shunne of our selues.
Moreouer sith there is not an euill, that presseth
others, that may not befall vs also, we are to
thinke, that the afflictions of another, frō which
God exempteth vs, be as many benefices of his
towards vs.

3. To consider, that all creatures de-
pend wholy of God, as well in regard of
their being, as of their operation, in
such sort as none can open his hand, moue a
foote, nor do the least thing of all, without Gods
concourse therein. And from hence we are to
deduce a great motiue of loue, by considering
how precisely he hath still contributed his help
to our operations, as though he had nothing els
to do: disposing & gouerning all the other creatures for our good & profit. We must also take
occasion hereby of humbling our selues before
God, because we see, that we cannot do any thing
of our selues, and know not how to doe any
thing without his help.

Medit.

Meditat. X X I X.   *Of Gods prouidence towardes his creatures. Wherin prouidence consisteth: and of the great good that commeth
vnto vs thereby.*

T O Consider, that the prouidence of God is
an ordination, and disposition of all those
meanes, that his maiesty hath foreseene as
good, for the execution of his designes, according to his infinite Knowledge, and Wisdome
from all eternity. For whereas nothing can, nor
could be hidden from him, he hath chosen the
meanes most proper, & most proportioned to
his creatures, according to the diuers & different natures of euery one of them, and according to the end, wherunto by nature they tend.
And this God doth continually obserue & prosecute, and nothing can or doth oppose agaynst
his will, for the desire he hath, that all creatures,
especially those that vse the benefit of reason, attayne the end, for which they were created.
And for this we haue iust occasion to reioyce,
when we consider, that we be all comprehended
vnder the conduct of this soueraygne prouidence.

2.   To consider the infinite good, that this
diuine attribute bringeth vs, that we may cast all
our hopes absolutely vpon this eternall Prouidence of God, reuerencing it as our mother,
nurse, maistresse, protectresse, comfortresse, that
exerciseth towardes vs all the offices of charity,
that

that may be imagined. To consider, hovv the
diuine Prouidence is the first origen, of all the
good of body and of soule, temporall, & eternall, that both we, & all other creatures haue
receyued, and still hope to receyue. For it hath
care of al creaturs only for this, that the diuinity cannot need prouidence, because it comprehendeth in it selfe the masse & perfection of all
that is good, and therfore it imployeth it selfe a-
bout the good of the creaturs, without exceptiõ
of any, God himselfe being the executor therof,
in regard of which there cãnot be eyther chaúce,
or fortune, though in respect of man it may o-
therwise well be. For by his infinite Wisdome
he foreseeth the accidents before they arriue, &
by his prouidence he gouerneth thẽ, or he permitteth, that they come to passe, as he hath for-
seene, for the supreme end of the wonderful gouernement of this Vniuerse, which is none o-
ther, then his owne glory, and the manifestation of his mercy, iustice, & goodnes, by conuerting all to the good of his elect, of whome he
hath a particular care.

    3. To consider, that the prouidence, that
God hath of all his creatures, and consequently
of euery one of vs, in gouerning vs by his omnipotency and wisdome, ought to cause our singular spirituall ioy, and giue vs assurance, that
nothing shall be wanting vnto vs, either for our
body, or for our soule, and that his diuine maiesty will be our assistant in all aduersities and
troubles, especially if we obserue his precepts, &
in the first place seeke after the Kingdome of

heauen. For if his prouidence extendeth it selfe
euen to the birdes and fowles of the ayre, to the
beastes of the earth, and to the fishes of the sea:
how much more care will it haue of men, created to Gods own image, and likenes, especially
of the good? They must assure themselues, that
it will protect them in their afflictions, and deliuer them from all tentations and treacheryes of
Sathan, the sworne enemy of soules, ransomed
with the price of our Sauiours most precious
bloud. To whome with the Father, and the holy
Ghost be benediction, honour, & glory for euer
and euer. Amen.

Meditat. X X X. *Of the great* Prouidence
of God in giuing vs an Angeil-guardian, &
the great benefitts that we receaue by him.

TO consider, the motiues for which it hath
pleased God to giue to euery one of vs an
Angell Guardian. The first was to manifest vnto vs his great loue, & the desire that he
hath of our saluation, making the Angelicall
Spirits his ministers in this worke & office. The
second was in regard of our great weaknesse, &
of the great necessities and dangers in which
we liue. Wherefore the Prophet Dauid hath
sayd, psal. 90. *Euill shall not approach thee, because*
God hath commaunded his Angells *to haue a care*
ouer thee, In which words Dauid obserueth three
fauours and benefits: the first, that God hath
not giuen vs in charge to one only Angell but to
diuers

diuers : the second , that they guard vs euery
where ; the third , that they beare vs in their
hands that we may not fall . The third motiue
was to defend vs from the Euill Angells, & that
for this consideration , that as they be inuisible,
so we might also haue inuisible friendes , to difcouer them , & defend vs from them . By all
which vve must stir vp our selues to giue God
thankes , for that he hath had so great a care &
prouidence of vs : & also take therby great courage & assurance agaynst the Diuells, as knowing that we haue alwaies by our side an Angell
who is more strong & powerfull then they .

2 . To consider, that not only the predesti-
nate , but also the reprobate haue their Angell
Guardians . Thinke heere how the diuine Prouidence hath giuen to euery one an Angell , al-
though one alone had byn sufficient to haue
guarded diuers. This ought to incite in vs a loue
& particular esteeme of our neighbour , how
poore and abased so euer he be , since that euen
in that his basenes, God hath dedicated an Angell
wholly to his guard . Meditate moreouer , that
since God giues likewise vnto Princes , Countreyes , & Cittyes , Archaungells to gouerne &
defend thē, we haue by that meanes besides our
own Angell Guardian the help & assistance also
of that Archangell or Principality , who hath
care of the Realme in which we liue . From
hence we may draw new occasion of prayse &
reioycing, for the loue that God hath shewed towardes vs , in this his most Fatherly prouui-
dence .

3. To confider what caufes of contentment the B. Spirits may haue in guarding of vs . The firft is , becaufe God hath giuen vs to them in charge whereby for that they thinke nothing vile or abiect that is commaunded vnto them by God, are as carefull to preferue a flaue, as an Emperor or Pope : the feeond caufe is, the wonderfull charity , that they beare towardes men , who feing the great fauours that God ftill beftoweth vpon them, cannot choofe but therfore loue them . From thefe two caufes proceedeth a third, which is the great defire they haue to fill vp thofe feates in heauen , in fo much that what lieth in them they follicite & further our faluation, & are very ioifull when any finner conuerteth himfelfe, & doth pennance ; yea help them alfo in the way of vertue euen beyond themfelues , for they are free from all enuy & iealoufy .

4. To confider the great & fpirituall good, with accreweth vnto vs by their mediatiõ , weighing the caufe of their great prouidence in feeing God face to face, whereby they receaue the three neceffary properties of perfect knowledg , to wit Wifdome, Goodnes, & Power . Ponder alfo the meruaylous effects thereof , how they purge, enlighten, & perfectionate our foules in all vertue and vnion with God, to wit, by prayer, meditation,& contemplation. How they do encite vs to prayer , and after our prayers offer the fame vnto God; and finally how they doe continually watch ouer vs & direct all our actions, taking away from vs all obftacles & impediments

diments that may any way hinder our saluation; as also fighting and warring continually a-
gaynst the Diuells our enemies in our behalfe.
Let vs greatly reuerence thē, & humbly thanke
them for this their care and vigilancy, who are
so much the more watchfull ouer vs, by how
much the Diuell our enemy is ready to hurt and
destroy vs.

5. To consider, the great care & regard
they haue also of our corporall goods, in as
much as they contribute to the spirituall of our
soule, as is our health, honour, goods, garments
&c. They also haue care to keep & conserue vs
according to the diuine prouidence; as also to
help & assist vs in our sicknes, sorrowes, dangers
& miseries which we dayly suffer, and this with
as great loue and sollicitude, as did the Angell
Gabriell the yong Toby. Heerehence thou art
to thinke in what manner thou oughtest to cary
thy selfe towards thy Good Angell for his so louing care towards thee. And first take heed least
thou do any thing that shalbe displeasing in the
sight of so great a friend & benefactour. Secondly behaue thy selfe towards him somtyme as thy
Mayster, other whiles as thy best Consellour;
sometymes as thy Defender, & sometymes a-
gaine as thy deerest friend. Thirdly thanke
him continually for the fauour he dayly sheweth vnto thee, and prayse God for so singular a
gift, as is the giuing thee so noble a Guardian.
And that which ought to excite & stir thee vp
the more to honour thy Good Angell, is the re-
mēbrance of thy own death, wherin, if thou liue

as

as thou oughteſt, thou ſhalt find him moſt fauo-
rable, and then will he moſt of all be diligent in
aſſiſting thee , in that paſſage and agony of thy
life, to preſet thy ſoule pure to God, for thy faithfull ſeruice heere whileſt thou liuedſt. For theſe
reaſons it will be neceſſary , that we davly offer
vnto our Angell Guardian ſome particular ſeruice, or els ſome prayer, like to this which followeth .

A prayer to our Angell Guardian .

O Angell of God, mighty Prince, my Guardian, & moſt louing Gouernour, I reioyce, &
am glad that God hath created you ſo great, and
ſanctifyed you with his grace , in which you always perſeuered vntill you aried vnto his glory: for all theſe great fauours that God hath beſtowed vpon you, I render him humble & harty thanks ; & to you alſo the like for thoſe great
benefits with which you haue honoured me, &
for that loue and affection likewiſe with which
you continually guard & keep me. I commend
vnto you this day (O my Bleſſed Angell) both
my body & ſoule , my Memory, Will, & Vnderſtanding, togeather with all my ſenſes & appetites, to the & that you may guard, rule, & defend them: & moreouer that it wold pleaſe you
to purify & illuminate me in ſuch ſort, as being
filled by you with all graces & bleſſings , I may
ſtill perſeuere in vertue & good life vntill I ſhall
be takē hence, to ſee & enioy my God, togeather
with you, in his euerlaſting glory . Amen.

FINIS.

✿✿✿✿✿✿✿✿✿✿j✿✿✿✿✿✿✿✿✿✿✿✿✿✿✿

THE TABLE OF THE CONTENTS.

Iii 4

The

The second Weeke.

Vocati-

Kkk   wrought

The third Weeke.

Kkk 3 vpon

The fourth Weeke.

THE preparations to the fourth Weeke : of the vnion of vnderſtanding : of the vnion of the will : & of the vnion of imitation in life. And of two wayes for the knowing of God. pa. 409

K k k 4

Medit.

Meditations of the B. Sacrament.

A TABLE OF THE

MEDITATIONS

which are found vpon the Gospells of the Sundayes
through the yeare .

For the first Sunday of Aduent, the 1. weeke, the 13. Meditat.

The 2. Sund. of Aduent, 2. weeke. 31. Medit.

The 3. Sund. of Aduent, 2. weeke, 32. Medit.

The 4. Sund. of Aduent, 2. weeke, 33. Med.

The Sunday in the Octaue of the Natiuity of our Sauiour, 2. weeke, 15. Med.

The Sund. in the Octaue of the Epiphany, 2. weeke, 28. Med.

The 2. Sund. after Epiphany, 2. weeke, 29. Meditation.

The 3 Sund. after Epiphany, 2. weeke, 62. & 63. Meditat.

The 4. Sund. after Epiph. 2. weeke. 48. Med.

The 5. Sund. after Epiph. 2. weeke, 74. Med.

The 6. Sund. after Epiphany, 2. weeke, 76. Medit.

Septuagesima Sunday, 2. weeke, 84. Med.

Sexagesima Sund. 2. weeke, 74. Med.

Quinquagesima Sund. 2. weeke, 65. Med.

The 1. Sund. of Lent, 2. weeke, 34. & 35. med.

The 2. Sunday of Lent, 2. weeke, 31. Med.

The 3. Sunday of Lent, 2. weeke, 64. Med.

The 4. Sunday of Lent, 2. weeke, 47. Med.

Passi-

Lll2   The

The 15. Sund. 2. weeke, 70. med.

The 16. Sund. 1. weeke, 19. med.

The 17. Sund. 1. weeke, 27. med. & 2. weeke, 43. med.

The 18. Sund. See the 4. weeke, 9. med. and the 16. med. of the B. Sacrament .

The 19 Sund. 2. weeke, 86. med.

The 20. Sund. 2. weeke, 55. med.

The 21. Sund. 2. weeke, 81. med.

The 22. Sund. 2. weeke, 81. med.

The 23. Sund. 2. weeke, 69. med.

The 24. Sund. 1. weeke, 13. 14. & 15. med.

ANOTHER TABLE

of the Meditations found vpon the Gospells of the principall Feasts of the yeare. And when you find not a Meditation proper, you are remitted to another like vnto it.

Ianuary.

THE Feast of the Circumcision, 2. weeke, 10 & 21 med.

The Epiphany, 2. weeke, 22. & 23. med.

S. Antony, 1. weeke, 15. med. & 2. weeke, 38. med.

The Chaire of S. Peter, 2. weeke, 50. med.

SS. Fabian & Sebastian, 2. weeke, 41. med.

S. Agnes, 2. weeke, 87. med.

The Conuersion of S. Paul, 2. weeke, 38. med.

S. Iohn Chrysostome, 2. weeke, 42. med.

Feb.

LII 3   Iuly.

FINIS.